Gender and Personality

Gender and Personality

Current Perspectives on Theory and Research

Edited by Abigail J. Stewart
and M. Brinton Lykes

Duke University Press   Durham 1985

The text of this book was originally published
without the present introduction or index
as Volume 53, No. 2 (June 1985)
of the *Journal of Personality.*

Printed in the United States of America
Library of Congress Cataloging-in-Publication Data
Main entry under title:
Gender and personality.
Derived from the Journal of personality, v. 53. no. 2.
Includes bibliographies and index.
1. Sex differences (Psychology)—Addresses, essays,
lectures. 2. Personality—Addresses, essays,
lectures. I. Stewart, Abigail J. II. Lykes, M. Brinton,
1949–   . III. Journal of personality. [DNLM:
1. Identification (Psychology)—collected works.
2. Personality—collected works. BF 698 G325]
BF692.2.G465   1985   155.3′3   85-
16240
ISBN 0-8223-0262-4

Contents

Gender and Personality

Conceptualizing gender in personality theory and research

Abigail J. Stewart and M. Brinton Lykes

This volume is based on a special issue of the *Journal of Personality* devoted to the question of how "gender" is, and (especially) should be, conceptualized in personality theory and research. It was designed for students and researchers. The idea for the issue grew out of our conviction that "gender" has played a curious and paradoxical role in personality theory and research to date. First, gender has been widely assumed to have an important role in personality. Indeed, according to some theories, an individual's gender provides a major "organizing principle" for personality development (Freud, 1905/1953, 1933/1964; Jung, 1926). Nevertheless, despite fairly elaborate conceptualizations, most aspects of these theories have not been submitted to empirical examination (Fisher & Greenberg, 1977; Flowerman, 1954). At the same time personality researchers have tended, like the theorists, to assume that "gender" (or biological sex) is an important "variable" and have routinely examined empirical differences between the sexes (Harris, 1972) in the absence of clearly articulated conceptualizations of the possible or real meaning of biological sex, or gender roles, for the phenomenon under study. The inevitable yield of these entirely separate endeavors is elegant theory with no grounding in data and an ever-growing but uninterpretable account of discovered differences—and nondifferences—between the sexes (Block, 1976).

The landscape of research and theory on gender and personality has also been substantially changed by theoretical and methodological developments within personality research (e.g., idiographic vs. nomethetic approach to personality research, qualitative vs. quantitative research methods) and by the impact of the women's liberation movement on research and theory about women. Within this latter context, psychologists concerned with women have developed theory and research that seek to correct many of the biases of traditional personality theory rooted in an analysis of the experiences of white, middle-class, college-educated males (Grady, 1981; Reardon & Prescott, 1977). Parlee (1975, 1979) and Henley (1974) enumerated several of the perspectives generated by psychologists concerned about women in their discussion of psychology of, against, and for

Author Note: We would like to thank Emily C. Hewitt, Marcia Johnston, David Winter, and Nicholas Winter for their generous help in many phases of this project.

women. Minimally, work that is "of" or "for" women requires that the researcher take women's experience as a serious starting point for the research endeavor, not as "noise" to be controlled. More basically, this critique has led to the reformulation of existing theories (e.g., Gilligan's 1982 theory of women's morality based on responsibility, in contrast to men's morality based on rights) and to the development of new theory (e.g., Miller's 1984 development of a theory of women's sense of "self-in-relation"). Parallel developments have emerged in the area of methodology (see, for example, Roberts, 1981). Each of these strategies has generated research and theory that have served as counterpoint to more traditional theorizing about males and females (see, e.g., Chodorow, 1978; Gilligan, 1982; Lewis, 1976) and generated entirely new questions for psychological research (see, e.g., Bem, 1974, on androgyny; Horney, 1972, on fear of success; Wolman & Frank, 1975, on token women).

Our goal in this text was to provide an opportunity for students, researchers, and theorists to consider the ways in which biological sex and social roles, social statuses, and life experiences linked to gender should be conceptualized in personality theory and research. Our aim was to encourage work that brought together: (a) those notions from classical and recent personality theories that are useful, (b) those findings from personality research that have implications for assessing the utility of theoretical concepts, and (c) those empirical explorations that give rise to entirely new conceptualizations of the meaning of gender for our work. The work presented here is both grounded in classical and recent personality theory and research and informed by the growing body of feminist theory in psychology. The papers do indeed challenge the adequacy of traditional theory, demonstrate the meaninglessness of piling up ad hoc findings, and point to several—sometimes divergent—approaches to conceptualizing gender in personality theory and research.

Moreover, these papers reflect a diversity of procedures and approaches quite different from the methodological narrowness of psychologists' usual practice. This diversity reflects our conviction that the challenge of conceptualizing gender in personality theory and research demands methods that go beyond experimental paradigms. Personality researchers (see, e.g., Carlson, 1985; Runyan, 1982) and feminist theorists (see, e.g., Eichler, 1980; Stanley & Wise, 1983) have critically evaluated the strengths and weaknesses of the experimental paradigm in the development of knowledge about women and men. Although no clear consensus about what constitutes "feminist" methodology has emerged from the critique of traditional methods and the debate this criticism has generated

(Reinharz, 1983), the discussion has fostered among many researchers (Lott, 1985) greater flexibility in approaches to studying women's and men's lives.

Despite the emergence of a body of critical theorizing about the limitations of the traditional experimental method (see, e.g., Buss, 1979; McKenna & Kessler, 1977; Manicas & Secord, 1983; Sampson, 1978; Unger, 1983) and growing consensus among psychologists that this reflects only one among many approaches to understanding, for example, gender and personality issues, the vast majority of *published* research in the field relies on this method (see, e.g., Lykes & Stewart, 1983). The papers in this volume depart from the usual practice in personality research and thus represent a broad range of procedures and approaches.

Methods of data collection reflected in the papers include conventional personality batteries, projective tests, interviews, and open-ended responses to written questions; and the subjects of research range in age from children through late middle-aged adults and include other than middle-class, college-educated people. Data are analyzed using content analysis of written and oral responses, factor analysis of quantitative and qualitative scores, and secondary analysis of existing data. Evidence for and against theoretical propositions is evaluated in terms of aggregate data as well as individual cases. The only major technique *not* represented is the traditional experimental method, in which subjects are asked to participate in an experimenter-defined and experimenter-controlled procedure.

Despite this diversity of approaches all of the researchers represented share one methodological commitment. They all try to use methods that allow the subjects of their research to respond in terms of personally meaningful experiences and issues.

While the articles in this volume vary in their dependence on either formal feminist theory or the critique of traditional personality theory, all of them share some elements of both. Each author has engaged these issues at a point unique to her or his experience and expertise. All of the work is informed by a generation of theorists and researchers about women who have sought new ways of conceptualizing age-old experiences. The research and theorizing presented here should therefore be examined in the context of this developing agenda for personality psychologists concerned with the study of gender. The volume includes both assessments of the current state of research and theory in several areas of personality research and proposed directions for future work. Each paper in this book clearly represents a unique and independent contribution and will provide direction and stimulation to particular inquiries within the field of personality. Taken as a group they provide some synthesis and direction for conceptualizing gender in personality theory and research; moreover, a number of common themes clearly emerge.

Substantive Themes

Several insights and concerns, with significant consequences for personality, recur in many of the papers: the role of relationships and relatedness in personality development; the significance of power and status; and the role of concrete, particular life experiences. These three themes (with variations) emerge most often in combination with recognition of two additional discoveries: that an understanding of "individuation"—at the core of many classical theories (e.g., Freud and Jung)—is inadequate to encompass personality development; and that sex differences are actually rather *un*important in the study of personality.

The Relative Unimportance of Sex as an Explanatory Variable

In areas as different as the domains of reported achievement successes, power motives and behaviors, and moral development, sex differences per se were found to play a very small role in other published research and in data reported here. In addition, sex-role identity also played a relatively small part. Even in areas with somewhat more consistent evidence for sex differences (e.g., women's greater sociability and emotional expressiveness; see the papers by Lewis, Lykes, and Brody), sex differences were smaller and more context-dependent than traditional notions would suggest.

The Inadequacy of "Individuation" as a Definition for Personality Development

Though most of the authors concede that individuation, or definition of a separate "self," is one element of personality development, many identified this conceptualization as exaggerated in contemporary understanding of personality. Thus, Lykes argues that "autonomous individualism" is only one form of self-definition, and Helson, Mitchell, and Hart find that some women's processes of self-definition within relationships cannot be understood using most existing personality theories. Similarly, Franz and White argue that the apparent sexism in Erikson's theory lies less in overvaluation of male personality than in an overvaluation of individuation.

The Importance of Connection and Relatedness for Personality Development

Most of the papers identify the experience of relationships, and the need to be connected to others, as important elements in personality. Most broadly, Franz and White argue that the development of a mature capacity for relationship is a process parallel to, and equal with, the development of the capacity for a separate, autonomous identity. Lykes argues in a different vein that alternative understandings of the self derive from different experiences of the self in relationship with others. Thus, a central element of self-definition is the particular relationships one has experienced. Lewis proposes both that sociability is a human universal and that women are (innately) slightly more disposed than are men to form and care about relationships. She argues that this bias in sociability then results in differential personality development and hence differential vulnerability to depression and paranoia.

Even in those papers *less centrally* concerned with this issue, the importance of relationships is discussed. Most often, the writings of Gilligan (1982), Chodorow (1978), and Miller (1976, 1984) are drawn upon to provide some theoretical context for understanding the consequences of relationships for personality (see, e.g., Helson, Mitchell, & Hart; Winter & Barenbaum; and Brody). In addition, some more traditional concepts—e.g., agency and communion (see Gaeddert) and the instrumental-expressive distinction (see Winter & Barenbaum)—are employed. In any case, the significance of relationships as a fundamental need, as well as a context for personality development, is a critical theme throughout these papers.

An important priority implied by the diversity of the *ways* in which this theme emerges, though, is even more precision and detail about the *different* meanings of relationship and the *different* forms of relating. Thus, Franz and White distinguish between abstract relationships to institutions and concrete interpersonal relations, while Lykes suggests that concrete interpersonal relations are importantly affected by larger institutional and social structural connections. Lewis proposes that there is an innate bias toward sociability in females. Brody suggests that social connectedness may have a different adaptive function where women have lower status; and Walker and Browne suggest that some women may overvalue relationships to the point of jeopardizing their own safety. The different understandings of relationships and relatedness implied by these different writers need to be developed; we need to better understand precisely how these notions are in conflict and convergence and to avoid prematurely collapsing these separate understandings into one another.

The Significance of Power and Status

Several of the papers attempt to incorporate women's lower status and lesser social power into the analysis of gender and personality. Thus, we see authors giving conscious attention to the power and status difference between women and men—a difference nearly always confounded with biological sex. Brody; Helson, Mitchell, and Hart; Lykes; Walker and Browne; and Winter and Barenbaum all argue that some observed personality differences between the sexes can be seen to flow directly from the different power resources and statuses of the sexes. This logic leads several researchers to argue that *intrasex* differences in status and experience should result in similar kinds of personality differences as those found *between* the sexes. In this way the significance of the structural relations between the sexes can be indirectly demonstrated.

Moreover, Winter and Barenbaum in their paper and Morawski argue that professional interpretations of sex differences are profoundly influenced by the ideological climate in which psychologists make them. These authors point out the distortions and collective misconceptions that result from professional norms and practices that reflect and reproduce power relations in the wider society. Thus, both papers suggest that psychology as a discipline must be more self-conscious about its past—and its present—capacity to hold inaccurate, unjustified views, and to ignore the data, when those views fit in with prevailing doctrines and justify the status quo. Morawski in particular shows how rapidly and enthusiastically psychologists can be recruited to ideas that lack "real" significance and violate common sense, if only they serve psychologists' need to defend and promote their professional interest. The self-reflective approach to psychological theory-building presented by Morawski provides an important strategy for correcting the tendency to recapitulate past errors in our development of new theory.

The Role of Concrete Life Experience

Nearly every paper in this volume argues for the importance of grounding our research and theory in concrete life experience. Morawski argues that we have often been led to ignore—or actively mistrust—the concrete, and at peril to our ideas. From a different angle Brody argues that few findings are so trans-situational or acontextual that we can afford to be so sublimely indifferent as we have been to the particularities out of which findings arise. Gaeddert and Lifton argue that subjects must be asked to engage in activities that grow out of their own life experiences. And Lykes, Walker and Browne, and Winter and Barenbaum all show that particular life experiences result in different personality outcomes. Thus, again, we see the power of exploring *within* the sexes the meaning of experiences that may differentiate the sexes on the average. Finally, both Lykes and (especially) Helson, Mitchell, and Hart examine personality issues in terms of individual lives—the clearest form of grounding the theoretical in the particular.

Organization of the Book

We believe that each of the papers in the volume makes a broad and individual contribution to the question of how to conceptualize gender and personality, and each deserves to be examined in its own terms, as well as in relation to the other papers. We note that nearly all of the papers depart at least somewhat from the traditional formats or models in "scientific writing." Few of them can be classified as theory *or* research—conceptual *or* empirical. Most of the papers include elements of review or analysis of data *and* development of theory. This derives in part, of course, from our goals in the volume. We believe the integration of theory and research in these papers reflects not only our encouragement to authors, but also our authors' appreciation of the need to shift from models of science as "theory-testing" or "fact-finding" to a more dialectical, reflexive model of theory development in which discovery and description have an important and valued place in defining and developing understanding.

Thus, the first three papers review significant research literatures on sex differences and discuss the accumulated empirical evidence in terms of major theoretical alternatives. In this way, Brody examines the theoretical and empirical literature on emotional development. She argues that many important theory-based questions have not been studied. For example, she shows that although many theories predict gender differences in affect experience (e.g., in the experience of shame), little research even attempts to document such differences. At the same time a fairly consistent finding of higher levels of fear in females—which is not predicted by major theories—remains unconceptualized. Perhaps worst of all, researchers continue to build extensive research studies on the basis of ad hoc findings about sex differences. Brody argues convincingly that we need: (1) new theoretical efforts, which encompass existing findings of gender differences and similarities; (2) systematic research exploring those areas in which gender differences are predicted by some or many theories. In a sense, then, this paper illustrates how even in an area in which gender has been conceptualized that conceptualization has rarely guided the research. Brody concludes with a proposal for research that could assess the notion she derives from her reading of the literature: that observed gender differences in emotion may result in part from the different social statuses and roles of women and men.

Lewis draws together a wide range of findings that grow out of many different theoretical and empirical traditions to try to understand the observed differences in men's and women's vulnerability to paranoia and depression, respectively. Many researchers have noted differential rates of these psychiatric diagnoses in men and women, but this paper provides an integrated conceptualization that accounts both for why men, when stressed, might tend to become paranoid, while women, when stressed, might tend to become depressed. Put most briefly, Lewis argues that the two patterns of response can be understood as resulting from distorted or extreme expressions of men's undervaluation and women's overvaluation of relationship. Her argument depends on an integration of psychodynamic theory and a reading of research evidence from a wide range of sources.

Again in this paper we see widely recognized findings about gender differences given meaning by an integrative conceptual framework that allows us to generate and test new, more complex hypotheses. Thus, if Lewis is right that depression in women results from their closer and stronger ties to others, then those men who appear to value relationships deeply should also be more vulnerable than other men to depression. Similarly, women who are less linked to others should be more prone to paranoia under stress. If these predictions are confirmed, we are able to move from a theoretical dead end (observation of sex differences) to a complex (if unmarked) trail, leading from prediction to finding to new prediction. By following the trail, we may hope to move beyond description of how men and women may differ to understanding of how those differences arise.

Finally, Walker and Browne evaluate the research findings about men and women's violent relations with each other, especially from the perspective of social learning theory. They argue that women's socialization can result in an exaggerated valuing of relationship even at the expense of their physical well-being, while men's socialization can result in a devaluation of relationship that allows them to express anger and frustrations in a violent and abusive way. This paper illustrates very clearly how adoption of a comprehensive theoretical framework results in a sharpened focus. Social learning theory demands explanation both of how tolerance for abuse may be learned and of how repeated behavior patterns are maintained.

By attending to these questions, the authors are able to select certain particular features of men and women's violent relations and attempt to develop a thorough account of how those relations may arise within a couple, and then what causes them to continue. This kind of selectiveness, or narrowness, is a likely product of clearer conceptualizations of gender within any research area. Sometimes it seems to exclude interesting aspects of the phenomena under study; however, it also enhances precision in the formulation of both research questions and explanations. Moreover, in a sense, the sharpening of a narrow focus tends rapidly to expose, by contrast, the large remaining unexplored terrain. Thus, greater clarity about smaller issues may help define the entirely uncharted territory.

These three papers, then, draw together a large number of findings and propose fresh and integrative theoretical perspectives on familiar research areas. Morawski suggests that we must be "critical" even of such proposed new perspectives. In a careful analysis of psychology's past she shows how psychologists have been engaged in a series of quests for ineffable "ideas": sex differences in personality, masculinity/femininity, and most recently, androgyny. This paper proposes that we need not only conceptualize "gender," but we need to conceptualize those conceptualizations themselves! She advocates, however, that we avoid pursuit of mere ideological chimera (such as "androgyny") and urges that we seek to understand "realities" in the experience of "human beings." Thus Morawski's is no counsel of despair; it is instead a call to ground investigations of gender in the lived experience of men and women rather than the ideological imperatives of scholars.

Franz and White begin their paper with a careful analysis of the meaning of gender in Erikson's theory of personality development, arguing that Erikson has been viewed as "sexist" when he is in fact more accurately described as "incomplete." They propose that his theory (which was developed in a period of unquestioned individualism) overemphasizes "individuation" in *all* people and underemphasizes "attachment" in *all* people. With Morawski's perspective in mind, we are mindful both of Franz and White's valuable correction of Erikson's bias, and that we too are located in history—at a time when connection and relationship are being affirmed and recognized. As Franz and White suggest, though, empirical exploration of these "twin" processes within human lives will help us evaluate whether a two-process model of personality development (a model including elements of separation and connection) captures "lived experience" better than past, more one-sided models.

Helson, Mitchell, and Hart present us with seven women's "lived experience"—seven women who, in mid-life, attained a high level of ego development. They explore these seven women's lives in terms of three broad theories: Loevinger's theory of ego development, Gilligan's theory of female moral development, and Levinson's theory of male development of a "life structure." They highlight the points of connection between theory and these women's lives, and at the same time they point to those elements of the women's lives that are least adequately illuminated by the theory. The themes of self-development and individuation, and connection or relationship, pervade both the paper and the women's lives. This paper, then, exemplifies how we can ground the theoretical in the particular and use what we know about the particular to develop theory.

Each of the four remaining papers presents new data on a major aspect of personality traditionally viewed as characterized by sex differences. Each paper presents some analyses primarily aimed at evaluating the adequacy of existing theoretical ideas and other analyses aimed at developing theory. Thus, Gaeddert explores sex and gender-role differences in the kinds of activities defined as achievement domains, as well as the kinds of rewards (inner or external) valued for performance in those domains. He finds that men more often report about achievement experiences in terms of extrinsic rewards and women in terms of intrinsic ones. Men and women do not, however, differ in their tendency to define affiliative or mastery activities as achievement activities. Instead, gender role (masculinity and femininity) predicts those tendencies among both women and men. This set of analyses, then, helps clarify exactly which achievement areas are affected by one's sex and which by one's sex role. Exploration of the factors or processes that produce each type of effect is clearly the next priority for research and theory in this area.

Lifton, in a similar line of reasoning, argues that the area of "moral development" (including both cognitive and personality elements) is characterized less by sex differences than by "gender" (or sex-role) differences. He shows, in addition, that moral development is strongly related to other aspects of personality development in both males and females. Thus, he makes a case for the study of intrasex differences in moral development and for the conceptualization of discovered sex differences in terms of sex role or "gender."

Similarly, Winter and Barenbaum argue that observed differences in the correlates of the power motive can be shown to derive from a personality characteristic (a sense of responsibility for others) that is not *intrinsically* gender-linked but which has been *historically* gender-linked. They argue both for analysis of the *precise* aspects of sex-role socialization that may underlie observed sex differences (in this instance, socialization for responsibility for others), as well as analysis of within-sex differences in that precise experience. This paper proposes not merely that sex role or gender generally accounts for observed sex differences but attempts to suggest precisely which aspect of sex role accounts for them, at least in this area, and how and why.

Finally, Lykes provides a critique of traditional conceptualizations of an individualistic "self," proposes an alternative conceptualization of the self as "social individuality," and seeks empirical evidence for this more relational self. In her study of community adults Lykes explores quantitative evidence for this alternative self-definition, finds a small sex difference (with women less inclined toward "autonomous individualism"), and shows that early and later experiences of connectedness (e.g., through collective activity and social group membership) are highly correlated with one's notion of the self. She concludes with detailed accounts of how several individual women's life experiences shaped and reflected their understandings of themselves. In this paper, sex differences are subsumed within a broader conceptualization of differences in self-experience that flow from differences in "lived experience" of social relations.

Two scholars with rich experience studying women's lives were asked to read and comment on these papers and to draw some conclusions. Rae Carlson, who wrote one of the earliest calls for richer conceptualizations of gender (see Carlson, 1972), first presents her "personological framework" for understanding personality generally, and gender and personality more specifically, and then discusses each of the papers. Deborah Belle, author of an important study of poor women's lives (see Belle, 1982), adopts a more explicitly "social" framework to comment on how the dualism of sex or gender pervaded past thinking but may be transcended in future work—as in this volume.

References

Belle, D. (1982). *Lives in stress.* Beverly Hills: Sage.
Bem, S. (1974). The measurement of psychological androgyny. *Journal of Consulting and Clinical Psychology,* **42,** 165–172.
Block, J. H. (1976). Issues, problems, and pitfalls in assessing sex differences: A critical review of *The Psychology of Sex Differences. Merrill-Palmer Quarterly,* **22,** 283–308.
Carlson, R. (1972). Understanding women: Implications for personality theory and research. *Journal of Social Issues,* **28,** 17–32.
Carlson, R. (1985). What's social about social psychology? Where's the person in

personality research? *Journal of Personality and Social Psychology, 47*(6), 1304–1309.

Chodorow, N. (1978). *The reproduction of mothering: Psychoanalysis and the sociology of gender.* Berkeley: University of California Press.

Eichler, M. (1980). *The double standard: A feminist critique of feminist social science.* Boston: Routledge & Kegan Paul.

Fisher, S., & Greenberg, R. P. (1977). *The scientific credibility of Freud's theory and therapy.* New York: Basic Books.

Flowerman, S. H. (1954). Psychoanalytic theory and science. *American Journal of Psychotherapy, 8,* 415–441.

Freud, S. (1953). Three essays on the theory of sexuality. In J. Strachey (Ed. and Trans.), *The standard edition of the complete psychological works of Sigmund Freud* (vol. 7). London: Hogarth Press. (Original work published 1905.)

Freud, S. (1964). Femininity. In J. Strachey (Ed. and Trans.), *The standard edition of the complete psychological works of Sigmund Freud* (vol. 22, pp. 121–135). London: Hogarth Press. (Original work published 1933.)

Gilligan, C. (1982). *In a different voice: Psychological theory and women's development.* Cambridge, Mass.: Harvard University Press.

Grady, K. E. (1981). Sex bias in research design. *Psychology of Women Quarterly, 5*(4), 628–636.

Harris, S. (1972). Who studies sex differences? *American Psychologist, 27,* 1077–1078.

Henley, N. (1974). Resources for the study of psychology and women. *RT: Journal of Radical Therapy, 4,* 20–21.

Jung, C. G. (1926). *Psychological types.* New York: Harcourt Brace.

Lewis, H. B. (1976). *The psychic war in men and women.* New York: New York University Press.

Lott, B. (1985). The potential enrichment of social/personality psychology through feminist research and vice versa. *American Psychologist, 40,* 155–164.

Lykes, M. B., & Stewart, A. J. (1983, August). *Evaluating the feminist challenge in psychology: 1963–1983.* Paper presented at the meeting of the American Psychological Association, Anaheim.

McKenna, W., & Kessler, S. J. (1977). Experimental design as a source of sex bias in social psychology. *Sex Roles, 3*(2), 117–128.

Manicas, P. T., & Secord, P. F. (1983). Implications for psychology of the new philosophy of science. *American Psychologist, 38,* 399–413.

Miller, J. B. (1976). *Toward a new psychology of women.* Boston: Beacon Press.

Miller, J. B. (1984). *The development of women's sense of self.* (Work in Progress Papers, No. 84-01). Wellesley, Mass.: Wellesley College, The Stone Center.

Parlee, M. B. (1975). Review essay: Psychology. *Signs, 1*(1), 119–138.

Parlee, M. B. (1979). Review essay: Psychology and women. *Signs, 5*(1), 121–133.

Reardon, P., & Prescott, S. (1977). Sex as reported in a recent sample of psychological research. *Psychology of Women Quarterly, 2*(2), 157–162.

Reinharz, S. (1983, May). *Feminist methodology in the human sciences: Creating alternative models for research.* Colloquium presented at Boston College, Chestnut Hill, Mass.

Roberts, H. (ed.). (1981). *Doing feminist research.* Boston: Routledge & Kegan Paul.

Runyan, W. McK. (1982). *Life histories and psychobiography.* New York: Oxford University Press.

Sampson, E. E. (1978). Scientific paradigms and social values: Wanted—A scientific revolution. *Journal of Personality and Social Psychology, 36,* 1332–1343.

Stanley, L., & Wise, S. (1983). *Breaking out: Feminist consciousness and feminist research.* Boston: Routledge & Kegan Paul.

Unger, R. (1983). Through the looking glass: No wonderland yet! (The reciprocal relationship between methodology and models of reality). *Psychology of Women Quarterly, 8*(1), 9–32.

Wolman, C., & Frank, H. (1975). The solo woman in a professional peer group. *American Journal of Orthopsychiatry, 45*(1), 164–171.

Gender differences in emotional development: A review of theories and research

Leslie Brody

Abstract

Theories, data, methodological and conceptual problems concerning the study of gender differences in the development of defenses, emotional expression, recognition, and experiences are reviewed. Data indicate gender differences in several areas of emotional functioning, including nonverbal sensitivity; expressiveness; self-reports of anger, fear, and sadness; the quality of defenses; and cognitive correlates of recognition abilities. Studies suggest that with development, boys increasingly inhibit the expression and attribution of most emotions, whereas girls increasingly inhibit the expression and recognition of socially unacceptable emotions, e.g., anger. These differences may be a function of different socialization processes for males and females, which may be adaptations to innate gender differences in temperament, or adaptations to existing sociocultural pressures.

The present paper argues that emotions motivate and regulate adaptive behaviors, and that researchers must explore gender differences in emotional development as a function of different familial, sociocultural, and interpersonal roles to which males and females must adapt.

Regardless of the relative emphasis placed on the social, cognitive, or biological determinants of emotion, the hypothesis that emotional expression, recognition, and experiences may differ dramatically for the two sexes is implicit in almost every theory of emotional development (cf. Brenner, 1980; Chodorow, 1978; Izard, 1971, 1977; Kemper, 1978 a and b; Miller, 1976). This hypothesis has important implications for theories about emotional change (including theories about psychotherapy), for theories about psychopathology, and for more general theories about personality development. For example, most personality theorists view emotions as either subsystems of, or as the primary determinants of, other aspects of personality func-

I would like to thank Ross Buck, Joseph C. Cunningham, Brinton Lykes, Abigail Stewart, Anne Thompson, Kathleen White, and an anonymous reviewer for their thoughtful comments and critiques of this manuscript. I would also especially like to thank Abigail Stewart for her patience and encouragement in waiting for the final version of this manuscript, and Louise True for her perseverance and help in typing the many revisions this manuscript underwent.

tioning, including self-concept, motivation, mood, cognitive style and traits such as extraversion-introversion (cf. Epstein, 1979; Kellerman, 1983; Tomkins, 1981). Furthermore, abnormal personality functioning, or psychopathology, is often defined as the inability to cope with emotions (cf. Peters, 1972), and/or as the expression or experience of inappropriately frequent or intense emotions. For example, flat affect is a diagnostic indicator of depression. Thus, if the two sexes do differ in their emotional development, these differences may account for or help to explain gender differences in mood, cognitive style, motivation, self-concept, and the incidence of various psychopathologies, such as depression (cf. Weissman & Klerman, 1977). Gender differences in emotional development would also argue for different strategies to be used with each sex in psychotherapy, since the appropriate labelling and understanding of feelings is an integral part of the psychotherapy process (cf. Pierce, Nichols, & DuBrin, 1983).

Whether or not there are gender differences in emotional development is also the subject of a great deal of popular speculation. In the midst of writing this paper, I happened to read letters to the editor of Time Magazine (June 25, 1984, p. 4) concerning readers' feelings about the possibility of a woman vice president. To my dismay (but not to my surprise) one male reader wrote, "Women are emotional. They are also unaware of the exigencies of life and they lack objectivity;" while another male reader wrote, "The ambitious female politician can come about only by an inborn androgyny, produced by a high level of that male hormone (testosterone) with its attendant aggressiveness." The idea that the emotional lives of women differ from those of men was supported both by a six-year-old female friend of mine who said to me, "You know why I'm scared? Because I'm a girl," and by a fortune cookie I received which informed me that "A woman either loves or hates; she knows no medium." The assumption of gender differences in emotional development has thus been used to argue for the kinds of roles women should and should not play in our culture. Given the hypothesized relationship of emotions to personality, psychopathology, psychotherapy, and social roles, it is clear that data concerning gender differences in emotional development are quite important and have both theoretical and practical significance.

In order to discuss gender in relation to emotional development, the present paper will be organized as follows. First, emotional development will be conceptualized, followed by a discussion of the methodological difficulties involved in studying gender differences. Next, theories of emotional development as well as empirical studies of emotional expression, recognition, experiences, and defenses will be reviewed with reference to their relevance for understanding and/or predicting gender differences. A discussion of the relationship between empirical and theoretical work on gender differences in emotional development will follow. It will be argued that there has been little overlap between research and theory, in that much of the important theoretical work about the interpersonal context in which emotions develop (cf. Chodorow, 1978; Lewis, 1976, 1983; Miller, 1976) has been neglected by researchers, and important data have been ignored by theorists (cf. Tomkins, 1981). Finally, recommendations for future research in this area will be proposed.

Conceptualizing Emotional Development

Emotional development (that is, how emotional functioning varies over the course of the lifespan) is difficult to conceptualize both because of the complexity of the construct "emotion" and because of widespread theoretical disagreements about the functions emotions serve (cf. Buck, 1983; Buechler & Izard, 1983; Plutchik, 1980). Emotions are multidimensional constructs, with physiological-experiential components (e.g., heartrate), cognitive components (e.g., interpretations of situations, recognition of facial cues), behavioral/ expressive components (e.g., facial expressions), attitudinal components (e.g., the values placed on emotional experiences) and regulatory components (e.g., coping or defense mechanisms to minimize, exaggerate, or distort emotions). Each of these components (or the interaction among different components) may have unique developmental etiologies and/or epigenetic timetables. The complexity of emotional functioning makes it difficult to generalize about the nature of emotional development as a unitary construct.

It is also difficult to conceptualize emotional development because theorists disagree about the function of emotions, and about the developmental changes and processes involved in these functions (cf. Buck, 1983; Buechler & Izard, 1983; Plutchik, 1980). Some theorists hypothesize that emotions serve motivating functions (Kellerman, 1983; Tomkins, 1981), the goals of which are interpersonal relationships (Buechler & Izard, 1983), object contacts (Buechler & Izard, 1983), or "the amplification of urgency" to ensure that adaptive behaviors occur, e.g., the feeling of pain causes us to tend to our wounds (Tomkins, 1981). Other functions which have been attributed to emotions include social referencing, that is, emotions help in the cognitive appraisal of ambiguous events (Klinnert, Campos, Sorce, Emde, & Svejda, 1983), and signalling, that is, emotions signal the emergence of new cognitive abilities (cf. Cicchetti & Hesse, 1983). Disagreements about whether or not emotions are primary motivating systems result in different theories about the nature of the interaction between emotional and cognitive development. For example, the emergence of fear at the end of the first year of life has been viewed as either the consequence or the cause of a new cognitive ability to recognize incongruities (cf. Cicchetti & Hesse, 1983). These differing theoretical perspectives on the functions served by emotions add to the complexity of any attempt made to conceptualize and study emotional development.

However, despite theoretical disagreements, theorists tend to concur and data indicate that there are several clear trends in the development of emotional functioning. It is generally agreed that a biological preparedness for emotional expressions (and, presumably, experiences) exists at birth (cf. Tomkins, 1981). This preparedness is hypothesized to occur in the form of either general arousal or discrete emotional states (e.g., anger vs. sadness), and plays a critical role in determining the quality and frequency of caretaker-infant interactions, as well as in motivating or interacting with the development of cognitive skills (cf. Buechler & Izard, 1983). With development, the expression and experience of emotions become more differentiated, more stable, and more internally and externally regulated (Cicchetti & Hesse, 1983). The expression of emotions becomes increasingly subject to voluntary controls as children begin to understand that there are culturally specific display rules which regulate the social acceptability of emotional expressions (Brody & Carter, 1982; Saarni, 1979). Although there are few data on the relationships between emotional expressions and the situations which elicit them, it has been hypothesized that with development, each emotion becomes elicited by or associated with, an increasing number of different situations (Piaget, 1981). Thus, for a six-month-old, the feeling of disgust may be limited to an aversive taste or odor; whereas, to a two-year-old, disgust may also include situations in which a standard of cleanliness is violated.

With development, the cognitive components of emotion become increasingly sophisticated. Children's abilities to label and recognize emotions on the basis of situations, facial expressions, and audio and visual cues becomes better with age (cf. Abramovich, 1977; Barden, Zelko, Duncan, & Masters, 1980; Borke, 1971; Brody & Harrison, 1984; Demos, 1975; Gilbert, 1969; Gnepp, 1983; Harter, 1982; Lewis, Wolman, & King, 1972; Reichenbach & Masters, 1983; Weiner, Graham, Stern, & Lawson, 1982). Several studies have indicated that with development, children increasingly recognize that feelings have internal, intrapsychic components in addition to external, situational components (Carroll & Steward, 1984; Donaldson & Westerman, 1984; Harris, Olthof, & Terwogt, 1981).

Thus, data and theories have indicated the existence of developmental trends in several components of emotions, that is, the expression, recognition, and cognitive understanding of emotions. The evidence for gender differences in these developmental trends is the focus of this paper. Research indicates that by adulthood, there are gender differences in many of the components of emotion previously specified. For example, adult women are more facially expressive of emotions than are men (cf. Buck, Baron, & Barrette, 1982; Buck, Miller, & Caul, 1974; Hall, 1979), and are better able to recognize nonverbal emotional cues than are men (cf. Hall, 1978; Rosenthal & DePaulo, 1979). Questions for researchers interested in gender differences in emotional development include the etiology of such differences; the ages at which such differences emerge; and the developmental patterns such differences follow. For example, are there gender differences in either the rate or the qualitative processes by which children begin to understand that emotions have both internal and external components? This review is focused on these developmental questions. The theories and empirical studies to be reviewed are limited to those which are helpful in illuminating these developmental issues and which concern nonpathological aspects of emotional development; therefore, theories and studies about, for example, gender differences in depression will not be included.

Methodological Complexities Involved in Studying Gender Differences

Conceptual and methodological difficulties abound in any attempt to study gender differences in emotional development. As previously discussed, emotions are multidimensional constructs, and there may be gender differences in any or all of the components of emotions, for example, in emotional expression but not in emotional experience. Furthermore, whether or not gender differences are manifested in any one component of emotions depends on other variables, such as the quality and intensity of the emotion experienced (e.g., happiness vs. anger/anger vs. irritation), the age of the person studied, the situational context in which the emotion is elicited, and whether emotions are studied with respect to the self or others. Given the multidimensional nature of emotions, it is difficult, if not impossible, to generalize about gender differences in emotional development.

Research on differential emotional development for the two sexes has been further constrained by both theoretical and methodological limitations. Despite the fact that theories of emotional development often include explicit and/or implicit predictions about differential emotional development by gender, and about the relationship between emotional development and personality development (cf. Field, 1982; Kemper, 1978 a and b; Lewis, 1976; Lewis & Michaelson, 1983; Miller, 1976), researchers tend to design studies in a theoretical vacuum. Typically, researchers who study gender differences in emotional development decide to explore such differences either because previous researchers found gender differences in the variable of interest, or more commonly, because previous studies were inconsistent in their findings concerning gender differences. When researchers do find gender differences, they briefly attempt to explain their findings on the basis of post hoc theories. The result has been a hodge-podge of theories about gender differences which are never systematically tested.

Furthermore, most of the research designs that have been used to study this question are seriously limited. Often, observers who rate subjects on various measures of emotionality, for example expressiveness or experience, are not blind as to the subjects' sex, which may bias them in their perceptions about sex differences. A highly consistent body of literature indicates that there are strong sex role stereotypes about the quality and intensity of emotions attributed to each sex. Happiness, sadness, fear, and general emotionality are associated with females; and anger with males, by children as young as preschool age (Birnbaum & Chemelski, 1984; Birnbaum, Nosanchuck, & Croll, 1980), and these differential emotional experiences have been found to be attributed to the same child as a function of whether that child is labeled male or female (Condry & Condry, 1976; Cunningham & Shapiro, 1984; Haviland & Malatesta, 1981). Such stereotypes undoubtedly have powerful effects, not only on experimental investigations of males' and females' emotional development, but on those who socialize males and females (i.e., teachers and parents), and also on children themselves, who may conform to such sex role stereotypes in certain contexts (perhaps when participating in experiments) because of social desirability pressures. In order to draw any conclusions about differential emotional development by sex, studies are needed in which observers are blind as to the sex of the subjects (often possible to do in work with infants and children, cf., Cunningham & Shapiro, 1984), and in which social desirability pressures on subjects are minimized. Recent studies of adults' emotionality have begun to explore within-sex variations in emotion as a function of gender identity (cf. Zuckerman, DeFrank,

Speigel, & Larrance, 1982). This paradigm is one that has been used very infrequently by developmental researchers (some exceptions are Cramer & Carter, 1978; Hall & Halberstadt, 1981), and it is certainly worth pursuing in order to avoid some of the methodological limitations just discussed, for example, observer bias (cf. Unger, 1979).

Theories of Emotional Development—What About Gender Differences?

Each theory of emotional development differs in the relative importance placed on cognitive, social, genetic, cultural, and physiological processes as etiological and conceptual variables, and consequently each has different predictions about emotional development for the two sexes (cf. Buck, 1982; Greenberg & Mitchell, 1983; Izard, 1971, 1977; Lewis, 1976; Miller, 1976; Plutchik, 1980). In order to discuss these theories with respect to gender differences, they will be categorized into those which emphasize biological-genetic processes and into those which emphasize social, cognitive, and cultural processes. These categories are somewhat arbitrary in that recent theorists have emphasized the role of both social and biological processes in emotional development (cf. Buck, 1983).

Biological/Genetic Theories

Perhaps the most widely written about biologically based theories of emotional development are genetic-evolutionary theories (cf. Izard, 1971, 1977; Plutchik, 1980), which posit that each emotion has an underlying neural or hormonal substrate with an adaptive social function. The purpose of emotions is to communicate about survival-related approach-withdrawal processes, for example, fear helps to identify potential aggressors. From this theoretical perspective, the important issue relevant to an understanding of gender differences in emotional development is that the two sexes historically differed in their interpersonal survival-related functions: Women were primarily responsible for child-rearing; men, for gathering and hunting food. While hunting required communication among peers who were at relatively similar levels of physical, cognitive, and social development, child-rearing required communication between a developmentally more advanced caretaker (in physical, social, and cognitive skills), and a developmentally immature, nonverbal, and physically vulnerable child (cf. Adkins, 1980; Daly & Wilson, 1978). These differences in gender-related interpersonal interactions have implications for two aspects of emotional functioning: Women should be more sensitive to nonverbal cues than are men, since nonverbal sensitivity is adaptive for child-rearing; and women should show anger less often than do men, since anger is theorized to be a precursor of aggressive behavior, and is nonadaptive for interactions with children (cf. Frodi, Macauley, & Thome, 1977).

Drive-based psychoanalytic theorists also conceptualize a biological basis to emotional development. The function of emotions is to maintain intrapsychic stability in the face of conflicts, often produced by environmental changes which impede or facilitate biological drive satisfaction (Brenner, 1980). Since the biological anatomies of the two sexes differ, both the nature and the resolution of the developmental conflicts they undergo are hypothesized to differ (cf. Cramer, 1980; Freud, 1925/1961; 1933/1965). These differences produce more aggression, competition, guilt, and outer-directedness in males; and more passivity, shame, inner-directedness, jealousy, and masochism in females (cf. Mitchell, 1974; Strouse, 1974).

Other theories which emphasize a biological conceptualization of emotions lead to less clear predictions about differential emotional development by sex. Neurochemical, hormonal, and neuroelectric processes have been associated with emotional experiences (Ekman & Oster, 1979; Lamandella, 1977; Pribram, 1980), and some researchers suggest that the two cerebral hemispheres may mediate different aspects of emotional functioning. For example, it has been suggested that the right hemisphere mediates facial recognition (cf. Ekman & Oster, 1979), as well as the more spontaneous aspects of emotional functioning (Buck, 1982), whereas the left hemisphere mediates more cognitive, analytic aspects of emotional functioning (Buck, 1982). Some researchers suggest that women rely on intuitive, right hemisphere modes for emotional processing, whereas men rely on analytic, left hemisphere modes for emotional processing (Buck, 1982), but there are as yet no clear data to support this hypothesis. Gender differences in most of these biological processes (cerebral lateralization, neurochemical, hormonal, and neuroelectric processes) are not well documented, particularly before puberty, and their meaning is controversial when they are documented (cf. McGlone, 1980).

Perhaps the clearest biology-behavior connection relevant to a discussion of gender differences is the well documented relationship between the male hormone androgen and aggression in animals, with aggression defined as an attack on another (cf. Daly & Wilson, 1978; Tieger, 1980). Increasing amounts of the hormone are associated with increasing frequency of aggression in many animals (cf. Tieger, 1980). However, the relationship between aggression and hormones in humans is not as clear (Tieger, 1980). Furthermore, the relationship between aggression and emotions is complicated, with many theorists positing that emotions such as anger and frustration precipitate a readiness to act aggressively, but that the experience of affect and aggressive acts do not have a one to one correspondence (cf. Frodi et al., 1977). Thus, although human males engage in more frequent aggression than human females do (cf. Maccoby & Jacklin, 1980), there is no evidence to suggest the existence of biologically mediated differences in the emotions preceding or accompanying aggressive behaviors. Thus, differential emotional development for the two sexes cannot be easily predicted by theories emphasizing biological concomitants of emotion.

Social/Cognitive Theories

Sociological, social learning, object-relations, and cognitive-developmental theories of emotional development all emphasize the importance of the social context for emotional development (cf. Greenberg & Mitchell, 1983; Kemper, 1978 a and b; Lazarus, 1982; Piaget, 1981; Schachter & Singer, 1962; Sroufe, 1979). Social learning theorists (cf. Lazarus, 1982; Schachter & Singer, 1962) posit that emotions are learned associations involving cognitive interpretations of physiologically arousing situations. In accordance with this theory, differential emotional development for the two sexes may occur if parents socialize the emotions of their sons and daughters differently (apply different contingencies to their behaviors) or if the behaviors or emotional reactions of adult males and females are observed to differ and children imitate those differences.

Cognitive-developmental theorists (Piaget, 1981; Sroufe, 1979) emphasize that the interaction among the infant's temperament at birth (which may be genetically determined), the mother's emotional style, the child's cognitive capabilities, and the quality of the situational context (which may vary over time) affect the course of children's abilities to recognize, express, experience, and cope with emotions. Cognitive-developmental theorists also emphasize that the increasing complexity of cognitive skills occurring with development is inextricably tied to greater complexity of emotional experiences (cf. Sommers, 1982). Gender differences in rates of cognitive and biological maturation, such as girls' superior language abilities at an early age, may be related to differential rates of emotional development for the two sexes (cf. Waber, 1976). In addition, if any one of the other variables hypothesized to be critical for emotional development differs for the two sexes (e.g., temperament), differences in the quality of mother-infant interaction will result, which will in turn differentially influence the emotional development of each sex.

Object relations theorists hypothesize that the quality of the mother-child relationship influences the child's ability to integrate and modulate feelings such as anger and loneliness, to be empathic, and to self-soothe (cf. Greenberg & Mitchell, 1983; Stechler & Kaplan, 1980). Recent feminist revisions of psychoanalytic and object relations theories (Chodorow, 1978; Lewis, 1976, 1983; Miller, 1976) emphasize differences in the quality of the mother-child relationship for girls and boys as well as differences in male and female sociocultural status as determining differences in emotional development.

Miller (1976) hypothesizes that women are characterized by greater sensitivity to nonverbal signals, greater envy, as well as greater expressions of vulnerability, self-directed hostility, weakness, and helplessness than are men. She theorizes that these qualities are due to the subordinate position of women which both requires them to please and accommodate men as well as to express for men socially unacceptable emotional experiences, for example, vulnerability and helplessness. Men need to deny such emotional experiences because they are incompatible with the characteristics of male identity, especially achievement.

Both Lewis (1983) and Chodorow (1978) argue that the quality and/or importance of attachment experiences and relationships differ for men and women, producing differences in emotional experiences. According to Chodorow (1978), girls are oriented toward affective, relational issues because they are parented by adults of the same sex (i.e., women), resulting in a lack of separateness in relation to others. In contrast, boys must clearly differentiate from mothers in order to develop separate, masculine sexual identities, producing repression of affective and relational issues.

Lewis (1976, 1983, and this issue) somewhat similarly argues that emotions are based on attachment systems, and that the threat of loss of attachment results in the emotions shame and/or guilt, which aim to restore the attachment. Lewis (1976, 1983, and this issue) further argues that women are more prone toward experiencing shame and men toward experiencing guilt. Her argument includes the following points: (1) Women's low sociocultural status causes women to feel (realistically) inferior, which predisposes them to experience shame, that is, to experience vicariously others' negative views of themselves; (2) because women care more about their relationships with others than do men (i.e., are more affiliative, a characteristic which Lewis [1983] argues may be biologically based), shame is more easily induced in women than it is in men. In other words, women experience more negative feelings about themselves because of the importance they place on the approval or disapproval of others; and (3) men's greater aggressiveness relative to women's (which again may be biologically based) leads them to experience more guilt. Guilt is aimed at actively making amends to another because of a wrong-doing or because of an injury inflicted on others, and both the initial act of injury and the feeling or act of reparation require aggressive behaviors, wishes, or feelings.

In his sociological theory of emotions, Kemper (1978 a and b) posits some ideas which are quite similar to those of feminist thinkers in the importance placed on the lower status, power, and sense of worth women have in relation to men as determining the quality of their emotional experiences. According to Kemper (1978 a and b), the function of emotions is to maintain or change social relationships, with the power and status inherent in the relationship determining the quality and intensity of the emotion to be experienced. For example, he theorizes that guilt results from an excessive use of power against others; shame from a sense of being unworthy of status; anxiety from the aversive use of power by others; depression when benefits felt to be deserved are denied. Although Kemper (1978 a and b) does not directly posit hypotheses about gender differences in emotional development, implicit in his theory is the prediction that women may experience more shame, anxiety, depression, and less anger than do men because of their low status, power, and sense of unworthiness.

To summarize the predictions about gender differences inherent in the theories reviewed above: Women should experience and express less anger and guilt than do men (according to psychoanalytic, genetic-evolutionary, and sociological theories); experience and express more self-directed hostility, envy, shame, depression, vulnerability, helplessness, and anxiety than do men (according to feminist psychoanalytic, drive-based psychoanalytic, object-relations, and sociological theories); direct feelings internally rather than externally (according to psychoanalytic theories); be more sensitive to nonverbal cues than are men (according to biological-evolutionary theories and feminist psychoanalytic theories); and be more emotionally expressive in general than are men (according to feminist psychoanalytic theories). It is noteworthy that theorists do not predict gender differences in the experience or recognition of fear, since the data to be reviewed below indicate that there are gender differences in the recognition and attribution of fear. From the perspective of cognitive-developmental theorists, predictions about gender differences are dependent on data concerning gender differences in the variables theorized to be of importance to emotional functioning: temperament, socialization practices, and cognitive maturation. These data will be reviewed and discussed below.

Interestingly, theorists do not seem to disagree about the direction or quality of gender differences, but rather in the relative emphasis they place on the developmental processes responsible for such differences, that is, biological-evolutionary processes vs. social-cognitive processes. These etiological differences lead to different hypotheses about the developmental timetable with which gender differences in emotions should emerge. Thus, biological-evolutionary theorists might predict the existence of some gender differences in emotional functioning at birth; whereas social-cognitive theorists would predict such differences emerging over the course of development as a function of socialization practices and of cognitive maturity. Object relations theorists would closely explore the development of gender differences during early mother-infant interactions. Drive-based psychoanalytic theorists would focus on Oedipal and adolescent life stages during which anatomical sex differences become critical for determining the nature of developmental conflicts. Theorists subscribing to a sociological view of emotions would explore gender differences in development as a function of power and status within cultural or subcultural groups.

The next sections of the present paper will review the empirical evidence for gender differences in emotional development, and for different emotional socialization practices for each sex. Gender differences in emotional development will be discussed with reference to the major components of emotion: emotional expression, recognition, experience, and defenses. Gender differences in defenses will be reviewed first, since defensive processes may affect the interpretation of gender differences found in any of the other components of emotions.

Gender Differences in Defenses and Display Rules

Defenses

Defenses are theorized to be processes which involve the distortion of a conflict-laden or socially unacceptable feeling, thought, or wish in order to mediate among impulses, internal and external prohibitions, and reality (A. Freud, 1936/1946; Vaillant, 1971), or in order to present the self in a socially acceptable light (Rogers, 1951). As previously discussed, theorists predict that females should use defenses that direct feelings internally while males should use defenses that direct feelings externally (Chodorow, 1978; Freud, 1925/1961, 1933/1965; Miller, 1976). In fact, research has indicated that projection (an outer-directed defense) is stereotyped as a masculine response and self-blame (an inner-directed defense) as a feminine response by fifth and sixth grade boys and girls (Dollinger, Staley, & McGuire, 1981). Contrary to work with adults in which masculine stereotypes are more socially desirable than are feminine stereotypes (Rosenkrantz, Vogel, Bee, Broverman, & Broverman, 1968), self-blame is viewed more favorably than is projection by elementary school children (Dollinger, Staley, & McGuire, 1981).

Projective measures of children's defensiveness, including the TAT and The Defense Mechanism Inventory, have tended to yield results consistent with such sex role stereotypes and with psychoanalytic theories: Boys use more externalized defenses, involving turning against others or projection, whereas girls use internalized defenses involving turning against themselves or denying or reversing an expected response (Cramer, 1979, 1983 a and b). These differences are more apparent in late adolescents, adults, and young children than in latency aged children and early adolescents. Cramer (1983b) suggests that the lack of sex differences in defenses during the latency period is consistent with Anna Freud's (1936/1946) hypothesis that the need for defense utilization is reduced during this relatively quiescent psychosexual stage.

Other measures of childrens' defensiveness have included self-report measures and tasks requiring children to attribute emotions to stories. Explorations of gender differences using these measures have yielded inconsistent results. Some studies have shown that girls use less denial and are less defensive than are boys (Brody, Rozek, & Muten, in press; Gilbert, 1969; Hill & Sarason, 1966), and that boys' defensiveness relative to girls' increases with age (Hill & Sarason, 1966). Other studies report no sex differences (Douglas & Rice 1979; Rothenberg, 1970). Brody, Rozek, & Muten (in press) also found no sex differences in mothers' ratings of preschoolers' use of internalization, denial, and stoicism.

Display Rules

Display rules are cultural standards about the quality and intensity of emotions that can be expressed in different contexts (cf. Saarni, 1979). Display rules thus represent reality prohibitions on emotional expression, and as such, may contribute to the use of and development of defenses. Age and sex differences in the understanding and application of these rules are beginning to be explored (Feldman,

Jenkins, & Poopola, 1979; Feldman & White, 1980; Saarni, 1979; Shennum & Bugental, 1982; Yarczower, Kilbride, & Hill, 1979). Children are either interviewed concerning their understanding of display rules, or they are asked to "pretend" to behave in certain ways by the experimenters. Several studies have indicated that with age, both boys and girls increasingly understand that emotional experience and expression do not have a one to one correspondence (Saarni, 1979), and that girls increasingly inhibit negative feelings (Feldman & White, 1980; Shennum & Bugental, 1982) whereas boys become better at neutralizing affects or decreasing overall expressiveness (Buck, 1977; Feldman & White, 1980; Saarni, 1982; Shennum & Bugental, 1982). Feldman, Jenkins, and Poopola (1979) found that both boys and girls had increasing control over emotional expressions with age, although girls had somewhat greater control over facial expressions than did boys and were rated as being better dissemblers in public than in private situations. Saarni (1979) found that girls tended to invoke the need for display rules in order to maintain relationships, whereas boys invoked them in order to maintain norms and rules.

Summary of Research on Defensiveness and Display Rules

The research on display rules and defenses suggests that gender differences in these processes are highly consistent with both cultural sex role stereotypes and theoretical predictions discussed previously. Girls tend to inhibit negative affects, and to turn them against themselves, and boys tend to neutralize the expression of most feelings and to project negative feelings externally. Developmental trends in these processes are inconsistent, with some studies indicating the existence of gender differences in young children and late adolescents, but not in latency aged children (Cramer, 1983b); and other studies indicating increasing gender differences in defensiveness with age (Feldman & White, 1980; Hill & Sarason, 1966; Saarni, 1982).

Further studies on defenses and display rules are needed to thoroughly explore the ways in which rules for the expression of affect vary as a function of age, culture, situational context. Existing research on defensiveness and display rules highlights the need for caution in interpreting the data on emotional expression, recognition, and expression to be discussed below. Since males and females are subject to different display rules and social pressures about the expression of affect, as the data suggest, then tendencies to conform to such pressures may confound or influence any interpretations of the data concerning gender differences in emotional development. For example, the greater emotional expressivity of women relative to men cited in many studies (cf. Hall, 1979) may not mean that women are more emotionally expressive than are men in all situations, but rather that they may be less subject to social constraints or display rules about emotional expression in experimental situations than are men.

Gender Differences in Emotional Expression

Theorists predict that women should express more vulnerability, helplessness, shame, anxiety, envy, depression, and less anger and guilt than do men. Furthermore, women should be more emotionally expressive in general than are men (Kemper, 1978 a and b; Lewis, 1976, 1983; Miller, 1976; Mitchell, 1974; Strouse, 1974). Emotional expressions have most often been measured in two different ways: Expressions are rated by judges (a) either after having been induced in subjects or (b) during the course of naturalistic observations. In studies of gender differences, there are several methodological problems with both types of measures. Judges are most frequently asked to compare the facial expressions of girls and boys without being blind to the sex of the child. Because of the strong sex role stereotypes concerning emotional expression discussed previously, observers may tend to be biased in their ratings of expressions. Researchers using these methodologies may actually be measuring how judges perceive males and females, rather than what males and females differentially express.

A second problem with this research is the relative lack of emphasis placed on the situational context in which the emotion is being studied. Research on sex differences in adult emotions as well as theories about emotional development suggest that an understanding of the situational context that provokes and maintains emotional expression may be critical for understanding gender differences. For example, very different precipitants have been found to elicit anger in women than in men (Frodi, MacCauley, & Thome, 1977). Developmental researchers make a serious mistake whenever they generalize about gender differences in expressiveness after studying only one situation. Although developmental researchers have emphasized the importance of context by interpreting the meaning of an emotional behavior differently depending on the situation that precipitates it (e.g., crying has been considered to be an index of fear when linked to separation- and stranger-anxiety [Kagan, 1978] and an index of anger/frustration when linked to peer interactions [Landreth,

1941]), they have failed to manipulate systematically the situational context as one of the predictors of sex differences in emotional expressiveness.

Another conceptual problem not adequately addressed in the emotional expression literature is that the same emotional expression may have a different meaning for each sex. Thus, smiling in adult females may be related to social anxiety and deference; whereas in adult males it may more often be related to sociability and appreciation (cf. Weitz, 1976). Keeping these limitations in mind, the studies on sex differences in emotional expression will be reviewed by dividing them into those using affect induction techniques, naturalistic observations, and other methodologies.

Affect Induction Techniques

The methodology common to these studies is that the emotional expressiveness of children's faces is rated by judges after children have watched slides or videotapes, have listened to stories, or have posed facial expressions according to experimenter's verbal directions. Judges have included parents, other children, or unfamiliar adults who have rated boys and girls on the intensity, appropriateness, and quality of their expressions (Brown & Cunningham, 1981; Buck, 1975, 1977; Feinman & Feldman, 1982; Field & Walden, 1982 a and b; Hamilton, 1973; Masters, 1981; Morency & Krauss, 1982). Most of these researchers have found no sex differences in rated expressivity (Brown & Cunningham, 1981; Buck, 1975, 1977; Field & Walden, 1982 a and b; Hamilton, 1973; Morency & Krauss, 1982). When sex differences do emerge they are often in a direction consistent with sex role stereotypes and theoretical predictions: Females are judged to be better at communicating affect than are males by undergraduate observers (Buck, 1975; Masters, 1981); females' anger is identified significantly less than chance, or is perceived as sadness or happiness (Feinman & Feldman, 1982) and males' expressivity is judged to decrease with age (Buck, 1977).

Felleman, Barden, Carlson, Rosenberg, and Masters (1983) found that among a sample of unfamiliar adults, spontaneous displays of anger by children were more recognizable than posed displays when the expressor was female, whereas the reverse was true when the expressor was male. Girls may pose anger less well than boys because of socialization pressures on the expression of anger by girls. These pressures may produce expressive inhibition when girls are made aware of their emotional expressions, as they would be in the process of posing.

One indication that these studies may be measuring the biases or perceptions of judges instead of providing an objective measure of children's expressiveness is that in some studies, judgments of expressivity have been found to vary depending on the familiarity of the raters with the infants and children (Condry & Condry, 1976; Feinman & Feldman, 1982). However, male and female raters from varying age and racial groups have been found to agree on their ratings of facial expressivity (cf. Eiland & Richardson, 1976; Gitter, Mostofsky, & Quincy, 1971). These findings suggest either that gender differences in rated expressivity may not be entirely a function of observer bias, or that the same sex role stereotypes about emotional expressivity are shared by members of different races, age groups, and by both sexes.

Naturalistic Observations

Naturalistic observations of children's emotional expressivity are quite inconsistent in their conclusions concerning gender differences, again possibly due to a failure to study situational context systematically. The context in which emotional expressions have been observed varies widely from study to study. Gender differences in newborn and infant emotional expression have been studied in the presence of siblings and mothers (Jacobs & Moss, 1976; Malatesta & Haviland, 1982; Moss, 1967); in the process of separating from mothers, with and without a barrier (Fiering & Lewis, 1979; Goldberg & Lewis, 1969; Jacklin, Maccoby, & Dick, 1973; Robson, Pederson, & Moss, 1969; Skarin, 1977; Trause, 1977; Van Lieshout, 1975); in the presence of unfamiliar adults (Kagan 1978; Lewis & Weinraub, 1979); and in the absence of any interpersonal or cognitive interactions (Feldman, Brody, & Miller, 1980; Osofsky & O'Connell, 1977; Phillips, King, & DuBois, 1978; Yang & Moss, 1978; Zeskind & Lester, 1978). Gender differences in preschoolers' emotional expressions have been studied in the context of interactions with peers (Camras, 1977; Landreth, 1941) and parents (Golding, 1982). As previously noted, differences in the situational context may help to account for the wide variations in results concerning gender differences in emotional expressiveness. For example, Landreth (1941) found that in an observational study of a preschool, girls cried more frequently as a result of accidental injury than did boys, whereas boys cried more frequently as a result of interactions with objects or conflicts with adults.

Many studies of gender differences in infant emotional expressiveness are studies of temperament, that is, the infants' reactive tendencies to external and internal stimulation. Cognitive developmental theorists hypothesize that gender differences in temperament should influence and be influenced by the quality of mother-infant interactions, which would in turn differentially affect the emotional development of each sex. Some reviews of infant temperament research indicate no evidence for any gender differences (Rothbart & Derryberry, 1981); yet Haviland and Malatesta (1981) review several studies which indicate that at birth, boys are more irritable, more emotionally labile, less consolable, startle more easily, and cry more intensely than do girls. The discrepancy between Haviland and Malatesta's conclusions and the conclusions based on reviews of infant temperament researchers may be partially understandable in that measures of temperament usually include patterns of behavior such as thresholds to stimulation and temporal response patterns which differ from those cited by Haviland and Malatesta (1981).

However, the studies Haviland and Malatesta review should be interpreted cautiously because in only two of the studies (Malatesta & Haviland, 1982; Phillips, King, & Dubois 1978) were observers blind to the sex of the infant. Observer bias may thus have been operating in many of the studies. Haviland and Malatesta (1981) also do not cite some of the neonatal studies that reveal no gender differences in variables related to emotional expressivity or infant temperament (cf. Ashton, 1971; Bell, Weller, & Waldrop, 1971; Caldwell & Leeper 1974).

In a well-designed study, Cunningham and Shapiro (1984) found that even when raters were deceived as to the correct sex of the infant, males were rated as producing more frequent anger, less frequent sadness, and more intense expressions of happiness, anger, sadness, and fear than were females. Malatesta and Haviland (1982) found that infant girls were rated as more frequently interested than infant boys during mother-child interactions. Replications of these studies in which context is varied are needed before it can be concluded that there are gender differences at birth in the intensity and quality of emotional expressiveness. For example, it may be that infant girls display more frequent expressions of interest than boys only when interacting with mothers and not in other social or cognitive interactions, which would certainly modify the conclusion to be drawn from Malatesta and Haviland's (1982) work.

Some studies have indicated no gender differences in the quality and intensity of angry, sad, interested, or happy facial expressions in preschool and young school-aged children (Camras, 1977; Golding, 1982). Lewis and Michaelson (1983) found a tendency for nursery school girls to display more anger, more intense fear, and more happiness than boys in their social interactions; while Goodenough (1931) also reported angry outbursts more frequently among girls than boys until 2 years of age, at which time girls' angry expressions decreased sharply. Observations of preschool children watching television which at times lost the video portion indicated that boys displayed more anger than did girls and that girls displayed more fear and happiness than did boys (Birnbaum & Croll, 1984). Angry expressions have also been observed by placing a barrier in front of children to prevent them from reaching a toy or a parent. While initial research in this area revealed gender differences in 13-month-olds consisting of more crying by girls and more instrumental action by boys (Goldberg & Lewis, 1969), further research showed no gender differences (Jacklin, Maccoby, & Dick, 1973), or gender differences which varied as a function of age or the type of barrier (Fiering & Lewis, 1979; Van Lieshout, 1975) and reversed the direction of gender differences found earlier.

Fearful behaviors have been observed in relation to separation from mothers, anxiety toward strangers, and in dentists' offices. Measures of fear have included crying, withdrawal from or wariness in novel situations. Again, results of these studies for gender differences have been highly inconsistent. Fear exhibited in dentists' offices has not been found to vary in quantity or quality as a function of gender in a large number of studies reviewed by Winer (1982). Lewis and Weinraub (1979) in a review paper, cite a large number of studies indicating that boys are more distressed at maternal separation than are girls of comparable ages; while Kagan (1978) in a paper that summarizes several studies of separation- and stranger-anxiety arrives at conclusions which are somewhat contradictory to those of Lewis and Weinraub: Girls exhibit stranger- and separation-anxiety earlier than boys, and thus within the same age levels they exhibit greater distress than do boys. Kagan (1978) attributes the gender differences in separation-anxiety to earlier cognitive maturation in girls than in boys.

Other Measures of Expressiveness

Other measures of children's expressiveness have included ratings by parents or teachers (Brody, Rozek, & Muten, in press; Buck, 1977; Buss, Iscoe, & Buss, 1979; Gilbert, 1969) and frequency counts of children's affective vocabularies (Bretherton & Beeghly, 1982). With the exception of Buck's (1977) finding that girls were rated higher in expressiveness by teachers than were boys, none of these other studies showed any evidence of sex differences.

Conclusions About Expressiveness

The literature on expressiveness discussed above reveals that theoretical predictions concerning gender differences in the expression of shame, guilt, vulnerability, helplessness, and jealousy have been virtually unexplored. Researchers have explored theoretical predictions about more general emotionality, and less frequent anger expressed by girls than by boys. This research reveals that there are as yet very little convincing data that such gender differences exist in children. Preliminary evidence is accumulating that neonatal boys may be more intensely expressive of affect than are neonatal girls, which suggests the existence of a biological basis underlying gender differences in the intensity of emotional expressions, but in a direction which is opposite to theoretical predictions. Other evidence indicates that boys may become worse at expressing affects with age (Buck 1977; Shennum & Bugental, 1982) perhaps because of socialization pressures that encourage them to neutralize or to mask emotions, as consistent with social-cognitive theories of emotional development. Boys may be taught to mask emotions because the intensity of their emotions is considered to be culturally inappropriate.

Overall, the developmental data on expressiveness do not support any theory about the development of gender differences clearly, but instead suggest that gender differences in emotional expressiveness vary as a function of age, cognitive abilities, quality of emotion, and situational context, in accordance with culturally determined display rules. The failure to confirm theoretical predictions, however, may be due to researchers having neglected to study important theoretical issues, as will be discussed more fully below.

Gender Differences in Emotional Recognition

Many theorists concur that females should be better at nonverbal emotional recognition than are males, and a review by Hall (1978) of studies of adult men and women indicates that this is indeed the case. The studies Hall (1978) reviewed consisted of adult men and women judging emotionally laden face, body, or vocal cues presented in drawings, photographs, films, videotapes, and filtered speech.

A review of the developmental studies in affect recognition indicates that the etiological and developmental processes underlying adult female superiority are far from clear. Gender differences in the development of the ability to decode or recognize affects in others have been studied with respect to the ability to discriminate affects in emotionally laden situations, in facial expressions, in tone of voice, and in music. Studies generally have been highly consistent in indicating that there are no gender differences in the ability to match affectively laden situations with appropriate facial expressions or with appropriate affective verbal labels (Abramovitch, 1977; Barden, Zelko, Duncan, & Masters, 1980; Borke, 1971; Brody & Harrison, 1984; Gove & Keating, 1979; Hughes, Tingle, & Sawin, 1981; Kurdek & Rogdon, 1975; Mood, Johnson, & Shantz, 1978; Rothenberg, 1970; Weiner, Graham, Stern, & Lawson, 1982). Exceptions are studies by Borke (1973) in which 3- to 6-year-old girls were better at matching appropriate facial expressions to stories than were boys, and by Chandler, Paget, and Koch (1978), in which it was found that girls were better at identifying the defenses implicit in affect-laden stories than were boys.

No gender differences have been found in infants' and children's abilities to discriminate among facial expressions using paired preference and habituation techniques, as well as matching and sorting tasks (Brown & Cunningham, 1981; Daly, Abramovitch, & Pliner, 1980; Eiland & Richardson, 1976; Field & Walden, 1982a; Gitter, Mostofsky, & Quincy, 1971; Hamilton, 1973; LaBarbara, Izard, Vietze, & Parisi, 1976; Morency & Krauss, 1982; Sherrod, 1979; Young-Browne, Rosenfeld, & Horowitz, 1977). One group of researchers did find that within a same race group, children could more appropriately identify the affect expressions displayed by same sex than by opposite sex children (Felleman et al., 1983), perhaps indicating differential attention paid to same sex children at this age. Furthermore, Field and Walden (1982b) found that girls tended to be more accurate than boys in matching their own videotaped expressions to photographs of expressions.

In a recent study involving childrens' abilities to discriminate the affects elicited by music, Cunningham and Smith (1984) required children to listen to music which had been previously categorized by adults as depicting happy, angry, sad, and fearful feelings. At ages 4, 5, 6, and adulthood, girls were better than boys at identifying sad and happy music, and 4-year-old girls were equivalent to adults and better than any other age group of children at identifying fear.

Rosenthal and his colleagues (Rosenthal, Archer, Hall, DiMatteo, & Rogers, 1979a; Rosenthal, Hall, DiMatteo, Rogers, & Archer, 1979b) did a series of studies on sensitivity to nonverbal cues using a measure called the Profile of Nonverbal Sensitivity (PONS). The test consists of twenty affect laden situations portrayed by an American woman in which channels of communication are varied in visual and auditory cues. In recent studies (Rosenthal et al., 1979b) a man has also been used to convey emotions. Subjects were asked to label these situations affectively, given multiple choice cues. Rosenthal et al. (1979b) report that as early as third grade, relative to males, females showed superior recognition skills, were better at judging negative emotions, and profited more from the presence of body cues. For high school, junior high school, and children's groups, males tended to exhibit more variability in their PONS scores than did females. Furthermore, in third through fifth grades, younger boys performed relatively better in comparison to younger girls than did older boys in comparison to older girls.

In a study of 9- to 15-year-olds, high school, and college students, Blanck, Rosenthal, Snodgrass, DePaulo, and Zuckerman (1981) found that relative to males, females became increasingly better with age in decoding nonverbal cues from controllable sources, such as the face, but less good at decoding nonverbal cues from "leaky," less controllable sources, such as bodily cues. The authors suggest that with development, females may become increasingly sensitive to the social consequences which may ensue from decoding cues which the communicator does not intentionally wish to convey. However, because the data were analyzed using the superiority of females relative to males as the dependent variable, it is not clear whether the results are due to developmental changes in females' nonverbal recognition skills, males' nonverbal recognition skills, or both.

Rosenthal et al. (1979b) also found that the relationship between PONS scores and verbal SAT scores was higher for males than for females. They suggest that analytic skills may be less related to nonverbal affect recognition skills in females than in males. This suggestion is consistent with biologically based theories of emotional development, which predict that emotional development in males is mediated by analytically oriented left hemisphere functioning, whereas emotional development in females is mediated by more intuitive right hemisphere functioning (Buck, 1982). This suggestion is also consistent with feminist psychoanalytic theories (cf. Chodorow, 1978) about the greater value placed on emotional processes for women than for men. Because of the importance placed on emotional sensitivity for females, female emotional recognition skills may be independent of cognitive ability level, whereas the deemphasis on emotional sensitivity in males may ensure that only males with better developed cognitive skills learn to recognize emotional cues. Rosenthal et al. (1979b) also hypothesize that females' superiority in nonverbal affect recognition may be due to greater eye contact made by females relative to males. However, when the amount of eye contact was partialled out, female superiority in nonverbal recognition skills was still evident.

In other developmental studies using the PONS, Hall and Halberstadt (1981) explored the relationship between gender identity (using 4 different gender identity measures) and nonverbal decoding skills. Contrary to predictions, they found that with increasing age, the ability to decode cues was increasingly positively correlated with masculine gender identity, and negatively correlated with feminine gender identity. However, neither masculine nor feminine gender identity scores significantly accounted for female superiority in decoding nonverbal cues. The authors suggest that female superiority in decoding cues may have less to do with traditionally assessed aspects of gender identity (e.g., passivity and dependence vs. activity and independence) than with the amount of attention paid to nonverbal cues. Another interesting finding was that the attitude toward female roles interacted with the ability to decode nonverbal cues: Nontraditional attitudes about women correlated with the ability to decode cues from women's voices; whereas traditional attitudes about women tended to correlate with the ability to decode cues from men's voices. These findings suggest that values and attitudes can significantly influence emotional recognition skills.

Discussion About Affect Recognition Studies

Most of the developmental studies concerning gender differences in affect discrimination or recognition indicate that there are no clear or consistent gender differences. As noted previously, this is surprising in light of the very clear gender differences found in adults' nonverbal recognition abilities (Hall, 1978), and suggests that adult gender differences in affect discrimination and recognition are not innate. The influence of socialization processes on gender differences is suggested by Rosenthal et al.'s finding (1979b) that younger boys do less badly relative to younger girls than do older boys relative to older girls in nonverbal recognition skills, and by Blanck et al.'s (1981) finding that with development, females become less superior to males in their ability to decode nonintentional cues which the communicator does not wish to convey. However, studies tend to be limited in the range of affects tested and often require children to discriminate or recognize obviously differentiable emotional cues. The few studies which do show female superiority in affect recognition may be testing subtle affect recognition skills not assessed by other studies (Blanck et al., 1981; Chandler et al., 1978; Cunningham & Smith, 1984; Hall & Halberstadt, 1981; Rosenthal et al.,

1979 a and b). It is also possible that the studies showing female superiority in affect recognition require various cognitive skills in addition to affect recognition, for example, concept formation. These cognitive skills may mature at different rates for girls vs. boys, thus affecting gender differences in affect recognition.

The developmental processes involved in gender differences in emotional recognition skills thus remain unclear. Developmental researchers need to explore the development of gender differences in the nonverbal recognition of a wide range of audio and visual emotional cues, using a variety of measures. Such measures might include increased use of videotaped or filmed interactions as well as more frequent use of naturalistic observations. Furthermore, theoretical predictions about the relationships among emotional recognition abilities and social and interpersonal issues, such as power and status; values, such as the importance males and females attribute to knowing how other people feel; and cognitive processing strategies, such as analytic vs. intuitive strategies, need to be systematically explored. All of these relationships have important implications for the development of gender differences in emotional recognition abilities. The relationship between gender identity and emotional recognition abilities is also clearly important. Hall and Halberstadt's (1981) work suggests that traditionally assessed aspects of gender identity, such as dependence vs. independence, are not related to nonverbal recognition skills; but some theories suggest that other aspects of gender identity may be related, for example, sense of self-worth and low status and power (Miller, 1976).

A final word of caution about the interpretation of the affect recognition studies reviewed above is that they may be measuring the child's own affective experiences. Work on projective testing has indicated that the quality of the feelings preschoolers project into ambiguous story characters relates to the quality of their emotional behaviors as rated by their mothers (Brody et al., in press). Thus, it is possible that the feelings children attribute to music, to story situations, or to facial expressions, may partially reflect the quality of their own affective experiences. This issue may be especially problematic when children are cognitively egocentric and are incapable of distinguishing self from other.

Gender Differences in Affect Experience

Theories predict that girls should experience less anger and guilt, and more vulnerability, shame, helplessness, envy, and self-directed hostility than do boys. Affective experience is perhaps the most difficult dimension of affect to measure. It has been assessed using physiological techniques, such as skin conductance; self-report measures, including interviews; and projective measures, such as story completion tasks. These measures are all somewhat limited in assessing the quality of emotional experience. Physiological arousal may not have a one-to-one correspondence with emotional experience, for example, it may vary inversely with facial expressiveness (cf. Buck, Miller, & Caul, 1974; Field, 1982). Interview and self-report techniques are undoubtedly subject to censorship in that children may monitor what they report in accordance with display rules and sex role stereotypes. Brody and Carter (1982) found that children attributed socially undesirable feelings (intense, negative feelings) more frequently to stories when the story protaganists were ambiguous characters than when the story protaganists were the children themselves, that is, "you." This work indicates that children will censor socially unacceptable feelings when asked directly about the quality of their emotional experiences. Projective measures are perhaps the least subject to social desirability constraints, but because they tend to have low face or content validity, they require extensive studies of their concurrent and criterion validity in order to be meaningfully interpreted. Studies using all of these measures will be reviewed below. In addition, studies of empathy (vicarious emotional arousal in response to another person's emotional state) will be reviewed separately in this section.

Physiological Measures

Physiological measures have rarely been used to study affective development. Buck (1977) measured skin conductance in 4- to 6-year-old children who were watching affect-laden slides, and asked mothers to rate the type of slide children had viewed (familiar vs. unfamiliar people, unpleasant, unusual), as well as the pleasantness of the child's emotional expression. He found that in boys, high ratings of facial expressivity related to few skin conductance responses, but this was not true for girls. However, there were no significant gender differences in the skin conductance measure. In contrast, Buck, Miller, and Caul (1974) found that adult males tended to internalize (to be facially nonexpressive and physiologically aroused), whereas adult females tended to externalize (to be facially expressive without physiological arousal). Field (1982) also reports an inverse relationship between the frequency of facial expressions and cardiac responsivity in infants, but she does not indicate whether she analyzed for gender differences.

Self-Report Measures

Studies using self-report, interview, or self-attribution measures to assess the nature of emotional experiences, find that relative to boys, girls report greater sensitivity to feelings (Mackie, 1980); are more willing to acknowledge affect states (Gilbert, 1969), including self-control problems (Karoly & Ruehlman, 1982); and can better discuss the experience of affect (Demos, 1975; Lutz, 1980). Brody et al. (in press) found that 4-year-old boys attributed less intense emotions to themselves than did girls, while Brody (1984) found that 7- to 11-year-old girls attributed sadness and fear more frequently and anger less frequently to themselves than did same age boys. As previously discussed, these self-report measures may be subject to censorship in that children may feel compelled to conform to emotional sex role stereotypes or display rules.

Projective Measures

Projective measures of children's emotional experiences have included story completion and story telling techniques (Brody & Carter, 1982; Hoffman, 1975; Rosenzweig, 1960) and emotional attribution tasks (cf. Brody & Carter 1982; Feshbach & Roe, 1968). The use of projective story telling techniques has indicated that males attribute less fear (Feshbach & Roe, 1968) and less intense fear to stories than do girls (Brody & Carter, 1982), perhaps due to social pressures on the expression of fear. In a contradiction of psychoanalytic theory, Hoffman (1975) found that girls were more likely to attribute guilt to same sex story characters than were boys. He also found that these gender differences were greater in adults than in 5th and 7th graders, suggesting that females developed a relatively greater tendency toward guilt with age. Using the children's Frustration–Aggression Measure, in which children are asked to report on what story protagonists would say in frustrating situations, Rosenzweig (1960) reports no consistent gender differences. However, he does report a study in which nine-year-old girls were found to show more angry and aggressive responses toward other children than toward adults; whereas boys were found to project angry and aggressive responses when in conflict with both other children and adults.

Empathy

Empathy has been defined as a vicarious affective experience in response to the affect of another. The developmental study of empathy is quite complex, in that some researchers have theorized that empathy requires several sophisticated cognitive skills: a self-concept, including the ability to differentiate self from others, the ability to take the role of another, and the ability to understand situation-emotion relationships (Deutsch & Madle, 1975; Shantz, 1975). None of these skills is characteristic of very young children and some may develop at different rates for boys and girls. Other work on empathy implies that there may be an innate biological preparedness for empathy, and that cognitive processes may actually interfere with the experience of vicarious affect (Buck, 1984; Sagi & Hoffman, 1976). In any case, the importance of cognitive skills in the measures used to study empathy complicates interpretations of the data to be reviewed below.

Although it is frequently reported that girls are more empathic than are boys (Feshbach, 1982; Hoffman, 1977; Hoffman & Levine, 1976) the evidence for sex differences in empathy is far from conclusive. Eisenberg and Lennon (1983), in their thoughtful review of gender differences in empathy, argue that sex differences in empathy are largely a function of the measures used to assess empathy. Self-report measures show the largest sex differences in favor of females, whereas studies using physiological or observational measures show little evidence of sex differences. Eisenberg and Lennon (1983) note the problems inherent in the use of several measures of empathy to study sex differences. Two of the most frequently used measures, the Feshbach and Roe Affective Situations Test for Empathy (FASTE), and measures of reflexive crying in infancy, will be reviewed here. The FASTE was developed by Feshbach and Roe in 1968, and was recently revised by Feshbach in 1982. It requires children to report about their own feelings after hearing affect-laden stories about other children. This task may not be measuring gender differences in the quality of vicarious affective experiences as is commonly assumed, but instead may be measuring either gender differences in children's tendencies to admit to and express their feelings or in children's cognitive abilities to understand the stories. As was previously discussed, children's expression of or admission to feelings may be subject to social desirability pressures or display rules, and may not accurately reflect the nature of their underlying affective experience. The hypothesis that these tasks reflect social desirability pressures is consistent with data indicating that boys are more empathic when the story protagonist in affect-laden stories is male, not female (Deutsch, 1975; Feshbach & Roe, 1968). These data suggest that boys' performance on empathic tasks may vary as a function of whether or not they feel they have permission to admit to affects (which the presence of a male model might encourage). Eisenberg and Lennon (1983) also summarize data which indicate that gender differences in the FASTE may vary as a function of the sex of the experimenter, with children tested by a same-sex experimenter scoring as more empathic than children tested by an opposite-sex experimenter. A further problem with using the Feshbach and Roe task to explore gender differences in empathy is that males and females may express affect via different modalities (e.g., physiologically vs. facially: cf. Buck, Miller, & Caul, 1974) which this task fails to assess. Also, the importance of verbal skills in successfully completing this task neglects nonverbal empathy, which may be more characteristic of very young children (cf. Eisenberg & Lennon, 1983).

Other studies which have frequently been cited to support gender differences in empathy are studies of newborns' spontaneous cries in response to the cries of another infant (cf. Sagi & Hoffman, 1976; Simner, 1971). The fact that female newborns cry responsively for longer periods of time than male newborns has been viewed as evidence for gender differences in empathy at birth. Eisenberg and Lennon (1983) discuss the problems with this conclusion. First, other interpretations can be made about the meaning of these data. For example, perhaps female neonates sustain attention to a task longer than do males, or perhaps they are better at imitation. Second, both male and female neonates were exposed to the cry of a female infant. The implications of this are particularly striking when it is noted that newborn's capacities to differentiate cries are sufficiently well developed that they can differentiate their own cry from that of another neonate (Martin & Clark, 1982). A recent study (Martin & Clark, 1982) using a male newborn cry as a stimulus, found no significant sex differences in responsive cry duration, although females still tended to cry longer than males. Interpretations about gender differences in empathy seem to have gone far beyond what the data can support.

Feshbach (1982) explored correlates of boys' and girls' empathic skills using an updated version of the Feshbach and Roe empathy measure. She found that for boys empathy was primarily a cognitive measure, correlating with vocabulary and reading skills; whereas for girls empathy was correlated with social skills, including prosocial behavior. Although affect labelling and not empathy or affect experience may be being measured, this work is intriguing and suggests different functions or etiologies of affect labelling for boys and girls. These results are consistent with the findings of Rosenthal et al. (1979 a and b) discussed previously, as well as with various suggestions in the literature that affect is a more integral part of relation-ships for females than for males (Mackie, 1980; Saarni, 1979). These differences are also consistent with the idea that males rely on left hemisphere strategies and that females rely on right hemisphere strategies to process emotions. Further exploration of patterns in affective development, as opposed to exploration of single variables, may help to further our understanding of sex differences in emotional development.

Discussion of Affect Experience Studies

What emerges clearly from this literature is that there is very little research that explores major theoretical predictions about gender differences in affective experiences. The theoretical predictions that girls experience more vulnerability, shame, helplessness, envy, and self-directed hostility than do boys are virtually untested. The data do indicate that girls report themselves to be more emotional and are more articulate in discussing emotions than are boys (Demos, 1975; Gilbert, 1969; Lutz, 1980; Mackie, 1980). How well these self-reports reflect the nature of underlying experience rather than conformity to social desirability pressures is an unanswered question. These self-reports vary as a function of the quality of the affect, with girls attributing more sadness and fear to themselves and boys attributing more anger to themselves (Brody, 1984). Similar self-ratings have been made by adult males and females (Allen & Haccoun, 1976). These data are in accordance with theoretical predictions that girls should experience less anger than boys. However, Rosenzweig's report (1960) that girls direct more hostility to peers than to adults, whereas boys direct hostility to both adults and peers, qualifies the conclusion that girls experience less anger than do boys, and suggests that affective experiences may be situationally specific.

Clearly, further work on gender differences in affective experi-ences as predicted by theories is needed. Hoffman's finding (1975) that girls attribute more guilt to stories than do boys contradicts drive-based psychoanalytic theories and Lewis' (1976, 1983) theo-retical predictions. It is not clear, however, whether Hoffman (1975) wrote stories which clearly differentiated feelings of guilt from shame. Feshbach's (1982) finding that empathic skills correlate with social skills in girls and cognitive skills in boys supports feminist psychoanalytic ideas that girls' emotionality is related to the value girls place on relationships. However, Feshbach's work (1982) leads to many unanswered and important questions, including the developmental etiology of such gender differences and other cognitive correlates of such differences.

Both behavioral measures and physiological measures indicate that there are developmental changes in gender differences in affective experience. Buck and his colleagues' work (1974, 1977) indicates that an internalized pattern of physiological arousal and lack of facial expressiveness is found in adult males, but not as clearly in preschool boys. The opposite pattern is found in adult females, but not in preschool girls. Hoffman's (1975) work suggests a developmental progression in females toward an increasing sense of guilt relative to males. Many of the age trends in gender differences suggest the influence of socialization processes, which will be discussed next.

Gender Differences in the Socialization of Emotion

Many theories of emotional development indicate that affect develops within an interpersonal context (cf. Greenberg & Mitchell, 1983; Lewis, 1976, 1978; Miller, 1976), and that gender differences in emotional development result partially from qualitatively different caretaker-child affective exchanges. There is a rapidly accumulating body of literature which supports the idea that mothers and fathers, teachers and peers do interact differently with each sex around affective exchanges. Some of this work suggests that these differential interactions are in directions consistent with emotional sex role stereotypes and theoretical predictions.

Block's (1973) work indicates that parents encourage their sons to be aggressive but unemotional, and their daughters to be emotional but unaggressive. Mothers are more consistent in their responses to their 8- to 14-month-old sons' aggressive behaviors than to their same aged daughters' aggressive behaviors (Kendrick & Dunn, 1983), and show more contingent responding to sons' than to daughters' emotional expressions, responding more frequently to their sons' expressions with imitative expressions (Malatesta & Haviland, 1982). Mothers tend to emphasize anger more frequently when generating stories for preschool sons than daughters, and fathers emphasize affect words more frequently overall when generating stories for preschool daughters than for sons (Greif, Alvarez, & Ulman, 1981). In a more recent study, both mothers and fathers generate affect words more frequently when telling stories to 3- to 5- and 9- to 11-year-old girls than when telling stories to same age boys, but more frequently when telling stories to 6- to 8-year-old boys than to same age girls (Greif, 1984). Greif (1984) speculates that there is a developmental lag in the socialization of affect for boys relative to girls. Very similar patterns are noted by Birnbaum and Croll (1984), who find that parents report greater acceptance of anger in boys than in girls and greater acceptance of fear in girls than in boys. In a retrospective study involving college students, daughters report that their parents discuss feelings more with them and show them more affection than sons report (Barnett, Howard, King, & Dino, 1980).

Three studies indicate that the relationships between parental emotions, parental child rearing practices, and children's emotional and empathic behaviors differ for sons and daughters. Feshbach (1982) reports a study showing that empathy in girls is related to positive mother-daughter relationships, whereas empathy in boys is inversely related to fathers' encouragement of competition. Eisenberg-Berg and Mussen (1978) report a relationship between maternal qualities of being affectionate, egalitarian, nonrestrictive, nonpunitive and sons' empathy, but no relationship between these same maternal qualities and daughters' empathy. (The authors suggest that the lack of a relationship between mothers' and daughters' empathy may be due to a ceiling effect on the daughters' empathy scores.) Bringle and Williams (1979) report a relationship between parental sensitivity to environmental cues and reported jealousy of college-aged daughters, but not of sons.

The influence of sibling interactions on the socialization of emotions has not been studied extensively, but the importance of these interactions is suggested by a study indicating that same sex sibling pairs are more similar in nonverbal decoding abilities than opposite sex sibling pairs (Blanck, Zuckerman, DePaulo, & Rosenthal, 1980).

The effect of teacher-student interaction on emotional development may also be quite dramatic, as suggested by studies on learned helplessness in classroom interactions (Dweck, Davidson, Nelson, & Enna, 1978; Dweck, Goetz, & Strauss, 1980). Although not directly related to the socialization of emotion, the findings that teachers praise girls more for intellectually irrelevant aspects of their behavior (Dweck et al., 1978, 1980), and reprimand them less frequently than boys (Serbin, O'Leary, Kent, & Tonick, 1973), suggests that it would be worthwhile to explore whether or not teachers also reinforce the expression of different emotions by males and females.

Peers and television programs may also be powerful socialization agents in emotional development. Lever (1976) finds that peer group quarrels do not disrupt boys' games but do disrupt girls' games, and she suggests that girls' preference to play in small intimate groups is a training ground for sociocultural skills. Birnbaum and Croll (1984) rated the frequency of anger, happiness, fear, and sadness displayed

by characters on children's television shows and report that male
characters display significantly more anger than female characters.

Although the research on teacher and peer socialization processes
is not directly related to the development of affect, it suggests that
the two sexes have different socialization experiences which may
lead to differences in affect experience, expression, and recognition.
For example, if boys receive loud reprimands more frequently from
teachers than do girls (Serbin et al., 1973), they may learn either to
attend to or to model angry or aggressive behaviors more than girls
do. More research is clearly needed in this area to understand the
effects of peer, teacher, sibling, and parental socialization practices
on the emotional development of each sex. Block (1976) also notes
that socialization practices vary as a function of the child's developmental stage, parental role concepts, and social-cultural pressures,
all of which change over time. Research does not yet reflect the
changing qualities of emotional socialization practices over time.

Conclusions

Developmental Changes in Gender Differences

Emotional development theories suggest that relative to males,
females should be more sensitive to nonverbal cues; more emotionally expressive; less angry and guilty; more shameful, masochistic,
anxious, envious, vulnerable, helpless; and direct their feelings internally rather than externally. Furthermore, many theorists hypothesize that the origins of these gender differences lie partially in the
socialization process. The research reviewed in the present paper
indicates that there are suggestive data to support some of these
hypotheses. However, the developmental processes involved in such
differences and the developmental timetable within which such
differences manifest themselves remain unclear. Furthermore, many
of the theoretical predictions remain untested.

What is the evidence that gender differences do indeed exist in
the emotional functioning of infants, children, and adolescents, independent of the question of the developmental timetable or etiology of such differences? The most consistent data about gender
differences in emotional functioning come from studies about emotional sex role stereotypes as well as self-report, interview, and self-
attribution studies. These studies indicate that females are both
stereotyped to be and report themselves to be more sad, more scared,
less angry, and more emotionally expressive than males. In general
females are more articulate about discussing emotions than are males.
They also attribute more guilt to story characters than do males. At

a very young age, both boys and girls seem to think about their emotional lives in accordance with culturally prescribed standards, or at the very least, they conform to such standards when an audience is present.

Other areas of emotional functioning in which there are indications that gender differences exist include nonverbal recognition skills (with females having superior skills); the quality of emotional defenses (females use internally oriented defenses; males use externally oriented defenses); and the correlates of the ability to label and recognize affects (males' abilities correlate with cognitive skills, females' do not).

Are there developmental changes in the nature and extent of gender differences in these areas of emotional functioning? A review of the research in these areas sheds surprisingly little light on developmental processes. Only a few studies indicate developmental changes. In adults, there are clear gender differences in emotional styles of internalization vs. externalization, whereas such gender differences are not as clear in preschoolers (Buck, 1977; Buck et al., 1974). Gender differences in patterns of internal vs. external defenses and experiences are clearer in adults and late adolescents than in latency aged children (Cramer, 1983 a and b). Boys' defensiveness in the form of denial increases relative to girls' defensiveness during the elementary school years (Hill & Sarason, 1966). Similarly, studies of expressiveness and display rules indicate that boys' overall expressiveness decreases with age, and that girls show fewer negative affects with age (Buck, 1977; Feldman & White, 1980; Saarni, 1982; Shennum & Bugental, 1982). Gender differences increase with age in the intensity of guilt attributed to story characters (i.e., adult women attribute more intense guilt to story characters than do adult men, whereas these gender differences are not as clear in 5th and 7th graders [Hoffman, 1975]). With age, females become more superior to males in decoding overt nonverbal cues, but less superior to males in decoding nonintentional nonverbal cues. These few studies suggest that with development, boys increasingly inhibit the expression and attribution of all emotions, whereas girls increasingly inhibit the expression and recognition of socially unacceptable emotions such as anger. These developmental trends suggest both the influence of socialization processes on gender differences, as predicted by object relations and social learning theorists, and the interaction between cognitive-psychosexual stages and emotional experiences, as predicted by psychoanalytic and cognitive-developmental theorists.

Etiology of Gender Differences: Temperament and Socialization

The clearest data on the variables that influence the development of gender differences in emotional development emerge from studies of the socialization of emotion. Parents have been found to socialize the emotional development of their infant sons and their daughters differently (cf. Malatesta & Haviland, 1982). Parental behaviors such as deemphasizing affects when communicating with preschool sons (Birnbaum & Croll, 1984; Greif, Alvarez, & Ulman, 1981; Greif, 1984) undoubtedly contribute to gender differences in self-report, self-attribution, and sex role stereotyping studies (Birnbaum et al., 1980; Brody, 1984), which are evident by early school age. Differential socialization practices for each gender may be adaptations to innate (genetic or biological) gender differences in temperament, if indeed infant boys are more intensely emotionally expressive than are infant girls (cf. Cunningham & Shapiro, 1984; Malatesta & Haviland, 1982). For example, parents may encourage boys to minimize or mask their affects because their affects are perceived to be, or may in fact be, overly intense. Alternatively, differential socialization practices may simply be attempts to conform to existing social and cultural pressures.

Socialization practices may also influence the cognitive processing strategies used by boys and girls in their emotional experiences and behaviors. Research has indicated that the cognitive abilities of boys, but not girls, correlate with their affect labelling and decoding skills (Feshbach, 1982; Rosenthal et al., 1979 a and b). It may be that boys are encouraged to think analytically about feelings, possibly relying on left hemisphere cognitive strategies, whereas girls are encouraged to think intuitively about feelings, relying on right hemisphere cognitive strategies. Alternatively, innate biological differences may account for these gender differences in the cognitive correlates of emotional development. Another possible explanation is that cognitively mature boys are more developmentally advanced in their emotional abilities than are cognitively immature boys, whereas girls' emotional abilities are independent of their level of cognitive maturity, since all girls are encouraged and socialized to value emotions (cf. Chodorow, 1978).

Thus, although data strongly suggest that socialization practices account for some of the developmental processes involved in gender differences in emotional development, more data are needed which explore the contributions of socialization practices and innate biological predispositions to emotional functioning, as well as changes in these processes over time.

Methodological and Conceptual Problems with the Literature

It is difficult to regard the conclusions of the studies reviewed in the present paper as anything other than suggestive, because as previously discussed, many of the studies do not test theoretical predictions directly and are plagued with methodological problems, including observer bias; stimuli that have been presented by only one sex (usually female); and reliance on self-report measures to assess emotional experience or expressiveness which are subject to social desirability constraints. Another serious limitation to this research is that emotional behaviors are commonly sampled in only one situation at only one point in time. Most personality theorists, including those subscribing to interactional models (Magnusson & Endler, 1977); situational models (Mischel, 1979); or trait models (cf. Epstein, 1979) agree that an individual's behavior may not be consistent across all situations. In fact, work by Weitz (1976) indicates that the quality of adult female nonverbal expressivity varies as a function of the personality traits of the men with whom they interact. Women become more nonverbally submissive with more dominant male partners, and more nonverbally dominant with more submissive male partners. Epstein (1979) cogently argues that an individual's emotions or behaviors need to be studied across multiple situations over an extended period of time in order to yield consistent individual differences. Recent work by Diener and his collegues (Diener & Larsen, 1984; Diener, Larsen, & Emmons, 1984) has begun to explore these issues, and indicates consistent levels of intraperson affect across situations, with continuity in affect being stronger than continuity in behaviors. In addition to cross-situational studies, studies of gender differences in emotional development as a function of cultural context are needed. There are clear indications that sex role stereotypes vary as a function of ethnicity and social class (Lutz, 1980; Romer & Cherry, 1980) and undoubtedly, emotional development does, too.

The failure of emotional development researchers to sample emotional behaviors from more than one situation or from more than one cultural context is only one example of the many discontinuities between theories of emotional development and theories of personality development. There is a striking lack of overlap between research papers published in the two fields, despite the fact that most personality theorists view emotions as integral to personality functioning. Personality constructs such as self-concept, cognitive style, and traits such as introversion vs. extraversion are often defined as enduring and consistent patterns of emotional behaviors. Gender differences in the relationships among emotional expressiveness, recognition, experience, and other aspects of personality functioning have been largely neglected by emotional development researchers and need to be more fully explored.

Theoretical Speculations About Gender Differences in Emotional Development

In order to be meaningful, research on gender differences in emotional development needs to be conducted within a larger theoretical framework. What most theories about emotional development share is the hypothesis that emotions partially serve an interpersonal communication or signalling function. It follows from this hypothesis that an emotional event (e.g., an expression or experience) is most likely to occur when there is either an internal or external stimulus which is perceived to be worth communicating about, and when there is a person available to communicate to. There may be both biological (e.g., temperament) and learned patterns in the quality and intensity of the internal and external states experienced and interpreted as worth communicating about, as well in standards for determining when and with whom emotional communication can occur. Males and females may differ in the ways in which emotions became activated, either because of innate differences in emotional functioning, learned differences, or because of the interaction between the two.

Some of the data and theories reviewed in the present paper provide clues as to the differential nature of these process for boys and girls. For example, Malatesta and Haviland (1982) report that mothers respond more contingently to sons than to daughters—that is, mothers are more attuned to responding to boys' emotional expressions than to girls'. In a related vein, Jacobs and Moss (1976) find that mothers interact less frequently with second-born daughters than with second-born sons or first-born sons and daughters. These data suggest that boys may not have to learn to express or recognize emotions as clearly as do girls because they have less need to. In other words, in order to receive the same level of emotional stimulation and response from mothers, girls may have to work harder than do boys. Boys' emotional functioning may not become as highly activated as girls' because they do not have as great a need to "amplify urgency", which Tomkins (1981) suggests is the primary motivating function of affects. Why do mothers respond more contingently to sons than to daughters? Perhaps, as previously mentioned, because boys' emotional expressions are more intense than are girls' (Cunningham & Shapiro, 1984), and therefore more compelling. These very speculative ideas would help to explain the superior emotional recognition and expressive abilities of females relative to males and differential parental socialization practices by gender.

However, an even broader theoretical context is necessary in order to understand gender differences in emotional development. Most importantly, an understanding of the *function* of emotions must be incorporated into relevant theories and research. Many theorists agree that emotions are adaptive: Emotions motivate or regulate interpersonal relationships, object contacts, and possibly self-concepts, personality traits, and cognitive skills as well (Buechler & Izard, 1983; Buck, 1983; Kellerman, 1983; Plutchik, 1980; Tomkins, 1981). Emotions are thus an integral part of personality, which can also be viewed as an adaptive process—an adaptation to or a compromise among needs, impulses, drives, constitutional traits, and sociocultural demands and supports. The significant question for researchers interested in gender differences in emotional development then becomes: Are different personality patterns adaptive for men and for women? And if so, what kinds of emotional functioning would ensure that those differing adaptive patterns occur?

According to many of the theories reviewed at the beginning of the present paper, including both biological-evolutionary theories and feminist psychoanalytic theories, it is indeed the case that different personality and emotional patterns are adaptive for men vs. women (cf. Lewis, 1976, 1983; Miller, 1976), partially because of differential roles in current social functioning. The emotional functioning of women should help them to adapt to the social role of child-caretaker and to their lower status and power relative to men. The qualities of emotional functioning which would help women to adapt to these social processes were discussed at the beginning of the present paper, and include nonverbal sensitivity, the minimization of anger, and the emotional expression of vulnerability and weakness. There are certainly data which support the existence of gender differences in the first two processes (cf. Brody,1984; Greif et al., 1981; Hall, 1978; Rosenthal et al., 1979 a and b).

In addition to having to adapt to low status, power, and a child-oriented social role, women also have to adapt to an interpersonal and physical world in which men are more aggressive than they are from a very young age (cf. Maccoby & Jacklin, 1980; Tieger, 1980).

Needs for safety may be primary personality motives (Maslow, 1968), and in order to be safe, females may need to avoid being the object of male aggression. Emotional processes such as self-blame, the use of internally directed defenses, the expression of sadness rather than anger, and the sensitivity to nonverbal cues may not only be adaptive for child-rearing, but may also protect women from aggression and ensure their safety. The studies indicating that girls attribute more frequent and intense fear to stories and tend to express more intense fear than do boys (Brody, 1984; Brody & Carter, 1982; Feshbach & Roe, 1968; Lewis & Michaelson, 1983) may also reflect female responsivity to male aggression, that is, fear may be an adaptive and appropriate emotional response which girls learn. Similarly, the importance females place on relationships (cf. Chodorow, 1978; Mackie, 1980) may also be viewed as adaptive: It is safer to be part of a group, or even a dyad (particularly a male-female dyad) than to be alone. This highly speculative argument does not necessarily imply that sex differences in aggression are biologically based (cf. the debate between Maccoby & Jacklin, 1980; and Tieger, 1980), but does imply that the emotional functioning of females may develop so as to protect them from the well-documented greater aggressiveness of males (cf. Maccoby & Jacklin, 1980), whether innate or learned. It would be quite interesting to explore the types of emotional and personality variables in children that are related to being the object of aggressive behaviors, since much research has indicated that aggression is context specific (cf. Maccoby & Jacklin, 1980). If the present argument is correct, emotional strategies such as greater sensitivity to feelings, less expression of anger, and greater use of internally oriented defenses, would be related to being the object of fewer aggressive attacks from others than the use of the reverse emotional strategies.

Studies related to this argument involve comparisons of the personality characteristics of wives who are abused with the characteristics of those who are not. The majority of studies indicate that there are no personality differences between wives who are the object of abuse and those who are not. It is the personalities of abusive vs. nonabusive husbands which have been found to differ (Walker & Browne, this issue). However, Walker and Browne suggest that abused wives may be less skilled at self-protective strategies than are nonabused wives. The argument in the present paper suggests that abused wives may differ from nonabused wives in their use of nonadaptive emotional strategies, for example, they may minimize their anger in contexts in which it is self-destructive to do so.

It is thus important to note that although emotional strategies such as nonverbal sensitivity and the minimization of anger may be adaptive for women in some contexts (e.g., while walking alone at night on a deserted city street), they may become nonadaptive and even self-destructive when used across all contexts in inflexible ways. For example, the minimization of anger once an attack has occurred may be clearly nonadaptive. It may be the situational flexibility with which such strategies are used that determines their ultimate usefulness and value. This point again highlights the need for researchers to explore situational context as a variable in understanding gender differences in emotional development.

The emotional functioning of males can also be viewed as motivating or regulating personality processes which are adaptive to their social and interpersonal worlds. Male social roles have traditionally included the processes of achievement and competition (cf. Miller, 1976). In order to maximize achievement, it may be adaptive for males to be less sensitive to nonverbal cues, to use externally oriented defenses, and to be more expressive of anger but less expressive of other emotions. For example, being sensitive to the feelings of others might prevent males from competing, since winning a competition may entail causing hurt feelings on the part of the person who loses and guilt on the part of the person who wins. Related arguments have been advanced by feminist psychoanalytic writers (Lewis, 1976; Miller, 1976). The relationships among achievement orientation, aggression, fear of aggression, and patterns of emotional functioning would not be difficult for researchers to explore, and would make a valuable theoretical contribution to our understanding of emotional development.

Exploring gender differences in emotional development with the hypothesis that emotions motivate or regulate adaptive behaviors and personality patterns (cf. Tomkins, 1981) thus requires a consideration of the complex multitude of sociocultural and interpersonal processes to which males and females need to adapt. Social roles, power, status, and aggression, which this discussion has focused on, include only one of these processes. Others may be as numerous and as complex as the theory of personality to which one subscribes, and may include needs, drives, impulses, and traits in both the self and in significant others (such as parents), as well as sociocultural and familial values, roles, demands, and supports.

One of the most powerful transmitters of sociocultural values and roles is the family. The data reviewed in the present paper have argued strongly that parents socialize the emotional development of boys and girls differently (cf. Greif, 1984; Greif et al., 1981; Malatesta & Haviland, 1982), thus contributing to differences in males' and females' emotional functioning. Researchers need to explore more fully gender differences in the familial processes associated with emotional development, such as familial values, the quality of relationships between parents' and children's emotional styles, and assigned familial roles. Several studies have demonstrated both similar and complementary relationships between parents' and children's emotional functioning (cf. Barnett et al., 1980; Brody & Landau, 1984; Cummings, Zahn-Waxler, & Radke-Yarrow, 1981; Daly et al., 1980), suggesting that emotional development partially reflects a process of accommodation among the emotional styles of all family members. For example, growing up with a depressed parent is likely to produce a very different pattern of emotional functioning than growing up with an overly intrusive parent. The existence of gender differences in these familial relationships seems likely, but is at present only suggested by data (cf. Bringle & Williams, 1979). Data are also needed on gender differences in assigned familial roles and on the relationships among these roles and emotional development. How often have we heard the maxim, "A daughter is a daughter all her life; a son is a son until he takes a wife"? This expression implies that females are expected to maintain familial relationships and to take care of elderly parents in ways that males are not (cf. Chodorow, 1978). This is yet another social and familial role of females which may require adaptive types of emotional functioning such as nonverbal sensitivity. Comparisons of emotional development in boys and girls growing up in families with traditional vs. nontraditional sex role patterns would be especially illuminating in understanding the relationships among familial values, roles, interaction patterns, and emotional development (cf. Hall & Halberstadt, 1981).

The theories and research reviewed in the present paper thus argue for the study of gender differences in emotional development in the context of personality, familial, social, and cultural variables. Emotions are adaptive processes (Tomkins, 1981), and cannot be studied independently of the sociocultural and familial variables to which males and females need to adapt. More theoretically based research and more data-informed theories cannot but help to advance our understanding of the differences and similarities between males and females in emotional development.

References

Abramovitch, R. (1977). Children's recognition of situational aspects of facial expression. *Child Development*, 48, 459–463.

Adkins, E. K. (1980). Genes, hormones, sex, and gender. In G. W. Barlow, & J. Silverberg (Eds.), *Sociobiology: Beyond nature/nurture?* Boulder, CO: Westview Press, Inc.

Allen, J. G., & Haccoun, D. M. (1976). Sex differences in emotionality: A multidimensional approach. *Human Relations*, 29(8), 711–720.

Ashton, R. (1971). Behavioral sleep cycles in the human newborn. *Child Development*, 42, 2098–2100.

Barden, R. C., Zelko, F. A., Duncan, S. W., & Masters, J. C. (1980). Children's consensual knowledge about the experiential determinants of emotion. *Journal of Personality and Social Psychology*, 39(5), 968–976.

Barnett, M. A., Howard, J. A., King, L. M., & Dino, G. A. (1980). Antecedents of empathy: Retrospective accounts of early socialization. *Personality and Social Psychology Bulletin*, 6(3), 361–365.

Bell, R. Q., Weller, G. M., & Waldrop, M. F. (1971). Newborn and preschooler: Organization of behavior and relations between periods. *Monographs of the Society for Research in Child Development*, 36(Serial No. 142).

Birnbaum, D. W., & Chemelski, B. E. (1984). Preschoolers' inferences about gender and emotion: The mediation of emotionality stereotypes. *Sex Roles*, 10, 505–511.

Birmbaum, D. W., & Croll, W. L. (1984). The etiology of children's stereotypes about sex differences in emotionality. *Sex Roles*, 10, 677–691.

Birnbaum, D. W., Nosanchuk, T. A., & Croll, W. L. (1980). Children's stereotypes about sex differences in emotionality. *Sex Roles*, 6(3), 435–443.

Blanck, P., Rosenthal, R., Snodgrass, S., DePaulo, B., & Zuckerman, M. (1981). Sex differences in eavesdropping on nonverbal cues: Developmental changes. *Journal of Personality and Social Psychology*, 41, 391–396.

Blanck, P. D., Zuckerman, M., DePaulo, B. M., & Rosenthal, R. (1980). Sibling resemblances in nonverbal skill and style. *Journal of Nonverbal Behavior*, 4(4), 219–226.

Block, J. (1973). Conceptions of sex role: Some cross-cultural and longitudinal perspectives. *American Psychologist*, 28, 512–526.

Block, J. (1976). Issues, problems, and pitfalls in assessing sex differences: A critical review of *The Psychology of Sex Differences*. *Merrill Palmer Quarterly*, 22, 283–308.

Borke, H. (1971). Interpersonal perception of young children: Egocentrism or empathy? *Developmental Psychology*, 5, 262–269.

Borke, H. (1973). The development of empathy in Chinese and American children between three and six years of age. *Developmental Psychology*, 9, 102–108.

Brenner, C. (1980). A psychoanalytic theory of affects. In R. Plutchik & H. Kellerman (Eds), *Emotion: Theory, research and experience* (Vol. 1, pp. 341–347). New York: Academic Press.

Bretherton, I., & Beeghly, M. (1982). Talking about internal states: The acquisition of an explicit theory of mind. *Developmental Psychology*, 18(6), 906–921.

Bringle, R. G., & Williams, L. J. (1979). Parental-offspring similarity on jealousy and related personality dimensions. *Motivation and Emotion*, 3(3), 265–286.

Brody, L. R. (1984). Sex and age variations in the quality and intensity of children's emotional attributions to hypothetical situations. *Sex Roles*, 11, 51–59.

Brody, L., & Carter, A. (1982). Children's emotional attributions to self versus other: An exploration of an assumption underlying projective techniques. *Journal of Consulting and Clinical Psychology*, 50, 665–671.

Brody, L., & Harrison, R. (1984). Children's abilities to match and label story situations depicting similar emotions. Manuscript submitted for publication, Boston University, Boston.

Brody, L., & Landau, I. (1984, August). Mothers' emotional styles and preschoolers' emotional attributions. Paper presented at the American Psychological Association, Toronto.

Brody, L., Rozek, M., & Muten, E. (in press). Age, sex, and individual differences in children's defensiveness. *Journal of Clinical Child Psychology*.

Brown, A., & Cunningham, J. G. (1981). Developmental interactions in the expression and interpretation of facial affect. Paper presented at The Society for Research in Child Development, Boston.

Buck, R. (1975). Nonverbal communication of affect in children. *Journal of Personality and Social Psychology, 31*(4), 644–653.

Buck, R. (1977). Nonverbal communication of affect in preschool children: Relationships with personality and skin conductance. *Journal of Personality and Social Psychology, 35*(4), 225–236.

Buck, R. (1982). Spontaneous and symbolic nonverbal behavior and the ontogeny of communication. In R. S. Feldman (Ed.), *Development of nonverbal behavior in children* (pp. 29–62). New York: Springer-Verlag.

Buck, R. (1983). Emotional development and emotional education. In R. Plutchik & H. Kellerman (Eds.), *Emotion: Theory, research, and experience* (Vol. 2, pp. 259–292). New York: Academic Press.

Buck, R. (1984, October 30). Personal communication.

Buck, R., Baron, R., & Barrette, D. (1982). The temporal organization of spontaneous nonverbal expression: A segmentation analysis. *Journal of Personality and Social Psychology, 42*, 506–517.

Buck, R., Miller, R. E., & Caul, W. F. (1974). Sex, personality, and physiological variables in the communication of affect via facial expression. *Journal of Personality and Social Psychology, 30*(4), 587–596.

Buechler, S., & Izard, C. (1983). On the emergence, functions, and regulation of some emotion expressions in infancy. In R. Plutchik & H. Kellerman (Eds.), *Emotion: Theory, research, and experience* (Vol. 2, pp. 293–314). New York: Academic Press.

Buss, A. H., Iscoe, I., & Buss, E. H. (1979). The development of embarrassment. *Journal of Psychology, 103*, 227–230.

Caldwell, H., & Leeper, H. (1974). Temporal patterns of neonatal vocalizations. *Perceptual & Motor Skills, 38*, 911–916.

Camras, L. A. (1977). Facial expressions used by children in a conflict situation. *Child Development, 48*, 1431–1435.

Carroll, J., & Steward, M. (1984). The role of cognitive development in children's understanding of their own feelings. *Child Development, 55*, 1486–1492.

Chandler, M. J., Paget, K. F., & Koch, D. A. (1978). The child's demystification of psychological defense mechanisms: A structural and developmental analysis. *Developmental Psychology, 14*(3), 197–205.

Chodorow, N. (1978) *The reproduction of mothering.* Berkeley: University of California Press.

Cicchetti, D., & Hesse, P. (1983). Affect and intellect: Piaget's contributions to the study of infant emotional development. In R. Plutchik & H. Kellerman (Eds.), *Emotion, Theory, research, and experience* (Vol. 2, pp. 115–170). New York: Academic Press.

Condry, J., & Condry, S. (1976). Sex differences: A study of the eye of the beholder. *Child Development, 47*, 812–819.

Cramer, P. (1979). Defense mechanisms in adolescence. *Developmental Psychology, 15*, 476–477.

Cramer, P. (1980). The development of sexual identity. *Journal of Personality Assessment, 44*(6), 604–612.

Cramer, P. (1983a, August). Defense mechanisms: A developmental study. In L. R. Brody & J. C. Cunningham (Chairs), *Emotional Attributions, Behaviors, and Defenses: Developmental Research with Clinical Implications.* Symposium conducted at the American Psychological Association meeting, Anaheim.

Cramer, P. (1983b). Children's use of defense mechanisms in reaction to displeasure caused by others. *Journal of Personality, 51*, 78–94.

Cramer, P., & Carter, T. (1978). The relationship between sexual identification and the use of defense mechanisms. *Journal of Personality Assessment, 42*(1), 63–73.

Cummings, E., Zahn-Waxler, C., & Radke-Yarrow, M. (1981). Young children's responses to expressions of anger and affection by others in the family. *Child Development, 52,* 1274–1282.

Cunningham, J., & Shapiro, L. (1984). Infant affective expression as a function of infant and adult gender. Unpublished manuscript, Brandeis University, Waltham.

Cunningham, J. G., & Smith, R. (1984). Developmental change in the understanding of affective meaning in music. Manuscript under review, Brandeis University, Waltham.

Daly, E. M., Abramovitch, R., & Pliner, P. (1980). The relationship between mother's encoding and their children's decoding of facial expressions of emotion. *Merrill-Palmer Quarterly, 26,* 25–33.

Daly, M., & Wilson, M. (1978). *Sex, evolution and behavior: Adaptations for reproduction.* North Scituate, MA: Duxbury Press.

Demos, V. (1975). Children's understanding of affect terms. Unpublished doctoral dissertation, Harvard University, Cambridge.

Deutsch, F. (1975). Effects of sex of subject and story character on preschoolers' perceptions of affective responses and interpersonal behavior in story sequences. *Developmental Psychology, 11*(1), 112–113.

Deutsch, R., & Madle, R. (1975). Empathy: Historic and current conceptualizations, measurement, and a cognitive theoretical perspective. *Human Development, 18,* 267–287.

Diener, E., & Larsen, R. J. (1984). Temporal stability and cross-situational consistency of affective, behavioral, and cognitive responses. *Journal of Personality and Social Psychology, 47,* 871–883.

Diener, E., Larsen, R. J., & Emmons, R. (1984). Person-situation interactions: chance of situations and congruence response models. *Journal of Personality and Social Psychology, 47,* 580–592.

Dollinger, S. J., Staley, A., & McGuire, B. (1981). The child as psychologist: Attributes and evaluations of defense strategies. *Child Development, 52,* 1084–1086.

Donaldson, S. K., & Westerman, M. A. (1984). The development of children's understanding of ambivalence and causal theories of emotion. Unpublished manuscript, New York University, New York.

Douglas, J. D., & Rice, K. M. (1979). Sex differences in children's anxiety and defensiveness measures. *Developmental Psychology, 15,* 223–224.

Dweck, C. S., Davidson, W., Nelson, S., & Enna, B. (1978). Sex differences in learned helplessness: II. The contingencies of evaluative feedback in the classroom and III. An experimental analysis. *Developmental Psychology, 14*(3), 268–276.

Dweck, C. S., Goetz, T. E., & Strauss, N. L. (1980). Sex differences in learned helplessness: IV. An experimental and naturalistic study of failure generalization and its mediators. *Journal of Personality and Social Psychology, 39*(3), 441–452.

Eiland, R., & Richardson, D. (1976). The influence of race, sex, and age on judgements of emotion portrayed in photographs. *Communication Monographs, 43,* 167–175.

Eisenberg, N., & Lennon, R. (1983). Sex differences in empathy and related capacities. *Psychological Bulletin, 94,* 100–131.

Eisenberg-Berg, N., & Mussen, P. (1978). Empathy and moral development in adolescence. *Developmental Psychology, 14*(2), 185–186.

Ekman, P., & Oster, H. (1979). Facial expressions of emotion. *Annual Review of Psychology, 30,* 527–554.

Epstein, S. (1979). The stability of behavior: I. On predicting most of the people much of the time. *Journal of Personality and Social Psychology, 37*(7), 1097–1126.

Feinman, J. A., & Feldman, R. S. (1982). Decoding children's expressions of affect. *Child Development, 53,* 710–716.

Feldman, J. F., Brody, N., & Miller, S. A. (1980). Sex differences in nonelicited neonatal behaviors. *Merrill-Palmer Quarterly, 26*(1), 63–73.

Feldman, R. S., Jenkins, L., & Poopola, O. (1979). Detection of deception in adults and children via facial expressions. *Child Development, 50,* 350–355.

Feldman, R., & White, J. (1980). Detecting deception in children. *Journal of Communication, 30,* 121–128.

Felleman, E. S., Barden, R. C., Carlson, C. R., Rosenberg, L., & Masters, J. C. (1983). Children's and adults' recognition of spontaneous and posed emotional expressions in young children. *Developmental Psychology*, 19(3), 405–413.

Feshbach, N. D. (1982). Sex differences in empathy and social behavior in children. In N. Eisenberg (Ed.), *The development of prosocial behavior* (pp. 315–338). New York: Academic Press.

Feshbach, N. D., & Roe, K. (1968). Empathy in six- and seven-year-olds. *Child Development*, 39, 133–145.

Field, T. (1982). Individual differences in the expressivity of neonates and young infants. R. S. Feldman (Ed.), *Development of nonverbal behavior in children* (pp. 279–298). New York: Springer-Verlag.

Field, T. M., & Walden, T. A. (1982a). Production and discrimination of facial expressions by preschool children. *Child Development*, 53, 1299–1311.

Field, T. M., & Walden, T. A. (1982b). Production and perception of facial expression in infancy and early childhood. In H. W. Reese & L. P. Lipsitt (Eds.), *Advances in child development and behavior* (Vol. 16, pp. 169–211). New York: Academic Press.

Fiering, C., & Lewis, M. (1979). Sex and age differences in young children's reactions to frustration: A further look at the Goldberg and Lewis subjects. *Child Development*, 50, 848–53.

Freud, A. (1946). *The ego and the mechanisms of defense.* (C. Baines, Trans.). New York: International Universities Press. (Original work published 1936).

Freud, S. (1961). Some psychical consequences of the anatomical distinction between the sexes. In J. Strachey (Ed. and trans.), *Standard edition of the complete psychological works of Sigmund Freud* (Vol. 19, pp. 248–258). London: Hogarth Press. (Original work published 1925)

Freud, S. (1965). Femininity. In James Strachy, (Ed. and trans.), *New introductory lectures on psychoanalysis* (pp. 112–135). New York: W. W. Norton & Company. (Original work published 1933)

Frodi, A., Macaulay, J., & Thome, P. R. (1977). Are women always less aggressive than men? A review of the experimental literature. *Psychological Bulletin*, 84(4), 634–660.

Gilbert, D. C. (1969). The young child's awareness of affect. *Child Development*, 40, 629–640.

Gitter, A. G., Mostofsky, D. I., & Quincy, A. J., Jr. (1971). Race and sex differences in the child's perception of emotion. *Child Development*, 42, 2071–2075.

Gnepp, J. (1983). Children's social sensitivity: Inferring emotions from conflicting cues. *Developmental Psychology*, 19, 805–14.

Goldberg, S., & Lewis, M. (1969). Play behavior in the year-old infant: Early sex differences. *Child Development*, 40, 21–31.

Golding, E. R. (1982). Five-year-old children's expression of affect and the parent-child interaction. Unpublished doctoral dissertation, Boston University, Boston.

Goodenough, F. (1931). *Anger in young children.* Minneapolis: University of Minnesota Press.

Gove, F. L., & Keating, D. P. (1979). Empathic role-taking precursors. *Developmental Psychology*, 15(6), 594–600.

Greenberg, J. R., & Mitchell, S. A. (1983). *Object relations in psychoanalytic theory.* Cambridge, MA: Harvard University Press.

Greif, E. (1984). *Developmental antecedents of sensitivity to emotions.* Progress Report to NIMH. (Grant No. 1R01MH39357–01)

Greif, E., Alvarez, M., & Ulman, K. (1981, April). Recognizing emotions in other people: Sex differences in socialization. Paper presented at the Biennial Meeting of the Society for Research in Child Development, Boston, MA.

Hall, J. A. (1978). Gender effects in decoding nonverbal cues. *Psychological Bulletin*, 85, 845–857.

Hall, J. A. (1979). Gender, gender roles, and nonverbal communication skills. In R.

Rosenthal (Ed.), *Skill in nonverbal communication* (pp. 32–67). Cambridge, MA: Oelgeschlager, Gunn, & Hain.

Hall, J. A., & Halberstadt, A. G. (1981). Sex roles and nonverbal communication skills. *Sex Roles*, 7(3), 273–287.

Hamilton, M. L. (1973). Imitative behavior and expressive ability in facial expression of emotion. *Developmental Psychology*, 8(1), 138.

Harris, P., Olthof, T., & Terwogt, M. (1981). Children's knowledge of emotions. *Journal of Child Psychology and Psychiatry*, 22, 247–61.

Harter, S. (1982). A cognitive-developmental approach to children's understanding of trait and affect labels. In F. C. Serafica (Ed.), *Social cognitive development in context* (pp. 27–61). New York: Guilford Press.

Haviland, J. J., & Malatesta, C. Z. (1981). The development of sex differences in nonverbal signals: Fallacies, facts, and fantasies. In C. Mayo & N. Healy (Eds.), *Gender and nonverbal behavior* (pp. 183–208). New York: Springer-Verlag.

Hill, K. T., & Sarason, S. (1966). The relation of test anxiety and defensiveness to test and school performance over the elementary school years. *Monographs of Society for Research in Child Development*, 31(2, Serial No. 104).

Hoffman, M. L. (1975). Sex differences in moral internalization and values. *Journal of Personality and Social Psychology*, 32, 720–29.

Hoffman, M. L. (1977). Sex differences in empathy and related behaviors. *Psychological Bulletin*, 34(4), 712–722.

Hoffman, M., & Levine, L. (1976). Early sex differences in empathy. *Developmental Psychology*, 6, 557–558.

Hughes, J., Tingle, B., & Sawin, D. (1981). Development of empathic understanding in children. *Child Development*, 52, 122–128.

Izard, C. (1971). *The face of emotion*. New York: Appleton Century Crafts.

Izard, C. (1977). *Human emotions*. New York: Plenum Press.

Jacklin, C. N., Maccoby, E. E., & Dick, A. E. (1973). Barrier behavior and toy preference: Sex differences (and their absence) in the year-old child. *Child Development*, 44, 196–200.

Jacobs, B. S., & Moss, H. A. (1976). Birth order and sex of sibling as determinants of mother-infant interaction. *Child Development*, 47, 315–322.

Kagan, J. (1978). Sex differences in the human infant. In T. E. McGill, D. A. Dewsbury, & B. D. Sachs (Eds.), *Sex and behavior: Status and prospectus* (pp. 305–316). New York: Plenum Press.

Karoly, P., & Ruehlman, L. S. (1982). Gender differences in adolescents' reports of self-control problems. *Cognitive Therapy and Research*, 6(2), 235–237.

Kellerman, H. (1983). An epigenetic theory of emotions in early development. In R. Plutchik & H. Kellerman (Eds.), *Emotion: Theory, research and experience* (Vol. 2, pp. 315–350). New York: Academic Press.

Kemper, T. D. (1978a). Toward a sociology of emotions: Some problems and some solutions. *The American Sociologist*, 13, 30–41.

Kemper, T. D. (1978b). *A social interactional theory of emotions*. New York: John Wiley and Sons.

Kendrick, C., & Dunn, J. (1983). Sibling quarrels and maternal responses. *Developmental Psychology*, 19(1), 62–70.

Klinnert, M. D., Campos, J. J., Sorce, J. F., Emde, R. N., & Svejda, M. (1983). Emotions as behavior regulators: Social referencing in infancy. In R. A. Plutchik & H. Kellerman (Eds.), *Emotion: Theory, research, and experience* (Vol. 2, pp. 57–86). New York: Academic Press.

Kurdek, L., & Rogdon, M. (1975). Perceptual, cognitive, and affective perspective taking in kindergarten through sixth grade children. *Developmental Psychology*, 11, 643–650.

LaBarbera, J. D., Izard, C. E., Vietze, P., & Parisi, S. A. (1976). Four- and six-month-old infants' visual responses to joy, anger, and neutral expressions. *Child Development*, 47, 535–538.

Lamandella, J. T. (1977). The limbic system in human communication. In H. Whitaker

& H. A. Whitaker (Eds.), *Studies in neurolinguistics* (Vol. 3, pp. 157–222). New York: Academic Press.

Landreth, C. (1941). Factors associated with crying in young children in the nursery school and the home. *Child Development*, **12**, 81–97.

Lazarus, R. S. (1982). Thoughts on the relations between emotions and cognition. *American Psychologist*, **37**, 1019–1024.

Lever, J. (1976). Sex differences in the games children play. *American Sociological Review*, **43**, 471–83.

Lewis, H. B. (1976). *Psychic war in men and women*. New York: New York University Press.

Lewis, H. B. (1983). *Freud and modern psychology*. New York: Plenum Press.

Lewis, H. B. (1985). Depression vs. paranoia: Why are there sex differences in mental illness? *Journal of Personality*, **53**, 150–178.

Lewis, M., & Michaelson, L. (1983). *Children's emotions and moods: Developmental theory and measurement*. New York: Plenum Press.

Lewis, M., & Weinraub, M. (1979). Origins of early sex role development. *Sex Roles*, **5**(2), 135–153.

Lewis, W. C., Wolman, R. N., & King, M. (1972). The development of the language of emotions: III Type of anxiety in the experience of affect. *Journal of Genetic Psychology*, **120**, 325–342.

Lutz, C. (1980). Emotion words and emotional development on Ifaluk Atoll. Unpublished doctoral dissertation, Harvard University, Cambridge.

Maccoby, E., & Jacklin, C. (1980). Sex differences in aggression; A rejoinder and reprise. *Child Development*, **51**, 964–980.

Mackie, M. (1980). The impact of sex stereotypes upon adult self imagery. *Social Psychology Quarterly*, **43**(1), 121–125.

Magnusson, D., & Endler, S. (1977). Interactional psychology: present status and future prospects. In D. Magnusson & N. S. Endler (Eds.), *Personality at the crossroads: Current issues in interactional psychology* (pp. 3–31). Hillsdale, NJ: Erlbaum.

Malatesta, C. Z., & Haviland, J. M. (1982). Learning display rules: The socialization of emotion expression in infancy. *Child Development*, **53**, 991–1003.

Martin, G. B., & Clark, R. D., III. (1982). Distress crying in neonates: Species and peer specificity. *Developmental Psychology*, **18**(1), 3–9.

Maslow, A. (1968). *Toward a psychology of being* (2nd ed.). New York: Van Nostrand Reinhold.

Masters, J. (1981). Adults' emotional states and the recognition of emotion in young children. Unpublished manuscript. Vanderbilt University, Nashville, Tennessee.

McGlone, J. (1980). Sex differences in human brain asymmetry: A critical survey and review. *Behavioral and Brain Sciences*, **3**(2), 215–227.

Miller, J. B. (1976). *Toward a new psychology of women*. Boston: Beacon Press.

Mischel, W. (1979). On the interface of cognition and personality. *American Psychologist*, **34**(9), 740–754.

Mitchell, J. (1974). *Psychoanalysis and feminism*. New York: Pantheon Books.

Mood, D. W., Johnson, J. E., & Shantz, C. (1978). Social comprehension and affect-matching in young children. *Merrill-Palmer Quarterly*, **24**(1), 63–68.

Morency, N. L., & Krauss, R. M. (1982). Children's nonverbal encoding and decoding of affect. In R. S. Feldman (Ed.), *Development of nonverbal behavior in children*. New York: Springer-Verlag.

Moss, H. A. (1967). Sex, age, and state as determinants of mother-infant interaction. *Merrill-Palmer Quarterly*, **13**, 19–36.

Osofsky, J. D., & O'Connell, E. J. (1977). Patterning of newborn behavior in an urban population. *Child Development*, **48**, 532–536.

Peters, R. S. (1972). The education of the emotions. In R. Dearden, P. Hirst, & R. Peters (Eds.), *Education and the development of reason* (pp. 446–483). London: Routledge & Kegan.

Phillips, S., King, S., & Dubois, L. (1978). Spontaneous activities of female versus male newborns. *Child Development*, 49, 590–597.

Piaget, J. (1981). *Intelligence and affectivity.* Annual Reviews Monograph. Palo Alto, CA: Annual Reviews, Inc.

Pierce, R., Nichols, M., & DuBrin, J. (1983). *Emotional expression in psychotherapy.* New York: Gardner Press.

Plutchik, R. (1980). A general psychoevolutionary theory of emotion. In R. Plutchik & H. Kellerman (Eds.), *Emotion: Theory, research, and experience* (Vol. 1, pp. 3–33). New York: Academic Press.

Pribram, K. H. (1980). The biology of emotions and other feelings. In R. Plutchik & H. Kellerman (Eds.), *Emotion: Theory, research, and experience* (Vol. 1, pp. 245–269). New York: Academic Press.

Reichenbach, L., & Masters, J. (1983). Children's use of expressive and contextual cues in judgments of emotion. *Child Development*, 54, 993–1004.

Robson, K. S., Pedersen, F. A., & Moss, H. A. (1969). Developmental observations of diadic gazing in relation to the fear of strangers and social approach behavior. *Child Development*, 40, 619–627.

Rogers, C. (1951). *Client-centered therapy.* Boston: Houghton Mifflin.

Romer, N., & Cherry, D. (1980). Ethnic and social class differences in children's sex role concepts. *Sex Roles*, 6, 245–263.

Rosenkrantz, P., Vogel, S., Bee, H., Broverman, I., & Broverman, D. M. (1968). Sex-role stereotypes and self-concepts in college students. *Journal of Consulting and Clinical Psychology*, 3, 287–295.

Rosenthal, R., Archer, D., Hall, J. A., DiMatteo, M. R., & Rogers, P. L. (1979a). Measuring sensitivity to nonverbal communication: The PONS test. In A. Wolfgang (Ed.), *Nonverbal behavior: Applications and cultural implications* (pp. 67–98). New York: Academic Press.

Rosenthal, R., Hall, J., DiMatteo, M. R., Rogers, P. L., Archer, D. (1979b). *Sensitivity to nonverbal communication: The PONS test.* Baltimore: Johns Hopkins University Press.

Rosenthal, R., & DePaulo, B. (1979). Sex differences in accommodation in nonverbal communication. In R. Rosenthal (Ed.), *Skill in nonverbal communication* (pp. 68–103). Cambridge, MA: Oelgeschlager, Gunn & Hain.

Rosenzweig, S. (1960). The Rosenzweig picture-frustration study, children's form. In A. I. Rabin & M. R. Haworth (Eds.), *Projective techniques with children* (pp. 149–176). New York: Grune and Stratton.

Rothbart, M. K., & Derryberry, D. (1981). Development of individual differences in temperament. In M. E. Lamb & A. L. Brown (Eds.), *Advances in developmental psychology* (Vol. 1, pp. 37–86). New York: Erlbaum.

Rothenberg, B. B. (1970). Children's social sensitivity and the relationship to interpersonal competence, intrapersonal comfort, and intellectual level. *Developmental Psychology*, 2(3), 335–350.

Saarni, C. (1979). Children's understanding of display rules for expressive behavior. *Developmental Psychology*, 15(4), 424–429.

Saarni, C. (1982). Social and affective functions of nonverbal behavior: Developmental concerns. In R. S. Feldman (Ed.), *Development of nonverbal behavior in children* (pp. 123–147). New York: Springer-Verlag.

Sagi, A., & Hoffman, M. L. (1976). Empathic distress in newborns. *Developmental Psychology*, 12, 175–176.

Schacter, S., & Singer, J. E. (1962). Cognitive, social, and physiological determinants of emotional state. *Psychological Review*, 69, 379–399.

Serbin, L. A., O'Leary, K. D., Kent, R. N., & Tonick, I. J. (1973). A comparison of teacher response to the preacademic and problem behavior of boys and girls. *Child Development*, 44, 796–804.

Shantz, C. (1975). Empathy in relation to social cognitive development. *Counseling Psychologist*, 5, 18–20.

Shennum, W. A., & Bugental, D. B. (1982). The development of control over affective expression in nonverbal behavior. In R. S. Feldman (Ed.), *Development of nonverbal behavior in children* (pp. 101–121). New York: Springer-Verlag.

Sherrod, L. R. (1979). Social cognition in infants: Attention to the human face. *Infant Behavior and Development*, 2, 279–294.

Simner, M. L. (1971). Newborn's response to the cry of another infant. *Developmental Psychology*, 5, 136–150.

Skarin, K. (1977). Cognitive and contextual determinants of stranger fear in six- and eleven-month-old infants. *Child Development*, 48, 537–544.

Sommers, S. (1982). Emotionality reconsidered: The role of cognition in emotional responsiveness. *Journal of Personality and Social Psychology*, 41(3), 553–561.

Sroufe, L. A. (1979). Socioemotional development. In J. Osofsky (Ed.), *Handbook of infant development* (pp. 462–516). New York: Wiley and Sons.

Stechler, G., & Kaplan, S. (1980). The development of the self: A psychoanalytic perspective. In A. J. Solnit, R. S. Eissler, A. Freud, M. Kris, & P. B. Neubauer (Eds.), *The psychoanalytic study of the child* (Vol. 35, pp. 85–105). New Haven: Yale University Press.

Strouse, J. (Ed.), (1974). *Women & analysis*. New York: Dell Publishing Co.

Tieger, T. (1980). On the biological basis of sex differences in aggression. *Child Development*, 51, 943–963.

Tomkins, S. (1981). The quest for primary motives: Biography and autobiography of an idea. *Journal of Personality and Social Psychology*, 41, 306–29.

Trause, M. A. (1977). Stranger responses: Effects of familiarity, stranger's approach, and sex of infant. *Child Development*, 48, 1657–1661.

Unger, R. K. (1979). Toward a redefinition of sex and gender. *American Psychologist*, 34(11), 1085–1094.

Vaillant, G. E. (1971). Theoretical hierarchy of adaptive ego mechanisms. *Archives of General Psychiatry*, 24, 107–118.

Van Lieshout, C. F. M. (1975). Young children's reaction to barriers placed by their mothers. *Child Development*, 46, 879–886.

Waber, D. P. (1976). Sex differences in mental abilities, hemispheric lateralization, and rate of physical growth at adolescence. *Developmental Psychology*, 12, 276–82.

Walker, L., & Browne, A. (1985). Gender and victimization by intimates. *Journal of Personality*, 53, 179–195.

Weiner, B., Graham, S., Stern, P., & Lawson, M. E. (1982). Using affective cues to infer causal thoughts. *Developmental Psychology*, 18(2), 278–286.

Weissman, M. M., & Klerman, G. L. (1977). Sex differences and the epidemiology of depression. *Archives of General Psychiatry*, 34, 98–111.

Weitz, S. (1976). Sex differences in nonverbal communication. *Sex Roles*, 2(2), 175–184.

Winer, G. A. (1982). A review and analysis of children's fearful behavior in dental settings. *Child Development*, 53(5), 1111–1113.

Yang, R. K., & Moss, H. A. (1978). Neonatal precursors of infant behavior. *Developmental Psychology*, 14(6), 607–613.

Yarczower, M., Kilbride, J. E., & Hill, L. A. (1979). Initiation and inhibition of facial expression. *Developmental Psychology*, 15(4), 453–454.

Young-Browne, G., Rosenfeld, H. M., & Horowitz, F. D. (1977). Infant discrimination of facial expression. *Child Development*, 48, 555–562.

Zeskind, P. S., & Lester, B. M. (1978). Acoustic features and auditory perceptions of the cries of newborns with prenatal and perinatal complications. *Child Development*, 49, 580–589.

Zuckerman, M., DeFrank, R., Spiegel, N., & Larrance, D. (1982). Masculinity-femininity and the encoding of nonverbal cues. *Journal of Personality and Social Psychology*, 42, 548–556.

Depression vs. paranoia: Why are there sex differences in mental illness?

Helen Block Lewis

Abstract

Sex differences in proneness to depression and paranoia are seen as reflecting caricatures of women's and men's stereotypical role in a male-dominated, exploitative society. Following its major hypothesis that mental illness arises out of failures in the sociability that is inherent in our species, the paper discusses some of the evidence for sex differences in sociability, and some evidence from studies of sex differences in field dependence which, taken together, suggest a sex difference in proneness to shame and guilt. This sex difference in "superego" style is a mediating factor in proneness to depression and paranoia.

That women in our society are more prone to depression than men, while men are more prone to paranoid schizophrenia than women, has been well known since accurate statistics began to be assembled well before World War II. In a paper published more than two decades ago (Lewis, 1958) I speculated on the basis of slight evidence that this sex difference in the two great functional mental disorders might be somehow related to what we now know is an almost ubiquitous (Berry, 1976), small but significant sex difference in field dependence (Wittig & Petersen, 1979). But it was not until the 1960s revival of the women's liberation movement that I began to glimpse the way in which women's depression and men's paranoia are both caricatures of women's and men's stereotypical roles in a male-dominated, exploitative society. The image of an affectively overwhelmed, selfless woman, helpless to stop her own suffering is in sharp contrast to the image of an emotionally shut-down man, ideationally overwhelmed by a compelling mission to rectify evil, even if this means killing people. Both sets of psychiatric symptoms reflect our own social norms for men and women, in grossly distorted, but now recognizable forms, thanks to Freud's

I am grateful to the two anonymous reviewers and to the editors of this special issue for their helpful criticisms and suggestions for improving my manuscript.

descriptions of symptom formation (Lewis, 1976, 1981). There is even some empirical evidence for the notion that sex role alienation is a factor in schizophrenia (Cheek, 1964; McClelland & Watt, 1968). Similarly, Bart's (1971) study of depression in middle-aged women comes close to describing their overinvolvement with others as a caricature of attachment.

In this paper I shall present the hypothesis that mental illness arises out of failures in the maintenance of our species' inherent sociability. The notion that psychiatric illness reflects the contradictory values of an exploitative society has been well developed, especially by the Freudian revisionists, Horney (1937), Fromm (1955), and Wilhelm Reich (1971). The hypothesis that mental illness arises out of failures in the maintenance of our species' inherent sociability explicitly assumes that human nature is "cultural" (Barash, 1977; LaBarre, 1954) or "social by biological origin" (Rheingold, 1969, p. 782). It thus expands the Freudian revisionists' critique of our society to include the concept of human sociability as a biological given. As an essential corollary hypothesis, I assume that women have a slight advantage over men in inherent sociability.

Before considering this question, however, it is necessary to confront some attitudes stemming from the values of our competitive, male-dominated society that may make it difficult to consider a genetic sex difference in sociability.

It is sometimes said that it is useless to consider the influence of genetic constitution on psychological differences between the sexes because genetic effects cannot be sorted out from the effects of women's social position. An analogy has been made between the problem of differences in intelligence between blacks and whites. In one respect this analogy is apt since genetic differences were widely assumed to be the basis of observed differences in blacks' and whites' IQ, just as genetic factors are readily assumed to be the reason for women's inferior social positions.

Although this analogy is appealing on the surface, it is actually misleading. In the case of so-called black and white "racial" groups, many of these are really "ethnic," and, in any case, the extent of common gene pool is extremely difficult to assess. In the case of male and female groups, however, the genetic basis for sexual differentiation is clearly known. Females have an XX and males an XY as one of their 23 chromosomal pairs. This is not to imply that all factors responsible for genetic sex differentiations are understood. But it does remind us that males and females are genetically homogeneous groups and different from each other in a way no racial groups could ever be. Furthermore, the anatomical and physiological end-products of having an XY rather than an XX are incomparably different. Having a body that can be host to a developing fetus and then suckle an infant is uniquely female. It can only be contrasted with having a body *not* so equipped. This is a different order of comparison from a variable number of points on the same scale of intellectual functioning. Woman's having a body equipped for nurturance coincides with the universal cultural recognition that women are "natural" infant caretakers. It connects as well to the universal cultural moral value for infant nurturance (Edel & Edel, 1968). It also dictates a universal pattern in which the "natural" caretaker of an infant is same-sex for females and opposite-sex for males. As we shall see later on, this difference may itself be an important determinant of differences in sociability between the sexes.

In their monumental *Psychology of Sex Differences*, Maccoby and Jacklin (1974) accept the genetic basis for aggression in males via the established fact that there is genetic control of differing sex hormones. This line of reasoning also directly suggests a genetic basis for maternal behavior via the same route of genetic control of hormones. Although Maccoby and Jacklin have "no doubt that women throughout the world are perceived to be the nurturant sex" (p. 215), they do not accord the notion that nurturant behavior in women is genetically based the status of an equal hypothesis with the genetic control of male aggression. This may be because, as their survey shows, nurturance has been much less studied than aggression.

The neglect of the possible genetic basis for women's nurturance (or sociability) also reflects an androcentric bias. The scientific respectability of the genetic basis for male aggression reflects a greater respect for aggression than for nurturance as a powerful psychological and historical force.

Maccoby and Jacklin (1974) emphasize that the picture which emerges from their survey is of "high sociability in both sexes" (p. 368). This view is congruent with my own hypothesis that human beings are social by biological origin. They also conclude that the greater sociability of women is a myth (1974, pp. 154, 275, 368). As I have shown elsewhere in greater detail (Lewis, 1976) this conclusion is not well supported by the evidence cited in their book.

As a result of a difference in sociability the two sexes experience the societal conflict of values differently, and are prone to different forms of mental illness. Women's greater sociability pushes them to bear the culture's devaluation of sociability by devaluing themselves, thus increasing their vulnerability to unresolved shame and depression. Men's lesser sociability increases their aggressive response to disruptions of their affectional ties. This increase in aggression still further disrupts their affectional ties leading to a mounting spiral of aggression and unresolved guilt. This increases their vulnerability to the paranoid and schizophrenic symptoms of emotional shutdown.

It requires an intuitive leap of understanding to connect women's greater sociability to their greater vulnerability to depression, which is above all the experience of sadness over social loss. The same intuitive leap of understanding connects men's lesser sociability with their proneness to schizophrenia, the illness of emotional shutdown. There are, however, some lines of evidence which support the connections between greater and lesser sociability and kind of mental illness. In particular, the work on field dependence, a cognitive style which I helped to develop (Witkin, Dyk, Goodenough, Faterson, & Karp, 1962; Witkin, Lewis, Hertzman, Machover, Meissner, & Wapner, 1954) can be used as a "tracer element" to illuminate these connections.

This paper is divided into three parts. In Part 1 I shall discuss the evidence on which I have based the contrast between depression and schizophrenia. Part 2 briefly reviews the evidence for a concept of innate human sociability, and for the corollary assumption of women's advantage in sociability over men. Part 3 uses the evidence from field dependence as a tracer element for discerning the connections between sex differences in sociability and sex differences in forms of mental illness.

Part 1: The Contrast Between Depression and Schizophrenia

While the contrast is between two very gross categories, each including a wide variety of subcategories, such as endogenous vs. reactive depression or paranoid vs. "simple" schizophrenia, there is cross-cultural evidence that primitive people distinguish between depression and schizophrenia pretty much in the same terms as we do. Two widely separated non-Western groups, the Eskimo of northwest Alaska and the Yoruba of tropical Nigeria both label as "crazy" such phenomena as "talking to oneself, screaming at someone who does not exist, making strange grimaces, becoming strange and violent" (Murphy, 1976, p. 1022). While they have no such single "crazy" label for anxiety and depression any more than we do, they have many phrases in their vocabulary for excessive emotional responses that sound like depression, for example; "extreme bashfulness which is like a sense of shame," "crying with sadness," "head down" and "shaking and trembling all over," "unrest that prevents sleep" (ibid., p. 1024).

The biochemists, looking for their biochemical markers of mental illness, also recognize the important distinction between schizophrenia, which involves the "stress of social interaction" and depression, which is a "stress reaction to social loss" (Barchas, Akil, & Elliot, 1978, p. 967). And while we do not as yet have any worldwide evidence that women are more prone to depression than men, or that men are more prone to paranoid schizophrenia than women, there is good evidence in our own society.

There are some difficulties in establishing the evidence about sex difference in proneness to depression and schizophrenia. Some researchers (for example, Phyllis Chesler, 1972) have concluded that women in our society are more prone to mental illness in general than men, as a reflection of their oppression by men. While I do not at all disagree with the idea that women are oppressed, and by men, a careful review of the evidence suggests that the important question is not which sex is more often mentally ill, but how they differ in kind of illness. There is unanimous agreement that women are more often depressed than men (Lewis, 1976, 1978). The evidence that men are more prone to fall ill of schizophrenia is more ambiguous, mainly because of changing use of diagnostic criteria in schizophrenia. When, however, rates for schizophrenia and manic-depressive psychosis are assessed by first-admissions (and by readmissions) to state hospitals, men—especially between the ages of 15 and 35— are more frequently admitted for schizophrenia, and women for manic-depressive psychosis (Malzberg, 1959). The rates for schizophrenia, moreover, far exceed the rates for bipolar depression. Schizophrenia is thus a more massive social problem than its counterpart, psychotic depression.

The statistics for schizophrenia also closely parallel the statistics for poverty and social disorganization (Dohrenwend & Dohrenwend, 1976; Faris & Dunham, 1939/1960; Levy & Rowitz, 1973). Highest admissions for schizophrenia come from areas where the population is poor, and where there is substandard housing, high residential mobility, high unemployment and high male delinquency. The rates for manic-depressive illness, in contrast, do *not* parallel social conditions. This difference in the extent to which the two major psychoses are influenced by socio-economic factors has been interpreted (Cohen, 1961) as a function of stereotypical sex differences in economic role. Men's proneness to schizophrenia is a reflection of their place in the front-line of economic battle. Women's greater proneness to depressive psychosis as well as depressive neurosis reflects the casualties of women's primary caretaking involvement with the family as their front-line of struggle.

It has been suggested by Hammen and Peters (1977, 1978) that women's greater proneness to depression is an artifact of their greater freedom to report illnesses, and to express their feelings, rather than to a genuine susceptibility to depressive illness. In an elegant study of the question of susceptibility, Radloff and Rae (1979) showed that even when various precipitating factors that might produce depression are controlled for both sexes, the sex difference in depression remains, leading to the conclusion that there is a genuine susceptibility factor in women's proneness to depression.

The sex difference in proneness to schizophrenia and depression parallels the question: Why do women live longer than men? (Waldron, 1976, 1978). A favorite shorthand statement among epidemiologists about sex differences in morbidity and mortality is: "Women get sick; men die." What this statement reflects is the fact that women in our society are more often chronically ill; they also report more psychosomatic symptoms. Women more often than men refer themselves to psychiatric clinics for help with "nervous" symptoms (Lewis, 1976). Men, in contrast, die ten years sooner than women, they are significantly more prone to coronary heart disease, which kills them, to alcoholism and cirrhosis of the liver, to smoking and cancer of the lungs, and to death by accident and suicide. Type A personalities, psychology's newest version of Freud's anal character (as transformed by Fromm, 1955, into the "bourgeois man"), are more often victims of heart attack, and they are much more numerous among men than among women. There is thus a parallel between the gender patterns of physical and of mental illness: Men die sooner of illnesses involving elements of self-destruction and they are more subject to the bizarre and severe distortions of the self that occur in schizophrenia. Women seek help, live longer, and are prone to the more benign, relatively mundane illness of depression. These patterns of physical and mental illness are congruent with lesser and greater sociability.

Part 2: The Biosocial or Cultural Nature of Humanity

Human beings are the most thoroughly domesticated primates on earth. Anthropologists tell us that everywhere they look they find human beings organized into a culture. Levi-Strauss (1969) puts it this way: "Mankind is inconceivable outside society" (p. 514). This fact suggests in turn the theoretical position that culture is humanity's unique evolutionary adaptation to life. LaBarre (1954), for example, suggested that human culture is the human being's ecology. More recently, Barash (1977), a sociobiologist, writes that "culture is a major biological adaptation of Homo sapiens; and certainly we possess a biologically evolved *capacity* for culture" (p. 319).

Culture has many facets, but one of its universals is that human beings everywhere are organized into a society governed by moral law (Edel & Edel, 1968). Although the content of morality varies enormously, moral law is thus immanent in human nature, beginning with infant nurturance. Infant nurturance in every society is guided by a set of mortal prescriptions. Although the content of these varies widely, all cultures thus institutionalize nurturance, a fact which surely fosters species survival. That human culture and with it, uniquely human morality are universals is no guarantee, of course, that human culture originated as an evolutionary adaptation. But the idea that human culture necessarily involves an immanent human morality can be a useful hypothesis.

It is instructive to observe, in passing, some of the political implications of a Darwinist position about human culture. Anchoring culture in biology can readily become social Darwinism, that is, a doctrine that rationalizes the inequities, oppression, and warfare that characterize many cultures, including our own. But human culture is Janus-faced: it *sometimes* comprises institutionalized oppression, warfare, and the inferiority of women, but it *always* involves the institutionalized nurturance out of which morality arises. Anchoring morality in biology calls attention to the profoundly social nature of our species, as well as to the destructive capacities that are unleashed when social bonds are threatened. Calling attention to the biology of nurturance can thus be a tool for the critique of particular cultures' institutionalized oppression and war.

The hypothesis that human beings are cultural by "nature" and that they are thus inevitably moral creatures brings with it the corollary hypothesis that there are sex differences in the way the culture's morality is experienced. It follows that some sex difference in proneness to depression vs. paranoia might be expected to occur in all cultures. Specifically, women, because of their closer connection to others, are likely to experience the aggressions resulting from loss of attachment in a form that is muted by these close connections. Men, in contrast, are likely to respond to threats to their affectional bonds by aggression and ensuing guilt. The difference in the acculturation process for the two sexes is enormously widened in societies like our own where aggression is both highly valued and the prerogative of men, while continuing attachment is devalued.

The present day sociobiologists' idea that culture is humanity's evolutionary adaptation is very different from earlier models of evolutionary biology in which superior intellectual skills and success in predation were the major factors guiding evolution. In this version, mankind was represented mainly by the male sex, and featured Tarzan the Mighty Hunter come down out of the trees with his opposable thumb for handling tools and large brain for outwitting other species. The androcentric character of this model has been criticized not only by feminists (see Elaine Morgan's *Descent of Woman*, 1972) but by present day comparative psychologists as well. Current thinking about the factors governing sexual selection is one example. To explain mating behavior, Darwin (1871) had invoked two main selection factors: competition between males and preference by females for certain characteristics of their mates. In subsequent years, evolutionists placed major emphasis on male size and aggressiveness as the prime natural selection factors. But, as Bernstein (1978) has shown, "no monkey becomes dominant merely on the basis of fighting skill, nor is dominance a permanent property of the individual" (p. 153). Bernstein points out further that the emphasis on male aggression, via male size and dominance, contains an implication that selection operates against smaller, less aggressive females. As he wryly suggests, no species that selects against females can be expected to survive.

Another line of investigation into evolutionary biology also emphasizes the importance of nurturance. Lovejoy (1981), for example, suggests that humanity's advances in brain development and material culture were the *result* not the *cause* of an "established hominid character system" that included "intensified parenting and social relationships" (p. 348).

Infant Sociability and Competence

A cultural theory of human nature predicts that infants should have some inborn capacity for sociability. The concept of infant sociability is very different from the individualistic model of infancy implicit in James' (1890) version of infancy as a "big, buzzing blooming confusion." It also differs from Freud's notion of the chaotic Id, and from more modern psychoanalytic notions of an original infantile autism (Mahler, Pine, & Bergman, 1975).

We now know that the human infant is equipped to respond to people from the very earliest (Rheingold, 1969). Newborn infants are much more competent (Stone, Smith, & Murphy, 1973) and much more social creatures than has been previously supposed. In fact, their sociability may be basic to the development of their intellectual functioning. There is some evidence, for example, that the infant's concept of people may normally have primacy over his or her concept of things (Bell, 1970). (It is certain that all experiments on infants' intellectual functioning are done when the infant is in a comfortable or peaceful state in relation to its caretaker.) Bell's important experiment grew out of Piaget's description of the development of perceptual constancy. Her hypothesis was that the infant's concept of person-constancy precedes its concept of thing-constancy. (The term, object-constancy, has to be avoided because it has been used to include both persons and things.) Bell was able to classify 33 infants from white middle-class homes into three categories: 23 infants who were more advanced in person-constancy ("positive decalage"); seven more advanced in thing-constancy ("negative decalage"); and three who were in neither category. The 23 infants who were more advanced in person-constancy were also more securely attached to their mothers as measured by the Ainsworth strange-situation assessment. The seven infants who were more advanced in thing-constancy were anxiously attached to their mothers. These results have been confirmed in subsequent studies (Ainsworth, Blehar, Waters, & Wall, 1978) and they may be taken to indicate that infants' secure attachment is basic to their early concept of others. They also suggest that anxious attachment is associated with an early salience of things over people; this may be a hint of later withdrawn pathological states.

Newborn infants respond to crying to the sound of other newborns' crying (Simner, 1971). Newborn infants synchronize their movements to adult speech (Condon & Sander, 1974). Newborn infants can discriminate and prefer the sounds of their mothers' voices (DeCasper & Fifer, 1980). Infants who are only 36 hours old can discriminate and imitate facial gestures (Meltzoff & Moore, 1977). These relatively new findings remind us of Kaila's pioneer work (cited in H. R. Schaffer, 1971) establishing that a visual Gestalt consisting of two eyes and a forehead "en face" is a key stimulus to the infant's smile. Kaila assumed that the human face is the first differentiated object in an infant's life-space and that its properties are apprehended as a Gestalt to which the nervous system is organized to respond.

Infant smiling, moreover, occurs even when infants are born blind (Freedman, 1964). Thalidomide babies, blind, deaf, and without arms to touch their mothers also smile at about three months (Eibl-Eibelsfeldt, 1974). Evidence exists, moreover, from studies of identical and fraternal twins that infant smiling at three months is under genetic control (Freedman, 1965). This study also suggested that "stranger-anxiety," an indicator that the infant is attached to its mother, occurs closer to the same age for identical than for fraternal twins. Studies of older children, using the same method of comparing identical and fraternal twins also suggest that a trait called sociability or person-orientation may be under genetic control (Lindzey, Loehlin, Manosevitz, & Thiessen, 1971). While the evidence for continuity between childhood and adult sociability is by no means unequivocal, some longitudinal studies (e.g., Sears, Rau, & Alpert, 1965) do suggest continuity for women.

It is instructive to note, in passing, that behaviorist theory, which assumes that people become important to infants as a result of infants' contingency analysis of the "games" they play (Watson, 1973) is like Gestalt theory in its explicit reliance on built-in genetic propensities for social response. Watson, for example, assumes that the infant is "specially sensitive and responsive to fellow members of our species" with built-in schemata for face and voice (p. 108). These studies of neonates' extraordinary capacity for social response, taken together with studies suggesting that sociability is under genetic control support the concept of sociability as a part of human equipment.

Infant-Caretaker Interaction: A Psychological Given

Along with the evidence for the existence of innate human sociability there is evidence for a biologically given attachment system between the infant and its caretaker (Ainsworth, Blehar, Waters, & Wall, 1978; Bowlby, 1969). The mother-infant attachment system involves mutual advantage and serves to protect the young. Its existence on the primate level was demonstrated by the Harlows (Harlow & Mears, 1979) giving further credence to the probability that the human infant-caretaker affectional system is biologically given.

Harlow and Mears review an enormous number of studies on primates showing the devastating effects of maternal deprivation not only on adult sexual behavior but on adult social behavior, individual initiative, curiosity, and learning. These results on primates are paralleled by Bowlby's findings on the negative effects of separation on human children although the evidence for a connection between maternal deprivation and adult human disturbance is much more complicated.

The evidence from studies of the mother-infant attachment system suggests that the development of a "secure self" is basic to intellectual functioning (Sroufe, 1979). In brief, then, there is evidence for the biosocial nature of human beings, both sexes.

Human Sociability: The Resulting Superego Experience

Human beings (both sexes) normally develop within a matrix of affectional bonds which remain operative throughout life. These bonds, in turn, assure the development of a quintessentially moral human nature, in which the moral emotions of shame and guilt play a compelling role.

Freud (1913) was one of the first scientists to hypothesize a uniquely human universal morality and to anchor it in evolutionary biology. (See Lewis, 1983, for a fuller account.) Freud sought the origins of morality not in God-given laws but in the Darwinian concept of adaptation to the conditions of existence. Freud's model of the origins of guilt relied on the Darwinian hypothesis that human society was organized around a dominant male, who excluded male juveniles from the group, thus fostering exogamous mating, ensuring the incest barrier and thereby contributing to increased chances of survival. Although Freud's concept of primordial human society was of a male-dominated horde, the origins of guilt were nevertheless understood as inhering in the son's conflict between the emotions of affection and hatred for the father. Reading *Totem and Taboo* some 70 years after it was written, one is struck by the irony that one of its most important, seminal ideas—the idea that identification with the injured party is the source of guilt—was almost buried in what now seem like trivial controversies over the historical reality of the primal patricide or the existence of a collective unconscious. These controversies reflect the epistemological uncertainty (still existing today) of anchoring emotions in "reality." In any case, with our newer knowledge of the attachment emotions, we may now anchor morality in attachment. Threatened attachment, which first evokes protest aimed at the caretaker is transformed, mainly by identifications with significant others, into states of shame and guilt that aim at restoring or maintaining the attachment. This view focuses on the origins of morality within the emotional transactions occurring between the individual and his or her principal caretakers. It regards shame and guilt as the two principal moral emotions arising out of the affectionate or "sociable" nature of the human species.

Sex Differences in Human Sociability

There are many clearly established sex differences in sensory capacity at birth. Girls have greater sensitivity to touch, taste, and pain (Garai & Scheinfeld, 1968). There is also some evidence for a greater sensitivity on the part of girl neonates to sound and light (Korner, 1973). Simner (1971) and Sagi and Hoffman (1976) have evidence that female infants are even more responsive than males to the sounds of other newborns' crying. Women, moreover, retain their greater sensitivity to sensory stimuli into adulthood (Garai & Scheinfeld, 1968), a fact which speaks against regarding the advantage of girl infants as solely the product of differences in developmental timetable. Thus, a "given" may be at work in the newborn girl which could permit adult women to be more sensitive than men, as befits their biosocial role as caretakers.

Newborn girls spend more time in reflex smiling than boys (Korner, 1969). While the newborn smile is not the same as the three-month social smile, it may be considered its precursor. In a follow-up study Korner (1973) also observed a sex difference in "oral organization." For girls a mouth-dominated pattern was more frequent. Korner hypothesizes that the androgens which circulate in fetal life to produce maleness may also suppress responsivity and sensitivity especially to mouth and skin.

Newborn boys, in contrast, "startle" more in both waking and sleeping states. This can be interpreted as a forerunner of the greater irritability that has been observed in boys (Moss, 1974) as well as of the finding that boys (not girls) have a constitutional level of fearfulness that follows them from infancy until they are eight years of age (Bronson, 1969). To the extent that sociability and fearfulness are "opposites," girls may be thought of as more social than boys.

Six-month-old girl infants are more interested in faces than in geometrical forms, which suggests that little girls are more interested in people, while boys are more interested in things (M. Lewis, 1969; Lewis, Kagan, & Kalafat, 1966). Again this line of evidence suggests that there are "givens" which push women into greater sociability than men. This edge in sociability may account, in part, for girls' well-known developmental advantage in early rate of growth.

Perhaps the most persuasive evidence supporting the idea that girls have an initial edge in sociability comes from studies of nonverbal communication. Hall's (1978) exhaustive and careful review of 75 studies of the accuracy of decoding nonverbal (emotional) signals suggests to her that females may be "wired" from birth to have an advantage in this respect. Hall also notes, of course, that the oppressed status of women may create a greater need for them to assess accurately the wishes of powerful others. But very young (4-year-old) girls are better than boys at decoding nonverbal messages, indicating a high level of consistency of the female advantage over the life-span, instead of a developmental increase which might be expected on a social learning basis alone.

Haviland and Malatesta (1981) surveyed the infant literature for sex differences in patterns of attention and temperament. Studies of eye-contact and gaze-aversion show that girls and women establish and maintain eye-contact much more than boys and men, beginning with neonates. Boys avert their gaze more. When it comes to memory for faces girls as young as four years of age have better recognition than do boys. From their literature review Haviland and Malatesta also are "forced to conclude that there is very definitely a female advantage in nonverbal sensitivity to emotional cues; in addition there appears to be developmental continuity" (p. 193). Haviland and Malatesta thus also suggest the influence of biogenetic as well as socialization factors in a female advantage in sociability.

Sex Differences in Language Ability

Human beings have developed their unique social and communicative skills because they have developed language and vice versa. In their updated review of the literature on language ability, Maccoby and Jacklin (1974) tell us that female superiority in verbal tasks is one of the most solidly established findings in the field of sex differences. (See Lewis, 1976, for a fuller treatment of this issue.) Language superiority may be a genetic "given" which is also fostered by women's culturally developed attachment to other people. As McCarthy (1953) suggested some years ago, girls' consistent advantage over boys in language development may result from the fact that girls, in identification with their mothers, may be better able to use an "echo quality" in learning language than boys. The evolutionary advantage of the endowment of a language advantage to women is that it fosters the "vocal or nonharmful control" of the infant (Kagan, 1971, p. 69).

Sex Differences in the Mother-Infant Interaction

Along with evidence for the greater sensitivity of girls there is evidence of a sex difference in the quality of the mother-infant interaction. Evidence on the primate level suggests that females are much less injured by maternal deprivation than are males (Sackett, 1974). Sackett has shown that male monkeys raised in isolation are totally unable to copulate in adulthood, while female monkeys are less impaired. Moreover, females reared in isolation are less injured in their curiosity, social behavior, and learning capacity. As Sackett puts it, summarizing the findings, females are the "buffered sex." Perhaps what they are buffered by is a slight edge in their sociability which makes them better able to withstand the injuries of isolation. Studies of monkeys show also that mother monkeys treat the two sexes differently. Mothers punish their male infants more than their females; they pay less attention to them and carry them around less frequently than their females. (This finding among primates has its forerunner among mice; female pups are retrieved by their mothers more often than are male pups.) No one yet understands the basis for this difference in mother-infant interaction among monkeys. One can speculate that male infants are innately more aggressive than are females and so induce more aggression in their mothers, in turn perpetuating male aggression. One can also speculate that a greater degree of sociability in females is expressed by and in turn perpetuates females' greater sociability.

The findings among monkeys are paralleled by findings about sex differences in the mother-infant interaction among ourselves. Differences in the symbolic meaning of boy and girl neonates to their parents have been demonstrated experimentally (Rubin, Provenzano, & Luria, 1974). Girl infants are perceived in the eyes of their beholders as "softer" than are boys; boys are "harder" than girls. When older infants (eight to fifteen months) were thought to be girls, videotapes of their faces were more often judged to be expressing joy, while infants identified as boys were more often judged to be expressing anger, fear and distress (Haviland & Malatesta, 1981). In infancy, at least, female gender symbolizes positive affect, while male gender symbolizes negative affect.

Close observation of middle-class mothers and their first infants has shown significant sex differences in mother's handling of their infants at three weeks and again at three months of age (Moss, 1974). Mothers held their boy infants farther away from their bodies. They more often held a boy baby in a sitting or standing position—"stressing the musculature." Mothers stimulated and aroused their boy infants more often than their girls, and they attended to them more than their girls. In sharp contrast, the only thing mothers did more of with their girl babies was imitate them. One does not need to be a psychoanalyst to interpret these findings as meaning that mothers are less comfortable with infants of the male sex and express their sense of sameness with girls by imitating them.

By the time the infants were three months old, an important sex difference had emerged in the mother-infant interaction. Male infants, even at three weeks, had cried more, fussed more, and been more irritable than had girls. Girl infants slept more and cried less than did boys. For males, who were more irritable to begin with, the correlation between the total time they cried and the amount of attention they got from their mothers was negative. The more boys cried, the less their mothers attended them. For girl infants, in contrast, the amount of time they cried and the amount of attention they got were positively correlated. As Moss (1974) points out, the evidence here joins the evidence of a number of other studies that boys are more subject to "inconsolable states," while girls can be seen as "responding more favorably to maternal intervention" (p. 29). A recent literature review by Haviland and Malatesta (1981) offers additional evidence supporting the "irritability" of male and the "consolability" of female infants.

This evidence is consistent with the finding that among nonhuman primates males are more injured by maternal deprivation. It also conforms to evidence from longitudinal studies that maternal deprivation has a more harmful effect on intelligence in men than in women (Bayley & Schaefer, 1964).

The reasons for this favorable treatment of girl infants and their smoother interaction with their mothers are still very mysterious. But being a same-sex or an opposite-sex first caretaker may be one factor.

If it is the mother-infant gender difference that is responsible for the greater difficulty in pacifying boy infants, one would expect to see Moss' findings duplicated cross-culturally. This would then be an instance of a biologically given sex difference which leads directly into a predictable difference in learned patterns of social interaction. It seems reasonable to suppose that the attitude toward her infant daughter will be different from her attitude toward her infant son if only in the recognition that her infant is same-sex or opposite-sex. Where there is serious devaluation of women, the maternal attitude might be expected to be grossly different. But even in egalitarian societies where there is less devaluation of women, a difference in the infant-mother interaction might be expected.

Girls may be expected to assimilate "sameness" from their relationship to their mothers, while boys assimilate "difference." It was Freud (1905) who first called attention to a difference in the self of men and women depending on first caretaker. Describing how adults find their mates, he wrote "The finding of an object [in adulthood] is a refinding of it" (p. 222). Freud was caught by the fact that men have an opposite-sex caretaker, but the same "love-object" all their lives. Women have a same-sex caretaker and an opposite-sex love object in adulthood. With his customary androcentric bias, Freud saw this as a harder task for women than for men, making it more difficult for women to develop sexual feeling for men and making them more prone to homosexuality (Freud, 1933).

Freud's androcentric bias was first criticized by Horney (1926/ 1967) who suggested that men's assumption of gender identity might be more difficult than women's precisely because men have an opposite-sex rather than a same-sex first caretaker. Margaret Mead (1949), largely under Horney's influence, also suggested that having an opposite-sex first caretaker made a boy's assumption of gender identity harder than is the case for women. Lynn (1961) also pursued this line of reasoning, suggesting that girls have only to learn a "lesson" in person emulation, while boys have to solve a "problem" in mother-person differentiation and then learn to model themselves on their distant fathers. Whether for this or for other reasons, adult men are, contrary to Freud's prediction, more prone to disturbances of gender identity than women. Although in general they apply less often than women for psychiatric help, men are more likely to apply for help in changing sexual deviation (Lewis, 1976). Fetishism, cross-dressing, voyeurism, and exhibitionism as a means of sexual excitement are all more prevalent among men (Stoller, 1968). These modes of sexual excitement all reflect a deficit in sociability. Incest (Herman, 1981) and rape (Brownmiller, 1965) are both crimes committed mainly by men. These disturbances of gender identity and the crimes they induce may be thought to reflect failures of human sociability. In any case, these distortions of their sexuality form an avenue along which men march into the statistics on schizophrenia.

Dinnerstein (1977) has recently argued that a family structure in which both sexes are reared predominantly by women fosters both male aggression against women and the subordinate position of women. Chodorow's (1978) cross-cultural studies of the reproduction of mothering and Baumrind's (1980) review of socialization research also call attention to the harmful effects of one-sided child-rearing vs. "parenting."

The question that must be disentangled from cross-sex vs. like-sex caretaking is the effect of egalitarian vs. stratified society. In societies where power and submission are relatively unimportant considerations, the aggression that arises in both sexes toward an opposite-sex or same-sex parent might be expected to dissolve by adulthood. Exploitative societies, which transmit the values of male competition and domination, are likely to enhance male aggressions against the gender that reminds them of their first (female) caretaker.

There is actually some cross-cultural evidence for this hypothesis. For example, societies where women and children are segregated from adult males are likely to have more severe initiation rites for males at puberty. Societies without such distance between adult males and the women and children are less likely to "brainwash" their boys into equating masculinity and toughness (Chodorow, 1971).

In any case, in our own society the picture of an aggressive male and a less aggressive *and* more sociable female has been overwhelmingly documented in psychological studies over the past thirty years (see Lewis, 1976 for a fuller treatment of this evidence). A man's level of aggression, moreover, becomes characteristic of him in his childhood. By age four, the "pattern of feminine-maternal qualities ... has all but broken down [in boys] under the requirement that males model themselves after male. The anaclitic quality of the initial socialization process is evident in girls but does not appear in boys" (Sears, Rau, & Alpert, 1965, p. 262). Aggression remains characteristic of boys through childhood and follow-up studies of persons in later life (Kagan & Moss, 1962) show unequivocally that aggressive boys turn into aggressive men. Mussen (1969) sums it up as follows: "Aggressive adolescent boys become aggressive, easily angered men ... appropriately sex typed, they become "instrumental," i.e., self-sufficient, lacking in sociability and introspection" (p. 712). As already indicated, this stereotypical sex difference is paralleled by the sex difference in field dependence.

Part 3: Evidence From Studies of Field Dependence

Field dependence is a very widely researched cognitive style (Kogan, 1976) involving more than 3,000 studies (Singer, 1984), which catches the self not only in its relation to the physical surround but in relation to other people.

Work on field dependence actually grew out of opposing theories about whether the self is "egotistical" or not. As a first step toward the empirical study of his hypothesis that the self is not egotistical but rather influenced by its relation to the surround, Wertheimer (1912) undertook to study how people perceive the upright in space. Using an ingenious technique to separate the postural and gravitational cues operating on the body from the visual cues reflecting horizontals and verticals in space, Wertheimer demonstrated that the perception of the upright is indeed influenced by the visual framework in which we live. His findings were extended by Asch and Witkin (1948) and Witkin and Asch (1948). Witkin then discovered a stable, consistent individual difference in the extent to which people's perception is influenced by the prevailing framework, and his hypothesis that people who are "egotistical" in their perception of the upright should also be egotistical personalities was empirically tested and confirmed (Witkin et al., 1954; Witkin et al., 1962). The early finding of a small but significant sex difference, with women more field dependent than men, was also clearly congruent with the difference in men's and women's stereotypical sex roles.

There is now some evidence for cultural differences in field dependence. Nomadic hunting groups, which of necessity foster autonomy in personal functioning, are predictably more field independent than sedentary agricultural groups whose organization requires more social interaction and cooperation (Berry, 1976). Cognitive style thus apparently arises in adaptation to cultural conditions. Witkin and Goodenough (1981) suggest, moreover, that the course of evolution has been from field independence to greater field dependence with the shift from early human hunting societies to the development of agriculture. Among the Eskimo, whose hunting economy relies on the work of men and women equally, there is no sex difference in field dependence.

The operation of the self in relation to other people clearly creates different demands than when the self is operating in relation to inanimate things. Specifically, the self in relation to other people requires more empathic and vicarious experience; the self in relation to things requires that the boundary between the self and the object be clearly articulated. In dealing with others as human beings (not as objects or things) the self necessarily engages in the vicarious experience of others' feelings. Encounters with people involve and animate feedback and the use of language in two-way communication. The transactions involved in dealing with people thus require a self with permeable boundaries. By contrast, when the self is engaged in grasping and changing the properties of a thing, the self is ordinarily not even aware of itself except as an automatic reference point. In dealing with things, moreover, the self is often required to adopt a field-independent or analytical cognitive attitude. In dealing with people, a field-dependent attitude is often more useful.

The personality characteristics of field-dependent and field-independent adults, as revealed in many empirical studies, clearly correspond to the categories of greater and lesser sociability, and to the stereotypical sex roles of women and men. A field-dependent person "likes being with others, [is] sociable, gregarious, affiliation-oriented, socially outgoing, prefers interpersonal and group to intrapersonal circumstances, seeks relations with others, shows participativeness, shows need for friendship, [is] interested in people, wants to help others, has a concern for people, has wide acquaintanceship, knows many people, and is known to many people" (Witkin & Goodenough, 1977, p. 672). A field-independent person, in contrast, "prefers solitary activities, [is] individualistic, cold, and distant in relations with others, aloof, never feels like embracing the whole world, [is] not interested in humanitarian activities, highly interested in intellectual activities, values cognitive pursuits, [is] concerned with philosophical problems, concerned with ideas and principles rather than people, task-oriented, has work-oriented values such as efficiency, control, competence, excelling" (Witkin & Goodenough, 1977, p. 672).

Field dependence in adulthood has thus been found to be related to two sets of factors—positive attitudes toward others or sociability and deficits in cognitive restructuring capacity (Witkin, Goodenough, & Oltman, 1979). Witkin et al. speculate that the "greater recourse of field-dependent people to external referents (meaning, in this case, other people) stimulated the development of interpersonal competencies but may be responsible for these people's lesser cognitive restructuring skills. Relatively field-dependent people may be seen as making their main developmental investment in different domains" (p. 1139).

What this formulation leaves unanswered, however, is why there should be an inverse relation between social skills and cognitive restructuring skills. Why should the two different domains of emotional and cognitive development not proceed in a positive interaction rather than a negative interaction? Why, for example, should women's greater ability to judge the warmth of other people's feelings go together with greater difficulty in cognitive restructuring skills? (Rapaczynski, Welkowitz, & Sadd, 1979).

It seems likely, in fact, that social skills and field independence do develop in positive interaction during childhood. Coates (1974) has evidence which suggests that there may be a relatively brief period, at age five, when preschool girls are more field independent than boys. Coates suggests that the superiority of five-year-old girls may be a result of girls's more rapid maturation, or it may come about because preschool boys are more aggressive than girls and at least among preschoolers, aggressiveness is a hindrance to analytic functioning. Coates, Lord, and Jakabovics (1975) also have evidence that better socialized preschoolers are more field independent.

This evidence suggests that the two tracks of self in relation to others and self in relation to things may begin by interacting positively and stop doing so when socialization processes begin to emphasize the culturally enforced contradiction between interpersonal relationships and individualistic, competitive strivings, when men begin to be trained to "agency" and women to "communion" (Bakan, 1966), compounding their advantage in sociability.

Another early finding of the studies on field dependence was of a correlation between field dependence and depression, and a corresponding correlation between field independence and paranoia (Witkin et al., 1954; Witkin, 1965). Subsequent studies have offered robust evidence for the connection between field dependence and depression (Levenson & Neuringer, 1974; Newman & Hirt, 1983). There is also additional evidence for the connection between field independence and paranoia (Johnson, 1980). These findings are also congruent with the lesser egotism of women.

Field Dependence and Superego Style

In the course of my work on field dependence, it became apparent that the relation of the self to transgression for which it is responsible (guilt) would be very different from the relation of the self to another person in unrequited love (shame). Some clinical observation of field-dependent and field-independent patients confirmed the usefulness of a phenomenological approach to the two affective states which constitute a person's superego: shame and guilt.

Studying neurotic patients with some of the insights gained in my work on field dependence suggested that differences in the way people determine the position of the self in the field reflect not only perceptual and cognitive style but important variables in patients' defensive style and in their relationship to significant others in their lives. In clinical accounts of psychoanalytic work with neurotic patients (Lewis, 1958, 1959), I used field dependence as a "tracer element" for following characteristic behavior and transference phenomena during treatment. In particular, the patients' perceptual style focused attention on the manner and extent of individuation of the self from significant "others." A field-dependent patient was described as readily merging herself with the surround. She was self-effacing; when she was self-conscious, it was in an awkward and shy way. A field-independent patient, also a woman, was described as having an organized self which took the initiative in vigilantly defending her place in the field. Differences between field-dependent and field-independent patients were also traced in the organization of the self in dreams.

In a case of "watching" in a child patient (Lewis, 1963) I suggested that shame functions particularly as a protection against the loss of self-boundaries which is implicit in absorbed sexual fantasy, i.e., in states of longing-for-attachment experience. Shame functions as a sharp, in fact, painful remainder that fantasy experience of the "other" is vicarious. Shame brings into focal awareness both the self and the "other," with the imagery that the "other" rejects the self. It thus helps to maintain the sense of separate identity, by making the self the focus of experience. This notion about the function of shame is similar to Lynd's (1958) description of how shame can spur the sense of identity. It also parallels Erikson's (1956) observation that shame is the opposite of autonomy, but with the emendation that it is the opposite of the autonomy of the *self* rather than of the ego. This formulation, while recognizing the apparent "narcissism" in shame, regards this as a phenomenon in which the self is experienced "at the quick," while the person is maintaining affectional ties.

Making a link between characteristics of the self and characteristic functioning of the superego was one step in a line of reasoning which supposed that the superego functioned differently in field-dependent and field-independent patients. A field-dependent mode of superego functioning would be shame; while a field-independent mode would be guilt. Both modes of superego functioning represent an equally developed superego. Both modes could also be associated with an equally severe or malfunctioning superego.

An empirical study undertaken to check these predictions was able to confirm them (Witkin, Lewis, & Weil, 1968).[1] Patients selected on the basis of their perceptual style, and their figure drawings, were placed in individual psychotherapy in "pairs" of matched groups, a field-dependent and field-independent patient each with the same therapist. Transcripts of their first two psychotherapy sessions were scored (by a "blind" judge) according to the method developed by Louis Gottschalk and his associates (Gottschalk & Gleser, 1969) for affect implied in verbal productions. As predicted, in the transcripts of field-dependent patients there were significantly more references to anxiety of "shame, humiliation, embarrassment, ridicule, and exposure of private details," then references to the anxiety of "guilt, fault, responsibility, being punished, scolded, or abused." The converse was true for field-independent patients.

We also made predictions about the direction of hostility which would be found in the "pairs" of transcripts. These predictions were based both upon the nature of shame and guilt and upon what differences might be expected between field-dependent and field-independent patients. Specifically, we found that field-independent patients were more prone to direct their hostility both outward and inward; while field-dependent patients were more prone to self-directed hostility. There was some evidence that, regardless of patient type, shame tended to be found in association with self-

1. This study was supported by Grants M-628 and MH 05518 from the National Institutes of Health, US Public Health Service.

directed hostility, and that this association was particularly strong in field-dependent patients.

Further evidence has since accumulated for a connection between field dependence and shame (Crouppen, 1976; Smith, 1972). The success in predicting a relation between cognitive style and shame and guilt thus led to the related hypothesis that shame is the salient factor in depression, while guilt is more salient in obsessional neurosis and paranoia.

Direct evidence for the role of shame in depression has not been easy to obtain mainly because there are too few easily usable, reliable, and valid shame measures. There is, however, now mounting evidence of a robust connection between shame and depression (Lewis, in press). Attention to shame is particularly helpful for understanding the role of retroflected hostility in depression. We can assume that the sequel of lost love is humiliated fury or shame-rage, which is a communication to the "other" of protest at the broken tie. Bowlby (1980) suggests that "the principal issue about which a [depressed] person feels helpless is his ability to make or maintain affectional relationships" (p. 247). As is apparent, I am equating shame-rage with Bowlby's "bitter" protest on separation (1963). Humiliated fury is a particularly difficult state to resolve, since shame or humiliation is a vicarious experience of the self in the other's eyes. On the one hand, its sequel is "turning the tables" in an effort to humiliate the (beloved) other, which risks even further rejection in turn and also involves the self in guilt for retaliatory hostility. On the other hand, humiliated fury is "only about the self" and is thus perceived as "inappropriate" and unjust. This turns attention away from the fury. A fall in self-esteem, without full consciousness of fury, can thus operate to maintain the affectional tie. The recognition of humiliated fury as a particularly difficult feeling trap because affectional ties are threatened thus clarifies the social interaction behind retroflected hostility.

A framework that posits the importance of shame in depression can help make sense of some findings from cognitive-behavioral models of depression. For example, the cognitive paradox in depression is: If depressed people are as helpless as they feel, logic dictates that they should not also feel self-reproaches for what they are unable to do (Abramson & Sackeim, 1977; Peterson, 1979; Rizley, 1978). This paradox vanishes, however, if we assume that depressed people are helpless to change the vicarious experience of another's negative feeling about the self—that is, to get out of a state of shame. Humiliated fury won't do it; expressing such fury is likely to get the self into even more trouble with the other, especially as humiliated fury is felt by the self to be inappropriate and blameworthy.

Peterson, Schwartz, and Seligman (1981) have found that depressed women undergraduates were more likely to blame their *characters* for bad events than they were to blame specific *behaviors*. (If anything, blame for behaviors was negatively correlated with depression.) If we equate blame of the self for its character with shame, and blame for behaviors with guilt, we may glimpse a convergence of evidence resulting from the accurate specification of the role of shame in depression. What attention to shame suggests is that the maintenance of an affectional tie, even at some expense to self-esteem, may also contribute to the perpetuation of faulty negative attributions. There is even some experimental evidence for this dynamic (see, for example, Forrest & Hokanson, 1975).

On the side of paranoia and guilt, the evidence comes mainly from the symptomatology itself, which is quintessentially the projection of guilt. Colby (1977), in his studies of computer-simulated paranoia, suggests that a shame-humiliation model is preferable to a homosexual, hostility, or homeostatic model. Although this is in apparent contradiction to my view that guilt is the more proximal state out of which paranoia forms, the discrepancy between Colby and myself may be more apparent than real. Colby actually suggests that the paranoid forestalls the threat of humiliation by a strategy of "blaming others for wrongdoing," that is, projecting guilt.

Sex Differences in Shame and Guilt

The formal evidence directly showing a sex difference between men and women in proneness to shame and guilt remains thin. This is a particularly promising area for future research. A number of tangential studies support the hypothesis (Lewis, 1976). One study, for example, invited men and women to describe their experience of conscience when tempted to do something wrong, that is, threatened by guilt. Women gave as their most frequent answer that they would take into account all the personal circumstances. Men's most frequent answer was that they would consult their own standards. Women said that they would consider the harm to others and the teachings of their parents, thus demonstrating their "other-connected" conscience, from which one could predict that they would more often experience shame of themselves in others' eyes as well as their own. In this same study, women chose as metaphors for their conscious images (representing an ideal of goodness) of their conscience: a "seeing eye dog," or "hidden lamp." Men, in contrast, chose punitive metaphors, as conscience such as a "concealed weapon," or "foreign agent." In a direct study of shame and guilt as assessed by an early memories test (Binder, 1970), women were more prone to shame than to guilt, while men were more prone to guilt than to shame. Women were also more prone to shame-anxiety and men to guilt-anxiety in a 5-minute sample of verbal productions (see Lewis, 1976, p. 212).

The suggestion of a difference between the sexes in proneness to shame or guilt fit neatly with Gilligan's (1982) results on sex differences in the considerations governing ethical choice. Faced with ethical dilemmas, women tried more often than men to find a solution by invoking the "ethic of care," that is, an ethic which is based on a caring relationship between people. Men, in contrast, more often invoked the "ethic of responsibility" that is, of individual guilt. Men's conscience, in short, operated much more according to Kant's categorical imperative, in keeping with men's lesser value for relationship to others.

Recapitulation of the Argument

Let me briefly recapitulate the main points in my understanding of sex differences in proneness to depression vs. paranoia. Human beings of both sexes are innately sociable creatures. This is indicated by anthropological evidence and also by many studies showing the social competence of infants and by studies of the infant-caretaker interaction.

Because they are sociable creatures, human beings are inevitably moral creatures as well. As predicted, the two principal moral emotions, shame and guilt, involved differing cognitive styles, field dependence/independence.

Women may have a slight edge over men in innate sociability. This is indicated by evidence from studies of infant sensitivity, from studies of infant-caretaker interaction, and from studies of language ability. Evidence also comes from studies of the effects of same-sex vs. opposite-sex first caretakers. From this slight edge in sociability and from the evidence that sociability and intellectual development initially proceed in tandem, it might be expected that little girls should be more field independent than little boys. There is, in fact, evidence that this is so at age five. But by adolescence, when the contradiction between the culture's value for (female) attachment and (male) aggression becomes salient, boys and men become more field independent than are girls and women.

From their slight edge in sociability, and their greater field dependence, we can predict, also, that their prevailing superego mode should involve women more often in the shame of "loss of love." Their proneness to shame predisposes them to depression. In addition, the contradiction in cultural values surrounding attachment and aggression operates to denigrate women, and still further increases their shame and depression.

This same contradiction of values places men at greater risk of becoming emotionally detached, impersonal, and field independent. The expectation that men should dominate also increases their likelihood of aggressive behavior with a resulting increase in their level of chronic, unresolved guilt. The way is thus paved for the development of paranoia and schizophrenia.

References

Abramson, L., & Sackeim, H. (1977). A paradox in depression: Uncontrollability and self-blame. *Psychological Bulletin, 84,* 32–48.
Ainsworth, M., Blehar, M., Waters, E., & Wall, S. (1978). *Patterns of attachment.* New York: Erlbaum.
Asch, S., & Witkin, H. (1948). Studies in space orientation. I and II. *Journal of Experimental Psychology, 38,* 603–614; 762–782.
Bakan, D. (1966). *The duality of human existence.* Chicago: Rand McNally.
Barash, D. (1977). *Sociobiology and behavior.* New York: Elsevier.
Barchas, J., Akil, H., & Elliot, G. (1978). Behavioral neurochemistry: Neuroregulators and behavioral states. *Science, 200,* 964–973.
Bart, P. (1971). Depression in middle-aged women. In V. Gornick & B. Moran (Eds.), *Women in sexist society* (pp. 163–186). New York: New American Library.
Baumrind, D. (1980). New directions in socialization research. *American Psychologist, 35,* 639–652.
Bayley, N., & Schaefer, E. (1964). Correlations of maternal and child behaviors with development of mental abilities. *Monographs of the Society for Research on Child Development, 29,* No. 97.
Bell, S. (1970). The development of the concepts of the object as related to infant-mother attachment. *Child Development, 41,* 291–311.
Bernstein, I. (1978). Sex differences in the behaviors of nonhuman primates. *Social Science and Medicine, 12,* 151–155.
Berry, J. (1976). *Human ecology and cognitive style.* New York: Wiley.
Binder, J. (1970). The relative proneness to shame or guilt as a dimension of character style. *Dissertation Abstracts International.*
Bowlby, J. (1963). Pathological mourning and childhood mourning. *Journal of the American Psychological Association, 11,* 500–542.
Bowlby, J. (1969). *Attachment and loss* (Vol. 1). New York: Basic Books.
Bowlby, J. (1980). *Attachment and loss* (Vol. 3). New York: Basic Books.
Bronson, G. (1969). Sex differences in the development of fearfulness: A replication. *Psychonomic Science, 17,* 367–368.
Brownmiller, S. (1975). *Against our will: Men, women, and rape.* New York: Simon & Schuster.
Cheek, F. (1964). A serendipitous finding: Sex roles and schizophrenia. *Journal of Abnormal and Social Psychology, 69,* 392–400.
Chesler, P. (1972). *Women and madness.* New York: Doubleday.
Chodorow, N. (1971). Being and doing: A cross-cultural examination of the socialization of males and females. In V. Gornick & B. Moran (Eds.), *Women in sexist society* (pp. 259–291). New York: New American Library.

Chodorow, N. (1978) *The reproduction of mothering*. Berkeley: University of California Press.

Coates, S. (1974). Sex differences in field dependence among preschool children. In R. Friedman, R. Reichert, & R. Vande Weile (Eds.), *Sex differences in behavior* (pp. 259–274). New York: Wiley.

Coates, S., Lord, M., & Jakabovics, E. (1975). Field dependence/independence, social nonsocial play and sex differences in preschool children. *Perceptual and Motor Skills*, **40**, 195–202.

Cohen, Y. (Ed.). (1961). *Social structure and personality*. New York: Holt, Rinehart and Winston.

Colby, K. (1977). Appraisal of four psychological theories of paranoid phenomena. *Journal of Abnormal Psychology*, **86**, 54–59.

Condon, W., & Sander, L. (1974). Neonate movement is synchronized with adult speech. *Science*, **183**, 99–101.

Crouppen, G. (1976). *Field dependence in depressed and normal males, as an indication of relative proneness to shame and guilt and ego functioning*. Unpublished dissertation, California School of Professional Psychology.

Darwin, C. (1871). *The descent of man and selection in relation to sex*. Parts I, II. New York: P. F. Collier & Son.

DeCasper, A., & Fifer, W. (1980). Of human bonding: Newborns prefer their mothers's voices. *Science*, **208**, 1174–1176.

Dinnerstein, D. (1977). *The mermaid and the minotaur*. New York: Harper & Row.

Dohrenwend, B., & Dohrenwend, B. (1976). Sex differences and psychiatric disorders. *American Journal of Sociology*, **81**, 1447–1454.

Edel, M., & Edel, A. (1968). *Anthropology and ethics* (rev. ed.). Cleveland: Western Reserve Press.

Eibl-Eibelsfeldt, I. (1974). *Love and hate*. New York: Schocken Books.

Erikson, E. (1956). Identity and the life-cycle. *Journal of the American Psychoanalytic Association*, **4**, 56–121.

Faris, R., & Dunham, H. (1960). *Mental disorders in urban areas*. New York: Hafner. (Original work published 1939)

Forrest, M., & Hokanson, J. (1975). Depression and autonomic arousal reduction accompanying self-punitive behavior. *Journal of Abnormal Psychology*, **84**, 346–357.

Freedman, D. (1964). Smiling in blind infants. *Journal of Child Psychology and Psychiatry*, **5**, 171–184.

Freedman, D. (1965). Hereditary control of early social behavior. In B. M. Foss (Ed.), *Determinants of infant behavior* (Vol. 3, pp. 149–159). New York: Wiley.

Freud, S. (1905). Three essays on sexuality. In J. Strachey (Ed. and Trans.), *Standard edition of the complete psychological works of Sigmund Freud* (Vol. 7). London: Hogarth Press.

Freud, S. (1913). Totem and taboo. In J. Strachey (Ed. and Trans.), *Standard edition of the complete psychological works of Sigmund Freud*. London: Hogarth Press.

Freud, S. (1933). New introductory lectures on psychoanalysis. In J. Strachey (Ed. and Trans.), *Standard edition of the complete psychological works of Sigmund Freud* (Vol. 22). London: Hogarth Press.

Fromm, E. (1941). *Escape from freedom*. New York: Farrar & Rinehart.

Fromm, E. (1955). *The sane society*. New York: Rinehart.

Garai, J., & Scheinfeld, A. (1968). Sex differences in mental traits. *Genetic Psychology Monographs*, **77**, 169–299.

Gilligan, C. (1982). *In a different voice*. Cambridge: Harvard University Press.

Gottschalk, L., & Gleser, G. (1969). *The measurement of psychological states through the content analysis of verbal behavior*. Berkeley: University of California Press.

Hall, J. (1978). Gender effects in decoding nonverbal cues. *Psychological Bulletin*, **85**, 845–857.

Hammen, C., & Peters, S. (1977). Differential responses to male and female depressive relations. *Journal of Clinical and Consulting Psychology*, **45**, 994–1001.

Hammen, C., & Peters, S. (1978). Interpersonal consequences of depression: Responses to men and women enacting a depressed role. *Journal of Abnormal Psychology*, **87**, 322–332.

Harlow, H., & Mears, C. (1979). *The human model: Primate perspectives*. New York: Wiley.

Haviland, J., & Malatesta, C. (1981). The development of sex differences in nonverbal signals. In C. Mayo & N. Henley (Eds.), *Gender and nonverbal behavior* (pp. 183–208). New York: Springer.

Herman, J. (1981). *Father-daughter incest*. Cambridge: Harvard University Press.

Horney, K. (1937). *The neurotic personality of our time*. New York: W. W. Horton.

Horney, K. (1967). The flight from womanhood. In H. Kelman (Ed.), *Feminine psychology*. New York: W. W. Horton. (Original work published 1926)

James, W. (1890). *Principles of psychology* (Vol. 1). New York: Henry Holt.

Johnson, D. (1980). *Cognitive organization in paranoic and nonparanoid schizophrenics*. Unpublished dissertation, Yale University.

Kagan, J. (1971). In H. R. Schaffer (Ed.), *The origin of human social relations*. New York: Academic Press.

Kagan, J., & Moss, H. (1962) *Birth to maturity: A study in psychological development*. New York: Wiley.

Kaila, E. (1971). Cited in H. R. Schaffer, *The growth of sociability*. London: Penguin Books, chap. 3.

Kogan, N. (1976). *Cognitive styles in infancy and early childhood*. New York: Wiley.

Korner, A. (1969). Neonatal startles, smiles, erections, and reflex sucks as related to state, age, and individuality. *Child Development*, **40**, 1039–1053.

Korner, A. (1973). Sex differences in newborns with special reference to differences in the organization of oral behavior. *Journal of Child Psychology and Psychiatry*, **14**, 19–29.

LaBarre, W. (1954). *The human animal*. Chicago: University of Chicago Press.

Levenson, M., & Neuringer, C. (1974). Suicide and field dependency. *Omega*, **5**, 181–186.

Levi-Strauss, C. (1969). *Totemism*. Middlesex, England: Pelican Books.

Levy, L., & Rowitz, L. (1973). *The ecology of mental disorder*. New York: Behavioral Publications.

Lewis, H. B. (1958). Overdifferentiation and underindividuation of the self. *Psychoanalysis and the Psychoanalytic Review*, **45**, 3–24.

Lewis, H. (1959). The organization of the self in manifest dreams. *Psychoanalysis and the Psychoanalytic Review*, **46**, 21–35.

Lewis, H. (1963). A case of watching as a defense against an oral incorporation fantasy. *Psychoanalytic Review*, **50**, 68–80.

Lewis, H. B. (1976). *Psychic war in men and women*. New York: New York University Press.

Lewis, H. (1978). Sex differences in superego mode as related to sex differences in psychiatric illness. *Social Science and Medicine*, **12B**, 199–205.

Lewis, H. B. (1981). *Freud and modern psychology* (Vol. 1). *The emotional basis of mental illness*. New York: Plenum.

Lewis, H. B. (1983). *Freud and modern psychology* (Vol. 2). *The emotional basis of human behavior*. New York: Plenum.

Lewis, H. B. (in press). The role of shame in depression. In M. Rutter, C. Izard, & P. Read (Eds.), *Depression in childhood: Developmental perspectives*. New York: Guilford Press.

Lewis, M. (1969). Infants' responses to facial stimuli during the first year of life. *Developmental Psychology*, **1**, 75–86.

Lewis, M., Kagan, J., & Kalafat, E. (1966). Patterns of fixation in the young infant. *Child Development*, **37**, 331–341.

Lindzey, G., Loehlin, J., Manosevitz, M., & Thiessen, D. (1971). *Behavior Genetics: Annual Review of Psychology*, **22**, 39–54.

Lovejoy, O. (1981). The origin of man. *Science*, **216**, 341–349.

Lynd, G. (1958). *On shame and the search for identity.* New York: Harcourt Brace.

Lynn, D. (1961). Sex role and parental identification. *Child Development,* 33, 555–564.

Maccoby, E., Jacklin, C. (1974). *The psychology of sex differences.* Stanford: Stanford University Press.

Mahler, M., Pine, F., & Bergman, A. (1975). *The psychological birth of the infant.* New York: Basic Books.

Malzberg, B. (1959). Important statistical data about mental illness. In S. Arieti (Ed.), *American handbook of psychiatry* (pp. 161–174). New York: Basic Books.

McCarthy, D. (1953). Some possible explanations of sex differences in language development. *Journal of Psychology,* 35, 155–160.

McClelland, D., & Watt, N. (1968). Sex role alienation in schizophrenia. *Journal of Abnormal Psychology,* 73, 226–240.

Mead, M. (1949). *Male and female.* New York: Morrow.

Meltzoff, A., & Moore, M. (1977). Imitation of facial and nonfacial gestures. *Science,* 198, 75–78.

Morgan, E. (1972). *The descent of woman.* New York: Bantam Books.

Moss, H. (1974). Early sex differences in the mother-infant interaction. In R. Friedman, R. Reichert, & R. Vande Weile (Eds.), *Sex differences in behavior* (pp. 149–163). New York: Wiley.

Murphy, J. (1976). Psychiatric labeling in cross-cultural perspective. *Science,* 191, 1019–1028.

Mussen, P. (1969). Early sex role development. In D. Goslin (Ed.), *Handbook of socialization theory and research* (pp. 707–731). Chicago: Rand McNally.

Newman, R., & Hirt, M. (1983). The psychoanalytic theory of depression: Symptoms as a function of aggressive works and field-articulation. *Journal of Abnormal Psychology,* 92, 42–49.

Peterson, C. (1979). Uncontrollability and self-blame in depression: Investigations of the paradox in a college population. *Journal of Abnormal Psychology,* 88, 620–624.

Peterson, C., Schwartz, S., & Seligman, M. (1981). Self-blame and depressive symptoms. *Journal of Personality and Social Psychology,* 41, 253–260.

Radloff, L., & Rae, D. (1979). Susceptibility and precipitating factors in depression: Sex differences and similarities. *Journal of Abnormal Psychology,* 88, 174–181.

Rapaczynski, W., Welkowitz, J., & Sadd, S. (1979). Affect judgment and field dependence. (ETS RR 79-5) Princeton, NJ: Educational Testing Service.

Reich, W. (1971). *The mass psychology of fascism.* New York: Farrar, Straus, & Giroux.

Rheingold, H. (1969). The social and socializing infant. In D. Goslin (Ed.), *Handbook of socialization theory and research* (pp. 779–790). Chicago: Rand McNally.

Rizley, R. (1978). Depression and distortion in the attribution of causality. *Journal of Abnormal Psychology,* 87, 32–48.

Rubin, J., Provenzano, F., & Luria, Z. (1974). The eye of the beholder: Parents' views of the sex of the newborn. *American Journal of Orthopsychiatry,* 44, 512–519.

Sackett, G. (1974). Sex differences in rehesus monkeys following varied rearing experiences. In R. Friedman, R. Reichert, & R. Vande Weile (Eds.), *Sex differences in behavior* (pp. 99–122). New York: Wiley.

Sagi, A., & Hoffman, M. L. (1976). Empathic distress in newborns. *Developmental Psychology,* 12, 175–176.

Schaffer, H. R. (Ed.). (1971). *The origin of human social relations.* New York: Academic Press.

Sears, R., Rau, L., & Alpert, R. (1965). *Identification and child rearing.* Stanford: Stanford University Press.

Simner, M. L. (1971). Newborn response to the cry of another infant. *Developmental Psychology,* 5, 136–150.

Singer, J. L. (1984). *The human personality.* New York: Harcourt Brace Jovanovich.

Smith, R. (1972). *The relative proneness to shame and guilt as an indicator of defensive style*. Unpublished doctoral dissertation, Northwestern University.

Sroufe, A. (1979). The coherence of individual development: Early care, attachment, and subsequent developmental issues. *American Psychologist*, 34, 834–841.

Stoller, R. (1968). *Sex and gender*. New York: Jason Aronson.

Stone, L., Smith, H., & Murphy, L. (Eds.). (1973). *The social infant*. New York: Basic Books.

Waldron, I. (1976). Why do women live longer than men? Part I. *Journal of Human Stress*, 2, 2–10.

Waldron, I. (1978). Type A behavior pattern and coronary heart disease in men and women. *Social Science and Medicine*, 12B, 167–170.

Watson, J. (1974). Smiling, cooing, and "The Game." In L. Stone, H. Smith, & L. Murphy (Eds.), *The social infant*. New York: Basic Books.

Wertheimer, M. (1912). Experimentelle studien uber das seben von bewegung. *Zeitschrift fur Psychologie*, 61, 165–265.

Witkin, H. A. (1965). Psychological differentiation and forms of pathology. *Journal of Abnormal Psychology*, 70, 317–336.

Witkin, H., & Asch, S. (1948). Studies in space orientation. III. and IV. *Journal of Experimental Psychology*, 38, 603–614; 762–782.

Witkin, H., Dyk, R., Goodenough, D., Faterson, H., & Karp, S. (1962). *Psychological differentiation*. New York: Wiley.

Witkin, H., & Goodenough, D. (1977). Field dependence and interpersonal behavior. *Psychological Bulletin*, 84, 661–689.

Witkin, H., & Goodenough, D. (1981). *Cognitive styles: Essence and origins*. New York: International Universities Press.

Witkin, H., Goodenough, D., & Oltman, P. (1979). Psychological differentiation: Current status. *Journal of Personality and Social Psychology*, 37, 1127–1145.

Witkin, H., Lewis, H., Hertzman, M., Machover, K., Meissner, P., & Wapner, J. (1954). *Personality through perception*. New York: Harper.

Witkin, H., Lewis, H., & Weil, E. (1968). Affective reactions and patient-therapist interactions among more and less differentiated patients early in therapy. *Journal of Nervous and Mental Disease*, 146, 193–208.

Wittig, M., & Petersen, A. (1979). *Sex-related differences in cognitive functioning*. New York: Academic Press.

Gender and victimization by intimates

Lenore E. Auerbach Walker and Angela Browne

Abstract

Recent data demonstrate that, although gender has an impact upon the experience of being a victim of an intimate's violence, there is no particular personality pattern that leads one to become a victim. Rather, women—who are socialized to adapt and submit, and who are likely to become victims of men's sexual violence or physical abuse—may not develop adequate self-protection skills as children, especially if they come from childhood homes in which females are victimized, leading to a later vulnerability to physical and sexual abuse. Men, however, socialized to express anger and aggression in an outward manner, learn to model the abuse witnessed or experienced in childhood and often learn that women are the "appropriate" recipients of this violence.

Social learning theories of modeling and aggression are used to explain how such personality patterns develop, and the theory of learned helplessness is used to explain battered women's coping responses to their partners' abusive behavior. The extreme situation, in which a battered woman kills her partner in self-defense, is analyzed in order to understand women victims' sense of desperation and entrapment in severely abusive relationships and the extent to which their behaviors are in reaction to the abuse perpetrated by the mate.

Suppositions concerning women who are battered by male partners abound in our society. The most prevalent of these involve theories of victim precipitation, suggesting that battered women invite abuse because of some personality deficit in themselves, sometimes labeled as masochism (e.g., Blum, 1982; Shainess, 1979). While such theories were accepted prior to the seventies, the past decade of research has provided evidence that women who are physically, sexually, or psychologically battered by their mates do not derive enjoyment from their suffering and do not feel a need to be punished or to seek out abusive treatment, as a masochism explanation would propose (see Finkelhor, Gelles, Hotaling, & Straus, 1983, for examples of recent research). However, living in constant fear of violent attacks and experiencing physical assault does create sufficient stress to affect women's responses in significant ways.

Until recently, most research on abusive relationships focused on the women involved, in an attempt to find out what factors in their personality structure resulted in their victimization. However, studies comparing abusive and nonabusive couples failed to find many significant differences between women; most of the differences occurred between abusive and nonabusive men (e.g., Rosenbaum & O'Leary, 1981; for a comprehensive review of comparative research see Bowen, Straus, Sedlak, Hotaling, & Sugarman, 1984). Differences in the women were primarily in areas relating to living with and responding to violence, either as a child or in an adult relationship. It is these reactions to violence, and the differential impact that gender socialization has on the occurrence of abuse between partners, that we wish to discuss in this paper.

Sex Role Socialization and Responses to Violence

There is ample evidence to suggest that girls and boys are socialized quite differently from one another into "gender-appropriate" role behaviors (Russo, 1984; Maccoby & Jacklin, 1974). Walker has suggested that rigid sex role stereotyping during childhood and in marriage or marriage-like relationships could cause distortions in the way women respond to violent behavior (Walker, 1978, 1979, 1981a). Little girls are typically taught to reach their goals by attempting to win the approval of others, adapting to dominant behavior, and suppressing angry or aggressive reactions in favor of peace-keeping maneuvers or persuasion. They do not learn the confrontation skills that may be necessary to stop abuse, and their realistic appraisal of being at greater physical risk in an argument with a male partner may dissuade them from responding assertively and may lead to acquiescence and acceptance of abusive behavior as unavoidable.

Women are also taught to be dependent on others for their sense of security and well-being, and to accept the responsibility for keeping intimate and family relationships intact. Miller (1976) and her colleagues (Kaplan & Surrey, 1984) hypothesize that women are likely to develop a "relational ego," dependent on personal relationships as a source of self-esteem, in contrast to the more male-identified standard of autonomy. They theorize that any interpersonal conflict would have a major impact on a woman's perception of herself. Thus theorists argue that, whatever the situational variables, the *impact* of those variables will be experienced differently by women than by men (Bernard, 1984).

In abusive situations, this differential impact can have quite dramatic effects, not only on the woman's immediate reactions to the violence, but on her perceptions of the alternatives available to her. Individuals facing the threat of harm choose responses based on their appraisal of whether a particular method of coping will further endanger them, and to what degree; a key factor in captive situations, for instance, is the perceived balance of power between the captor and the victim, and the coping strategy selected is weighed against the aggressor's perceived ability to control or to harm (Lazarus, 1967). Women who have been taught that they are unsuited to deal with aggressive behavior—when confronted with a man who has been taught that the hands and feet may sometimes be used as weapons, and that dominance and aggression are justified expressions of his emotion or intent—may believe that they have little choice but to endure. Unfortunately, society contributes to this belief by its acceptance of aggression and dominance on the part of males, and the general expectation that a woman should submit, rather than defend herself, particularly against a mate.

Early Development: Childhood Experiences with Violence

Consistent with the more general findings on the differential impact of experience by gender, childhood experiences with violence seem also to affect males and females differently. There is much interest in what causes men to hurt women, especially those they love. Epidemiological studies indicate that at least one out of four women will be battered by their mates (Straus, Gelles, & Steinmetz, 1980), while those studying rape suggest a similar statistic (Finkelhor, 1979; Russell, 1982). The number of female victims expands when we add those who are victims of childhood sexual abuse in which the perpetrator is a male relative or a close family friend. Researchers estimate that a more accurate figure of how many women will be abused by intimate men is closer to 50% (Finkelhor, et al., 1983). In a study of over 400 battered women (Walker, 1981a, 1984a), it was found that two-thirds of these women reported violence in their childhood homes, and approximately half had been sexually molested as children.[1] The women also reported that 85% of their battering mates came from abusive homes. The extremity of these figures lends credence to the theories that vio-

1. This research was supported by NIMH Grant #RO1MH30147, Lenore E. Walker, Principal Investigator.

lence, and the acceptance of violence, can be transmitted from generation to generation, and that childhood socialization is crucial in the development of this pattern.

Developmental issues and violent men. Violence in men is viewed by social learning theorists as largely attributable to the interactional styles in the men's families of orientation, rather than as an innate personality characteristic (Carroll, 1977; Fagan, Stewart, & Hansen, 1983; Gelles, 1974; Kalmuss, 1984; Rouse, 1984; Telch & Lindquist, 1984). Bandura's (1973) theory of modeling is frequently cited to explain the occurrence of violence within families, with the hypothesis that individuals learn the behavior from being abused or observing abuse in their childhood homes, and later reproduce those behaviors as adults (Bandura, 1973; Bandura & Walters, 1963). This social learning explanation suggests that abusive behavior is influenced primarily by its social consequences. Those actions that are allowed and that elicit desired responses are maintained, while those that fail to elicit attention or reinforcement decrease in frequency (Bandura, 1977).

The effect that witnessing violence may have on a child's future interactional styles is further underscored by recent studies comparing the differential impact of witnessing parent-to-parent violence vs. experiencing violence oneself. Although exposure to violence in the childhood home—whether as a victim or a witness or both—is highly associated with later involvement in violent relationships, men who witness parental violence appear to be much more likely to later perpetrate abuse against a female partner than men who were the victims of child abuse but did not witness abuse between their parents (Kalmuss, 1984; Rosenbaum & O'Leary, 1981; Rouse, 1984). This suggests that specific modeling occurs in many adult relationships, with individuals reproducing the types of family agression to which they were exposed (Kalmuss, 1984).

Sonkin & Durphy (1982), reporting on their clinical treatment of violent men, contend that one reason men batter is because it works. They note that such instrumental violence "puts a quick stop to an emotional argument or a situation that is getting out of control," and also acts as a relatively safe outlet for frustration, whether that frustration arises from inside or outside the home (p. 3). Thus it may be that those who commit violence have seen it successfully used as a coping mechanism by a male authority figure in childhood, and have developed learned behaviors that lead to the perpetuation of violence as a personal style of relating in adulthood.

Abusers tend to respond to close personal interactions with a deficit of positive behaviors and an overabundance of negative acts.

Further, as is often found with abused children, the abusers' needs for attention and reassurance are extreme and their expectations of intimacy unrealistic, and this can lead to angry and frustrated feelings when such expectations are not met. This is evidenced in an intrusive personal style, easily triggered responses of anger, pathological jealously, and violent outbrusts in response to a threat of loss of control (Walker, 1979). Although social learning concepts such as modeling portray how deviant behavior is learned and help explain the transmission of violence from parent to child, they still do not fully explain why some men who witness violence as children do not grow up to batter their intimates, while others who did not come from abusive backgrounds later become violent. On the basis of his empirical research, Burgess (1984) has suggested that positive peer interactions in childhood may be an intervening variable, and that the resulting competency in social relationships may serve to offset violent adult reactions in some men who were exposed to violence as children.

Childhood violence and its effect on women. The effect on women of witnessing or being the victims of abuse as children is less clear than its effects on men. Studies of battered women do suggest that a high percentage come from abusive homes (Coleman, Weiman, & Hsi, 1980; Frieze, Knoble, Zomnir, & Washburn, 1980; Walker, 1981a, 1984a). If children tend to model behavior along gender lines, then a female child whose mother is abused would grow up with a perception of women as men's victims, and might later be more susceptible to the acceptance of that role herself. Research on incest victims indicates a strong tendency for them to be revictimized in later life, and Herman (1981) has suggested that a history of sexual abuse may be associated with an "impairment of the normal adult mechanisms for self-protection" in dealing with later relationships (p. 30). Consistent with this hypothesis, a study of first-time and repeat rape victims, conducted by Miller, Moeller, Kaufman, Divasto, Pathak, & Christy in 1978, found that 18% of the repeat victims had incest histories, compared to only 4% of first-time victims. Thus, childhood physical or sexual abuse may have the effect of making a woman less skilled at self-protection, less sure of her own worth and her personal boundaries, and more apt to accept victimization as a part of the role of being female. This could lead to the development of a particular personality style, but the majority of findings on abused women argue against such stable personality characteristics; they suggest instead a more temporary reactive style, more strongly related to the current experience and threat of assault than to prior childhood variables.

Patterns in Abusive Families

Patterson (1982) and his colleagues, Reid, Tapling, and Lorber (1981) have spent 15 years studying families with antisocial and aggressive boys. In sending observers into the homes of these families to catalog actual behaviors, they identified two dominant family types: one, the dysfunctional family, which contained an aggressive child but in which the physical interactions were not violent, and the second, families in which physical abuse occurred. These families were then compared to a control group of families without an aggressive boy, who had responded to newspaper advertisements and were matched to the clinical families on demographic variables.

When further analyzed, the significant differences found in studying families with aggressive sons were in the performance pattern of negative acts (Patterson, 1982). With dysfunctional and normal families, both positive and negative acts occurred in a fairly regular pattern. However, in abusive families, the negative acts seemed to follow one another rapidly, like beads on a chain. Such chaining of abuse seems to create what Patterson calls a "fogging" effect, reducing the ability of the target victim to make any effective response. This finding is consistent with what women in the Battered Women Syndrome Study (Walker, 1984a) reported about the occurrence of violent acts in their relationships. Typical battering episodes involved a combination of physically assaultive acts, threats, verbal abuse, and often the destruction of property. Victims felt overwhelmed by the rapidity with which one act followed another, and the feeling that they were trapped in a situation that was totally out of control led to a sense of being unable to take any action except to endure.

The ratio of positive to negative interactions between members of the abusive or dysfunctional families differed significantly from "normal" families as well. Many more negative behavioral interactions occurred in both abusive and dysfunctional family types. However, in abusive families, the negative interactions more often crossed gender lines, and treating females in a negative manner was positively reinforced. This was especially true of interactions with the mother. Fathers were less likely to demonstrate a consistent alliance with her than in other families, and children often modeled his coercive style.

Violent behavior against others also tends to escalate: Geen, Stonner, and Shope (1975) found that acts of aggression increased, rather than decreased, the likelihood of an individual aggressing again. In addition, Berkowitz theorized that aggressive tendencies are stimulated and reinforced when a victim evidences pain or submits to the aggressor (1977, 1983). Thus, in meeting the abuser's demands for compliance and submission, a wife or child in an abusive family may actually reinforce the very pattern by which they are being victimized. Azrin and his colleagues have demonstrated that violence in families also escalates because of victims' tendencies to habituate to punishment—this then leads to an intensification of the aggression against them, as the abuser attempts to achieve the same level of impact as in earlier interactions (Azrin, Holz, & Hake, 1963).

Victims' Reactions to Abuse

Reactive violence. Our research on abused women indicates that battered women rarely initiate or respond with physical attacks toward their abusers, and that they perceive their behavior in the relationship as primarily reactive to their mates' real or threatened violence (Browne, 1983 a and b, in press; Walker, 1981a, 1984 a and b). Although Straus, Gelles, and Steinmetz (1980) found that the rate of abusive acts was similar between partners, they noted that husbands had a higher rate of the most dangerous and injurious forms of violence (such as physical beatings or using a gun or a knife), and that violent acts were repeated more often by husbands than by wives. They also cautioned that their data did not show what proportion of the acts by wives were in self-defense, or in response to violence initiated by their mates. Bureau of Justice Statistics indicate that, when a victimization occurs, 95% of the time it is the woman who gets hurt (1980). The work of researchers such as Berk, Berk, Loseke, and Rauma (1983), Sonkin and Durphy (1982), and Russell (1982) also supports the finding that the woman is the partner most likely to be injured, and that violence perpetrated by a woman in an abusive relationship is usually in response to ongoing abusive behavior by the man.

There is some evidence that those living with violence display a higher incidence of child abuse than those not living in a violent situation. According to self-reports in the Battered Women Syndrome Study, women respondents who were living with an abusive man were eight times as likely to abuse their children as when they did not live in violence. This inconsistency of behaviors, that is, battering or not battering a child depending on whether the woman was or was not living with an abusive man, further supports the contention that abused women do not develop stable personality characteristics from living with violence; rather, their behaviors are a response to the situation itself.

The battered woman syndrome. Battered women's affective, cognitive, and behavioral responses often become distorted by their single focus on survival. Women use phrases such as, "He can't break my spirit like he does my bones," or "I can't stop what he does to my body, but I try not to let him have my mind." They may develop a whole range of behaviors—such as controlling their breathing during attacks or learning not to cry out when in pain—that seem to mitigate the severity of the abuse during a violent episode, but not have any developed plans for escaping the abusive situation. They may also exhibit signs of having lived with noncontingent violence, such as hypervigilance toward the possibility of further attacks, acquiescence to the abuser, lack of trust or fearfulness resembling paranoia, denial of the seriousness of the abuse, and a strong protection of the inner self while appearing suggestible or easily manipulated by others. Many of these outward characteristics resemble symptoms of personality disorder and would indeed be maladaptive if there was no threat of harm. They are, however, adaptive and usually temporary personality features, understandable for an individual faced with ongoing and unpredictable assaults (Browne, 1980).

These and other clinical symptoms often seen together are now called the battered woman syndrome, and are included as part of the diagnosis for post traumatic stress disorders in the third edition of the Diagnostic and Statistical Manual of Mental Disorders (APA, 1981). Most post traumatic stress disorders are considered temporary disruptions of an individual's normal personality pattern, occurring as a result of an extreme pyschosocial stressor. They generally run their course subsequent to removal of the stressor, although after effects may be noticeable for from one to five years after removal. Rosewater (1982) recently developed a battered woman syndrome profile for the widely used Minnesota Multiphasic Personality Inventory (MMPI), and discovered marked similarities between the profiles of individuals usually diagnosed as schizophrenic or borderline personalities and the profiles of battered women. These similarities indicate that a careful interpretation of all standardized tests and diagnostic assessments is necessary, to avoid labeling as personal pathology the coping characteristics exhibited by women who are currently or have recently been the victims of ongoing relationship violence (Rosewater & Walker, 1985).

In the Battered Women Syndrome Study, half (200) of the women reported on a nonviolent intimate relationship, as well as on an abusive one (Walker, 1984a). Subjects were asked the same series of questions for both the violent and nonviolent relationships, thus acting as their own control group for some analyses. Their self-reported behaviors indicated a marked difference between responses in relationships with abusive and nonabusive mates. Women indicated that they were able to be more assertive, friendly, emotional, trusting, genuine, and sexual with the nonviolent men. When living with violence, they were more fearful, emotionally restricted, isolated from others, and guarded. Much of their affect, cognition, and behavior seemed related to the batterer's state of mind. Again, these findings suggest that the emotional and behavioral responses of abused women are reactive to situational variables and do not represent a core personality pattern.

Learned helplessness. The construct of learned helplessness, first observed in the laboratory by Seligman (1975), is one way to conceptualize battered women's reactions—or lack of reactions—to abuse. It was discovered that when laboratory animals (usually dogs, in the early experiments) were repeatedly and noncontingently shocked, they found ways to control or adapt to the pain and quit trying to escape the aversive situation, even when escape was possible and readily apparent to animals who had not undergone helplessness training. Seligman likened this helplessness to human depression, and theorized that the two conditions would have similar cognitive, motivational, and behavioral components.

Learned helplessness does not mean that the victim is actually powerless to effect any change over the situation. Rather, it is a process of learning to believe that nothing one can do will bring about a predictable positive result. Like animals or human subjects in Seligman's experiments, a physically, sexually, or psychologically abused woman who has experienced a series of painful, noncontingent attacks begins to perceive fewer and fewer options for dealing with or escaping the violence; her focus is on minimizing injury and coping with pain and fear. She may fail to perceive or to attempt confrontational or escape behaviors, even when, to an outside observer, these alternatives seem obvious and possible. Although she sometimes appears not to be taking any action on her own behalf, she may actually be choosing the only option that she believes will facilitate her survival.

As with other findings on gender differences, sex role training that encourages girls to be passive and dependent seems to create a tendency toward a sense of helplessness (Radloff & Rae, 1979, 1981; Dweck, Goetz, & Strauss, 1980). Seligman's research with animals indicated that experiences of helplessness early in an animal's development increased that animal's vulnerability to helplessness in later life, and led to the hypothesis that the same principle applied to human child-raising (1975). To the extent that these findings can be generalized to humans, they would suggest that childhood experiences of victimization, often found in the histories of battered women—in combination with gender socialization into traditional feminine roles—would increase their later vulnerability to helplessness in a violent relationship. This factor may only come into play, however, if the woman experiences violence later on in life; it does not seem to dispose women to seek out abusive relationships.

In studying abused women we found that certain factors, both in the women's childhoods and in the adult battering relationship, did apparently leave them more susceptible to the development of a learned helpless response to violence. Childhood factors included: (1) witnessing or experiencing abuse in the childhood home, (2) sexual abuse or molestation, (3) experiencing critical life-events, (4) rigid adherence to traditional sex role stereotypes in the home, and (5) health problems. Factors which are implicated in the development of learned helplessness in an adult battering relationship include: (1) the pattern of abuse, including the frequency of abusive incidents, the number of abusive acts within a typical incident, and the number of injuries sustained from the incident, (2) the frequency with which the woman is sexually assaulted by the batterer, (3) pathological jealousy and overpossessiveness on the part of the batterer, (4) psychological abuse, (5) threats to kill the woman and her perception that those threats are likely to be carried out, (6) child abuse, violence toward others, destruction of property, and cruelty toward pets, and (7) alcohol and drug abuse on the part of the batterer.

Victimization and the Response of Homicide

Almost all of the women in the Battered Women Syndrome Study believed that the abuser could or would kill them (Browne, 1983b; Walker, 1981a, 1984a). For some, the battering had become so severe that they only narrowly escaped death in later incidents, and many felt they could not escape the danger by leaving. Abused women's primary fear—that the abuser will find them and violently retaliate against their leaving—is justified. Some women who had fled abusive partners have been followed and harassed for months or even years (Jones, 1980, pp. 298–299; Lindsey, 1978). The combination of an increase in the violent behavior and a perception that escape is not possible can produce a sense of desperation in a victimized woman. Many feel trapped in a deadly situation in which staying means the possibility of being killed, but attempting to leave carries with it the threat of reprisal or death (Browne, 1983a, in press). It is when hope is gone, and the woman perceives her life or the lives of her children to be in extreme danger, that she sometimes responds with violence toward the abuser, usually in self-defense.

Factors precipitating homicide. In a study by one of the authors comparing 42 homicide cases in which the battered woman was the perpetrator of a lethal incident with 205 abuse cases in which no lethal incident occurred, results again indicated that the significant differences were primarily on variables related to the behavior of the men (Browne, 1983a). Men in the homicide group used drugs and alcohol much more often than in the nonhomicide group; for example, 80% of men in the homicide group reportedly became intoxicated every day or almost every day by the end of the relationship, compared to 40% of men in the nonhomicide group. Men in the homicide group were also reportedly more apt to have a history of arrest (92% vs. 77%), abuse the children (71% vs. 51%), and make threats to kill (83% vs. 59%).

In addition to these variables, the frequency with which abusive incidents occurred, and the severity of the women's injuries, were more extreme in those relationships that culminated in a homicide by the woman. Forty percent of women in the homicide group reported that abusive incidents occurred more than once a week by the end of the relationship, whereas only 13% of the nonhomicide group reported incidents occurring that often. Women in the homicide group also sustained more, and more severe, injuries from these attacks. In addition, over 75% of victims in the homicide group reported that they had been raped by their mates on at least one occasion, compared to 59% in the nonhomicide group; and 62% of the homicide group—vs. 37% of the nonhomicide group—reported that their mates had forced or urged them to perform other sexual acts against their will, such as forced anal or oral sex, sado-masochistic sex, forced sex with others, or sex with animals.

A discriminant analysis was conducted which identified seven variables that, in linear combination, best discriminated battered women who had killed or seriously injured their abusers from those who had not. These variables included: severity of the woman's injuries, the man's drug use and frequency of intoxication, the frequency with which abusive incidents occurred, forced or threatened sexual acts by the man, and the man's threats to kill. The only variable relating specifically to differences between the women was in threats to commit suicide: 48% of women in the homicide group had talked of killing themselves, compared to 31% in the nonhomicide group. Thus, women in the homicide group were subjected to more frequent and severe attacks from partners who were also likely to be sexually assaulting them, using drugs, drinking heavily, and threatening murder. Women in the homicide group were more apt to sustain injuries from the abuse than were women in the nonhomicide group, and were more suicidal. Most of these women had no prior history of violent, or even illegal, behavior; yet in these relationships, the women's attempts to survive with an increasingly violent and unpredictable mate eventually resulted in an act of violence on their part as well (Browne, 1983a; in press). Such a severe act of violence from an otherwise nonviolent individual would seem inexplicable, unless the pattern of victimization was understood.

Women who kill and the legal system. Although threatening or attacking another person is illegal, when it happens between partners, the episodes rarely come to the attention of authorities. Even when such assaults are reported, they are usually not accorded the serious treatment given to similar attacks by strangers. Often it is not until someone is seriously hurt or killed that direct action is taken. Yet studies of murder cases in the United States indicate that many spousal homicides are preceded by a history of abuse, and that many women jailed for the slaying of their mates had been assaulted by them (Benke, 1980; Bourdouris, 1971; Crimes of Violence, 1969; Jones, 1980; Stephens, 1977; Wolfgang, 1967). Often these women sought help from the police or others prior to the lethal incident, but either the urgency of their situation was not understood, or the alternatives offered were inadequate to allow them to escape (Lindsey, 1978).

Women charged with the death of a mate have the least extensive criminal records of any female offenders. Women who kill are also more likely to do so in self-defense. A report by a government commission on violence estimated that homicides committed by women were seven times as likely to be in self-defense as were homicides committed by men (Crimes of Violence, 1969). However, these women often face harsher penalties than do men who kill their partners. FBI statistics indicate that fewer men are charged with first or second degree murder for killing a woman they have known than are women who kill a man they have known; and women convicted of these murders are frequently sentenced to longer prison terms than are men for similar crimes (Schneider & Jordon, 1981). Even with a history of physical abuse by the deceased and evidence that the woman was in reasonable fear of her life at the time of the incident, battered women who kill their mates are not afforded the same self-defense considerations as are extended to those who protect themselves against attacks by strangers. Gender role expectations often result in women being taught to react passively to actions by others, even when those actions are abusive (although they are sometimes labeled masochistic when they do so); however, these same role expectations do not allow them the defense of their own persons against a husband or other male partner.

Conclusions

Early studies of battered women often focused on the personality characteristics of the women, in a search for factors that might lead them to seek abusive treatment, or to stay in an abusive relationship because of a personality disturbance that caused them to prefer punishing interactions to more positive styles of relating. These theories suggested that the pathology resided in the woman victim, and largely ignored the initiation and effect of violence by the man. However, more recent research findings indicate that women's behavior in battering relationships is primarily in *reaction* to the level of violence and threat perpetrated by the abuser. Women choose those responses that seem most likely to minimize the danger and to facilitate at least their short-term survival. While reactions geared to the possibility of becoming a victim of men's violence affect a great deal of women's behavior in this society, and the experience of victimization certainly has a major impact on the expression of women's personalities, behaviors specifically related to victimization often disappear when the threat of violence is no longer present.

Victims' reactions to abuse—and the severity of the abuse they are confronted with—are at least partly determined by the sex role attitudes and interactional styles that were modeled in their families of origin. Children who were raised in abusive environments are particularly at risk for later problems with violence. Much more research is needed on situations or factors that mediate this risk. Early experiences in an abusive environment may cause a man to develop aggressive behavior patterns, especially if he watched his mother assaulted by his father or another male partner. Similar experiences in a woman's childhood may teach her to become a victim and leave her less effective in protecting herself from violence she encounters as an adult. In a violent situation, she may concentrate on her immediate survival, rather than escaping early, before the violence escalates to life-threatening proportions.

This susceptibility to remaining a victim has been described in the theory of learned helplessness, and is exacerbated by traditional sex role stereotyping, which encourages women to respond with passivity and acquiescence to aggression and dominance by males. If women are to escape violent relationships, they must overcome their tendency to helplessness by, for instance, becoming angry rather than depressed; active rather than passive; and more realistic about the likelihood of the relationship continuing on its aversive course rather than improving. In so doing, they must also overcome the sex role socialization they have been taught from early childhood.

Descriptions of violent men indicate that there are sufficient similarities in their behaviors to suggest a violence-prone personality pattern, originating in childhood and becoming more severe as a man practices aggression. More research focused on violent men is needed to confirm this hypothesis, but their resistance to treatment and high recidivism rates suggests that there may well be such a long-standing personality disorder. Clinicians note that at least half of the small percentage of abusive men who receive treatment continue their violent behavior with new partners (Sonkin, Martin, & Walker, in preparation). More effective intervention with abusive men is needed, as well as intensive research on the etiology of violent behavior in men. Positive parenting techniques, which value women as highly as men, can also help to prevent the development of the coercive relational styles so often found in abusive families.

Tacit social support exists for abuse of family members in our society's traditions of a man's "rights" in dealing with his family and the gender stereotyping that favors a male's expression of dominance and control. Lack of effective system response to assaults in which the victim is a wife, and the lack of adequate and established alternatives to assure the victim's protection from further aggression, allows this violence to escalate, leaving the woman in a potentially deadly situation from which there seems no practical avenue of escape. Given what we know of battering relationships—the tendency for the abuse to escalate in frequency and severity, the women's sense of helplessness, and the desperation this produces—it is clear that informed, effective responses to early contact with these cases cannot be overemphasized.

Homicides that result from abusive relationships remind us of the seriousness of "domestic" violence, and highlight how a lack of adequate intervention strategies and responsiveness by all facets of society can greatly exacerbate the dangers already present in these situations. A society that condones violence against women by forcing the individual woman, rather than its institutions, to stop an abusive man's behavior, encourages continued victimization. Psychologists who study human behavior and offer theories for change have a particular moral obligation to use their research and intervention skills to prevent another generation of perpetrators and victims of violence.

References

American Psychiatric Association (1981). *Diagnostic and statistical manual of mental disorders* (3rd ed.). Washington, DC: Author, p. 236.

Azrin, N. H., Holz, W. C., & Hake, D. F. (1963). Fixed ratio punishment. *Journal of Experimental Analysis of Behavior*, 6, 141–148.

Bandura, A. (1973). *Aggression: A social learning analysis*. Englewood Cliffs, NJ: Prentice-Hall.

Bandura, A. (1977). *Social learning therapy*. New York: General Learning Press.

Bandura, A., & Walters, R. H. (1963). *Social learning and personality development*. New York: Holt, Rinehart and Winston.

Benke, P. D. (1980, December). Prosecuting women who use force in self-defense: Investigative considerations. *Peace Officer Law Report*. California Department of Justice, 8–15.

Berk, R. A., Berk, S. F., Loseke, D. R., & Rauma, D. (1983). Mutual combat and other family violence myths. In D. Finkelhor, R. Gelles, G. Hotaling, & M. Straus (Eds.), *The dark side of families* (pp. 197–212). Beverly Hills, CA: Sage.

Berkowitz, L. (1977). Simple views of aggression: An essay review. In J. C. Brigham & L. S. Wrightsman (Eds.), *Contemporary issues in social psychology* (3rd ed., pp. 42–50). Monterey, CA: Brooks/Cole.

Berkowitz, L. (1983). The goals of aggression. In D. Finkelhor, R. Gelles, G. Hotaling, & M. Straus (Eds.), *The dark side of families* (pp. 166–181). Beverly Hills: Sage Publications.

Bernard, J. (1984). Mental health issues of women in a time of transition. In L. E. Walker (Ed.), *Women and mental health policy* (pp. 181–195). Beverly Hills, CA: Sage Publications.

Blum, H. P. (1982). Psychoanalytic reflections on "The beaten wife syndrome." In M. Kirkpatrick (Ed.), *Women's sexual experiences: Explorations of the dark continent* (pp. 263–267). New York: Plenum.

Bourdouris, J. (1971). Homicide in the family. *Journal of Marriage and the Family*, 33, 667–676.

Bowen, G. L., Straus, M. A., Sedlak, A. J., Hotaling, G. T., & Sugarman, D. B. (1984). *Domestic violence surveillance system feasibility study*. Phase 1 Report: Identification of outcomes and risk factors. Centers for Disease Control, The Violence Epidemiological Branch, Atlanta, GA.

Browne, A. (1980, April). *Comparison of victim's reactions across traumas*. Paper presented at the meeting of the Rocky Mountain Psychological Association, Tucson, AZ.

Browne, A. (1983a). *When battered women kill*. Unpublished doctoral dissertation, University of Experimenting Colleges and Universities, Cincinnati, OH.

Browne, A. (1983b, October). *Self-defense homicides by battered women: Relationships at risk*. Paper presented at the meeting of the American Psychology-Law Society, Chicago, IL.

Browne, A. (in press). Assault and homicide at home: When battered women kill. In L. Saxe & M. J. Saks, (Eds.), *Advances in applied social psychology* (Vol. 3). Hillsdale, NJ: Erlbaum.

Bureau of Justice Statistics. (1980). *Intimate victims: A study of violence among friends and relatives* (U. S. Department of Justice). Washington, DC: U. S. Government Printing Office.

Burgess, R. L. (1984, November). *Social incompetence as a precipitant to and consequence of maltreatment*. Paper presented at the Third International Victimology Conference, Lisbon, Portugal.

Carroll, J. C. (1977). The intergenerational transmission of family violence: Long term effects of aggressive behavior. *Aggressive Behavior*, 3, 289–299.

Coleman, K. H., Weiman, M. L., & Hsi, B. P. (1980). Factors affecting conjugal violence. *Journal of Psychology*, 105, 197–202.

Crimes of violence. (1969). A staff report to the National Commission on the Causes and Prevention of Violence. Washington, DC: U. S. Government Printing Office.

Dweck, C. C., Goetz, T. E., & Strauss, N. L. (1980). Sex differences in learned helplessness: An experimental and naturalistic study of failure generalization and its mediators. *Journal of Personality and Social Psychology*, 38, 441–452.

Fagan, J. A., Stewart, D. K., & Hansen, K. V. (1983). Violent men or violent husbands? In D. Finkelhor, R. J. Gelles, G. T. Hotaling, & M. A. Straus (Eds.), *The dark side of families: Current family violence research* (pp. 49–67). Beverly Hills: Sage Publications.

Finkelhor, D. (1979). *Sexually victimized children*. New York: Free Press.

Finkelhor, D., Gelles, R., Hotaling, G., & Straus, M. (1983). (Eds.). *The dark side of families*, Beverly Hills, CA: Sage.

Frieze, I. H., Knoble, J., Zomnir, G., & Washburn, C. (1980, March). *Types of battered women*. Paper presented at the meeting of the Association for Women in Psychology, Santa Monica, CA.

Gelles, R. J. (1974). *The violent home: A study of physical aggression between husbands and wives*. Beverly Hills, CA: Sage Publications.

Geen, R. G., Stonner, D., & Shope, G. L. (1975). The facilitation of aggression by aggression: Evidence against the catharsis hypotheses. *Journal of Personality and Social Psychology*, 31, 721–726.

Herman, J. L. (1981). *Father-daughter incest*. Cambridge, MA: Harvard University Press.

Jones, A. (1980). *Women who kill*. New York: Fawcett Columbine Books.

Kalmuss, D. (1984). The intergenerational transmission of marital aggression. *Journal of Marriage and the Family*, 11–19.

Kaplan, A. G., & Surrey, J. L. (1984). The relational self in women: Implications for developmental theory and public policy. In L. E. Walker (Ed.), *Women and mental health policy* (pp. 79–94). Beverly Hills, CA: Sage.

Lazarus, R. S. (1967). Cognitive and personality factors underlying threat and coping. In M. H. Appley & R. Trumbull (Eds.), *Psychological stress*. New York: Appleton-Century-Crofts.

Lindsey, K. (1978, September). When battered women strike back: Murder or self-defense. *Viva* (pp. 58–59; 66–74).

Maccoby, E., & Jacklin, C. (1974). *The psychology of sex differences*. Stanford, CA: Stanford University Press.

Miller, J. B. (1976). *Toward a new psychology of women*. Boston: Beacon Press.

Miller, J., Moeller, D., Kaufman, A., Divasto, P., Pathak, D., & Christy, J. (1978). Recidivism among sexual assault victims. *American Journal of Psychiatry*, 135, 1103–1104.

Patterson, G. (1982). *Coercive family processes*. Eugene, OR: Cataglia Press.

Radloff, L. S., & Rae, D. S. (1979). Susceptibility and precipitating factors in depression: Sex differences and similarities. *Journal of Abnormal Psychology*, 88, 174–181.

Radloff, L. S., & Rae, D. S. (1981). Components of the sex difference in depression. *Research in Community Mental Health*, 2, 111–137.

Reid, J. B., Taplin, P. S., & Lorber, R. (1981). A social interactional approach to treatment of abusive families. In R. B. Stuart (Ed.), *Violent behavior: Social learning approaches to prediction, management, and treatment*. (pp. 3–19). New York: Brunner/Mazel.

Rosenbaum, A., & O'Leary, K. D. (1981). Marital violence: Characteristics of abusive couples. *Journal of Consulting and Clinical Psychology*, 49, 63–71.

Rosewater, L. B. (1982). *An MMPI profile for battered women*. Unpublished doctoral dissertation, University of Experimenting Colleges and Universities, Cincinnati, OH.

Rosewater, L. B., & Walker, L. E. (1985). *A handbook of feminist therapy: Women's issues in psychotherapy.* New York: Springer.

Rouse, L. P. (1984). Models, self-esteem, and locus of control as factors contributing to spouse abuse. *Victimology: An International Journal,* 9, 130–141.

Russell, D. (1982). *Rape in marriage.* New York: Macmillian.

Russo, N. F. (1984). Women in the mental health delivery system: Policy, research, and practice. In L. E. Walker (Ed.), *Women and mental health policy* (pp. 21–41). Beverly Hill, CA: Sage Publications.

Schneider, E. M., & Jordan, S. B. (1981). Representation of women who defend themselves in response to physical or sexual assault. In E. Bochnak (Ed.), *Women's self-defense cases: Theory and practice.* (pp. 1–39). Charlottesville, VA: The Michie Company Law Publishers.

Seligman, M. (1975). *Helplessness: On depression, development, and death.* San Francisco: Freeman Press.

Shainess, N. (1979). Vulnerability to violence: Masochism as a process. *American Journal of Psychotherapy,* 33, 174–189.

Sonkin, D., & Durphy, M. (1982). *Learning to live without violence: A handbook for men.* San Francisco: Volcano Press.

Sonkin, D., Martin, D., & Walker, L. E. (in preparation). *Learning to live without violence: The group treatment of men who batter women.*

Stephens, D. W. (1977). Domestic assault: The police response. In M. Roy (Ed.), *Battered women: A psychosocial study of domestic violence* (pp. 164–172). New York: Van Nostrand Reinhold Company.

Straus, M., Gelles, R., & Steinmetz, S. (1980). *Behind closed doors: Violence in the American family.* New York: Doubleday.

Telch, C. F., & Lindquist, C. U. (1984). Violent vs. nonviolent couples: A comparison of patterns. *Psychotherapy,* 21, 242–248.

Walker, L. E. (1978). Learned helplessness and battered women. *Victimology: An International Journal,* 2, 499–509.

Walker, L. E., (1979). *The battered woman.* New York: Harper & Row.

Walker, L. E. (1981a). *The battered woman syndrome: Final report.* NIMH Grant #R0130147.

Walker, L. E. (1981b). Battered women: Sex roles and clinical issues. *Professional Psychology,* 12, 81–91.

Walker, L. E. (1984a). *The battered woman syndrome.* New York: Springer.

Walker, L. E. (1984b). (Ed.), *Women and mental health policy.* Beverly Hills, CA: Sage.

Wolfgang, M. E. (1967). A sociological analysis of criminal homicide. In M. E. Wolfgang (Ed.), *Studies in homicide.* New York: Harper & Row.

The measurement of masculinity and femininity: Engendering categorical realities

J. G. Morawski

Abstract

The study of gender attributes, masculinity and femininity, has comprised a major research program in twentieth-century psychology. Historical examination reveals that this research program has produced not cumulative discovery but a pattern of repetition and reification. Researchers have repeatedly attempted to ensure the reality of masculinity and femininity, and have even introduced methodological techniques that privilege their observational statements on that reality. Similar patterns have occurred in the case of androgyny research, despite expectations that the androgyny construct would remedy the shortcomings of masculinity and femininity concepts. When analyzed in historical context, these gender concepts are found to share ethnopsychological origins—roots in social practices and prescriptions. Contextual analysis also provides telling details about researchers' normative interests. If we choose to terminate such fruitless ventures and to generate novel understandings of the social world, then we must undertake critical self-appraisal and adopt a new metatheoretical grounding.

When the protagonist of Virginia Woolf's *Orlando* is suddenly transformed from male to female, he/she has minimal difficulty adjusting to a new form. The recent shift from the bipolar, apparently antiquated concepts of masculinity and femininity to one of androgyny, though purportedly a major reformulation, actually intimates a similar facile accommodation. While different in kind, both changes rely on mundane oppositions—those cultural concepts that ordinarily signify masculine and feminine. Both changes constitute fairly undramatic revisions rather than radical transformations.

The study of femininity and masculinity, comprising a massive scientific project across 90 years of experimental psychology, depicts a curious recurrence of these cultural concepts. The research exemplifies the repetition, with minor modifications, of several central stipulations about masculinity and femininity. Conventional literature reviews strive to identify significant advances in gender research, to chart the "breakthroughs" or "discoveries" as it were, but they neglect what is stable and common to the studies. A perspective that acknowledges the repeated similarities is needed to begin to appreciate the virtual reification of the existence, contents, and evaluative dynamics of masculinity and femininity concepts. Such a perspective attends to the procedures through which those stipulations were defended and sustained. It illuminates some of the nonempirical reasons for maintaining certain categorical stipulations about femininity and masculinity and, in turn, intimates how these categories bolstered prescriptions for appropriate social behavior.

The contents of the masculinity and femininity categories are familiar even to those uninitiated into gender-role research. They are constituted by global polarities found in common personality dimensions: instrumental vs. expressive, agentic vs. communal, active vs. passive, independent vs. dependent characteristics. At this level the categories are straightforward and represent nothing more than what is ordinarily meant when one is said to be like a man or woman in our culture. In addition, it is presupposed that the categories are consistent within the individual and that the individual has a sincere desire to manifest them appropriately. The enduring presence of the categories is readily apparent, and in the light of recent feminist studies, so is the unhappy coincidence that the dichotomous personality signifiers indicate behavior norms for social relations between men and women. The present exploration, then, moves beyond these acknowledged conditions in order to locate the means by which scientific psychologists (while avowing an ethos of objectivity, disinterestedness, and impartiality) retained the categories. How, in the face of contradictory empirical findings and of nonobservable postulates, were they sustained? The answer involves more than just revealing unreasonable or unscientific practices, because the assumptions under question were also maintained through normal and legitimate scientific procedures. For their maintenance it was necessary that psychologists occasionally override scientific knowledge as well as the knowledge of ordinary people.

The first section of this study examines the procedures and rhetoric whereby even scientific knowledge was rendered dubious in order to uphold the reality of femininity and masculinity. The second section describes the ways in which psychologists were able to verify the nearly ephemeral gender entities as a psychological *reality* and claim *privileged* access to *observing* and *assessing* that reality. Once this psychological phenomenon was secured, the study of masculinity and femininity seemed to consist simply of healthy competition for the most efficient and elegant assessment techniques. The apparent breakdown of the extended research tradition came primarily through challenges raised by feminist scholarship, and even the subsequent revisions of androgyny theory ultimately proved insufficient to meet those challenges.

The methodology of the present study departs from conventional criticism by looking not at faulty scientific ideas but at how the research practices themselves were constructed to foster certain interests and even to confect certain realities. Historical studies have identified some of the misogynists and androcentric theories in psychology. Yet we must look beyond cranks and heresies to understand how normal scientific practices were integral to the construction and maintenance of an "engendered" psychological reality. The study does not deny the existence of gender differences but rather questions the particular forms ascribed to these differences and the means by which they were sustained. The fact that these practices confirmed the mundane realities of social life, the ethnopsychology of gender categories, makes it surprising that psychologists even had the troubles they did in locating masculinity and femininity.

Discovering Masculinity and Femininity through Science

In his comprehensive review of sex difference research, Havelock Ellis (1894) noted the ideological distortions frequently imposed on the subject. For these ideological biases, Ellis prescribed the remedy of empirical inquiry, particularly the "new" scientific psychology which "lays the axe at the root of many pseudoscientific superstitions" (p. 513). However, he cautioned that science reveals only factual, not potential, conditions, for "our present knowledge of men and women cannot tell us what they might be or what they ought to be, but what they actually are, under the conditions of civilization" (p. 513). Within a decade, numerous American psychologists had taken up the question of sex differences. While acknowledging the precedent of Ellis's work, they professed closer alignment with the empirical spirit of providing what Helen Thompson Woolley (1903) described as the "original investigation" that his study lacked (p. 2). As did many of her cohorts, Thompson Woolley reached somewhat different conclusions than Ellis, for though she admonished pseudo-scientific theorizing and anticipated the fruits of objective experimentation, she believed that modifications in social life could or would alter psychological sex differences. With agreement on the correct methods for knowledge acquisition, Ellis and Thompson Woolley disagreed on whether or not the psychology of the sexes might change, or be perfected, with the former betting on nature's desires and the latter on the effects of social organization. Nevertheless, the psychologist's task was not to explore the dynamics of social perfectibility but to better the process of knowledge production. The normative notion of bettering gender arrangements was taken to be another problem altogether.

Thompson Woolley's careful laboratory research resembles a host of similar studies, many of them conducted by women (such as Mary Whiton Calkins, Leta Hollingworth, Catherine Cox Miles, and Margaret Floy Washburn) who, with the new opportunities for higher education, turned to intellectual questions that were not far removed from their own lives (Rosenberg, 1982). Thompson Woolley's dissertation (1903) reported experiments on sex differences in motor, affective, sensory, and intellectual abilities. Within the next three decades hundreds of studies assessed these sex differences as well as those to be found in the association of ideas, color preference, handwriting, remembering of advertisements and moving pictures, motor efficiency, nervous behavior of nursery school children, fear responses, reading speed, credulity regarding fortune telling, stammering, scope of attention, reasoning, and ideals and tastes, not to mention knowledge of psychology after the first course (see Allen, 1927, 1930; Hollingworth, 1916, 1918; Johnson & Terman 1940; Thompson Woolley, 1910, 1914).

The research on the psychology of sex created some confusion because many of the studies reported no or minor sex differences and those finding differences often indicated female superiority. Probably no study equalled the impact of the intelligence research as measured by the new mental tests. In revising the Binet-Simon Intelligence Scale, Lewis Terman (1917) tested 1,000 children and found slight superiority of girls. The results led him to consider why women had not attained eminence and ultimately to suggest that their failure "may be due to wholly extraneous factors." Even before Terman's standardized test, other investigators found few significant sex differences on measures of mental abilities. In her 1914 review of the psychology of sex, Thompson Woolley reported these findings with a cynical conclusion: "On the whole then, girls have stood better than boys in measures of general intelligence. So far as I know, no one has drawn the conclusion that girls have greater native ability than boys. One is tempted to indulge in idle speculation as to whether this admirable restraint from hasty generalization would have been equally marked had the sex findings been reversed!" (p. 365). The reported differences were often so slight that Hollingworth (1918) claimed that any reviewer who restricted himself to

reporting sex differences on mental traits would "automatically tend
to do himself out of his review. He would have very little to report"
(p. 428).

Despite such enthusiasm, the wide-scale operation to attain objective scientific knowledge of the psychology of sex faltered, and by
1930 was mired in complications due to inconsistent findings and a
paucity of studies on social factors as well as to professional difficulties of the women psychologists who undertook a substantial amount
of the research (see Rosenberg, 1982). Yet, the persistent spirit
behind the project was far from exhausted though the problems
encountered by experimentalists were serious. For those who had
posited the superiority of males on tasks involving general mental
ability the ground had fallen away, for the new intelligence tests left
their position unsubstantiated. While experimental studies were
indicating that males and females diverged on some measures, they
gave no coherent explanation of these differences. They ultimately
provided no final test of theory—no indication of whether the
differences were environmentally or biologically determined. And
because a number of variables could not be controlled, the critical
experiment to ascertain the respective natures of males and females
could not be performed, at least not on conventional ethical grounds.
This limitation plagued more than John B. Watson who, in his
autobiography claimed "regret" at not having established "a group
of infant farms" where various races could be reared under controlled
conditions (1936, p. 281), a variation on his earlier proposal for a
human laboratory "where squads can be kept at work. Their food,
water, sex, and shelter could then be kept under very definite
control" (1924, p. 214). In describing these impracticable experiments, some contemplated such perfect controls as Arcady, for their
constitution required elimination of all gender-related discrimination
(Hinkle, 1920; Thompson Woolley, 1903). What several decades of
research apparently had disclosed is that males and females differed
on some psychological measures and were similar on others, and that
the decisive experiment for ascertaining the essence of gender, while
resembling a nonsexist environment, was unfeasible.

The solutions to these problems were of several types. Some
psychologists seemed indifferent to the experimental research and
proceeded to publish theoretical statements on the psychology of
men and women. These researchers frequently intimated that the
actualization of psychology as a true science had not yet happened,
but they took license as professionals to conjecture, to proffer
scientific expertise, on an important psychological and social issue.
While lacking experimental evidence, these statements nevertheless

represented knowledge of the new "scientific intelligence" as Lippmann (1922) called them, the social scientific experts who had gained a public spotlight during the reform period and later through involvement in the war effort. Thus, G. Stanley Hall (1922) explained that the flapper, rather than exemplifying the demise of femininity in the American woman, actually represented "the bud of a new and better womanhood, and the evolutionary progress of civilization toward maternal femininity." He added, "Our Simon-Binet tests can grade and mark, at least for intelligence, but here they baulk, stammer, and diverge" (p. 780). Watson (1927) identified the dangerous characteristics of modern women which guaranteed that men would opt out of marriage in the next fifty years and suggested behaviorist femininity through careful hygiene for sexual attractiveness. Others turned toward the new "glandular psychology" to learn the final word on masculinity and femininity.

While these respondents exhibited what charitably could be called benign neglect of empirical evidence, others, assured that psychology as science had arrived, stipulated the means for discovering the *real* nature of masculine and feminine. A minor study published in 1922 epitomizes the general logic behind these newer explorations and, therefore, is worthy of extended quotation:

> The mental test seems to have said its utmost on the subject of sex differences, and the results have been on the whole surprisingly at variance with the insistent prejudices of the average man and woman.
>
> When common sense and science clash it is more often science that has the last word, but not always. Occasionally the worm turns, and a supposedly scientific doctrine unacceptable to common sense continues to be scrutinized until a glaring flaw is discovered either in the method or the interpretation of results that led to the doctrine. The history of medicine is strewn with the wrecks of such doctrines, and psychology bids fair to number at least its fair share of derelict 'scientific' notions. . . .
>
> Very much the same may be said of the small differences apparent in the test scores of men and women. So far as these results suggest the interpretation that the mental differences between the two sexes are after all comparatively insignificant, they suggest something that common sense and universal experience refuse to allow. Such results again promise to stand as the mark of the inadequacy of the psychological test to get at the most important features of mental differentiation (Moore, 1922, p. 210).

Moore depicted the important feature of maleness and femaleness in "natural emotional aptitude, of an unyielding innate divergence that predominates the enthusiasms that are to be expected from the two sexes in identically the same environment" (p. 211). He proceeded to test his hypothesis by measuring these "natural aptitudes" as they were expressed in conversations of men and women on Broadway. He found that male-to-male conversations were typically about money and business while woman-to-woman conversations were about persons of the opposite sex. His hypothesis was confirmed.

In addition to natural aptitudes, other researchers looked for maleness and femaleness in such phenomena as levels of "mental energy" (Leuba, 1926), the "unconscious" (Hamilton, 1931), and in "mind" (Jastrow, 1918, p. 303). Jastrow found the intelligence test to be both "partial" and "artificial," claiming that "deeper and more comprehensive are the allied and supporting processes which gave the cutting edge to the instrument, and determine the temper of the mind, the manner and spirit of its use." Real psychological processes corresponding to masculinity and femininity in everyday life are located "in the habitat of deep psychology, where traits are at once subtle and profound. Here the feminine mind, as all minds in the specialized aspects, becomes most revealing" (p. 314). Discontented with the extant empirical research, this last group of psychologists was convinced that the *real* substance of masculinity and femininity existed but not in what was measured by the myriad mental tests. They argued from the logical premise that *if other* human sciences, notably anatomy, physiology and pathology reveal man as man and woman as woman, then "What reason is there to suspect psychology to enter a dissenting opinion?" (Jastrow, 1918, p. 303).

Producing the Subject of Psychological Science

Given these general trends in psychology, and given the rather audacious ad hoc theorizing without supporting "facts," or without any facts, it appears that some psychologists were engaging in sex role stereotyping. Perhaps they were subjects of a "cultural lag" similar to that which Eagley (1978) detected in some psychologists of a later period. But while investigations of masculinity and femininity seem to have diverged from conventional research practices, perhaps to accommodate particular sex role stereotypes, they also converged with those practices in several revealing ways. They emphasized detached objective observation and the consequential devaluation and even denigration of subjective observations. The ordinary observer or self-observer came to be seen as an incomplete psychologist at best (Watson, 1919; Robinson, 1926); he or she was unable to identify the true causes of behavior (Dashiell, 1928). The image of the incompetent subject gained support not only with the intensified dedication to rigorous objective techniques but also with concurrent assumptions about the complexity and causal interdependence of human actions (Haskell, 1977). The idea of the causal complexity of human action gained adherents throughout the early twentieth-century, and it dovetailed with another social assumption adopted by psychology: the increasing human disorder and the consequent need for rational control. While these concerns were voiced in the progressive era (Haber, 1964; Wiebe, 1967) and reinforced with the successes of applied social science in the war effort, they were amplified by psychologists in the 1920s and 1930s (O'Donnell, 1979; Samelson, 1979; Sokal, 1984). Scientists in general showed escalated concern about human ignorance and about the scientists' leadership responsibilities (Kaplan, 1956; Tobey, 1971). For instance Edward Thorndike (1920) suggested that the average citizen, the "half-educated man," should relinquish decision making to the experts.

Similar portraits of human irrationality were depicted by psychologists as were the pleas for scientific, particularly psychological, control (Danziger, 1979; Morawski, 1982, 1983, 1984b). Psychologists became more vocal about their role in bringing social problems under control (Allport, 1924; Angell, 1929; Dunlap, 1920, 1928; Terman, 1922 a and b). For many, control became a fundamental component of the definition of psychology: "Ultimately it is a desire to get *control*" (Dashiell, 1928, p. 6). Even the seemingly most detached researchers saw the world in "dire need" of control over human conduct (Hull, 1935, p. 515).

Of the institutions needing control, marriage and family life were thought to be central for they constituted the primary source for individual well-being and for socialization of adjusted adults. Researchers proceeded with several premises: that the family is universal, the nuclear family being the most natural form; that the role of the mother is primary in the socialization of children; and that childrearing failures were to be interpreted as failures of mothers. Intimated in these premises is the preference for studying only adult heterosexual relationships in the context of the nuclear family (Morawski, 1984b).

The shifts in research orientations over the four decades indicate more than innovative conceptual strategies for pursuing an empirical question; they represent an intriguing deviation from mainstream psychology. The conceptual changes proceeded from a search for corporeal differences, then to cognitive and behavioral differences, and eventually to postulates about hidden but salient, nonconscious substrates of masculinity and femininity. To some extent the changes resemble the broader transition from structuralism and introspectionism to behaviorism which was then occurring in American psychology. However, the study of the sexes deviates significantly from that pattern. The rise in behaviorism, although meeting more resistance than is typically believed, involved an extensive exorcism of nonobservable or mentalist phenomena. Even excluding extremists such as John B. Watson and Karl Lashley there was an emerging consensus that psychology consisted of the objective study of observable events. Mind, self, consciousness, and personality traits were like epiphenomena. Personality traits were taken as merely descriptive aspects of more fundamental causal mechanisms since they are, behaviorally speaking, "the individual's characteristic reactions to social stimuli, and the quality of his adaptations to the social features of his environment" (Allport, 1924, p. 101). The ascendency of objective and behavioral psychology foreshortened the search for any real mental mechanisms; even though individual differences research continued, behaviorism challenged the plausibility of interior mental entities such as ethnic and racial traits (Cravens & Burnham, 1971; Samelson, 1978, 1979).

Psychologists' particular interests in the diagnoses and eventual remediation of social disorders provides an important clue to the persistent intrigue with male and female psychological functioning. These interests help explicate the continued discourse on masculinity and femininity which often deviated from current theoretical and methodological trends and disregarded empirical findings. At least hypothetically, standardized tests promised to rectify some of the empirical problems while serving the overall practical interests in control. Hence there ensued a quiet transition from the study of sex differences to the exploration of "masculinity" and "femininity."

The Solution of Terman and Miles

Challenged by the muddled state of masculinity and femininity research and specifically "by the lack of definiteness with respect to what these terms should connote," Lewis Terman and Catherine Cox Miles (1936, p. vi) undertook an extensive project in the early 1920s. They were moved by the questioning of the very existence of such entities which was being made by some psychologists and anthropologists, notably Margaret Mead. Nevertheless, they began with the premise that masculinity and femininity were real. Terman and Miles understood their task to resemble the earlier efforts to eradicate misconceptions about intelligence: like Binet's transformation of intelligence research, they sought "a quantification of procedures and concepts" (p. vi). They believed that despite the failures to determine the origin of sex-related attributes and the inability to attain observer agreement on the content of these attributes, there existed considerable clarity in the composite pictures of femininity and masculinity. Hence, the only assumption Terman and Miles suspended was that about origins; however, like previous researchers they lamented the ethical impossibility of conducting the study, the experimental rearing of infants, that could reveal those origins (p. 464).

Terman and Miles (1936) constructed a test to give "a more factual basis" to ordinary concepts of masculinity and femininity by accumulating test items on which males and females differed (p. 3). A preliminary version of the test was given to members of Terman's group of gifted children, and in this pretesting they observed their first case of a high cross-sex scorer displaying homosexual tendencies, or "sexual inversion." The final product of the psychometric project was a 910-item test with seven subtests: word association, ink-blot association, general information, emotional and ethical attitudes, interests, opinions, and introvertive response. Most subtests were compiled by modifying existing tests on those phenomena according to two criteria: selection of items that best discriminate the responses of males and females, and maximization of the efficiency and economy of test administration. Items were converted to multiple-choice format where two of the response alternatives were feminine and two masculine. Validity was assessed by ascertaining overlap of score distributions for male and female samples and by correlations with independent measures of femininity and masculinity. Since there was no other psychometric measure for ascertaining validity, comparison data were obtained from clinical studies.

The contents of the test perhaps now appear as an intriguing cultural artifact, but it did discriminate successfully between females and males. Scores of the sexes differed on average by 122 points and only about 10 out of 1000 subjects of each sex had scores exceeding the mean of the other sex (Terman & Miles, 1936, p. 371). The Attitude-Interest Analysis Test (AIST), as the M-F scale was titled to mask its purpose, contains masculine response items such as those requiring negative responses to the questions "Do you like to have people tell you their troubles?", "Do you usually get to do the things that please you most?", "Do you sometimes wish you had never been born?", and "Do you feel that you are getting a square deal in life?" Femininity points are attained by responding negatively to the questions "Do people ever say you are a bad loser?", "Do you feel bored a large share of the time?", and "Were you ever fond of playing with snakes?" Masculinity points are gained by replying that you dislike foreigners, religious men, women cleverer than you are, dancing, guessing games, being alone, and thin women. Femininity points are accrued by indicating dislike for sideshow freaks, bashful men, riding bicycles, giving advice, bald-headed men, and very cautious people.

AIST correlated with only a small number of other personality inventories and poorly with measures of marital adjustment. The scores varied consideraby for different age groups (for both sexes, scores declined in older samples), and the test was susceptible to faking. Qualitative comparison of the test results and clinical measures of abnormalities such as homosexuality and female delinquency was more promising: The AIST detected "roughly, degree of inversion of the sex temperament, and it is probably from inverts in this sense that homosexuals are chiefly recruited" (p. 467). Despite its limitations, Terman and Miles endorsed the scale and its potential. Use of the AIST promised to "help clean up the confused notions which are current with regard to what constitutes masculinity and femininity of personality. The fact seems to be that most of us have not acquired the ability to discriminate very clearly the genuinely masculine from the genuinely feminine" (pp. 465–466).

Convinced of the everyday inability to make such discriminations and of the detrimental effects of such judgment errors, Terman and Miles conducted a study on psychologists showing that even professionals, without the use of scientific techniques such as the AIST, were inadequate judges of masculinity and femininity (pp. 454–459). Such findings supported the hypothesis that "the test scores do have behavioral correlates but that ordinary observers lack adeptness in detecting them" (p. 465). The authors confidently anticipated use of the test in clinical diagnosis and in ameliorating familial and marital maladjustments. They refrained from relating their results to the environment-heredity controversy over the origins of sex differences. However, they offered a clear conception of psychological well-being, a model equating mental health with definitive correspondence between psychological and biological sex ascriptions. The subsequent research of Terman and Miles further attests to their interest in relating mental health to gender-based psychological characteristics (Miles, 1942; Terman, 1938).

Production of M-F

Theirs was the first major attempt to assess quantitatively the existence of masculinity and femininity in the psychological realm of temperament and to do so without postulating causality or nature/ nurture influences. Terman and Miles had introduced a way of accessing the reality of masculinity and femininity that became a model for constructing scales over the next 25 years. Most of the tests shared with their predecessor three assumptions: that masculinity and femininity existed but at a level that could not be readily identified by the ordinary observer; that the attributes were so psychologically charged that subjects had to be deceived of the true nature of the test lest they fake their response in order to appear socially desirable; and that femininity and masculinity were distinct qualities which were somehow related to psychological stability and deviancy, notably homosexuality and familial troubles. The first two assumptions were supported by the popularity of social theories that conceptualized human action as complex, causally interdependent, and beyond the self-knowledge attainable by the ordinary observer. Later investigations confirmed these conjectures when empirical evidence was found to contradict everyday analysis: Psychometric assessments were showing pedestrian attributions of femininity and masculinity to be in error. The third assumption, that of adjustment and mental health, corresponds with the mandates for reconstructing psychology into a more objective behavioral science that would better serve social control. As stated by two psychologists engaged in an extensive study of sex and marriage: "Some of us feel that if we were permitted to train the management, fewer of the exploring children would get hurt, and more of them would find the happiness they are looking for" (Hamilton & MacGowan, 1928, p. 287). Understanding intimate heterosexual relationships, sexuality, and family life comprised a substantial obligation for socially responsible psychologists.

Just as these assumptions directed conceptualizing about the form and location of "gendered" psyches, so Terman and Miles (1936) also indicated their content. In a qualitative analysis of the findings, they described the masculine psyche as adventurous, mechanically and object oriented, aggressive, self-asserting, fearless, and rough, and the feminine psyche as aesthetically and domestically oriented, sedentary, compassionate, timid, emotional, and fastidious. The two composite minds resemble the Victorian sex role schema of separate spheres (Lewin, 1984 b and c; Rosenberg, 1982). This reconstituted schema lent certainty to the increasingly fuzzy question of the nature of the sexes, and was similar in content to the one Robert Yerkes (1943) generated from his studies of male and female chimpanzee behavior (see Haraway, 1978). This gender schematization can be contrasted with the concurrent changes in the actual social positions of men and women and the alterations and confusions of gender images and roles (for examples, see Filene, 1974; May, 1980; Showalter, 1978). Given the social conditions of the period, the M-F scale itself may have served more than a taxonomic or descriptive function; it offered prescriptions for a moral order. Here the case of Ernest Hemingway's writing is suggestive. While portraying rigidly sex typed characters in his published fiction, his unpublished works include characters who betray, escape, or eschew conventional gender attributes (Latham, 1977). A somewhat different example of two levels of reality is apparent in writings of John B. Watson in which the strong argument for total conditioning and environmental adjustments were to provide behavior directives primarily for certain classes, including that of women (Harris, 1984). Invoking certainty can appear to arrest the flux of an uncertain social reality. Whatever the intended or unintended prescriptive function of the AIST may have been, and whatever the discrepancy between the test findings and other social indicators may mean, the form and content of the scale are significant, for they came to inform later assessment techniques and normative evaluations.

Reproduction of M-F Inventories

Although the AIST was developed according to a psychometric procedure of selecting test items for their ability to discriminate the criterion groups of men and women, it lacked theoretical coherence due to the variety of psychological phenomena tapped by the subscales. Later attempts to construct M-F instruments often focused on a more specific range of psychological phenomena and were considered in terms of particular personality theories. For instance, in the same year that Terman and Miles published their study, two quite specific inventories were reported, one by Edward K. Strong and the other by J. P. and Ruth Guilford. Strong (1936) prepared a Masculinity-Femininity subscale for his general inventory of vocational interests, the Strong Vocational Interest Blank (SVIB). He reported that although both sexes exhibited more feminine interests with age, sex differences were a major indicator of occupational interest. Strong suspended pronouncement on the origin of these differences, and simply concluded his study by asking, "Are the differences in interest of engineers and lawyers to be found in differences in hormone secretions, or in early attachment to father instead of mother, or in the possession of certain abilities in which the sexes differ?" (p. 65). On the one hand, Strong (1943) cautiously noted that the interests of males and females were more similar than different and that because his inventory also assessed similarities, it was in this sense superior to Terman and Miles' test. On the other hand, he admitted that his inventory was limited in the psychological dimensions it assessed; in the end, he deferred to the findings of Terman and Miles. A later test of occupational preferences also incorporated a M-F subscale (Kuder, 1946).

Guilford and Guilford (1936) attained a sex temperament measure through factor analysis of a test of introversion-extroversion. Guilfords' 101-item Nebraska Personality Inventory contains five factors, one of which is M. Although initially viewing the factor as "masculine-ideal," the investigators chose the "more noncommittal letter M" (p. 121) to signify a factor that was "perhaps masculinity-femininity, or possibly a dominance or ascendance-submission factor" (p. 127). The tentative identification of the masculinity factor later was described with considerable certainty (Guilford & Zimmerman, 1956; Lewin, 1984c). Both the scales of Strong and of the Guilfords, while ostensibly appraising different psychological dimensions, indicated greater aggressiveness, dominance, and fearlessness in males and greater emotionality, subjectivity, and sympathy in females. In both cases checks on external validity were limited and inconclusive.

Masculinity and femininity comprised a subarea of interest in other inventories designed primarily to assess psychological abnormalities. S. R. Hathaway and J. C. McKinley devised the Minnesota Multiphasic Personality Inventory (MMPI) in 1940 to measure traits of importance to the practitioner who "wishes to assay those traits that are commonly characteristic of disabling psychological abnormality" (Hathaway & McKinley, 1951, p. 5). Many of their items were inspired by Terman and Miles' inventory; others were original. The MMPI manual gives no information about the construction of the M-F subscale although other evidence suggests that it was compiled using only a criterion group of 13 male homosexuals (Lewin, 1984b). In developing a subscale of psychological femininity for the California Psychological Inventory (CPI), Harrison Gough (1952) attempted to create a less obtrusive instrument than the MMPI or SVIB. Gough selected items according to both their differentiation between male and female responses and their subtlety. The resultant 58 true-false questionnaire, containing items like "I am inclined to take things hard," discriminated between males and females but was only moderately successful in identifying psychological abnormalities and in correlating with judgements of trained observers. (Femininity, as interpreted in this scale, is characterized as sensitivity, timidity, compassion, acquiescence, subjectivity, and sentimentality.) A shortened version of the scale, the version that was integrated into the CPI, was examined for cross-cultural validation, accurate identification of adjustment problems, and correlation with other M-F scales; these checks were only moderately successful (Gough, 1966, 1975). A third scale of this type is the M-F subscale of the Depauw Adjustment Inventory (Heston, 1948).

Most of these researchers were concerned that their tests might be susceptible to either faking or reflecting cultural ideals. Yet they typically concluded, as did Guilford and Guilford (1936), that their test was sufficiently complex to elude the acumen or disingenuous calculations of the normal subject. Other researchers were not so readily convinced and sought to eliminate two possible contaminants of the conventional scales: (1) "cultural" biases and (2) the possibility that subjects could deceive testers, and themselves, given the ostensibly common tendency to obscure issues of sex identity. Solution to these problems of cultural and psychological "noise" was sought by testing symbolic representation through projective techniques; symbolic representation was believed to be beyond cultural constraints and the subject's awareness of self. Kate Franck (1946) designed a projective test of M-F based on the subjects' choices of pictures with male or female symbols. This and other studies assumed that normal subjects would prefer opposite sex symbols. The projective study of drawing styles indicated that men close off areas, expand the stimulus, seek unity, and use angular and sharp lines while women leave areas open, elaborate within the stimulus area, and blunt or enclose sharp lines (Franck and Rosen, 1949). Men tend to create objects such as towers, tools, and mechanical vehicles. Women tend to construct vases, windows, flowers, and human figures. Franck and Rosen compared their findings to Erik Erikson's analysis of children's play constructions and to Freudian psychoanalysis; they suggested the universality of symbols, and offered guidelines for evaluating maladjustments in role identification. Other attempts to appraise the "hidden" or "unconscious" of masculinity and femininity identification employed projective devises such as draw-a-person (Caligor, 1951; Machover, 1949), the Thematic Apperception Test (Webster, 1953), and open-ended word association (Goodenough, 1946).

During the 40-year period, 1930–1970, projective tests were not the sole means for circumventing cultural artifacts and subject biases. Several researchers adopted rating scales to permit the subject to evaluate self and others; by indirectly assessing social "ideals" or "stereotypes," they could check deviations from those baselines (Berdie, 1959; Reece, 1964). Berdie (1959) claimed that the adjective check list, because it enabled self-other statements, could measure not just "dimensions" of personality but also "processes" including "such things as identification, repression, self-acceptance, and perception" (p. 327). These researchers presumed the primacy of sex role identification for mental health, and that direct behavioral responses which reflect these underlying processes comprised valuable information for clinical practice. Measurement of other behavior indices of masculinity and femininity sometimes (Gray, 1957) though not always (Rosenberg & Sutton-Smith, 1959) linked sex role identification with these elusive or unconscious psychological processes.

The qualitative definitions of masculinity and femininity were consistent among these tests, though quantitative reliability checks did not always confirm such consistency (Constantinople, 1973). The tests were routinely constructed with the three core assumptions originally adopted by Terman and Miles: that masculinity and femininity were unavailable to the ordinary observer, that deception was required to deter the subject's natural tendency toward complicity, and that masculine and feminine traits were indicators of psychological adjustment. But the later scales had added grounds for making more adamant claims. By the late 1930s the idea of psychological femininity and masculinity located beyond the awareness of the person was being corroborated by depth psychology. The works of Freud, Jung, and Erikson, all of which gained popularity during the period, hypothesized that potent gender attributes were nonconscious. In addition, experimental research in general psychology was disclosing the various ways that subjects could bias responses, and these findings prompted attempts to design methods for circumventing such "faking" (Caligor, 1951). Thus, the constructs of masculinity and femininity, concepts which more than one researcher compared to atoms and genes, came to be described as knowable but not without calculated pursuit. Note how the search for the phenomena is described:

> . . . when we come to deal with what is often called the "private world" of the individual, comprising as it does, the feelings, urges, beliefs, attitudes, and desires of which he may be only dimly aware and which he is often reluctant to admit even to himself, much less to others, the problems of measurement are of a very different nature. Here the universe which we wish to assay is no longer overt and accessible but covert and jealously guarded (Goodenough, 1946, p. 456).

The subject typically complicated this search by deceptive behaviors: "A man may be an athlete, may know all about automobiles and fly a plane—and yet be afraid of women. Everyone has known such people, for there are many, who use behavior labeled masculine or feminine by our society to hide their disorientation, often from themselves" (Franck & Rosen, 1949, p. 247).

Other test compilers checked to ensure that subjects' stereotyped ideas about masculinity and femininity did not interfere with the more "subtle" or "true" indices (Nichols, 1962; Reece, 1964). Despite such precautionary circumventions, the constructs of the gender types, when put in verbal form, did not vary much from test to test. Masculine is powerful, strenuous, active, steady, strong, self-confident, with preference for machinery, athletics, working for self, and the external/public life. Feminine is sensitive, compassionate, timid, cautious, irritable, acquiescent, sentimental, preferring artistic and sendentary activities, and the internal/private life. Nevertheless, with the near certainty of the constructs' existence few researchers pronounced on their origins.

Feminist Difference: Complaint or Challenge?

Although problems of validity were occasionally noted, the general techniques of assessing masculinity and femininity were continued until the 1970s. A serious challenge to the tests appeared with Anne Constantinople's (1973) examination of three central postulates: the unidimensionality of femininity and masculinity, their bipolarity, and their definition in terms of sex differences in item-response. She offered convincing evidence of the theoretical vacuity of the masculinity-femininity construct. While Constantinople's critique examined M-F tests specifically, related research on sex and gender further compromised the tests' accepted validity. Theories of sex roles and sex role socialization were criticized for positing conventional norms for appropriate gender behavior (Block, 1973; Carlson, 1972), for making differential evaluations of male and female attributes (Helson, 1972; Rosenberg, 1973), and for assuming temporal stability of gender-linked traits (Angrist, 1972; Emmerich, 1973). These researches, and those in feminist studies generally, imperiled not only the credibility of M-F scales but the very reality of "masculine" and "feminine."

An expedient solution to the resulting quandary was offered with the concept of androgyny and the accompanying techniques for its assessment. Introduced in 1974, the Bem Sex Role Inventory (BSRI) measured the ideals of masculinity and femininity in a manner enabling comparison of the degree to which an individual rates high on both attributes. It measured the degree to which an individual is "androgynous," and hence psychologically healthy (Bem, 1974, 1977). During the next few years several similar scales were created (Berzins, Welling, & Wetter, 1978; Heilbrun, 1976; Spence, Helmreich, & Stapp, 1975). Initially, the most popular of these androgyny measures, the BSRI, was recognized as successful in predicting gender-related behaviors, in expanding the range of appropriate or healthy responses (Bem, 1974, 1977), and in detecting life-span changes (Maracek, 1979; White, 1979). The concept was expediently adopted to help explain a wide range of human behaviors, especially those for which clear gender differences were found. The scale became a popular tool for explaining activities in the hospital and boardroom, in the school and romantic encounters. The very idea of androgyny was received as a solution to the ostensible "sexism" of talking about masculinity and femininity. In fact, it offered an escape from openly endorsing those gender categories and a new ideal for evaluating behavior (Bem, 1977; Kaplan, 1976; Lee & Scheurer, 1983). That ideal has little if any relevance to psychosexual matters and illustrates a heightened concern with complex cognitive competencies. While the initial M-F scale of Terman and Miles was intended to tap psycho-sexual maladjustments, the androgyny scales exhibit little relation to sexuality (Storms, 1980). Androgyny researchers have tended to eschew consideration of sexuality in favor of correlating androgyny and those complex cognitive styles believed to be essential in, for example, the workplace (see Colwill, 1982).

The concept has also received both empirical and theoretical challenges, some of which fault androgyny research with incorporating the very same presuppositions that it was intended to eliminate. The critics noted that the newer models retain, even if unintentionally, certain values associated with masculine and feminine, and thus contribute to their ossification as universals (Lott, 1981; Hefner & Rebecca, 1979). Associated with these normative stipulations are untenable prescriptions for psychological health (Kenworthy, 1979). For instance, Sampson (1977) indicated how the "self-contained individualism" assumed in the concept of the androgynous person is a dubious yet essentially unquestioned norm. Others noted how the androgyny models neglect negative attributes and gender similarities (Rosen & Rekers, 1980; White, 1979). And although purportedly sensitive to changes in gender attributes within the individual, these models do not explicate the broader cultural conditions that may mediate or transform these attributes (Kaplan, 1979; Kenworthy,

1979; Sherif, 1982; Worell, 1978). The concept of androgyny has also yielded a questionable record in empirical investigations. The findings of a recent meta-analysis of androgyny research not only confirm some of the theoretical complications but also suggest that neither the BSRI nor the PAQ even adequately predicts psychological well-being (Taylor & Hall, 1982).

The androgyny models were advanced to replace theories that were circumscribed by history and culture; yet they apparently failed to confront their own historically constituted limitations (particularly by assuming transhistorical stability). They renovate rather than replace the rejected presuppositions about the ontology, structure, and desirability of gender concepts (Morawski, 1984a). The criticisms essentially demonstrate that androgyny research proceeded without critical scrutiny of the arguable metatheoretical foundation that subtly guided the entire enterprise of explaining the psychology of gender (Sherif, 1982; Taylor & Hall, 1982; Unger, 1983). Bem (1979) has also come to question the concept. She has suggested that the androgyny concept would sow the seeds of its own destruction by immobilizing the cultural categories of masculinity and femininity and, hence, by undermining its own foundation in those very categories. Bem's (1983) reconsideration of the androgyny construct does acknowledge the historical and cultural processes involved in the construction of gender dichotomies. However, to end the repetitions and sanctioning of a particular reality requires more than acknowledging history. It demands a comprehensive reevaluation of our scientific practices, particularly the reflexivity and empowerment of psychological knowledge.

Repetition in Discoveries

Androgyny research exhibits telling resemblances to the earlier work on femininity and masculinity. Undoubtedly androgyny models no longer prescribe correspondence between biologically ascribed sex and psychologically ascribed gender roles, and they dismiss altogether the issue of sexual deviancy. These "liberating" implications have tended to obscure other qualities of the androgyny scales, most notably their retention of the categorical constructs of femininity and masculinity along with the cultural values associated with them. As such, androgyny may be viewed as extension of an enduring process of pursuing the "real." It forms part of an ostensibly progressive and maybe interminable scientific search for psychological essences by reference to somatic body types, to mind stuff, to personality matter, and eventually to roles and cognitive styles.

Androgyny research is part of a pattern whereby appeals to these hypothetical constructs are invoked to locate the hypothetical constructs which were posited initially (those of the masculine and feminine). The process consists of continued indexicality of constructs where, even in the case of androgyny, the idea of gender types is substantiated by indexical relation to previously conjectured constructs. The process in turn engenders objectification and ossification of the constructs. The polarities of masculine and feminine, retaining qualities such as "instrumental" and "expressive" or "agentic" and "communal" action, become fixed, even reified. They come to represent ahistorical entities that potentially can be treated as referents of particular behaviors, traits, or ideals. Masculinity and femininity, then, become symbolic signifiers *and* the signified. Despite the apparent emancipatory implications of the androgyny theories, they, too, are embedded with limiting conditions and valuational underpinnings dictated by these polarities.

A further process operating throughout, by way of protecting the theory from external contamination, might be called "assessment control." There has developed an increasing wariness toward the commonsensical: independent reports or everyday interpretations have become a bias to be minimized or eliminated by implementing deceptive techniques and psychometric complexities. One consequence of this last procedure is the distancing of theory from everyday life. Further, regarding questions of power and privilege, distancing has significant implications for the establishment of norms of conduct. Here we approach the issue of perfectability and must recognize that any conception of betterment—be it of health, working life, or gender arrangements—requires some notion of the good. The masculinity-femininity theorists, purportedly by detaching their conceptual work from social life, have tacitly defined normative objectives by way of reference to an ideal of society and individual behavior within that society. For the earliest theorists the ideals were framed by the nineteenth-century division of labor in both the private and public realms. The test makers of the 1930s and 1940s aligned their ideals with social relations as typified by the nuclear family (hence the concern with marital adjustment, homosexuality, parenting). Their norms were also tied to perceptions of the possible collapse of these social relations. The implicit objectives of the androgyny theorists mirror the virtues of corporate democracy where self-contained individualism and role flexibility (behavioral inconsistency) are desired.

These normative stipulations need not be purposively imposed; their indirect infusion into theoretical work can be seen in the periodic occurrence of unintended reflexivity. The history of gender theorizing illustrates how psychologists' participation in and reflection upon cultural life can affect the primary stipulations in their work (Eagley, 1978; Rosenberg, 1982). Although these occurrences were not the focus of the present study, it is clear that research strategies were altered as a consequence of psychologists' experiences of the world wars, suffrage, the feminist movement of the 1960s, and general transitions in public life.

The support given to the idea of androgyny by feminist psychologists raises several obvious questions. Why did feminists not only subscribe to but participate in the reiteration of cultural concepts and consequently endorse the underlying moral edicts? On one level it is apparent how the concept was, in some senses self-serving: feminist psychologists have been primarily white, professional women who could find in androgyny theory an inspiring model for their own roles in a predominantly male world (not to mention their interests in the desired roles of their male peers). Here may be one case of unintended reflexive thinking. On another level, feminist psychologists may have been vulnerable to the lures of scientific ideals, and to the essentialist psychology that historically underlay the scientific ethos of skeptical empiricism, disinterestedness, and impartiality. Science has been extolled as the primary if not sole technique to work against prejudice and discrimination. Especially for those trained in scientific methods, it is not easy (or sometimes permissible) to acknowledge how scientific rationality itself is fallible (see Lykes & Stewart, 1983); yet the grounds of rationality are derived by social consensus and can be renegotiated and even transformed during normal scientific practice (Knorr-Cetina, 1981; Shapin, 1982). That feminist psychologists throughout the century would entrust their work to the superior rationality of scientific knowledge makes sense (as does the particular faith in psychology with its legacy of social reformism). This adherence is even more comprehensible given the resistance of the discipline to critically confronting the positivist metaphysics and naive realism which has both prefigured our observations of psychological reality as well as foreshortened our understanding of epistemological alternatives.

Toward New Theory

The exploration of masculinity and femininity is but one aspect of the history of gender research, and although highly informative work on the subject is now appearing (Lewin, 1984a; Rosenberg, 1982; Shields, 1975, 1982), further investigation is needed. Such historical ventures, along with those on the history of the actual practices of gender relations, offer correctives to current research (Morawski, 1984a). The history reviewed here suggests a reconsideration of the entire project of developing theory through a critical unpacking of our habits of theorizing and the generation of new theoretical frameworks. Such reconsideration begins with a critical and historical framework. It is critical in the sense of holding that all attempts to establish knowledge claims should be evaluated not simply in terms of empirical confirmation but also in terms of the very criteria of reliable knowledge and rationality that are attributed to the knower (psychologist). It is historical in the sense that knowledge claims must be understood as historical products, as constructions guided by particular interests and problematics. Neither of these provisions necessarily implies any radical relativism (Rorty, 1982, pp. 160–175).

Given this general superstructure, several issues fundamental to constructing gender theory must be considered. Most obvious is the need to take the broader context, and consequently reflexivity, seriously (Unger, 1983). The comprehensive social context must be understood if, borrowing Sherif's (1982) illustrations, we are to understand why the androgynous person may not be a political feminist or how social power relates to gender-linked behaviors. Such contextualist understanding requires sociological, anthropological, and historical studies (Morawski, 1983; Sherif, 1982) and is inescapably political (Parlee, 1979). A corollary is the need for the researcher to undertake critical self-appraisal as well as assessment of the stipulated canons of rationality (Addelson, 1983; Harding, 1984; Jaggar, 1984) and of the social and political facets of his or her work (Buss, 1979; Eagley, 1978; Flanagan, 1981; Sampson, 1977). Masculinity and femininity research demonstrates how the scientific questions of gender necessarily imply political questions in that even the androgyny theorists posit an idealization of society. Mere tacit endorsement of this idealization (in the case of androgyny an idealization where advances in technology and welfare may mitigate the bases for some gender distinctions) harbors debatable stipulations about the kind of world we are promoting.

The second major area of reconsideration concerns replacing conceptions of human nature that have either distorted or impeded research on gender. In light of the history of gender and of psychology generally, it seems prudent if not profitable at least to consider a working conception of human beings *as* human beings. And if we require any metaphors of powers or essences, those atoms of psychological actions, we consider that they be located in the act of the search, in *language* and its context of use. Simply assuming that human beings are active social agents involved with moral ambitions and with the construction of psychological realities generates numerous possibilities for future research. Some contributions in this direction include the study of the phenomenology of gender labeling (Kessler & McKenna, 1978), dialectics of sex role transcendence (Hefner & Rebecca, 1979), alternatives to the orthodox psychoanalytic theories of socialization (Chodorow, 1978; Dinnerstein, 1976; see Steele, in press), and gender styles in moral decision making (Gilligan, 1982). These basic conceptions also imply reappraisal of the conventional modes of assessment control: it is necessary to examine how we empower certain voices (the researcher's) and not others with inordinate privilege, and how we define authority and rationality (Addelson, 1983; Harding, 1984). Whether this empowering is seen as the hegemony of masculine science or as a concomitant of everyday life, in gender research it has profoundly affected theory as well as empirical findings.

These general architectonics simply intimate possibilities for theory construction which are informed by a systematic rereading of the historical record. They address some of the repeatedly evaded temporal, epistemological, and moral dimensions of research. Yet if we choose to participate in generating novel ways of looking at the social world as, at least hypothetically, scientists have sought new ways of viewing the natural world, then we must first audit our inventory of artifactual and conventional beliefs.

References

Addelson, K. P. (1983). The man of professional wisdom. In S. Harding & M. B. Hintikka (Eds.), *Discovering reality* (pp. 165–186). Boston: D. Reidel.
Allen, C. (1927). Studies in sex differences. *Psychological Bulletin*, 24, 294–304.
Allen, C. (1930). Recent studies in sex differences. *Psychological Bulletin*, 27, 394–407.
Allport, F. H. (1924). *Social psychology.* Boston: Houghton Mifflin.
Angell, J. R. (1929, April 19). Yale's Institute of Human Relations. *Yale Alumni Weekly* (pp. 889–891).
Angrist, S. (1972). The study of sex roles. In J. M. Bardwick (Ed.), *Readings on the psychology of women* (pp. 101–106). New York: Harper & Row.
Bem, S. L. (1974). The measurement of psychological androgyny. *Journal of Consulting and Clinical Psychology*, 42, 155–162.
Bem, S. L. (1977). On the utility of alternative procedures for assessing psychological androgyny. *Journal of Consulting and Clinical Psychology*, 45, 196–205.
Bem, S. L. (1979). Theory and measurement of androgyny: A reply to Pedhazur-Tetenbaum and Locksley-Colten critiques. *Journal of Personality and Social Psychology*, 37, 1047–1054.
Bem, S. L. (1983). Gender schema theory and its implications for child development: Raising gender-aschematic children in a gender-schematic society. *Signs*, 8, 598–616.

Berdie, R. F. (1959). A femininity adjective check list. *Journal of Applied Psychology,* **43**, 327–333.

Berzins, J. I., Welling, M. A., & Wetter, R. E. (1978). A new measure of psychological androgyny based on the Personality Research Form. *Journal of Consulting and Clinical Psychology,* **46**, 126–138.

Block, J. H. (1973). Conceptions of sex role: Some cross-cultural and longitudinal perspectives. *American Psychologist,* **28**, 512–526.

Buss, A. R. (Ed.). (1979). *Psychology in social context.* New York: Irvington.

Caligor, L. (1951). The determination of the individual's unconscious conception of his own masculinity-femininity identification. *Journal of Projective Techniques and Personality Assessment,* **15**, 494–509.

Carlson, R. (1972). Understanding women: Implications for personality theory and research. *Journal of Social Issues,* **28**, 17–32.

Chodorow, N. (1978). *The reproduction of mothering: Psychoanalysis and the sociology of gender.* Berkeley: University of California.

Colwill, N. L. (1982). *The new partnership: Women and men in organizations.* Palo Alto, CA: Mayfield.

Constantinople, A. (1973). Masculinity-femininity. An exception to a famous dictum. *Psychological Bulletin,* **80**, 389–407.

Cravens, H., & Burnham, J. C. (1971). Psychology and evolutionary naturalism in American thought, 1890–1940. *American Quarterly,* **23**, 635–657.

Danziger, K. (1979). The social origins of modern psychology. In A. R. Buss (Ed.), *Psychology in social context* (pp. 27–45). New York: Irvington.

Dashiell, J. F. (1928). *Fundamentals of objective psychology.* Boston: Houghton Mifflin.

Dinnerstein, D. (1976). *The mermaid and the minotaur: Sexual arrangements and human malaise.* New York: Harper & Row.

Dunlap, K. (1920). Social need for scientific psychology. *Scientific Monthly,* **11**, 502–517.

Dunlap, K. (1928). The applications of psychology to social problems. In C. Murchison (Ed.), *Psychologics of 1925* (pp. 353–379). Worcester: Clark University Press.

Eagley, A. H. (1978). Sex differences in influenceability. *Psychological Bulletin,* **85**, 86–116.

Ellis, H. H. (1894). *Man and woman: A study of human secondary characters.* London: Walter Scott.

Emmerich, W. (1973). Socialization and sex role development. In P. B. Baltes & K. W. Schaie (Eds.), *Life-span developmental psychology: Personality and socialization.* New York: Academic Press.

Filene, P. G. (1974). *Him/her/self: Sex roles in modern America.* New York: Harcourt Brace Jovanovich, 1974.

Flanagan, O. J., Jr. (1981). Psychology, progress, and the problem of reflexivity: A study in the epistemological foundations of psychology. *Journal of the History of the Behavioral Sciences,* **17**, 375–386.

Franck, K. (1946). Preference for sex symbols and their personality correlates. *Genetic Psychology Monograph,* **33**, 73–123.

Franck, K., & Rosen, E. (1949). A projective test of masculinity-femininity. *Journal of Consulting Psychology,* **13**, 247–256.

Gilligan, C. (1982). *In a different voice: Psychological theory and women's development.* Cambridge: Harvard University Press.

Goodenough, F. L. (1946). Semantic choice and personality structure. *Science,* **104**, 451–456.

Gough, H. G. (1952). Identifying psychological femininity. *Educational and psychological measurement.* **12**, 427–439.

Gough, H. G. (1966). A cross-cultural analysis of the CPI Femininity Scale. *Journal of Consulting Psychology,* **30**, 136–141.

Gough, H. G. (1975). *California psychological inventory: Manual* (rev. ed.). Palo Alto: Consulting Psychologists Press.

Gray, S. W. (1957). Masculinity-femininity in relation to anxiety and social acceptance. *Child Development*, 28, 203–214.

Guilford, J. P., & Guilford, R. B. (1936). Personality factors S, E, and M and their measurement. *Journal of Psychology*, 2, 109–127.

Guilford, J. P., & Zimmerman, W. S. (1956). *The Guilford-Zimmerman temperament survey: Manual of instructions and interpretations*. Beverly Hills, CA: Sheridan Supply.

Haber, S. (1964). *Efficiency and uplift: Scientific management in the progressive era, 1890–1920*. Chicago: University of Chicago Press.

Hall, G. S. (1922). Flapper Americana novissima. *Atlantic Monthly*, 129, 771–780.

Hamilton, G. V. (1931). The emotional life of modern woman. In S. D. Schmalhausen & V. F. Calverton (Eds.), *Woman's coming of age* (pp. 207–229). New York: Horace Liveright.

Hamilton, G. V., & MacGowan, K. (1928). Marriage and love affairs. *Harpers*, 157, 277–287.

Haraway, D. (1978). Animal sociology and a natural economy of the body politic. Part I: A political physiology of dominance. *Signs*, 4, 21–36.

Harding, S. (1984). Is gender a variable in conceptions of rationality? A survey of issues. In Carol C. Gould (Ed.), *Beyond domination: New perspective on women and philosophy* (pp. 43–63). Totowa, NJ: Rowman & Allanheld.

Harris, B. (1984). Give me a dozen healthy infants: John B. Watson's popular advice on childrearing, woman, and the family. In M. Lewin (Ed.), *In the shadow of the past: Psychology portrays the sexes*. New York: Columbia University Press.

Haskell, T. L. (1977). *The emergence of professional social science*. Urbana: University of Illinois Press.

Hathaway, S. R., & McKinley, J. C. (1951). *Manual for the Minnesota multiphasic personality inventory* (rev. ed.). Minneapolis: University of Minnesota Press.

Hefner, R., & Rebecca, M. (1979). The future of sex roles. In M. Richmond-Abbott (Ed.), *The American woman: Her past, her present, her future* (pp. 243–264). New York: Holt, Rinehart & Winston.

Heilbrun, A. B., Jr. (1976). Measurement of masculine and feminine sex role identities as independent dimensions. *Journal of Consulting and Clinical Psychology*, 44, 183–190.

Helson, R. (1972). The changing image of the career woman. *Journal of Social Issues*, 28, 33–46.

Heston, J. C. (1948). A comparison of four masculinity-femininity scales. *Educational and Psychological Measurement*, 8, 375–387.

Hinkle, B. M. (1920). On the arbitrary use of the terms "masculine" and "feminine." *Psychoanalytic Review*, 7, 15–30.

Hollingworth, L. S. (1916). Sex differences in mental traits. *The Psychological Bulletin*, 13, 377–384.

Hollingworth, L. S. (1918). Comparison of the sexes in mental traits. *Psychological Bulletin*, 15, 427–432.

Hull, C. L. (1935). The conflicting psychologies of learning—A way out. *The Psychological Review*, 42, 491–516.

Jaggar, A. (1984). Human biology in feminist theory: Sexual equality reconsidered. In Carol Gould (Ed.), *Beyond domination: New perspectives on women and philosophy* (pp. 21–42). Totowa. NJ: Rowman & Allenhead.

Jastrow, J. (1918). The feminine mind. In J. Jastrow (Ed.), *The psychology of conviction* (pp. 280–325). New York: Houghton Mifflin.

Johnson, W. B., & Terman, L. B. (1940). Some highlights in the literature of psychological sex differences published since 1920. *Journal of Psychology*, 9, 327–336.

Kaplan, A. G. (1976). Androgyny as a model of mental health for woman: From theory to therapy. In A. G. Kaplan & J. P. Bean (Eds.), *Beyond sex role stereotypes: Readings toward a psychology of androgyny* (pp. 352–362). Boston: Little Brown.

Kaplan, A. G. (1979). Clarifying the concept of androgyny: Implications for therapy. *Psychology of Women Quarterly*, **3**, 223–230.

Kaplan, S. (1956). Social engineers as saviors: Effects of World War I on some American liberals. *Journal of the History of Ideas*, **17**, 347–369.

Kenworthy, J. A. (1979). Androgyny in psychotherapy: But will it sell in Peoria? *Psychology of Women Quarterly*, **3**, 231–240.

Kessler, S. J., & McKenna, W. (1978). *Gender: An ethnomethodological approach.* New York: John Wiley & Sons.

Knorr-Cetina, K. D. (1981). *The manufacture of knowledge.* New York: Pergamon Press.

Kuder, G. F. (1946). *Revised manual for the Kuder preference record.* Chicago: Science Research Associates.

Latham, A. (1977, October 16). A farewell to machismo. *New York Times*, **6**, (pp. 52–55, 80–82, 90–99).

Lee, A., & Scheurer, V. L. (1983). Psychological androgyny and aspects of self-image in women and men. *Sex Roles*, **9**, 289–306.

Leuba, J. H. (1926). The weaker sex. *Atlantic Monthly*, **137**, 454–460.

Lewin, M. (Ed.). (1984a). *In the shadow of the past: Psychology portrays the sexes.* New York: Columbia University Press.

Lewin, M. (1984b). Psychology measures femininity and masculinity. II: From "13 Gay Men" to the instrumental-expressive distinction. In M. Lewin (Ed.), *In the shadow of the past: Psychology portrays the sexes* (pp. 197–204). New York: Columbia University Press.

Lewin, M. (1984c). Rather worse than folly? Psychology measures femininity and masculinity. I: From Terman and Miles to the Guilfords. In M. Lewin (Ed.), *In the shadow of the past: Psychology portrays the sexes* (pp. 155–178). New York: Columbia University Press.

Lippmann, W. (1922). *Public opinion.* New York: Macmillan.

Lott, B. (1981). A feminist critique of androgyny: Toward the elimination of gender attributions for learned behavior. In C. Mayo & N. M. Henley (Eds.), *Gender and nonverbal behavior* (pp. 171–180). New York: Springer-Verlag.

Lykes, M. B., & Stewart, A. J. (1983). Evaluating the feminist challenge in psychology: 1963–1983. Paper presented at the 91st Annual Meeting of the American Psychological Association, Anaheim, CA.

Machover, K. (1949). *Personality projection in the drawing of the human figure.* Springfield, IL: Charles C. Thomas.

Maracek, J. (1979). Social change, postive mental health, and psychological androgyny. *Psychology of Women Quarterly*, **3**, 241–247.

May, E. T. (1980). *Great expectations: Marriage and divorce in post-Victorian America.* Chicago: University of Chicago Press.

Miles, C. C. (1942). Psychological study of a young man pseudohermaphrodite reared as a female. In J. F. Dashiell (Ed.), *Studies in personality contributed in honor of Lewis M. Terman* (pp. 209–228). New York: McGraw-Hill.

Moore, H. T. (1922). Further data concerning sex differences. *Journal of Abnormal and Social Psychology*, **17**, 210–214.

Morawski, J. G. (1982). On thinking about history as social psychology. *Personality and Social Psychology Bulletin*, **8**, 393–401.

Morawski, J. G. (1983). Psychology and the shaping of policy. *Berkshire Review*, **18**, 92–107.

Morawski, J. G. (1984a). Historiography as metatheoretical text for social psychology. In K. J. Gergen & M. Gergen (Eds.), *Historical social psychology* (pp. 37–60). New York: Erlbaum.

Morawski, J. G. (1984b). Not quite new worlds: Psychologists' conceptions of the ideal family in the twenties. In M. Lewin (Ed.), *In the shadow of the past: Psychology portrays the sexes* (pp. 97–125). New York: Columbia University Press.

Nichols, R. C. (1962). Subtle, obvious, and stereotype measures of masculinity–femininity. *Educational and Psychological Measurement*, **22**, 449–461.

O'Donnell, J. M. (1979). The "Crisis of Experimentalism" in the twenties: E. G. Boring and his uses of historiography. *American Psychologist*, 34, 289–295.

Parlee, M. B. (1979). Psychology and women. *Signs*, 5, 121–133.

Reece, M. (1964). Masculinity and femininity: A factor analytical study. *Psychological Reports*, 14, 123–139.

Robinson, E. S. (1926). *Practical psychology: Human nature in everyday life.* New York: Macmillan Co.

Rorty, R. (1982). *The consequences of pragmatism.* Minneapolis: University of Minnesota.

Rosen, A. C. & Rekers, G. A. (1980). Toward a taxanomic framework for variables of sex and gender. *Genetic Psychology Monographs*, 102, 191–218.

Rosenberg, B. G., & Sutton-Smith, B. (1959). The measurement of masculinity and femininity in children. *Child Development*, 30, 373–380.

Rosenberg, M. (1973). The biologic basis for sex role stereotypes. *Contemporary Psychoanalysis*, 29, 374–391.

Rosenberg, R. L. (1982). *Beyond separate spheres: Intellectual origins of modern feminism.* New Haven: Yale University Press.

Samelson, F. (1978). From "Race psychology" to "Studies in prejudice." Some observations on the thematic reversals in social psychology. *Journal of the History of the Behavioral Sciences*, 14, 265–278.

Samelson, F. (1979). Putting psychology on the map: Ideology and intelligence testing. In A. R. Buss (Ed.), *Psychology in social context* (pp. 103–167). New York: Irvington.

Sampson, E. E. (1977). Psychology and the American ideal. *Journal of Personality and Social Psychology*, 35, 767–782.

Shapin, S. (1982). History of science and its sociological reconstructions. *History of Science*, 20, 157–207.

Sherif, C. W. (1982). Needed concepts in the study of gender identity. *Psychology of Women Quarterly*, 6, 375–398.

Shields, S. (1975). Functionalism, Darwinism, and the psychology of women. *American Psychologist*, 31, 739–751.

Shields, S. A. (1982). The variability hypothesis: The history of a biological model of sex differences in intelligence. *Signs*, 7, 769–797.

Showalter, E. (Ed.). (1978). *These modern women: Autobiographical essays from the twenties.* Old Westbury, New York: The Feminist Press.

Sokal, M. M. (1984). James McKeen Cattell and American psychology in the 1920s. In J. Brozek (Ed.), *Explorations in the history of psychology in the United States* (pp. 273–323). Lewisburg, PA: Bucknell University Press.

Spence, J. T., Helmreich, R., & Stapp, J. (1975). Ratings of self and peers on sex role attributes and their relation to self-esteem and conceptions of masculinity and femininity. *Journal of Personality and Social Psychology*, 32, 29–39.

Steele, R. (in press), Paradigm lost: Psychoanalysis after Freud. In C. Buxton (Ed.), *Points of view in the modern history of psychology.* New York: Academic Press.

Storms, M. D. (1980). Theories of sexual orientation. *Journal of Personality and Social Psychology*, 1980, 38, 783–792.

Strong, E. K., Jr. (1936). Interests of men and women. *Journal of Social Psychology*, 7, 49–67.

Strong, E. K., Jr. (1943). *Vocational interests of men and women.* Palo Alto: Stanford University Press.

Taylor, M. C., & Hall, J. A. (1982). Psychological androgyny: Theories, methods, and conclusions. *Psychological Bulletin*, 92, 347–366.

Terman, L. (1917). *The Stanford revision and extension of the Binet-Simon Scale for Measuring Intelligence.* Baltimore: Warwick and York.

Terman, L. M. (1922a). The control of propaganda as a psychological problem. *Scientific Monthly*, 14, 234–252.

Terman, L. M. (1922b). The psychological determinist, or democracy and the I. Q. *Journal of Educational Research*, 6, 57–62.

Terman, L. M. (1938). *Psychological factors in marital happiness*. New York: McGraw-Hill.
Terman, L. M., & Miles, C. C. (1936). *Sex and personality*. New York: McGraw-Hill.
Thorndike, E. L. (1920). Psychology of the half-educated man. *Harpers*, **140**, 666–670.
Tobey, R. C. (1971). *The American ideology of National Sciences, 1919–1930*. Pittsburgh: University of Pittsburgh Press.
Unger, R. K. (1983). Through the looking glass: No wonderland yet! (The reciprocal relationship between methodology and models of reality.) *Psychology of Women Quarterly*, **8**, 9–32.
Watson, J. B. (1919). *Psychology from the standpoint of a behaviorist*. Philadelphia: J. B. Lippincott.
Watson, J. B. (1924). *Behaviorism*. New York: Norton.
Watson, J. B. (1927). The weakness of women. *Nation*, **125**, 9–10.
Watson, J. B. (1936). Autobiography. In. C. Murchison (Ed.), *A history of psychology in autobiography* (pp. 271–282). Worcester: Clark University Press.
Webster, H. (1953). Derivation and use of the masculinity-femininity variable. *Journal of Clinical Psychology*, **9**, 33–36.
White, M. S. (1979). Measuring androgyny in adulthood. *Psychology of Women Quarterly*, **3**, 293–307.
Wiebe, R. (1967). *The search for order, 1877–1920*. New York: Hill & Wang.
Woolley, H. B. T. (1903). *The mental traits of sex: An experimental investigation of the normal mind in men and women*. Chicago: University of Chicago Press.
Woolley, H. B. T. (1910). A review on the recent literature on the psychology of sex. *Psychological Bulletin*, **7**, 335–342.
Woolley, H. B. T. (1914). The psychology of sex. *Psychological Bulletin*, **11**, 353–379.
Worell, J. (1978). Sex roles and psychological well-being: Perspectives on methodology. *Journal of Consulting and Clinical Psychology*, **46**, 777–791.
Yerkes, R. M. (1943). *Chimpanzees: A laboratory colony*. New Haven: Yale University Press.

Individuation and attachment in personality development: Extending Erikson's theory

Carol E. Franz and Kathleen M. White

Abstract

The question of whether Erikson's theory of psychosocial development is a complete and coherent view of development in males and females is considered. After a thorough review of Erikson's views on the role of sex in psychosocial development, the authors suggest that an important element is neglected in Erikson's account of personality development in both sexes. That is, due to his focus on issues of identity, Erikson does not account fully for the development of intimacy or other expressions of interpersonal attachment. The authors conclude that the major shortcoming of Erikson's theory is not, as some feminists have argued, that it is a male theory but that it fails to account adequately for the processes of interpersonal attachment that are essential to the development of both males and females. Preliminary elements of a two-path model of development are proposed.

In recent years, a major theoretical model for understanding life-span personality development has been that of Erik Erikson. Using psychoanalytic-psychosexual concepts as a foundation, Erikson (1963, 1964, 1968, 1977, 1978) traces the ego's progressive integration of the social world and the psychosexual experience of the individual. He describes personality development as an hierarchically ordered sequence of stages which progress from initial narcissistic involvement with oneself, through stages of identification and socialization, to increasing individuation and establishment of an individual identity. While Erikson emphasizes that this development occurs within an expanding network of significant persons, we believe that his theory does not account adequately for the development of various forms of interpersonal connectedness or attachments. While Erikson views identity and intimacy (the psychosocial "virtues" emerging from his stages 5 and 6) as equal in value, his

The authors gratefully acknowledge the assistance of Brinton Lykes, Abigail Stewart, and two anonymous reviewers in reading and commenting on earlier drafts of this paper. For typing this manuscript, our gratitude goes to Deborah Reed and Marcia Johnston.

emphasis on the antecedents and consequences of identity to the neglect of the antecedents and consequences of intimacy means that his theory fails to do justice to the coherence and interrelatedness of both sets of processes in both sexes. It is our belief that a truly universal theory of personality development must provide an adequate account of the personality processes that are fundamental to both male and female development; specifically, a theory of personality development (as opposed to a more limited theory of a single personality component such as identity) must account adequately for both individuation and interpersonal attachment.

The principal purpose of this paper is to demonstrate that Erikson's notion of a single developmental pathway does not account adequately for the life-span process of interpersonal *attachment*—a construct sometimes assumed to represent a predominantly female orientation or concern. Indeed, because attachment as a life-span developmental process, or pathway, is neglected in Erikson's theory, violence is also done to the coherence of the construct of *individuation*, typically seen as a predominantly male orientation or concern. A number of theorists have argued that fundamental to all human experience and development are two modalities—sometimes labelled agency and communion (e.g., Bakan, 1966), sometimes labelled individuation and attachment or connectedness. One major attack on theories and methodologies emphasizing "agentic" values such as autonomy and separateness, objectification and quantification, and hierarchical relationships comes from feminists (e.g., Carlson, 1972; Gilligan, 1979) who characterize such approaches as neglectful of half the human experience—that is, the communal, interpersonally connected part that is essential to the well-being of both males and females.

Because a number of feminist and other social scientists have criticized Erikson for his neglect or misportrayal of female experience, we believe that a thorough review of Erikson's treatment of sex differences in psychosocial development is valuable. Some feminists consider Erikson's positive allusions to the valuable features of women's "inner space" to be just as insulting and stereotyping as Freud's more negative focus on penis envy; however, it is hard to find a full treatment of Erikson's views on the sexes in the literature. As will be seen, it is our position that the greatest limitation to Erikson's rich and ambitious theory lies not in his mystification of the female's "inner space" or in his presumption that identity precedes intimacy, but in his formulation of a single developmental pathway for the maturing male and female ego. This limitation prevents Erikson from achieving his goal of a universal theory of human development, even though the eight "values" or "virtues" he attributes to his developmental stages (trust, autonomy, initiative, industry, identity, intimacy, generativity, integrity) can easily be translated into the two modalities of individuation and attachment which constitute the two-pathway model we are proposing. Indeed, the logical weaving together of Erikson's eight ego-elements into two pathways rather than one appears to be a useful way of accounting fully for male as well as female experience. After demonstrating that a mere elaboration of Erikson's classic epigenetic chart will not suffice to correct the areas of imbalance in his theory, we will propose a preliminary version of the form a two-path model of development might take.

Sex Differences in the Developmental Stages in Erikson's Theory

Erikson holds several basic assumptions concerning the relation of sex to psychosocial development—two of which are particularly relevant to our analysis. First, he assumes that the developmental crises are in the same sequence for males and females, and that the ego-strengths associated with resolution of each stage are also the same regardless of sex. Second, Erikson describes three interactive components in development: Soma (anatomy), Psyche (individual dispositions), and Polis (the socio-cultural context). These components enter into the crisis of each stage, the resolution and synthesis of which influences each subsequent stage. Because there are these three elements, it becomes possible that males and females bring to any particular developmental crisis a different "Soma" and "Polis;" as a consequence, their experience of each crisis, as well as the way in which they resolve it, could be different. The ego-strengths stemming from adequate resolution of each crisis are, however, the same.

Many readers of Erikson have tried to grapple with the question of whether or not his theory has different implications for male and female development. Erikson addresses this issue when he asks: "But how does the identity formation of women differ by dint of the fact that their somatic design harbors an 'inner space'. . . ?" (1968, p. 266). An analysis of his many books and articles reveals that Erikson provides no simple or clear cut answers to his own question. On the one hand, he warns (1974) against the overinterpretation and decontextualization of sex differences in his theory; on the other hand, he consistently emphasizes the necessity for acknowledging and affirming any uniqueness of experience associated with sex. Indeed, he has

sometimes suggested (Erikson, 1968) that although males and females are similar in many ways, it may be useful to explore women's
identity separately from that of the male. A tension concerning sex
and personality persists throughout Erikson's writing. In his theory,
sex is sometimes treated as very important and sometimes as not
important to personality; he believes that one must recognize and
accept one's sex (e.g., in heterosexual relationships), yet in many
spheres (e.g., cognitive functioning) sex makes little difference in
how a person functions. In regard to the place of anatomy in his
theory, Erikson (1968) perceives it as "the physiological rock-bottom
which must neither be denied nor given exclusive emphasis. For a
human being, in addition to having a body, is *somebody*, which
means an indivisible personality and a defined member of a group"
(p. 285).

One way in which sex permeates personality, as conceived by
Erikson, is in his notion that a woman is never-not-a-woman; a man
is never-not-a-man. Erikson (1968) argues that there is a uniqueness
in female identity, yet he waivers when he has to pinpoint the extent
of this uniqueness or the degree to which it changes any aspects of
identity formation. It is possible to interpret Erikson (in particular,
"Womanhood and the inner space," 1968) as proposing major sex
differences in personality; however, this interpretation is not supported by all of Erikson's writing.

In Erikson's theory, the importance of sex is most clearly articulated at certain points in the life cycle—particularly, in the Oedipal
period, as well as the identity, intimacy, and generativity stages of
development. In the following section of the paper we will review
the stages in which Erikson delineates the place of sex in his larger
developmental scheme.

*Trust vs. mistrust, autonomy vs. shame (oral and anal stages, ages
birth–3)*. Erikson's early stages parallel and build on those of Freud.
Erikson, however, emphasizes the social context (connectedness) of
the child and the evolving psychosocial skills—ego-strengths—that
lay the foundation for later stages. According to both Freud and
Erikson, psychosexually and psychosocially there should be no sex
differences in the first two life stages—that is in the trust vs. mistrust
(oral) and autonomy vs. shame and doubt (anal) stages. Erikson,
however, does not elaborate on aspects of the young child's social
context in this stage that may allow different behaviors for males and
females (e.g., autonomy seeking may be restricted or encouraged in
sex-related ways).

Initiative vs. guilt (phallic stage, ages 4–5). In Erikson's theory, sex
differences become polarized in the resolution of the Oedipal crisis

at the end of the phallic stage (initiative vs. guilt). In his treatment
of the phallic stage, Erikson is still closely tied to a Freudian framework and to Freudian assumptions concerning the significance of
Oedipal crisis resolution for subsequent personality development.
Erikson, however, adds two elements to the phallic stage; these
additions change some of the ramifications of the Oedipal crisis and
are particularly pertinent to sex differences. The first element,
socialization, concerns the impact of the child's social context on his
or her ego-development. The second element, which Erikson calls
"inner space," is a positive addition to the Soma of the developing
girl.

The major socializing context of children in the third stage of
psychosexual/psychosocial development is the family; both parents
and siblings are significant figures who can contribute to the socialization of the child. It would appear that the extent to which the
family emphasizes sex differences and gender roles in the child's
expression of initiative could have a significant impact on gender
identity and personality. It is clear in Erikson's theory that both girls
and boys display initiative in this phase; the extent to which this
initiative is stifled hinges both on the child's social experiences and
resolution of Oedipal issues.

Erikson's delineation of the impact of Polis on the initiative vs.
guilt stage child helps to clarify the role of nonbiological forces in
shaping sex differences. Erikson also suggests, however, that biology
(Soma) should shape society (Polis); in Polis, claims Erikson (1968),
"the influence of women will not be fully actualized until it reflects
without apology the facts of the 'inner space' and the potentialities
and needs of the feminine psyche" (p. 290). What then is the
contribution of Soma to the initiative vs. guilt stage? Erikson's
description of the boy's experience of the initiative vs. guilt stage
closely parallels the Freudian analysis of the phallic stage, in which
the combination of phallic intrusiveness and successful identification
with the father provides the foundation for the active/masculine
roles expected in adulthood. The outcome of the phallic stage for
the girl is less optimal than that of the boy in Freudian theory, due
to her "lack" of a penis and the complexities of her attachment-
identification issues. According to Erikson (1963), in psychoanalytic
theory:

> Girls have a fateful experience at this stage in that they must
> comprehend the finality of the fact that although their locomo-
> tor, mental, and social intrusiveness is equally increased and as
> adequate as that of the boys', they lack one item: the penis.

While the boy has this visible, erectable, and comprehensible organ to attach his dreams of bigness to, the girl's clitoris cannot sustain dreams of sexual equality (p. 88).

In Eriksonian theory, by contrast, an "inner space" (that is, female reproductive organs) counteracts the negative impact of the girl's recognition that she is missing a penis. Femaleness, according to Erikson, neither produces a sense of inferiority and lack of purpose nor causes regression to earlier phases of development; rather, it carries its own sense of *having* something, a "fullness, warmth, and generosity . . . the existence of a productive inner-bodily space set in the center of the female form" (Erikson, 1968, p. 267). Erikson theorizes that owing to the sense of "inner space," the female has (*a*) a sense of being sexually equal but different—a sense of having something (as opposed to lacking a penis), (*b*) a basis for positive identification with her mother, and (*c*) a sense of purpose arising from her ability to be (or become) productive. According to Erikson (1968), the girl's desire for a baby is not necessarily a longing for a penis or penis-substitute as in Freudian theory; rather, it is a fulfill-ment of her inner space, her "procreative drive." Erikson's strong emphasis on motherhood in women, however, is not paralleled in his discussion of the male's experience of his anatomy. Moreover, it appears that positive psychosocial development in women occurs at the expense (or theoretical avoidance) of female sexuality; pleasure from genital sensations and phallic intrusiveness is sacrificed for the more abstract "procreative drive."

With Erikson's theoretical modification of the Freudian Oedipal crisis—where "penis envy" is supposed to have a regressive impact on female development—the girl is seen as experiencing an inner space which allows her to resolve Oedipal issues with as much potential as the boy for further healthy ego-development. Erikson does suggest that the dangers of this stage may be sex related; thus, phallic-aggressiveness and overinvestment in initiative can be as problematic for the boy's development as can be the girl's potential passive-dependency for her development. In addition, a social system that overemphasizes gender-related identifications and activities also hinders the potential for psychic wholeness in either males or fe-males.

For Erikson the anatomical functions of males and females, while not constituting the totality of the personality, provide an unavoid-able basis for further development; he holds that, "boys and girls are differentiated not only by differences in organs, capacities and roles, but by a unique quality of experience" (Erikson, 1963, p. 91). The unique quality of the female's experience is her disposition for care, warmth, and generosity through which she can express initiative. Erikson also suggests that the basic elements of the generativity (adult) stage first become apparent in the initiative vs. guilt (phallic) stage when the potential for productivity emerges in a way that is sex differentiated—that is, oriented towards work in males and towards procreation in females.

Despite the addition of the inner space concept, Erikson's analysis of the age 4–5 period is clearly based on Freudian assumptions concerning the phallic intrusiveness of pre-Oedipal girls and the pre-Oedipal relationships of children to their mothers as well as the assumption of the necessity of the Oedipal crisis for later development. Erikson is not willing to diverge from the Freudian viewpoint—as have numerous others, e.g., Chodorow (1974), Horney (1973), Mitchell (1974), Strouse (1974)—to analyze female development systematically. In consequence, in Erikson's theory the model for psychosocial development is still that of the male. Erikson does not question the assumptions and consequences of applying that model to female development. If a "phallic" girl is aware of and proud of her "inner space," it would appear to us that the sequence of the Oedipal complex initiated by penis envy need not occur as such. Thus, on the one hand, Erikson postulates what he believes is a more positive developmental sequence for females than that of Freud; on the other hand, Erikson accepts many of Freud's assumptions regarding sex differences and does not thoroughly reanalyze early development in light of the addition of socio-cultural influences and the concept of the inner space.

In Erikson's theory, the resolution of the Oedipal crisis at the end of the initiative vs. guilt stage is a crucial time in the child's differentiation of self as male or female. The resolution, moreover, has long-term consequences for personality. Erikson concludes that despite differences in experience of Soma and Polis, males and females can successfully resolve the psychosexual and psychosocial issues of the stage. Thus, individuals of each sex can emerge with a sense of purpose expressed through initiative—that is, the sense of being able to satisfy oneself and others. Is this initiative, however, expressed in different ways, based on anatomical differences? Is the initiative of a young girl expressed only in caring-oriented imaginative play, imitation, and role anticipation, or is her expression of initiative less Soma-linked? Although Erikson supports the latter view, it is clear in his writing that unique aspects of a girl's experience of inner space—warmth, caring, generosity, fullness—permeate her developmental path.

Industry vs. inferiority (latency stage, ages 6–12). Sexual differentiation during latency (the industry vs. inferiority stage) appears to play a minor role in Erikson's theory. From the perspective of socialization and identification, however, the roles and skills a child learns during this period can have a significant impact on his or her later life choices. For example, Erikson holds that the internalizations of earlier developmental lessons in the adolescent identity stage have a foundation in what the latency stage child thinks she or he can do or be. Karen Horney (1926/1973), elaborating on the cultural sources of anxiety and inferiority in women, cites the fact that men have the satisfying and prestigious jobs in Western cultures, leaving women with few, inferior, and inadequate life-options. To the extent that Horney's observation has a validity in our culture, the choices of spheres of competence a girl thinks she has for later life will affect her expression of industriousness significantly. Polis is not independent of Soma for Erikson; in entering the realm of Polis, women—Erikson believes—should not have to mimic male roles; rather, women should be able to bring their femaleness into society either in the jobs they choose or by adapting male jobs to themselves.

Identity vs. role-confusion (adolescent/genital stage, ages 12–18). The next stage in which Erikson emphasizes a crucial role for sex differences is the adolescent stage of identity vs. role-confusion. Erikson, like Freud, describes the male adolescent as successfully identifying with the father, repressing related hostilities and fears, and maintaining an affectionate relationship with his mother. The male adolescent's latent bisexuality is now oriented toward the masculine/active pole so that he can engage in "appropriately" heterosexual relationships. He is experiencing the pain and pleasure of puberty. The possibility of being an adult genitally brings the social demands of adulthood and requires, according to Erikson, a new level of ego-synthesis and integration unlike any prior resolution. An expanded social context introduces adolescents to new identifications, roles, rules, demands, and opportunities for growth and change.

The process of identity formation in Erikson's scheme of development is not a simple additive function of childhood experiences, biological maturation, and ego-growth; it is rather:

> . . . an evolving configuration—a configuration that gradually integrates constitutional givens, idiosyncratic libidinal needs, favored capacities, significant identifications, effective defenses, successful sublimations, and consistent roles. All of these, however, can only emerge from a mutual adaptation of individ-

ual potentials, technological worldviews, and religious or political ideologies (Erikson, 1982, p. 74).

Thus, adolescent identity resolution is neither a complete break from nor total continuity with the past. Gender is one significant element, among many, to be integrated into a new personality configuration. For a woman, gender-related issues include both the recognition of an inner space—child-bearing capacities and responsibilities—as well as the integration of this self-knowledge into an identity and life-choices.

In Erikson's theory, the female adolescent finds her experience of her anatomy particularly salient in resolving her identity. "Inner space," however, is only one aspect of identity formation. The adolescent female, like the adolescent male, can experience a time of moratorium in which careers and ideological concerns are pondered and pursued. The female's moratorium, like that of the male, ends when she chooses a path which integrates her abilities, social responsibilities, and anatomy. In the woman's case, however, many of her life-choices may be intertwined, since one aspect of a woman's social responsibility, in most cultures, is motherhood. According to Erikson (1968):

> But since a woman is never not-a-woman she can see her long-range goals only in those modes of activity which include and integrate her natural dispositions . . . . As an individual person, finally, she utilizes her (biologically given) inclinations and her (technologically and politically given) opportunities to make the decision which would render her life most continuous and meaningful without failing the task of motherhood and citizenship (pp. 290–291).

It is remarkable to us that Erikson implies that motherhood is an indispensable element in women's identity struggle, yet barely mentions fatherhood as a male identity issue. Rewording the above quotation for the male—that is, that the man "make[s] the decision which would render [his] life most continuous and meaningful without failing the task of [fatherhood] and citizenship"—we would complain either that (a) Erikson's theory has not led us to an adequate explanation or understanding of the relation between the male identity crisis and male sexuality, or (b) that a consideration of fatherhood in the context of a discussion of adolescent identity is somehow absurd. The quotation appears to reflect a case of values and attitutes toward women permeating the theory and/or a theory failing to account equally for the life-experience of both sexes.

In Erikson's theory, the male is no less embedded in the dictates of anatomy and history than is the female; both male and female development can be hampered or enhanced by these dictates. Erikson himself seems bewildered by the impact of sex on psychosocial personality development in our society:

> But it is clear where in girls a certain inner directedness and, indeed, a certain self-contained strength and peace was cultivated, they were also forced to abandon (and sometimes later overdo) much of the earlier locomotor vigor and the social and intellectual initiative and intrusiveness which, potentially girls share with boys; while most boys in pursuing the male role beyond what comes naturally have to dissimulate and to disavow what receptivity and intuitiveness they shared with the girls. How each sex overdeveloped what was given; how each compensated for what it had to deny; how each managed to get special approbation for a divided self-image; and to what extent "oppressor" and "oppressed" (beyond the blatant arrangements for political and economic dominance) colluded with each other in enslaving each other and themselves—that is what I mean by the deals which men and women must learn to study and discuss (Erikson, 1974, pp. 382–383).

It is interesting that Erikson appears to be describing two major orientations here, one focused on intrusion and individuation, the other on receptivity and attachment, and that he sees the abandonment of either orientation by members of a particular gender as a "deal" and a form of enslavement. As we shall demonstrate later, these two orientations and their relation with gender are not effectively handled within the theory.

Although males and females may focus on different areas of concern in adolescence, identity formation, in Erikson's view, is more closely related to a *process* of questioning and synthesizing than to the actual content of the deliberation. Nevertheless, sex differences in the content of adolescent experience need to be analyzed in terms of their implications for Erikson's theory as it is currently elaborated. Gilligan (1982), in a critique of Eriksonian (and other) theories, suggests that

> From the different dynamics of separation and attachment in their gender-identity formation through the divergence of identity and intimacy that marks their experience in the adolescent years, male and female voices typically speak of the importance of different truths, the former of the role of separation as it

defines and empowers the self, the latter of the ongoing process of attachment that creates and sustains the human community (p. 156).

Although Gilligan is oversimplifying when she equates Erikson's concepts of identity and intimacy with the more general notions of separation and attachment, she does provide a clue to an important unelaborated element in Erikson's scheme—the epigenesis of attachment. Erikson's "person" exists in an expanding social context to which she or he is always connected; this connectedness, which for Erikson is an important component in development, does not adequately convey the relational aspects of attachment. However, the "connections" which Erikson emphasizes (except, perhaps, in his treatment of the trust and intimacy stages) are to an expanding series of "institutions"—the family, school, society, etc. While Erikson locates development clearly within a social "niche," he does not provide a clear picture of how individuals become progressively able to form intimate dyadic bonds characterized by openness, reciprocity, and sharing. Thus, Erikson's theory provides a framework for understanding how successful identity development produces adults who are productive citizens with commitments to the institutions of their society; however, the theory, through its neglect of attachment issues, does not provide a framework for understanding how the individual moves from the dependency of the trust/mistrust stage to the mature interdependence of the intimacy stage.

Transition to adulthood. According to Erikson, "ideal" identity stage resolution for both males and females advances them toward becoming and functioning as well-adjusted adults—that is, toward becoming creative, productive, and procreative, as well as being concerned for the well-being of the next generation. The key contribution of the identity stage to the later stages is the sense of fidelity. The capacity to give fidelity to work, to beliefs, and to other persons arises from the ability to make choices based on an awareness of one's own self; the female's choice of a husband or a career necessitates the same kind of ego-resolution as males achieve. Stereotyped interpersonal relationships or overinvestment in social, artistic, or occupational tasks reflect inadequate identity-resolution for either sex and hamper the formation of truly intimate and generative relationships.

The healthy adolescent, in Freudian terms, is becoming the genital adult with the capacities for love and work. Erikson argues that genitality—as defined by the capacity for heterosexual mutually orgasmic sexual relations—is too narrow a concept to account for the experience of adult intimacy and generativity. Erikson believes that development beyond genitality is necessary to ensure the nurturing of the following generation: identity is turned toward an "other" in the intimate relationship, and, in turn, develops into concern for the next generation.

Intimacy vs. isolation (young adulthood). The intimacy of the young adult stage of intimacy vs. isolation, according to Erikson, involves an ability to make and keep commitments to relationships, with the recognition that these commitments will involve "significant sacrifices and compromises" (Erikson, 1963, p. 263). Love, the ego-strength of this stage, is expressed by mutual concern and commitment. To the extent that it can bridge the adolescent polarization of maleness and femaleness, love is the achievement that facilitates a full expression of sexuality. Intimacy, for both Freud and Erikson, implies a valuing of genital, heterosexual experience. True intimacy involves recognition of, allowance for, and enjoyment of genital differences as well as a willingness to risk the ego-synthesis of the identity stage to form a new, joint identity with another person. Intimacy, then, involves not only relationships with others but intimacy with oneself—in the sense that a knowledge of and security with oneself (identity) is a necessary consolidation prior to intimacy with others. Love, according to Erikson (Erikson & Erikson, 1981), is not found through "intimacies" (sexuality, relationships) when those "intimacies" are an attempt to gain a sense of one's own identity.

A controversial issue for Erikson and readers of Erikson (e.g., Chodorow, 1974; Gilligan, 1982; Janeway, 1971; Millett, 1970) is the relation between identity and intimacy in women. From a careful analysis of Erikson's writing on identity, it is clear that he believes that resolution of identity issues prior to intimacy issues is as crucial for women as for men. Excessively early commitments to another person prior to identity resolution would have profound (negative) implications for negotiating later adult issues. Erikson (1980) emphasizes that, for women, being in a relationship and having children (which have in the past been labeled by some authors as forms of "intimacy") is not the same as being able to care for children in the context of a loving faithful relationship; neither does male occupational commitment ensure the capacity to be intimate. Women, like men, must develop fidelity in order to become truly intimate and generative.

Erikson's statements regarding such issues as woman's inner space, his ties with psychoanalytic theory, and his vagueness concerning woman's identity (including remarks to the effect that women find their identity through relationships) are identified by his critics as evidence that Erikson says either that (a) women have less adequate identity resolution than males, or (b) that there may be a separate developmental sequence for females in which intimacy precedes identity. The key to the validity of either of these conclusions lies in the concept of "inner space." As we have stated earlier, Erikson believes that the positive development of females through the psychosexual and psychosocial stages is made possible by the "inner space." The concept of "inner space," when combined with Erikson's stress on autonomous ego-functioning, allows for a theoretical argument that females can and do adequately resolve their identity issues. Even if women (or men) are involved in or overly concerned with adolescent relationships, these relationships, according to Erikson, are identity-seeking and are qualitatively different from the type of intimate relationships that follow identity resolution. Once again, although adolescents may differ in the content of their identity issues (due to such factors as individual experiences of Soma and Polis and differently evolving Psyches), the process (questioning) and the outcome (virtue) of the identity stage is similar. The ideal stage sequence whereby identity precedes intimacy is the same regardless of sex.

What *is* problematic for women's identity, though, is the cultural support (or lack thereof) for adequate resolution of earlier developmental issues. Although many men also struggle through identity issues without satisfactory resolution and may be unable to be intimate or generative, it may be that as a group women have, in their identity resolution, suffered from more obstacles than men. Female development becomes more complicated when one considers society's expectations for the particular roles the female is to fulfill. Erikson (Evans, 1967) comments:

> All this is a little more complicated with women because women, at least in yesterday's cultures, had to keep their identities incomplete until they knew their man. Yet, I would think that a woman's identity develops out of the very way in which she looks around and selects the person with whose budding identity she can polarize her own. Her selection is already an expression of her identity, even if she seems to become totally absorbed in somebody else's life (p. 49).

A woman's disposition to care or to value relationships does not preclude her involvement in a career or ideological involvements. Erikson (1974) admits that exploitation of and prejudice against women exists yet suggests that the solution is not that women take on men's roles. Erikson claims, instead "it is as yet unpredictable what the tasks and roles, opportunities and job specifications will be once women are not merely adapted to male jobs in economics and politics but learn to adapt jobs to themselves. Such a revolutionary reappraisal may even lead to the insight that jobs now called masculine force men, too, into inhuman adjustments" (p. 361).

In summary, intimacy stage issues involve sex differences in a number of ways—(a) the possibility of a premature step into intimacy (without adequate identity resolution) by women because of cultural norms for motherhood and wifehood; (b) the importance of the recognition of sex differences in order for heterosexual, mutually orgasmic relationships to occur; (c) an emphasis on heterosexuality, showing disregard or disavowal of singleness or homosexuality as acceptable forms of adulthood; (d) the division of sexual activity by sex, which may be extended into a division of other roles by sex (e.g., household, work, etc.). Such a sex differentiation of roles, according to Erikson, prepares the intimate couple for the next life-stage, that of generativity.

Generativity vs. stagnation (adulthood). Erikson's concept of generativity, like intimacy, embraces Freud's notion of what the normal person should do well—love and work. However, Erikson's (Evans, 1967) description of generativity goes beyond genital love and work productiveness to focus on the ego-strength of caring: "I use 'care' in a sense which includes 'to care to do' something, to 'care for' somebody, to 'take care of' that which needs protection and attention, and 'to take care not to' do something destructive (p. 53). The caring of the generative adult is a unique ego-synthesis of psychosexual and psychosocial demands beyond genitality, identity, or intimacy.

Erikson (1963, 1968) suggests that the generativity stage is a psychosexual as well as a psychosocial stage; he believes this notion is supported by psychobiological observations of nonhuman, mammalian parents as well as by the disposition of children to play at caretaking (e.g., girls playing with dolls). As already noted, the roots of a girl's generativity can be found in her awareness of her "inner space" in the phallic stage. Erikson (Erikson & Erikson, 1981) assumes that males also have a disposition for generativity, even though he does not locate its biological roots. Although female anatomy is most clearly relevant to the productivity of bearing children, to Erikson males as well as females are libidinally oriented to care for their own or others' children.

At the generative stage, one's own life-cycle becomes enmeshed with the life-cycle of the next generation, which is dependent on the older generation for sustenance—physical, social, psychological, emotional. The generative adult must be ready to "feed"—literally and figuratively—the younger generation. The care expressed by the generative adult can take many forms. In Erikson's earlier writings (1963, 1968), it appeared that females were more likely to express procreative generativity, while males were more likely to express productive and creative generativity. It becomes apparent in Erikson's later writing (1974; Erikson & Erikson, 1981) that both work and procreation can occur with or without generative caring; it is not so much the form generativity takes that is crucial to development but the internal orientation to be caring. Development, for males and females, is a matter of integration and reintegration of stage-relevant issues into the ever evolving personality; in adulthood, this might include reintegration of different aspects of identity— work, sex, politics, or religion—so as to reflect the changing demands of one's life-situation (that is, parenthood).

The generative stage, like the identity stage, can reflect what Erikson (1974) calls "collusions"—the "deals" which men and women have made with each other—ostensibly to meet individual needs. One of these collusions is expressed in society's overemphasis, historically, on sex specific roles, functions, traits, and identities which limit the female's generativity to procreation and the male's to work productivity. Blocks to generativity—whether as a result of problems in earlier stages of development or current problems with the issues of generativity—result in stagnation, self-absorption, and, ultimately, the passing on of problems of development from one generation to the next.

Erikson states that the core issue of a woman's identity commitment stems from the libidinal demand to bear and care for the offspring of a chosen man. This commitment constitutes the core issue, whether or not it is combined with a career or actual children. Erikson's conceptualization of identity (fidelity) in women can be understood as assuming that part of the identity struggle of women (not men) includes the integration of women's unique ability to bear children. However, he also appears to assume that the problem— for personality theory—is to account for the developmental, psychological, and sociological meaning of the biological capacity for care.

We believe that Erikson has had some success in liberating his theory from some of the "anatomy is destiny" shackles of the theory that fathered his own (that is, psychoanalytic theory). However, Erikson's theory remains incomplete—not so much because it is a male theory as because it fails to explain adequately how an individual can become truly intimate and generative through the identity pathway of development. Erikson has seen human development from the perspective of adolescence and individuation, yet in that exclusive focus he has neglected the important growth of the capacity for attachment. One could even argue that Erikson's theory represents progress from an extremely masculine sex typed orientation (in Freudian theory) towards a more androgynous perspective, but that instead of integrating "masculine" and "feminine" concerns Erikson juxtaposes them by focusing on individuation in his childhood stages and attachment (intimacy and generativity) in his adult stages. This lack of integration appears to be related to Erikson's difficulty in resolving the implications of sex for his theoretical constructs (and vice versa). The goal of the remainder of this paper is to begin the discussion of gender in personality again by pursuing one issue—the possibility of a developmental pathway for attachment that parallels and interacts with the pathway of identity described by Erikson. Our analysis constitutes an attempt to synthesize into Erikson's theory what has been considered a female mode of development (attachment).

Individuation and Attachment: Modifying Erikson's Theory

Erikson, in a 1974 critique of his earlier (1968) paper on "Womanhood and the inner space" wrote to Jean Strouse, the editor of a psychoanalytic anthology on women:

> You may remember the Vermont farmer whom I quote as saying to a motorist what critics often say less succinctly: "Well now, if I wanted to go where you wanted to go, I wouldn't start from here." With your anthology in hand like a map, it is clearer why I couldn't possibly be anywhere else and that, considering where I came from, I was doing all right being where I was (p. 367).

In one sense, Erikson believed his personality theory had made major advances beyond psychoanalytic theory through the synthesis of concepts such as psychosocial crises, life-span development and ego-autonomy. His construct of the "inner space" made a positive, healthy female development possible within a modified psychoanalytic framework; anatomy was relegated to one aspect of a tripartite system—anatomy plus personality (ego) plus history is destiny. This system, however, still contributes to the maintenance of sex stereotypes. On the other hand, we believe that inadequacies in Erikson's theory become apparent through an analysis of his views on sex. Erikson's theory is most complete as a description of the process of identity development whereby a person's ego becomes increasingly individuated; the theory is most clear, perhaps, when it deals with male ego-development. Although this process of individuation occurs within a social context providing a form of connectedness, we argue that the forms of connectedness Erikson describes are forms associated with an orientation toward individuation rather than toward attachment. When we think of the demands and positive outcomes of the early stages of development—autonomy, initiative, industry, and identity—in relation to the demands and virtues of the adult stages—intimacy (to love) and generativity (to care)—we might well ask: "*Can* you get there from here?"

To answer this question, it is important to understand Erikson's notion of the epigenetic principle. In discussing the classic "epigenetic diagram" of his eight stages of personality development, Erikson (1968) notes the following: "(1) that each item of the vital personality . . . is systematically related to all others, and that they all depend on the proper development in the proper sequence of each item, and (2) that each item exists in some form before 'its' decisive and critical time normally arrives" (p. 93, 95).

The clear implication of this position is that intimacy and generativity, like the components of personality that emerge before them, and integrity, which emerges subsequently, exist from the beginning. Indeed, if we take Erikson's approach seriously, every state preceding the stages of intimacy and generativity represents a step in the evolution of intimacy and generativity, with their attendant virtues of love and care. Again, the question is, "Can we get there from here?"

We believe that Erikson's portrayal of the path to generativity is incomplete. It is clear from Erikson's theory that to achieve generativity, one must have successfully resolved both the identity crisis of adolescence and the intimacy crisis of young adulthood. The evolution of identity has been described by Erikson in detail. That is, much of his theorizing has focused on how, true to the epigenetic principle, the developmental stages that begin at birth lead up to and influence the outcome of the adolescent identity crisis—and how that crisis recapitulates the crises of earlier stages. Very little attention has been paid, however, to the precursors of the processes of attachment that would seem essential to intimacy and generativity. In Erikson's epigenetic sequence, there is very much the implication of a single developmental path whereby the healthy personality or ego begins by being trusting and then becomes autonomous, initiating, industrious, committed to an identity, intimate, generative, and finally having integrity. Although Erikson asserts that each component of the personality and each vital ego-strength or virtue has its own developmental history as well as its own time of ascendence, the only developmental pathway described in real depth is identity formation. Considering whence he began, we agree with Erikson's feeling that "he was doing all right being where he was" (particularly in his elaboration of a heuristic approach to the life-span); at another level, however, we think there is a long way to go before Erikson's theory can be seen as complete. One step in this direction is to formulate a description of the intrapsychic development of attachment.

Modifications of Erikson's Epigenetic Chart

Perhaps one solution to problems with Erikson's theory is simply to fill in a row and column (which he suggests is possible) of his classic epigenetic chart so that processes of attachment receive as much emphasis as processes of identity-formation. Erikson has discussed the antecedents of generativity in terms of the libidinal instinctual urge to procreate—as is expressed by the female's early discovery of her "inner space" and the concomitant predisposition to care; the "sense of generativity" is, as we discussed in the preceding pages, present from early in development. Building on Erikson's own statements about generativity, as well as his description of the "social modalities" associated with each stage, we have tentatively modified one version of Erikson's epigenetic chart to include material on attachment which parallels Erikson's material on identity formation. (See Figure 1.)

In Figure 1, the diagonal (from top left to bottom right), the fifth column and the fifth row are all traditional components of Erikson's portrayal of the epigenetic cycle—representing, in turn, the eight psychosocial stages (on the diagonal), the forms which the "sense of identity" takes during each of these life stages (the fifth column) and the antecedents and consequences of the identity vs. identity diffusion crisis during the other stages (the fifth row). These components are classic features of Erikson's epigenetic chart, designed to illustrate his notions about the epigenetic process of identity formation. To the Eriksonian diagram we have added material in the seventh row and seventh column to illustrate the forms which the "sense of generativity" takes in other life stages as well as the antecedents of generativity.

A brief overview of representative Eriksonian statements about early forms of attachment should help clarify our expansion of the identity pathway to include elements of generativity. These state-

Figure 1. Adaptation of Erikson's epigenetic chart to illustrate developmental pathway of intimacy and manifestations of sense of intimacy in other psychosocial stages.

Age periods during which normative psychosocial crises occur	Stage Issues Characterizing Each Age Period							
	1	2	3	4	5	6	7	8
I Infancy	Trust vs. Mistrust				Unipolarity vs. premature self-differentiation		Acceptance and Primitive Identification vs. Rejection of Generative Parent	
II Early Childhood		Autonomy vs. Shame, Doubt			Bipolarity vs. Autism		Secure Attachment vs. Narcissism	
III Play age			Initiative vs. Guilt		Play Identification vs. (Oedipal) Fantasy Identities		Imaginative Playfulness and Identifications vs. Inhibition	
IV School age				Industry vs. Inferiority	Work Identification vs. Identity Foreclosure		Secure Sense of Extendable Self and Comradeship vs. Duty Dependence	

	Time Perspective vs. Time Diffusion	Self-certainty vs. Identity Confusion	Role Experimentation vs. Negative Identity	Anticipation of Achievement vs. Work Paralysis	Identity vs. Identity Diffusion	Sexual Identity vs. Bisexual Diffusion	Leadership Polarization vs. Authority Diffusion	Ideological Polarization vs. Diffusion of Ideals
V Adolescent	Time Perspective vs. Time Diffusion	Self-certainty vs. Identity Confusion	Role Experimentation vs. Negative Identity	Anticipation of Achievement vs. Work Paralysis	Identity vs. Identity Diffusion	Sexual Identity vs. Bisexual Diffusion	Leadership Polarization vs. Authority Diffusion	Ideological Polarization vs. Diffusion of Ideals
VI Young Adult					Solidarity vs. Social Isolation	Intimacy vs. Isolation	*Embeddedness in social networks vs. Solitariness*	
VII Adulthood	*Symbiosis or Interdependence vs. Withdrawal*	*Pleasure in Social Relations vs. Self-insistence*	*Sense of Equality of Worth and Companionship vs. Jealousy and Rage*	*Cooperation and a Sense of a Shared World vs. Self-restraint*	Interdependence and Tolerance vs. Totalitarianism (over/under identifications)	Communality vs. Pseudointimacy	Generativity vs. Self-absorption	*Human Connectedness vs. Rejection and Humanity*
VIII Mature age								Integrity vs. Disgust, Despair

Note:—Italicized terms represent the authors' additions of the early forms and antecedents of attachment to Erikson's epigenetic chart. Adapted from *Identity and the life cycle* by Erik H. Erikson, with the permission of the publisher, W. W. Norton & Company, Inc.
Copyright © 1980 by W. W. Norton & Company, Inc.
Copyright © 1959 by International Universities Press, Inc.

ments, however, are not theoretically elaborated or integrated by Erikson into his stages or identity sequence; they merely suggest or hint at the importance of attachment.

Infancy (0–16 months). Erikson has noted that the groundwork for later generativity is established in the very first life stage (trust vs. mistrust). Specifically, he states ". . . in *getting what is given* and in learning to *get somebody* to give what is wished for, the infant also develops the necessary ego-groundwork to, some day, get to be a giver." (Erikson, 1980, p. 23, emphasis his.) Indeed, in one discussion of his epigenetic chart, Erikson himself has posed the question "How could anything like generativity appear?" in the row associated with infancy. His answer is that "after all, if this is infancy then the infant depends on the mother's generativity first and must experience from the very beginning, even if in a most rudimentary way, a very basic identification with that person who cares about and for it" (Erikson & Erikson, 1981, p. 252). Thus, the sense of generativity is experienced by the child both internally (libidinal) and externally (from the mother). (A future discussion of generativity needs to analyze the deficits and long term consequences of the over- or undergenerative mother.)

Drawing from Erikson's statements, we can tentatively formulate some descriptors of the "sense" of generativity during the first stage as "acceptance and primitive identification vs. rejection" of the generative parent (Figure 1, row 1, column 7). [Although Erikson refers to an early form of identification here, we think that the term identification has too many conceptual links to later developmental processes and use of the term would lead to confusion if used here.] The antecedent to mature generativity (Figure 1, row 7, column 1) from this stage is a type of mother-child mutuality which could be labeled "symbiosis and interdependence vs. withdrawal."

Toddlerhood (17–36 months). According to Erikson, the second life stage is characterized by a severe test of the processes of mutual regulation between parent and child. In reference to the social modalities associated with this stage, Erikson notes that "to hold" can be a destructive and cruel retaining and restraining or a pattern of caring (as captured by the phrase "to have and to hold"). Moreover, the related modality, "to let go," can involve an unleashing of destructive forces or a relaxed attitude of "letting pass" or "letting be." Erikson sees this stage as decisive for the ratio between loving good will vs. hateful self-insistence and between cooperation and willfulness. We have transposed these stage 2 issues into a generative sense of secure attachment vs. narcissism (row 2, column 7) and an antecedent to generativity in the form of the child's "beginning pleasure in and desire for social relations vs. self insistence" (row 7, column 2).

Early childhood. Associated with stage 3 in Erikson's theory are the sexual and social modalities of intrusion and inclusion—both of which are seen by Erikson as "developmentally essential for both boys and girls" (1980, p. 35). The inclusive mode—for both sexes—can be expressed through taking care of oneself and younger children, receptivity and tender identification. According to Erikson, the inclusive mode may also express itself in the often surprising alternation of aggression (associated with the intrusive mode) and readiness to form "tender and protective relationships" with peers and smaller children. In this stage the child develops the prerequisites for the later differentiation of roles that Erikson attributes to generativity as well as finding an arena for exuberant imaginative playfulness in the company of peers. "Imaginative playfulness and identifications vs. inhibition (self-restriction)" (row 3, column 7) seem to be early manifestations of the sense of generativity while "a sense of equality of worth and companionship vs. jealousy and rage" (row 7, column 3) can be seen as stage 3 antecedents to generativity.

Childhood. In discussing stage 4 (industry vs. inferiority), Erikson puts considerable emphasis on mastery of the technology of a society. Although this stage is distinct from earlier stages in its lack of psychosexual upheaval, it is "socially a most decisive stage" which can provide a "lasting basis for cooperative participation in productive adult life" (Erikson, 1980, p. 93). A successful entry into the realm of school, peers, and new adults with concomitant new attachments is based on the child's previously developed trust and a recently developed sense of self that can be safely extended into this broader social world. In Figure 1 we have identified "secure sense of extendable self and comradeship vs. duty-dependence" as early forms of the sense of generativity and "cooperation in a world shared with others vs. excessive self-restraint" as the stage 4 antecedents of generativity.

Adolescence. Erikson himself identified "leadership polarization vs. authority diffusion" as the form which the sense of generativity takes during the adolescent stage (stage 5). Along with his emphasis on values of individuation, Erikson (1968) acknowledges "tolerance" and interdependence as attributes of a "democratic identity" which he counterparts to the "simple and cruel totalitarian doctrines" which may have appeal to young people from countries which have lost (or are losing) their group identities. This tolerance for others is based on the young person's capacity for self-tolerance; "it is difficult to be tolerant if deep down you are not sure that you are a man (or a

woman), . . . and that you will know how to make the right decisions
. . . " (Erikson, 1968, p. 98). This capacity for tolerance or democratic interdependence is an orientation of the self toward others
and becomes a core aspect of the potential for mutually satisfying
relationships (sexual and otherwise). For the adolescent antecedent
of generativity we would suggest, then, "tolerance and interdependence vs. totalitarianism."

Adulthood. In his discussions of generativity, Erikson makes frequent reference to the issues of identity and intimacy which directly
precede the crisis of generativity vs. self-absorption. As we already
noted, the connections between intimacy and generativity appear
most obvious and coherent. To round out our expansion of the
epigenetic chart, we have identified "communality vs. pseudo-inti-
macy" as the antecedent to generativity and "embeddedness in social
networks vs. solitariness" as the prior sense of generativity. Finally,
we find support in Erikson's writings for the notion of "human
connectedness vs. rejection of humanity" as the consequent of generativity in the final life stage.

Such an expansion of the Eriksonian model might contribute a
great deal to our understanding of how well-functioning adults
become capable of both love and work, how they become both
attached and individuated. We believe that many committed Erik-
sonians would see such an elaboration as all that would be needed
to provide a complete account of a developmental history of attachment which complements the epigenesis of identity. However, we
also believe that this expansion does not solve the limitations in
Erikson's model. One problem stems from the fact that there is a
single diagonal, a single developmental path composed of the eight
strands representing the eight fundamental human conflicts, a single
developmental path in which strands of individuation (autonomy,
initiative, and industry) predominate through childhood, only to
relinquish their predominance, somehow, to the adult expressions
or achievements (love and care) of a connectedness which seems to
imply vital attachments. Erikson does not convince us that the
developmental path to identity will also prepare the young adult to
be intimate.

A second problem is that Erikson's treatment of the content of the
adult stages also seems to be incomplete. Leaving aside the issue of
integrity (the crisis of old age), more is missing in Erikson's discussion
of intimacy and generativity than a full description of their antecedents, consequences, and expressions ("part conflicts") in all the other
stages. Acknowledged but scarcely developed are intimacy as sharing, openness, and caring, and generativity as part of a vital, trans-

actional family process. Virtually omitted are alternative forms of intimate sexual relationships and nonsexual intimate relationships such as friendship. To account adequately for intimacy and generativity as major adult developmental tasks, Erikson needs, we believe, not simply to fill in another vertical and horizontal in his chart, but to elaborate a second developmental strand, that of attachment, which has its own birth to death history. Attachment, in addition, is a part of the development of personality that is decisive for and essential to adult identity (cf. Mahler). We propose that a two-strand "double helix" model of development can be formulated drawing primarily on the constructs of Erikson but also incorporating concepts from other theorists where Erikson is most incomplete. It may be argued that an eight-path model—one for each stage—could rightfully be developed; however, we believe that the two types of development—individuation and attachment—can account for most of the intrapersonal life-span change.

A Two-Path Model of Development

Erikson has suggested that his epigenetic chart might best be expressed as a *helix*—that is, a "three-dimensional curve that lies on a cylinder or cone and cuts the elements at a constant angle; . . . any spiral form or structure . . . " (Webster, 1979, p. 527). Other theorists (e.g., see Kegan, 1982) have also used such a model to describe development. We believe, however, that to account fully for "healthy" human development, even in Erikson's own terms, the field might better be served by the model of a *double helix* in which two separate but interconnected strands of psychological individuation and attachment ascend in a spiral representing the life-cycle. Each stage represents an intrapsychic developmental change in both individuation and attachment; experiences in any one realm will have ramifications for the other. Like the twisted strands making up a rope, tension on one strand will pull the other.

Building directly on concepts derived from Erikson's model, we have constructed a tentative preliminary model of a two-path model of life-span development. If one accepts Erikson's notion that there are eight stages of development, each defined by a particular psychosocial crisis and contributing to the evolution of a particular psychological virtue (or ego-strength), then a model with two strands or threads could take the form outlined in Figure 2. As can be seen in Figure 2, the crises characterizing the individuation strand are generally the same as those described by Erikson, except for intimacy and generativity, which have been shifted to the attachment strand.

Figure 2. Tentative adaptation of Erikson's theory to a two-path model.

	Infancy	Early Childhood	Play Age	School Age	Adolescence	Young Adulthood	Adulthood	Old Age
Individuation Pathway	Trust vs. Mistrust	Autonomy vs. Shame, Doubt	Initiative vs. Guilt	Industry vs. Inferiority	Identity vs. Identity Diffusion	Career and Life-style Exploration vs. Drifting	Life-style Consolidation vs. Emptiness	Integrity vs. Despair
Attachment Pathway	Trust vs. Mistrust	Object & Self-constancy vs. Loneliness & Helplessness	Playfulness vs. Passivity or Aggression	Empathy and Collaboration vs. Excessive Caution or Power	Mutuality Interdependence vs. Alienation	Intimacy vs. Isolation	Generativity vs. Self-absorption	Integrity vs. Despair

New crises have been identified as characteristic of the individuation path during the young adult and adult stages, and of the attachment path during most of the other stages.

This preliminary and very tentative outline of a stage model comprising two threads of development represents the introduction of concepts drawn partly from Selman's (1981) work on interpersonal competence and from object-relations theory (Horner, 1979; Mahler, 1968; Mahler & McDevitt, 1980; and McDevitt & Mahler, 1980) into a framework drawn primarily from Erikson. All three approaches cite and indeed draw upon the developmental notions of Jean Piaget to reinforce their own conceptions of development. Moreover, in all three approaches, it is assumed that psychological structures evolve through an ongoing transactional process between organism and environment—including, especially, the interpersonal environment. It is primarily because Erikson has not specifically developed a separate eight-stage pathway for attachment that we needed to draw on other frameworks for notions concerning the development of attachment relationships during infancy and childhood. While Selman provided a useful framework for conceptualizing sociocognitive development (Selman, 1976) and the development of interpersonal negotiation strategies (Selman, 1981) from the grade school years on, he, like other sociocognitive and ego-developmental theorists, treats the earliest years of life as a stage zero—that is a stage characterized more by the absence of any capacity for relatedness than by core elements of the capacity for relatedness that will develop. Object-relations theory, by contrast (particularly object-relations theory as it has been developed by such psychoanalytic thinkers as Horner, 1979; Mahler, 1968; Mahler & McDevitt, 1980; and McDevitt & Mahler, 1980) has a good deal to say about infantile relationships and their role in development. Thus, these two frameworks together, despite some important differences in general theoretical assumptions, were a source of constructs drawn for their consistency with Eriksonian theory and relevance to preadult relationships.

Infancy (0–16 months). In turning to object-relations theory to find a foundation for attachment in infancy, we are not suggesting that object-relations theory provides the only or even the best starting point for the elaboration of a second strand of development. However, the approach does provide a fairly well-elaborated starting point; it is a framework in which considerable attention has been given to the intrapsychic aspects of relationships, particularly during the earliest years of life.

While Erikson and the object-relations theorists often use a very different language, they seem to be in considerable agreement that the first 16 months of life are characterized by the emergence of attachment and the roots of identity-formation. In particular, the infant moves from a period of normal autism to normal symbiosis in which the child experiences a partnership with its mother which provides relief and gratification of needs. Mahler and McDevitt (1980) use Lichtenstein's expression that the child now "becomes the child of his particular mother." For the next 10 months the child's internal experience of separation and individuation of the self occurs with mother as the central framework for differentiation. The child's successful attempts at autonomy (e.g., playing away from the mother) occur in the context of the reliable availability and accessibility of the mother. McDevitt & Mahler (1980) note, for example, that an adequate degree of trust and confidence, and successful early identifications from this period, are essential prerequisites for the later emergence of both object-constancy (a stable love object) and self-constancy (a solid sense of self) and, ideally, a sense of self-esteem.

Comparing Erikson's approach with that of Mahler and McDevitt, it is evident that both approaches emphasize the importance of a close, secure relationship between mother and child at this stage. The descriptor of the attachment crisis as well as the individuation crisis of the first stage of life remains "trust vs. mistrust" (Figure 2).

Early childhood (17–36 months). Paralleling Erikson's early childhood stage of autonomy vs. shame and doubt, one finds, in object-relations theory, the emergence of self- and object-constancy. According to McDevitt and Mahler (1980), libidinal object-constancy implies: (a) a primarily positive attachment to a maternal representation, (b) an integration of "good" and "bad" (including, we suggest, "trustworthy" and "untrustworthy") components of the maternal representation, and (c) the achievement of a maternal image which is intrapsychically available to the child in the same way as the actual mother is available—that is, for sustenance, comfort, and love. This libidinal object-constancy, according to McDevitt (McDevitt & Mahler, 1980), "has its origins in infancy, begins to be attained in the third year [that is, 24 to 36 months]" (p. 408).

Using the language of McDevitt and Mahler, we will identify the second stage in the attachment pathway as the crisis over object-constancy. McDevitt and Mahler indicate that a successful resolution of this crisis in the third year of life provides relief from the "threats of helplessness and loneliness" as well as "a close relationship with . . . love objects" combined with "autonomy, individuation, self-constancy, and cohesiveness of the self" (p. 420). The child's rela-

tionship with the primary care-giver (love object) later in life provides a basis for mature relationships in which the other person is
esteemed, valued, and treated with consideration (McDevitt & Mahler, 1980). The crises of this stage represent particularly well the
interlocking relation between the attachment and individuation pathways: The toddler must have a new type of attachment to the mother
or care-giver in order to separate and become autonomous. Later in
life both the autonomy and the lessons of attachment contribute to
the adult capacities for love and work. McDevitt and Mahler (1980)
describe object-constancy as a process which, though becoming
functionally available by the age of three, "continues to develop
throughout childhood and adolescence, and in all probability is rarely
completely attained" (p. 408). The crisis of this phase may extend
into the third year of life and interfere with resolution of Oedipal
issues. As a result, we see object-constancy as overlapping two stages
in Erikson's model—early childhood (stage 2) and play age (stage
3).

Play age (ages 4–5 years). Mahler and McDevitt (1980) focus on
the child's structural intrapsychic changes from birth to approximately three years. In order to develop the next few stages of the
attachment pathway paralleling Erikson's identity pathway, we turn
to the work of Robert Selman (1981) on interpersonal competence—
a construct which goes beyond Selman's earlier work on sociocognitive development to account better for the affects and behaviors
that are part of the development of interpersonal competence. Drawing on Werner's (1964) orthogenetic approach and Piaget's (e.g.,
1932) notions of structural developmental change, as well as his own
field and clinical observations, Selman has identified four levels of
interpersonal understanding and behavioral negotiations (following
a stage zero). These cognitive developments, we believe, *permit*
developments in the child's capacity for and experience of relationships. Thus, Selman's levels of the child's interpersonal competence
can point the way to stages 3–6 of our attachment pathway.

During early childhood (corresponding to stage 3 or "initiative vs.
guilt" in Erikson's model), the child can understand that another
person has thoughts, feelings, and intentions separate from his or
her own. This differentiation includes and elaborates on the object-
constancy achieved around age 3 in Mahler and McDevitt's analysis
of child development. Although the child can recognize the other
person as psychologically separate, the child's perspective on relationships is essentially egocentric. The change in the child's internal
orientation toward self and others is manifested outwardly in the
changes that occur in play behavior during this stage—e.g., the

capacities for role playing either adult roles or those of the "family romance" or the switch from parallel play to cooperative play. Thus the cognitive shift allows for a new kind of relating. The playfulness of the child is not just an early attempt at "world" mastery (of *what* "I imagine I will be" [Erikson, 1968, p. 87]) but also *who* the child imagines she or he will be like and playfulness *with* other children. Thus, we can describe the attachment crisis of this stage as the capacity for playfulness vs. aggression and/or passivity.

School age (ages 6–12). The school age period (Erikson's stage 4: industry vs. inferiority) corresponds roughly with Selman's levels 2 and 3. In middle-childhood (level 2), the child goes beyond knowing that another person's subjective experience is distinct from his or her own, to a recognition that the other person can think about the child's own attitudes, feelings, and motives. The self and other each can be viewed as being self-reflective and reciprocal. Selman (1981) describes behavioral interactions at this level as manifesting a "tit-for-tat" self-interest. Level 3, interpersonal competence, includes the perspective-taking capacities of level 2, plus a new ability to see the other person as autonomous as well as related and interdependent. As a result of these new abilities relationships can be collaborative and mutually beneficial; how one's needs are met is based on communication and negotiation of "an equilibrated feeling between self and other" (Selman, 1981, p. 410).

These emerging capacities for mutuality, empathy, concern, and perspective-taking are not adequately accounted for in Erikson's description of the "industry" stage crisis or its resolution. All of these capacities, however, appear to be crucial elements in adult intimacy and generativity. To summarize the elements of the attachment crisis in the fourth stage, we have chosen "empathy and collaboration" vs. "excessive caution or power."

Adolescence and adulthood. Interpersonal orientation at Selman's level 4 (Erikson's stage 5: adolescence) integrates the aforementioned levels and includes a more sophisticated and complex knowledge of self and other as well as the interrelationship between the two. According to Selman (1981) "at level 4, affective and cognitive aspects of conduct are integrated by the self's capacity to identify in self and other, the relation between action and underlying affect and motives. . . . Higher levels reflect a [an observing] self that has the capacity to negotiate and communicate in ways that ultimately, over time, lead to the establishment of a mutual relationship" (p. 415). The adolescent functioning at higher levels is able to: (*a*) facilitate negotiation, (*b*) tolerate a broad range of emotions, (*c*) give and take, and finally, (*d*) perceive accurately, understand compassionately, and take action on the feelings of self and others. Again, these developments in interpersonal understanding should allow for new forms of relationship with others. In keeping with Selman, possible labels of the attachment crisis in adolescence could be described as "mutuality/interdependence vs. alienation."

Erikson's adult stages of intimacy and generativity follow nicely, we believe, on the earlier resolutions in the attachment pathway that we have just described. Now, when we ask the question "Can you get there from here?" the answer appears to be a clear "Yes." Moreover, the adult achievements on the identity pathway also seem to follow more coherently from such early crises as autonomy and initiative than was true in Erikson's original model. In addition, appropriate experiences of attachment foster individuation and vice versa. The proposed model also has the advantage of being conceptually consistent with Bakan's (1966) conception of two life modalities, agency and communion, and with Parson's notion (1964) that all social life is characterized by an instrumental/expressive division of function. While Bakan and Parsons, like Erikson, see one major modality (the intrusive, agentic, instrumental orientation) as linked with the male gender role and the other major modality (the receptive, communal, expressive orientation) as linked with the female gender role, all of the theorists acknowledge the possibility that both orientations can exist and be cultivated or suppressed in both sexes.

In research by one of the authors (White, Speisman, & Costos, 1983; White, Speisman, Jackson, Bartis, & Costos, in press), we have repeatedly found that gender role is more powerful than sex as a predictor of a number of individual and relationship variables. For example, we have found no statistically significant differences between men and women in either ego-development (related to processes of individuation) or intimacy development (related to processes of attachment). Moreover, even on measures of gender *role*, there are a dearth of sex differences: while men have scored somewhat higher than women in agency (measured through an adaptation of Bem's Sex Role Inventory), the genders do not differ on communion. Communion but not agency is related to intimacy maturity in both men and women. In a sample of married couples, communion in husbands is positively associated with intimacy maturity in their wives while communion in wives is negatively associated with their partner's intimacy maturity.

Also of relevance is the fact that despite a general dearth of sex differences on major individual and relationship variables, *patterns* of relationships among variables do vary greatly by sex. For example, gender role identity (agency, communion, and androgyny) is predicted by level of ego-development in men but not in women and by parental socialization practices in women but not in men. Intimacy maturity is associated with ego-development in women but not in men, and with marital adjustment in men but not in women. All of these findings suggest the importance to us of going beyond a simple search for sex differences in psychological functioning to an examination of the ways in which processes of individuation and attachment may be related to other psychological issues.

We believe that in psychological research, psychological variables—such as attachment and individuation—are more valuable to the goal of understanding psychological processes than are static, summarizing variables such as sex. Whether psychological processes are rooted in biology or socialization or both, the explanatory variables are likely to be *process* variables that are poorly represented by such global designations as male and female. We are not advocating that the goal of identifying and understanding sex differences in psychological functioning be abandoned. Instead, we are suggesting that research questions be phrased so that the potential role of psychological processes such as individuation and attachment can also be assessed—both independently and possibly in interaction with sex.

In his brief discussions of adulthood, Erikson often refers to the division of labor between men and women as well as the complementarity they bring to their relationships. There may indeed be different—and complementary—orientations, experiences, and roles that traditionally have been associated with sex. Traditionally, and to some extent currently, the developmental pathway of individuation may have been most emphasized in males, with a corresponding neglect of the separate but interconnected pathway of attachment. In females, the reverse pattern may hold true. We would argue that if, with changing times and mores, attachment processes were to undergo fuller development in men and individuation processes were to undergo fuller development in women, sex differences might become more elusive than ever, but individuation and attachment would retain their power as psychological variables associated with other psychological variables in important nomological nets.

Finally, Erikson's theory of identity development has been attacked at times on the grounds that it is more descriptive of male than of female development (Gilligan, 1982). This criticism may be historically/culturally accurate, but we would argue, instead, that the more serious weakness of the theory is that it emphasizes the development of the individuated, socially connected personality at the expense of the attached, interpersonally connected, care-oriented personality—and indeed, emphasizes one component of all personalities at the expense of the other component of all personalities.

References

Bakan, D. (1966). *The duality of human existence: Isolation and communion in Western man.* Boston: Beacon.

Carlson, R. (1972). Understanding women: Implications for personality theory and research. *Journal of Social Issues, 28*(2), 17–32.

Chodorow, N. (1974). Family structure and feminine personality. In M. Z. Rosaldo & L. Lamphere (Eds.), *Women, culture, and society* (pp. 43–66). Stanford: Stanford University Press.

Erikson, E. H. (1963). *Childhood and society* (2nd ed.). New York: W. W. Norton. (Original work published 1950)

Erikson, E. H. (1964). *Insight and responsibility.* New York: W. W. Norton.

Erikson, E. H. (1968). *Identity: Youth and crisis.* New York: W. W. Norton.

Erikson, E. H. (1974). Once more the inner space: Letter to former student. In J. Strouse (Ed.), *Women and analysis: Dialogues on psychoanalytic views of femininity* (pp. 365–387). New York: Dell.

Erikson, E. H. (1977). *Toys and reasons.* New York: W. W. Norton.

Erikson, E. H. (1978). Reflections on Dr. Borg's life cycle. In E. H. Erikson (Ed.), *Adulthood* (pp. 1–31). New York: W. W. Norton.

Erikson, E. H. (1980). *Identity and the life cycle.* New York: W. W. Norton.

Erikson, E. H. (1982). *The life cycle completed: A review.* New York: W. W. Norton.

Erikson, E. H., & Erikson, J. M. (1981). On generativity and identity: From a conversation with Erik and Joan Erikson. *Harvard Educational Review, 51,* 249–269.

Evans, R. (1967). *Dialogue with Erik Erikson.* New York: Harper & Row.

Gilligan, C. (1979). Women's place in man's life cycle. *Harvard Educational Review, 49*(4), 431–446.

Gilligan, C. (1982). *In a different voice: Psychological theory and women's development.* Cambridge, MA: Harvard University.

Horner, A. J. (1979). *Object relations and the developing ego in therapy.* New York: Jason Aronson.

Horney, K. (1973). The flight from womanhood. In H. Kelman (Ed.), *Feminine psychology* (pp. 54–70). New York: W. W. Norton. (Original work published 1926)

Janeway, E. (1971). *Man's world, woman's place.* New York: Morrow.

Kegan, R. (1982). *The evolving self: Problem and process in human development.* Cambridge, MA: Harvard University Press.

Mahler, M. S. (1968). *On human symbiosis and the vicissitudes of individuation: Vol. 1. Infantile psychosis.* New York: International Universities Press.

Mahler, M. S., & McDevitt, J. B. (1980) The separation-individuation process and identity formation. In S. I. Greenspan & G. H. Pollock (Eds.), *The course of life: Psychoanalytic contributions toward understanding personality development, Vol. 1: Infancy and early childhood* (pp. 395–406). National Institute of Mental Health.

McDevitt, J. B., & Mahler, M. S. (1980). Object constancy, individuality, and internalization. In S. I. Greenspan & G. H. Pollack (Eds.), *The course of life: Psychoanalytic contributions toward understanding personality development, Vol. 1: Infancy and early childhood* (pp. 407–423). National Institute of Mental Health.

Millett, K. (1970). *Sexual politics.* New York: Doubleday.

Mitchell, J. (1974). On Freud and the distinctions between the sexes. In J. Strouse (Ed.), *Women and analysis* (pp. 39–50). New York: Dell.

Parsons, T. (1964). *Social structure and personality.* New York: Free Press.

Piaget, J. (1932). *The moral judgment of the child.* New York: Free Press.

Selman, R. L. (1976). Toward a structural-developmental analysis of interpersonal relationship concepts: Research with normal and disturbed preadolescent boys. In A. Pick (Ed.), *Tenth annual Minnesota symposium on child psychology* (pp. 156–200). Minneapolis: University of Minnesota Press.

Selman, R. L. (1981). The development of interpersonal competence: The role of understanding in conduct. *Developmental Review*, 1, 404–422.

Strouse, J. (1974). *Women and analysis: Dialogues on psychoanalytic views of femininity.* New York: Dell.

Webster's new collegiate dictionary. (1979). Springfield, MA: G. & C. Merriam.

Werner, H. (1964). *Comparative psychology of mental development.* New York: International University Press.

White, K. M., Speisman, J. C., & Costos, D. (1983). From individuation to mutuality. *New Directions for Child Development*, No. 22, 61–76.

White, K. M., Speisman, J. C., Jackson, D., Bartis, S., & Costos, D. (in press). Intimacy maturity and its correlates in young married couples. *Journal of Personality and Social Psychology.*

Lives of women who became autonomous

Ravenna Helson, Valory Mitchell, and Barbara Hart

Abstract

We examine the lives and growth processes of women who have achieved considerable development of personality. Subjects of study are seven women in a longitudinal sample who, at ages 42–45, are classified by the Loevinger Sentence Completion Test at the highest ego-levels. As a way of describing their lives, all seven are analyzed in terms of Levinson's model of male development, one case is presented in terms of Gilligan's model of female development, another in terms of Loevinger's general model, and linkages among theories are observed. Characteristics of Loevinger's *autonomous* stage are illustrated and the extent to which they are gender-related is discussed. Findings show that women with very different personalities, problems, and ways of life can attain a high level of ego-development; that their lives tend not to have been orthodox or easy; and that theories of adult development are useful but uneven in application.

It was Freud's impression (1933) that young men near age 30 were going to continue to develop, where in women of the same age a creeping rigidity already foretold a greater limitation of their scope as persons. The research of Broverman, Broverman, Clarkson, Rosenkrantz, and Vogel (1970) on sex role stereotypes and judgments of mental health is widely interpreted to show that clinicians still expect greater maturity in men than in women. Though biographies portray women of exceptional character, devotion, or achievements, there is little contact between biography and research in personality. Our ideals for personality development in women are unclear, and how women's lives should be conceptualized is itself a disputed question.

This essay studies the lives of seven women in a longitudinal sample who, at ages 42–45, were classified by the Sentence Completion Test (SCT) (Loevinger & Wessler, 1970) at the highest ego-levels.

This research was supported by a grant from the National Institute of Mental Health. We wish to thank the seven "autonomous" women for their rich accounts of their lives and for helpful comments on our presentation of them in a preliminary draft of this paper.

One reason for studying this small group was to be able to examine in some detail what the lives of women with highly developed personalities, in Loevinger's terms, were like. Would such women be homemakers, career women, bohemians, mystics? If they faced the usual feminine dilemmas, how had they coped with them? Were their lives hero stories with an emphasis on plot, articulation, and forward movement (Levinson, 1978), or perhaps love stories with the emphasis on unfolding and realizing through relationships (Gilligan, 1982)?

A second reason for using these women as subjects of study was that Loevinger describes individuals at the *autonomous* and *integrated* stages as insightful, interested in their lives, and able to express themselves well. Thus, as informants, they should make possible an exploration of the fruitfulness and areas of application of different theories of development.

The three main theories to be presented vary in scope and character. Loevinger's (1966, 1976) is a general theory of ego-development, applicable to both men and women. A considerable literature supports its cogency and the utility of the SCT as a quantitative measure of its constructs (Hauser, 1976; Loevinger, 1979). The other two theories are more recent, and in each case the empirical base consists in interviews with small samples of individuals. Levinson's (1978) is a theory of evolving "life structures" in adulthood, originating in intensive interviews with middle-aged men and in some specific ways intended to apply only to men. Gilligan's (1982) is a theory of stages of moral development which grew out of her feeling that the developmental theories of Erikson, Kohlberg, and Levinson did not fit the lives of women. Gender differences are built into her theory, and she is primarily concerned with development in women.

We will use these theories in ways that are asymmetrical but suited to best describe and understand the course and texture of the lives. Loevinger's work provides, first, a basis for identifying individuals who have achieved considerable development of personality, and, later, concepts with which to describe stages and aspects of this development. Levinson offers a way to break the life into chronological segments in which certain kinds of characters, events, and sequences are expected. These make a useful frame for describing the lives of all seven women, comparing subgroups, and looking for sex differences. Gilligan's theory treats a sequence of complex attitudes toward oneself and others. Here we find it most informative to take one case and examine the feminine roots and growth with Gilligan's concepts. Then we shall move on to a woman whose account of her life illustrates especially well a progression through the stages described by Loevinger, at the same time that one perceives themes of Levinson and Gilligan. This case will lead to a discussion of characteristics of individuals at Loevinger's *autonomous* stage, as illustrated by our seven, and the relations of these characteristics to gender.

The study of lives is notoriously complex and laborious. To construct theories and measures of development that organize some significant aspects of life experience in adulthood is a creative and valuable contribution. For our subjects of study, the living and understanding of their own lives is also complex and creative. With only seven women from closely adjacent cohorts who graduated from one elite college, our aim cannot be to establish generalizations or conclusions. Rather, our approach to both theories and data will emphasize listening and looking for connections.

When Loevinger says that the ego develops, she is saying that there are systematic changes in style of life, method of facing problems, opinions about self and others, character, cognitive style, interpersonal relations, impulse control, conscious preoccupations, and moral judgment. These changes have a broad range of manifestations because the ego is the synthetic function. Ego-development is not synonymous with ego-dominance; it has aspects of what other theorists have termed individuation (Jung, 1966) or the development of the self (Kohut, 1977) because conflicting and less conscious aspects of the psyche enter the conscious domain as ego-development progresses.

Loevinger suggests that the average adult in the U.S. is at what she calls the *self-aware* level, just past the *conformist* stage. At the higher stages of development (*conscientious, individualistic, autonomous,* and *integrated*) impulse control is increasingly based on internal, long-term, choice-based motives. Cognitive style becomes increasingly complex, interpersonal relations increasingly differentiated, and conscious preoccupations less superficial and concrete.

Because the seven women at the *autonomous* stage and the sample of which they are a part were studied first as college seniors, then about five years after their graduation, and again at age 42–45, the data lend themselves to analysis in terms of Levinson's study of the life course of 40 men from late adolescence to middle adulthood (1978). Levinson and his colleagues conceive of adulthood as a process of building, maintaining, and changing life structures. The life structure consists primarily of relationships to one's work, to significant others, and to oneself. Because it is a *structure* with interdependence of parts, it resists change. However, when conditions become sufficiently different, change takes place. (What develops is not necessarily an optimal structure; the most obvious change could be an increase in rigidity.) Levinson believes that life structures at particular points in the life course have features with considerable generality across cohort and culture.

Levinson's theory has aroused much skepticism (Costa & McCrae, 1980; Lacy & Hendricks, 1980; Rossi, 1980; Wrightsman, 1981), and its applicability to women in particular has been questioned (Barnett & Baruch, 1978; Gilligan, 1982; Rossi, 1980). Two of the issues that have been raised are especially relevant in this study. One is whether women have the resources and opportunities to change their life structure in the optimal ways that Levinson describes. Many men may not have them either, but certainly women have been expected to adapt to men's moves and children's needs, and may thus not be in a position to change their life structure according to their own needs—or not at regular six-year intervals. Another issue is whether Levinson's emphasis on individual achievement is inappropriate for the lives of women. Gilligan (1982) maintains that "the elusive mystery of women's development lies in the recognition of the continuing importance of attachment in the human life cycle" (p. 23). We will be interested to see whether the seven women of our study, with their unusual resources of personality, change their life structures at the times and in the ways that Levinson has outlined, and whether their lives emphasize the themes of achievement or attachment.

Background

In 1958 and 1960, 140 seniors at a private women's college participated in a study described to them as concerned with creativity, leadership, and other aspects of effective functioning. About five years later, 99 of the women and 65 of their husbands participated in a study by mail (Helson, 1967). In 1981–82, 110 of the women provided personality and life history data (Helson, Mitchell, & Moane, 1984; Helson & Moane, 1984). The Sentence Completion Test (SCT) was obtained in the last wave of the study. Ninety protocols were scored in accordance with the SCT Manual (Loevinger, Wessler, & Redmore, 1970).[1] The sample falls in roughly equal

1. Raters were Barbara Hart and James Picano. Picano was an experienced rater and trained Hart according to the program outlined in the scoring manual (Loevinger & Wessler, 1970). A reliability coefficient of .87 was obtained between the Total Protocol Ratings assigned by the two raters independently. Raters agreed on the TPR for 68% of the sample, and for 98% they were within half a stage in agreement. Nine women were rated at the *autonomous* stage or above by at least one rater. In four cases there was agreement between raters; in the other five cases one rater had assigned a rating at the adjacent *individualistic* stage. In three of the five cases, discussion led to classification at the *autonomous* stage.

parts into the Self-Aware, Conscientious, and Individualistic categories, with a few women below these three categories and the seven women of this study above. Relations between ego-level and measures of personality and adaptation are described elsewhere (Picano, 1984). Here we will rely primarily on open-ended questionnaire data from the seven women classified by the SCT at the *autonomous* stage.

The Seven: Childhood and Adolescence

It is beyond the confines of this study to discuss in any detail the lives of our subjects before college. However, it seems important to state that there was more trouble in the backgrounds of the Seven than was typical of the sample as a whole. For example, there were three cases of disruption or painful malfunctioning and poverty in the family. There were two women who grew very tall (5'11", 6'2") in early adolescence. There were several serious illnesses and distressing health conditions. None of the seven grew up without the experience of loneliness and marginality, and without the need to exercise their coping abilities. *All* of them reported a concentration of interest in childhood in imaginary-artistic or tomboy activities, both of which are associated with creativity or effective coping (Helson, 1966).

Life Structures and Transitions

Early Adult Transition (18–22)

In Levinson's theory, the period between 18 and 22 is one in which a young man begins to "leave home." He becomes more independent and imagines what form his participation in the adult world might take. He has a dream of what he wants to do and become that will guide his choices.

College is an environment in which many young people experience "leaving home" in a partial and transitional way, and our sample were all seniors when the study began. On a questionnaire administered at this time, most of the seniors expressed an ideal future of a family-centered life with opportunity to pursue cultural interests, community activity, or a job. Very few gave a high priority to their own achievement. Of the seven, three had views that could be called typical, but the other four put more emphasis on work and/or less emphasis on marriage and children. For the seven, their dreams were highly predictive of future life styles.

Entering the Adult World (EAW) (22-27)

In the years of EAW, says Levinson, the young man needs both to explore the world and to achieve a structured place. The period is difficult, not only because these needs conflict, but also because, while still immature, he has to tolerate considerable uncertainty and encounter new demands and expectations.

Most of the seven did some exploring in their pursuit of structure. For example, one drove a tractor and harvested wheat during the summer before she started graduate school. For two others, graduate school itself was an exploration: After a year they dropped out and started families. Others traveled or took exploratory internships. But the EAW years were even harder than Levinson suggests. One woman encountered discouraging restrictions of opportunities for women in the first work she chose after graduate school. Another found herself pregnant by a man not ready to marry. In addition, there were four cases of fairly serious depression. One woman became depressed in graduate school, another after an unfortunate love affair, another after the birth of her first child, and another after severe illness and medical complications following her fourth pregnancy in four years, during which period she had worked, studied, and given birth to three children. We will reserve the question of why the seven had so much difficulty in these years for a later section.

By age 27, despite their problems, all were committed to a first life structure and trying to make a go of it. The life structures are easily described in terms of centrality of commitments: Three women had families and no jobs, three had careers and no families, and one women had a life structure that included both. For the women with children, the first life structure was "for real"—it lacked the provisional quality that Levinson ascribes to the first life structure in men.

Age 30 Transition (28-32)

Between the ages of 28 and 32, Levinson says, young men feel a need to evaluate their first life structure. If they don't change it soon, it will be too late. During these years they may switch fields or be promoted, or otherwise modify the structure to befit the fact that they wish no longer to be apprentices or novices but regulars. They may marry at this time, or change from one wife to another who is more congenial for the new structure they hope to achieve. Levinson describes two relationships of primary importance in the "novice phase" of early adulthood (ages 22 through the age 30 transition). The special woman loves and is loved by the young man.

She believes in his dream and enriches his vision of himself with the magic and support of the feminine. She may or may not be the wife. The mentor is typically an older man who is model, guide, and sponsor in the occupational world. Both special woman and mentor are transitional figures who aid the man through the era of his incomplete independence.

The concept of the age 30 transition applies powerfully to the lives of the seven. Here is what happened during these four years: Three single women had serious love relationships that ended disappointingly, after which they renewed their commitment to their careers; two women with children divorced and entered a new marriage or marriage-like relationship; another wife-mother and her husband tried out a variety of new approaches to breaking down rigidities and increasing awareness, after which they recommitted themselves to the marriage and a new lifestyle; the woman with career and family raised the level of her career dramatically. Something fairly decisive happened in each life.[2] In all but the last case, the attempt was made to achieve a satisfactory relationship with a special man.

One career woman had already met her special man. He was a paratrooper who had "dropped into" a bar. They fell in love almost at first sight, married, and for a long time through quite a bit of hell and high water they supported the dreams of each other. Another career woman, asked to describe four "important people" in her life (on the questionnaire), grouped a series of lovers into one "important person." They had all believed in her worth (supported her dream) throughout her alcoholism and bouts of depression. Two other career women did not find a lover who affirmed their way of being-in-the-world, though the encounter with their hoped for lover was a turning point in the age 30 transition.

For the noncareer women, husbands had seemed to affirm the dream of intimate partnership and family life, but when the woman tried to develop this dream beyond the *conformist* level, it became apparent in two of three cases that the husband was either unable or unwilling to support her. During the age 30 transition the women became attracted to other men who at first and in some important ways affirmed the dream of mutual sharing and enjoyment of each other as individuals. The partner who did not affirm the dream and upon whom the family woman was dependent became a "special

2. In an ongoing attempt to code women's lives between ages 28–32, we find many instances of continuation or modest expansion of the "first life structure." The number of dramatic alterations or heavily invested risks among the seven thus seems high.

man" in a negative sense. It was the woman's task in the 30s and age 40 transition to decrease or outgrow her dependence on him.

All career women among the seven had mentors whom they classified as important people. The family women did not have equivalent relationships. Mothers, husbands, friends, relatives, or psychotherapists sometimes provided orientation, support, or counsel, but a mentor encourages individual achievement, and this was not the dream of the family women among the seven. Only in the late 30s or early 40s when some of them developed interest in individual achievement did any mentor-like relationships develop.

Settling Down and Becoming One's Own Man (BOOM) (33–40)

Levinson uses the imagery of the ladder to describe the 30s. At the start of the period a man is on the bottom rung of a self-defined ladder, entering a world in which he is a junior member. He tries to anchor his life more firmly, develop competence, become a valued contributor, and be affirmed in a valued world. From about 36–40 there is an intensification of effort to become a senior member—to speak with one's own voice and have authority. If the man succeeds in these ambitions, he usually has heavy pressures and responsibilities. Heavy pressure and his need to "call the tune" may lead to severing of relationships with wives or mentors and to impulsive career decisions.

This description of the thirties applies fairly well to the four career women among the seven, all of whom—like Levinson's men—had a life structure in which work had been central since EAW. In the early 30s they were at the lower rungs of a ladder and they all climbed. One of them formed her first mentor relationship in her early 30s, stuck to one job for the first time (a good example of "settling down"), and then at 35 made the decision to give up alcohol, after which her successes were uninterrupted. At 37, another suffered the break-up of the dance group she headed, then achieved a peak of success. She also separated from her husband. She made a new integration, but this explosion was of the nature Levinson describes. Job shifts and decisions of the career women suggest that they wanted recognition and the opportunity to exercise their talents more than they wanted the positions of authority that Levinson himself describes as "male."

For family women without careers, the ladder image is less apt. All three of them had made considerable alteration in life structure during the age 30 transition, so there was some settling *into* the new life structure, which in all cases was one intended to give attention to the needs and goals of the woman herself as well as to those of partner and children (O'Connell, 1976). But there were no rungs to climb. In the late 30s, "becoming one's own woman" was certainly the dominant concern of the three women who had been "family-centered," but this was not a question of obtaining authority or public recognition. It was an emotional and often invigorating process of self-discovery, of becoming more independent of the partner, and accepting the approaching "loss" of children. This process involved learning to cope in the outer world to some extent. For many women in the larger sample, entry into the labor force was the conspicuous event of the late 30s. But all three of the noncareer women among the seven were faithful to a relational dream. They worked for pay as might be necessary, but the important development was a turn inward—to become related to the self. The spiritual interests of these three are almost without parallel in the larger sample. Two of the three had already had important encounters with the unconscious during the early twenties, in association with childbirth or early motherhood. Perhaps one could say that these first experiences were associated with loss of centrality of the ego in the life structure as the nuclear family began, and that they were associated in the late 30s with another reconstellation of personality associated with the diminishing responsibility for young children.

One woman had become deeply involved in a study group in which the members were reading philosophy, history, and religious thought. After a day of excited immersion in the sources of two particularly meaningful religious symbols, she had a mystical experience that requires to be described in full if at all. Suffice it to say that afterwards she had a new perspective that would not be shaken. At first, this perspective was discrepant with her daily life and set her apart from herself.

> When I got my own sight straightened out, I put down my own order for grounding the rest of my life. No need for compromise or schizoid deals with myself. Life got greatly simplified, enlarged, and more substantial.

But this change came about during the midlife transition, after she and her husband were divorced.

Midlife Transition (40–45)

According to Levinson, the period from 40–45 is another time when a man reevaluates his life in terms of his dream. In the effort

for success, certain aspects of the personality have been developed
at the cost of others, which now press for attention. The reevaluation
is given urgency by the awareness that life is finite and by his
anticipation of declining powers. During the midlife transition, a
man tries to integrate the polarities of young/old, destruction/crea-
tion, masculine/feminine, and attachment/separateness. He begins
to modify the second life structure in order to build a third that will
be vital and generative in middle adulthood (40–65).

The changes in a majority of the women between 40–45 consoli-
date or add to emphases of the late 30s rather than turn against
them, as one might observe in a man who repudiates the "bitch
goddess" at midlife. The seven had already been working to transcend the polarities of masculine/feminine, attachment/separate-
ness, and creation/destruction. Perhaps the tension between young
and old afforded some additional push. At any rate, changes in the
life structure have certainly occurred. Two of the three single career
women married. Two women with families divorced: One of them
started at graduate school and the other has shifted emphases in her
work away from "physical pyrotechnics" in the direction of her
deepened symbolic interests and broader experience. Another family
woman had a depression, then began a new venture with her husband.

Summary

The lives of the seven are organized in a helpful way by Levinson's
concepts. Where there are discrepancies, one can appreciate differences in the lives of men and women, or of career women and family
women. Levinson has been criticized for lack of evidence that his
normative concepts actually apply even in the lives of his 40 men
(Wrightsman, 1981). Many lives are not clear. We found the sharp-
ness of life structures and the eventfulness of transitional periods
among the seven somewhat surprising, and believe they may be
related to ego-development. These women were aware of aspects of
their lives that were unsatisfactory, they were able to envisage
alternatives, and they had the energy, courage, and coping ability to
effect change. In addition, they were interested in their development
and could articulate well the changes that took place.

The seven experienced a great deal of suffering during the period
of entering the adult world. We wonder whether entering a world
that is new requires coping at the level of the *self-protective* and
conformist stages, and is especially difficult for people who have to
regress in order to cope in these ways. They conform to young adult

roles at the cost of authenticity or fail to conform at the cost of loneliness. Another factor affecting the adjustment of the seven may be that the same early problems that had stimulated ego-development now increased the difficulties in forming attachments, negotiating marriage, and undertaking the emotional stresses of pregnancy and early motherhood. All of the seven, after graduating from a women's college, had to come to terms with a sexist culture. Many of the EAW experiences would seem to require more alteration of the previous self-concept and life structure than young men in peacetime have to undergo.

The career women fit Levinson's model better than do the family women. The young mothers without careers did not lead provisional lives in their 20s, they had no mentors, they had "settled down" *before* the early 30s, and they did not seek recognition and status in their late 30s. For careerists, individual achievement was a central commitment throughout the period of life we have studied, as it was for Levinson's men, but the noncareer family women had first to develop a life structure that was family-centered and then to change it to one more individual as children became independent.

Of course, a model of the male life course cannot be expected to fit even career-oriented women very well. In Levinson's men, for example, occupation is "figure" and relational needs are in the "ground." None of the career women among the seven had, or wanted to have, a wife at home whose existence and whose responsibility for relational needs could be taken for granted.

The faithfulness of the seven to their dreams may perhaps be attributed to a combination of resourcefulness associated with their ego-level and the persistence of early problems that engendered either the career woman's need for independence and achievement or the family woman's need to be related and accepted. We turn now to Gilligan's conceptualization of women's development in terms of relationships.

Development in Relationships

The importance for women of forming and maintaining relationships is a steady theme in the literature of adult development. It is, however, a theme that conflicts with Levinson's emphasis on separation and independence. Gilligan (1981) suggests, as Chodorow did (1974), that the role of separation may assume different meanings in the personality development of men and women:

> For boys and men, separation and individuation are critically tied to gender identity since separation from the mother is

essential for the development of masculinity. For girls and women, issues of femininity or feminine identity do not depend on the progress of individuation. Since masculinity is defined through separation while femininity is defined through attachment, male identity is threatened by intimacy while female gender identity is threatened by separation. Thus, males tend to have difficulty with relationships while females tend to have problems with individuation (p. 8).

Following this line, Gilligan says that women have a view of maturity that is fundamentally different from that of men—one that is founded on "an ethic of care" instead of on "an ethic of rights." From this perspective, relationships serve as a context for a unique sequence of feminine development in which "the major transitions . . . involve changes in the understanding and activities of care" (p. 171).

Gilligan has proposed a three-stage model for feminine growth. Initially, there is a focus on "caring for the self in order to ensure survival" (p. 74) which recalls Loevinger's *self-protective* ego-level. A woman's relationships are limited by a view of herself as isolated, and the good is identified with what serves her self-interest. This is followed by a phase in which she criticizes this attitude as "selfish" and develops a connection between self and others that is articulated by the concept of responsibility:

> Women's sense of integrity appears to be entwined with an ethic of care so that to see themselves as women is to see themselves in a relation of connection. When the distinction between helping and pleasing frees the activity of taking care from the wish for approval, the ethic of responsibility can become a self-chosen anchor for personal integrity (p. 171).

At the second stage, the good is equated with caring for others according to conventional notions of feminine virtue. According to Gilligan, a woman progresses within the second stage from a reliance on conforming to the opinions of others (Loevinger's third, *conformist* stage) to a more self-cognizant care for others (Loevinger's fourth, *conscientious* stage). This stage, however, carries a particular danger for further growth which Gilligan characterizes as a form of feminine "blindness." Because the notion of responsible care has become confused with self-sacrifice, women at this stage are left unaware of their own needs and agency. The transition to the next stage is thus preceded by a recognition of the "illogic of the inequality between the other and the self" (p. 74).

Inclusion of herself in the ethic of care enables a woman to reconcile the hitherto blinding opposition between responsibility and selfishness that "left her suspended between an ideal of selflessness and the truth of her own agency and needs" (p. 138). This latter stage corresponds well to Loevinger's *autonomous* stage of ego-development in which there is both a new recognition of one's own powers as well as a new respect for the fact that "others have a responsibility to their own destiny" (p. 21). Responsible care can thus become a "self-chosen" value which takes into account both the possibilities and limitations of one's actions in the lives of others as well as one's responsibility for self-development.

A Life Lived in Relationships

The member of the seven whose life best illustrates Gilligan's ideas about the character and sequence of adult feminine development has remained in a prototypic feminine world of marriage and home-making since college. We will see the struggle she has made through-out her life to free herself from excessive dependence, and the growth of awareness that led her to expand her view of herself to include a balanced sense of responsibility for others and responsibility for her own individual growth.

Writing at age 45 about her college years, this woman spoke of herself as having been "emotionally asleep except for the mating call." She remembered her relational dream in vivid detail.

I had a strong emotional urge to have a mate/partner/lover to share my life. I wanted the love (the specialness, the twosome, the secret sharing) that I had seen between my parents, and to have happy, productive, healthy children.

This account is consistent with what she had written on her questionnaire as a college senior. Her aspirations were inextricably connected with the creation of intimate, positive relationships. Otherwise, S "floated through" college in unconscious conformity with a minimum of personal investment.

Fulfilling the first part of her dream, S married after graduating from college. For the next few months, she alternated between following her husband's naval ship and returning to her parent's home. She then settled with him in a foreign port of duty where she felt "isolated" and had no close relationships except with her spouse. (Recall that the view of oneself as isolated is characteristic of Gilligan's first stage.) At 23, she had her first child and suffered a depression that lasted for six months. She describes this period of her life as "the first getting in touch with an inner world—a painful awakening. Having a child made me realize how undeveloped I was in relation to myself." This confrontation with the first demand to take care of others created a conflict between her relational dream and the reality of her developmental level, and stimulated growth.

Following the birth of her second child, she experienced another severe depression. Soon after this, at the beginning of what was to be four years of psychoanalysis, she said:

> I . . . am more aware of my inadequacies because for the first time I have been called upon to fulfill a mature, independent role. I would not return to my sheltered previous life at college or before, but neither am I content to remain at my present stage of development.

During the transition to the stage of responsible care, S criticizes her "undeveloped" state and wishes to become able to "fulfill a mature, independent role." Her depression and fear that she was "an abnormally deficient human being" demonstrate her dawning sense of the need for self-knowledge and of the pressure of the real-life rigors of motherhood. She struggles to become responsible for the day-to-day organization of her household while engaging in a process of painful self-inquiry. At this time (age 27) she says:

> I love to cook. I love doing things with my husband. I love certain aspects of motherhood—especially sharing things with my children. The responsibility I have towards my children sometimes frightens me. I hate the routine—budgets, check balancing, cleaning, dishwashing, care of clothing, etc., but can, in a burst of righteousness, attack one of these jobs with enjoyment. I have become more organized.

The story of subsequent years is based on the account of S's life that she gave at age 45. At age 29 (during the "age 30 transition"), S and her family move to accommodate her husband's new job and she enters upon a new phase of growth. The children are older and she is now able to turn more of her attention to herself. She and her husband become active in the human potential movement, attending seminars and investigating the new therapies and eastern philosophies. During this time, she discovers that "emotions are acceptable" and feels "in charge" of her destiny.

> My husband and I had an affair with another couple which I started (for excitement) and ended (for feeling threatened). I

liked the idea of it as being the first thing I'd ever done that my mother wouldn't approve of.

This statement signals the beginning of S's ability to experience a new degree of separation from her internalized dependence upon her mother's approval. Initially, she shows delight in opposing conventional notions about feminine goodness. She also has her first serious argument with her mother.

It was the first time I rebelled against my mother. As a child I felt repressed, because my mother could never understand my negative emotions.

At 32, reconfirming her marriage, S has her third and last child. For ten years she had supported her husband's occupational dream. Now they seek to fulfill a shared dream. They move to the country to start a commune with eight other couples. At first, she is happy with her "new family" but two years later, at age 36, she enters "a time of rebellion and reevaluation." She has an affair with a man whom she felt could give her "a level of tenderness and understanding" her husband couldn't provide. This event reflects a recognition of the conflict between her own need and the inadequacies of her role as a loving wife to fulfill them. She ends the affair two months later and recommits herself to her marriage and family. Her outlook has broadened (a hallmark of both Gilligan's third and Loevinger's *autonomous* stages) to include an appreciation for her husband's "imperfections." Nevertheless, her regard for her own needs takes an active form and she builds a dome away from her family home in which she can experience herself free from the demands of her husband and children. A poem expresses the transformation in her understanding at this time.

Again her life assumed / a shared home, a dependable love. / She fought to banish inanity / from conjugal conversation, / to give to her rechosen family, to him, / the rose of herself. / At times, it seemed a small persistent heartache / was too high a price to pay / for her love learning. / She vowed to seek . . . her own spirit.

S has developed in the context of her marriage relationship, but this relationship has developed too.

We were innocent college sweethearts with no great skills at communication but strong physical and emotional attraction. We have been married over 20 years, have grown tremendously as individuals and in our love and acceptance and encouragement of each other. I more and more value the richness of our shared lives . . . My husband is sensitive, active, energetic, Yang! creative, and manipulative. For the past ten years, at least, I have always felt his spiritual support of whatever path I chose in my individuation process—though his emotional reaction would seem to deny this. [This support] is an encouraging factor when I begin new adventures.

In a similar manner, S's relationship with her mother has matured. S described an intense childhood attachment to her mother who "appeared so much stronger" than she was. At the same time, she felt misunderstood and seems to have been left with an unsatisfied yearning for close, caring relationships. She used denial to cope with conflicts. When her parents divorced, she told herself she was lucky to be more "grown-up" (at age 14) than her siblings, and felt her best chance of security was to help her insecure, emotional, and unpredictable mother to be happy. She sometimes feared her mother would take too many sleeping pills. S found it difficult to leave home for college, or to go from one home to the other:

A kind of inertia kept me emotionally tied to whichever parents' sphere I currently inhabited (West Coast or East Coast). Inertia and my parents' competition for my loyalty.

Her mother, especially, "hated having me grow up and away."

Some years later, after the birth of her children, S's relationship with her mother changed.

I have felt a great deal more empathy for her and feel I have more in common with her now. Our family has always been close with emphasis on loving relationships but a problem I have had with my mother is her refusal to accept my adult separation from her.

With this statement, S demonstrates her enhanced ability to differentiate herself. Still later, after the death of her stepfather, S undergoes a further change in her attitude toward her mother in which she begins to feel a less dependent "emotional responsibility" for her mother and begins "to be regular" with weekly telephone calls.

I think how daily my mother handles her aloneness, her life. I know it is difficult to be without her mate and she is an inspiration in that she is still finding joy in her life. I feel more equal, more tolerant, less judgmental concerning our differences. I love and respect her more for what she has done than I find fault with what she hasn't. We have more in common.

At age 40, S had another serious depression. Commenting on this depression, she says:

> I think I periodically lose myself on the way to further growth. In the early years, I didn't know who I was and later when the children grew older my role was so uncertain. I [still] feel anxious, panicky at all my freedom—and exhilarated. I feel sad at their leaving and glad at less responsibility. I have fears that I will never do anything as important or as well as raising them.

These statements reveal the central position that responsible caring has had for this woman. But though S mourns the emptying of her nest, she does not remain in despair. She has deepened her marriage relationship and become a dedicated teacher of Tai Chi. Though she rejects the idea of "going to graduate school for some degree" as not right for her, she embarks upon a new undertaking with her husband.

> [Through my work], I am an integral part of this community and the town community. I am a teacher and student, artist and writer. I am not always sure what I have to teach, which leaves me feeling vulnerable, but many people tell me I teach them. My aim is to become a stronger, more unified person.

This woman has progressed through a series of decisive experiences of conflict in relationships. First, she struggled to leave home and then, recognizing the contradiction between her relational dream and her stage of development, she worked hard to know and to discipline herself in order to care responsibly for her family. Later, she began to modify and to expand her conception of responsible care to include herself. The tension between responsible care for others and her need to become more whole has resulted in an increasingly more differentiated and conscious struggle to become herself within the context of her important relationships. She has become a more active participant in a wider human community.

The positive aspect of relationships within the lives of some of the women who develop to the *autonomous* stage seems to be that they provide a context of value and tension within which development takes place. In order to tell the story of this woman, it is necessary to change "the lens of developmental observation from individual achievement to relationships of care (in which) women depict ongoing attachment as the path that leads to maturity" (Gilligan, 1982, p. 170).

Development across Loevinger's Stages

In the preceding sections of this paper, we have described the lives of the seven, using Levinson's concepts of life structures and

age-linked transitions; and we have traced the adult life of one of
the seven, using the developmental sequence that Gilligan has described as a prototypic feminine path. In this section, we will trace
the developmental history of another of the seven. But this time, our
intent is to document the journey across the stages of ego-development themselves.

The Self-Protective Stage

Cognitive simplicity, a manipulative interpersonal style, a preoccupation with control, and a desire to protect oneself are characteristics of this stage. One fears being caught, and externalizes blame.

The woman whose development we will chart in this section began
graduate school immediately after completing her bachelor's degree.
The characteristics of the *self-protective* stage emerge as salient in
her description of her entry into the adult world:

> I told myself all the time [in graduate school] how silly society's
> pressures about marriage were. But underneath I am sure they
> were a prime cause for emotional ups and downs.
>
> After graduation [from college], I had really made up my mind
> to marry G . . . then the tables turned and the previously steady
> and persistent man decided he wanted to date other people and
> concentrate on his work in law school. This really "did me in,"
> and I spent almost the whole year reacting to it. For a week or
> so I would attempt to see G, and then would get fed up and rush
> off into some brief but intense relationship with some new
> person. These usually turned quite sour after a few dates and I
> would begin again to pester G.
>
> This wild year ended when I became pregnant and G and I
> were married in June . . . It has occurred to me that perhaps
> after making the decision [to marry G] and then having G declare
> his intentions [to date others]—added to the subtle social pres-
> sures to get married—that maybe my pregnancy was not such
> an accident.

This autobiographical vignette was written retrospectively, about
five years after the events described. In it, one senses the young
woman's embarrassment as she recalled having been buffeted by
"silly" pressures into an anxious cycle of "pestering" and "running
off." Although the behavior she described was most characteristic of
the *self-protective* stage, by age 26, when the sketch was written,
she had begun to question her "accidental" pregnancy, to assert a
more internal locus of control, and to view herself as a person who

chooses. These changes signify her distance from that earlier mode and suggest higher levels of ego-development.[3]

The Conformist Stage

A desire to belong, to be "normal" and "happy," to fill one's role, and a preoccupation with appearance and acceptability are keynotes of this ego-stage. In her retrospective account of the early years of her marriage, this woman writes as if slightly mocking her former way of living. One reason for the caricature quality of life at the *conformist* stage may have been that it was a false self for her, a persona that she adopted because she felt she had to, but one that shielded a very different and still nascent self. (This and subsequent quotations are from retrospective accounts obtained when she was 42.)

> I thought marriage would be nice . . . and didn't think much about the future as I moved into the married years. Significant events were the births of three children, settling down . . . to what was a "normal" (then) relationship . . . We just did all the [expected things] and people thought we were happy. I tried to look and dress like other young homemakers should—tried to please this man.

Describing her husband, she sketches a prototypic *conformist* stage character, for whom helping and superficial niceness characterize the interpersonal manner.

> Everyone thought him a nice guy. He always joked and made people laugh, and offered his help to everyone (except his family). Otherwise, he was and is particularly *un*distinctive.

Soon, however, this woman moved out of the *conformist* stage into the *self-aware* phase, where the felt necessity of one (*conformist*) way of life yields to a dawning sense of alternatives. Perhaps as a result, one becomes preoccupied with the self as separate from the group. Introspection and self-consciousness emerge anew. She writes:

3.   At age 42 she did not discuss the issue of the pregnancy, but after receiving a draft of this paper she commented that she no longer engaged in self-blame as she had in former days. She had not wanted the pregnancy—it caused her to miss a bicycling trip through Europe that she had planned with much enthusiasm. She thought an unreliable method of birth control was a sufficient explanation. "I was at least taking my temperature; he wasn't doing anything." If one considers this last interpretation to show the objectivity of the *autonomous* stage, then the same critical event was perceived differently at three stages of ego-development.

I drew farther and farther away from the people our age where we lived . . . I looked longingly at people in the Peace Corps or civil rights activities . . . I became tense and distraught long before I knew why. I got more and more depressed—felt things were my fault somehow.

The Conscientious Stage

In the *conscientious* stage a sense of choice emerges, and the self is seen as the origin of a person's destiny. One lives more by self-evaluated standards, yet is also "one's brother's keeper." The interpersonal style is intensive, with great concern for communication. She writes that:

It was impossible to get G to deal with all the stuff I was unhappy about . . . I sought out counseling over G's objections. [He said], "*I* like it as it is, *I'm* not unhappy," but [I] gave up counseling when they decided tranquilizers were the answer to my emotional ups and downs . . . Our personal life was zero—sex-life bad because there was nothing going on between us mentally . . . .

Inwardly, a person at the *conscientious* stage steps away from cliché and stereotype toward an awareness of patterning and motive and a concern for ideals and self-respect. Interpersonally, the superficial is replaced by a desire for authentic mutuality:

As a direct result of how awful it became, I developed a huge commitment to being real, honest. I will never let things slide by again, nor will I ignore or deny how I really feel.

It seems in hindsight that I am a person who has a great curiosity about human behavior, my own and others', plus a desire for very close intimate relationships. I married someone who did not want to do that kind of sharing and exploring and growing at all. I had no idea that someone would not want to be close. . . .

Anyway, I was ripe for something to happen. What gets me now is how reluctant I was to really deal out loud with my despair. Reluctant even to think about separation or divorce, I just let myself become terribly attracted to someone else.

Despairing of the depth and intimacy that her own development now demanded of her relationships, she fell in love and left her husband. With her children, she moved from her town to a rural area where she began a very different style of life. In so doing, she launched herself out of the last vestiges of conformist ways and zealous *conscientiousness*, and into a strongly *individualistic* phase. Her heightened sense of individuality and concern for emotional independence/dependence are evident:

> The move I made created a lot of concern in my extended family—but I was going on gut level feeling and would not be dissuaded. These years I learned to work hard physically, handle all sorts of situations, trust myself, and stand up for myself. I made new friends with values more like mine—and began to be really in touch with myself. I'm sure I seemed insane to those I left behind. It was several years before anything very stable or intelligent began to form itself out of the dust of the chaos I stirred up. . . .
>
> I got real quiet and let my true feelings and wants and needs surface. That took a couple of *years* and I felt could only happen because I wasn't trying to please anyone—or be what they expected me to be. I developed deep spiritual attitudes. I've realized more about myself and had the strength to continue growing and learning.

The Autonomous Stage

Now at the *autonomous* stage, rejection of *conformist* values, *conscientious* championing of a set of ideals, or adamant assertions of individual selfhood seem almost superfluous. Acknowledgement of inner conflict, an intra- and interpersonal atmosphere of autonomy, tolerance for ambiguity, and the cherishing of individuality and personal ties give this stage a flavor of lively maturity.

> Now there is a place established by me in this community. M has come to live here, and that feels good 95% of the time as we deepen our knowing of each other. A genuine mutual caring and enjoyment exist. My kids are like young birds perched on the edge of the nest . . . all three finding their way in this strange, materialistic world. My house is building—small, simple, nice. I know I trust myself and my abilities to handle nearly any situation. I still don't have any goals except to stay connected to that serene place within and let the energy coming through me handle what I need to do. It feels like an ever-expanding and enjoyable future.

Interfacing Theories of Adult Development

This is an interesting case of a life that can be seen well from the vantage point of all three theories. The applicability of one theory does not diminish the descriptive power of others with different emphases. We have shown that this woman's experience, as recounted in her own words at ages 26 and 42, appears to follow the stages of ego-development described by Loevinger. Her life was a *conformist* one during the years of building what Levinson would call the "early adult life structure." The introspection of the *self-aware* phase, and the sense of choice that is characteristic of the *conscientious* stage were manifest in her life during the years closely surrounding age 30—the age thirty transition. Divorce and a move from an urban to rural milieu mark this transition, and subsequent events may be construed to include a "settling down" and "becoming one's own woman." That her present social matrix, cultivated interests, and self-concept allow for an "ever-expanding and enjoyable future" suggests a structure within which the middle adult era can be welcomed.

Still, though this life may be viewed in the agentic, structure-building language of Levinson, it is no less a feminine one in which family and relatedness play central parts. From Gilligan's perspective, the life shifts from self-protection, through a studied attempt to please others and take care, until "the illogic of the inequality between others and self" surged into consciousness and entailed a lengthy discovery and uncovering of self to accompany the nurturance of others.

What It Means to Be an Autonomous Woman

Independence is considered problematic for women, and some aspects of the psychology of people at the *autonomous* stage may seem "unfeminine." For this reason, it may be of interest to look closely at some of the characteristics of *autonomous* people, whose lives may be expected to illustrate a broadened repertoire of behaviors and experiences and the transcendence of polarities. We turn first to those qualities which have been considered incompatible with the feminine sex role.

The Capacity to Acknowledge and to Cope with Inner
Conflict

A hallmark of the *autonomous* stage is a willingness, almost a desire, to articulate and grapple with conflicting needs, or needs and duties. This desire forms a motivational nexus in a larger concern for growth and personal development. Such a spirit of inquiry is at odds with an image of the feminine as requiring a strategy of passivity or endurance.

One of the seven, a single women who taught fifth grade, met the deaths of two relatives who had lived with her, the award of a major honor in her work, and a job termination, all in the same year. Until this time, she had held wholeheartedly to a set of guiding values built around service to society. Now a conflict arose between the desires to give and to receive. Although hers was a career conflict, we can recognize the Gilligan theme.

> I took a new look at life. Now in my forties, with no stable career, where was I going? Where had my years of devotion gotten me? Who really cared about me? . . . [I began] searching, broadening my horizons, reaching out, contacting old friends and making new freinds. [My] need for positive innovations, new job, travel [led to my] marriage, contentment, and satisfaction . . . I have suffered, matured, become more realistic and basic in taking each day as it comes. I know my limitations more and I am more tolerant of others. I am looking more for what life has to offer me than what I have to offer life.

Self-fulfillment Emerges as a Salient Goal

The quotation above illustrates another characteristic of the *autonomous* stage that may be seen as inconsistent with the feminine sex role: the importance granted to self-fulfillment. During the *conformist* stage, one desires the approval of others. Then, during the *conscientious* stage, one seeks to appease those internalized others who have formed the super-ego. Now, with consolidation of the *autonomous* stage, there is an increase in intrapsychic autonomy— relative freedom from the oppressive demands of conscience. Because the feminine is associated with the "communal" motivation of keeping others in harmony, the shift away from pleasing others and toward pleasing oneself may appear rather masculine.

This lessening sense of the press of others, and an accompanying redefining of sex role, are described by an exhomemaker among the seven who supports her family in an area of high unemployment by working as piano tuner, substitute teacher, and manager of a pizza parlor:

> Before, I found it hard to be around people who had rigid opinions about how one should be—I could only relax at home,

where whatever happened was ok . . . [Now] I can calm myself
no matter what's going on . . . I feel like a very strong woman. I
know *whatever* the energy does through me is feminine. I like
that. I am continuing to play my piano by ear and by mood—I
have taken some voice lessons—in short, I'm going to do what
I want and see where it leads.

Interest in Psychological Causation

We have described two characteristics of Loevinger's *autonomous*
stage that appear more compatible with masculine than feminine sex
role prescriptions. Other qualities of this stage seem especially
congenial to women.

Where the masculine is often portrayed as a mode of functioning
that emphasizes action that affects the environment, a feminine mode
is conducive to reflection, gestation, and inner transformation. In
the *autonomous* stage, the acceptance of inner conflict and an internal
locus of control seem to foster psychological interest, objectivity,
and a reconstruction of the past that emphasizes motives.

A lawyer who represents a multinational corporation writes:

I'm much more my mother's daughter now, after years of trying
to hurt her by hurting myself (stupid, isn't it?) . . . She feels
guilty for the problems she thinks she caused me to have.
Actually, now I realize I was a real pain—and caused most of
my own problems.

The sense of ease with which one can move in an internal landscape
may be one indication of feminine intraception. This capacity is
amply illustrated by a woman who has assumed considerable respon-
ability in the Foreign Service. Here, she discusses the change in her
life over the last decade:

In the early 30s there are still so many painful uncertainties in
your work and love relationships; by your forties you're past the
establishment to the established period . . . Warts, scars, and all,
you know who you are, and can look toward future self-building
without so many fears of the unknown.

Recognition of the Limits of Autonomy, Cherishing
Personal Ties

At the same time that the *autonomous* stage brings an intrapersonal
focus, a sense of inner autonomy, and a granting of greater autonomy

to important others, it also brings an awareness of emotional inter-dependence and a pleasuring in this facet of human experience. Here is an excerpt from an interview with a career woman who was recently divorced:

> It's good to have an older woman for a friend. J and I just sit for a whole day and talk, with wonderful ideas going between us. With J there is this combination of brilliant perceptions, and at the same time she has all the traditional female behaviors—it's like an enclosure in her own house. She doesn't venture into the open, but she's so bold in her mind! . . . I have a sense of building up my own values with her.

Ability to See Objectively and from Multiple Perspectives

Still other aspects of autonomy in the *autonomous* stage may be understood as exempt from sex-linked connotations. Among these is a capacity for observation that coexists with vivid feelings and keenly honed personal values. The juxtaposition of these traits contributes to the complexity of outlook characteristic of the seven. This almost odd impartiality is apparent in the following comment by a woman of fierce loyalties, delighted with her recent marriage:

> [My husband is] coming to terms with the fact that in every institution merit, hard work, and loyalty don't assure promotion if you insist on rocking the boat.

Openness to the Future

Fear of the unknown is conspicuously absent among most of the seven, despite the considerable tumult of their recent pasts. They not only "tolerate" ambiguity, but even relish its unlimited options. At age 45, the dancer-choreographer says:

> I'm feeling betwixt and between right now . . . But I *like* that sense. Maybe you can justify trying to be comfortable—it's a task of life. But I love complexity. It's second nature to me.

The divorced graduate student in philosophy, mother of five, writes:

> Now, when others my age are committed, I am experimenting with lifestyle and relationships. I am in a position to appreciate better some of the alternatives available, and more relaxed about calculated risks, all to my growth and pleasure.

". . . All to my growth and pleasure," and yet, as a look at their lives has shown, the seven have experienced struggle, confusion, pain. That they have consolidated an autonomous orientation suggests that their perspective on self and life includes both masculine and feminine modes. The seven have had the problems of women—dependency and sex role conflicts required persistent ego-effort in the lives that we have described most thoroughly. But these women acquired capacities that span and eclipse sex role.

Discussion

We have described the lives from college to middle age of seven women who, in terms of the SCT, have attained a high level of ego-development. We have illustrated how their personalities changed, discussed their characteristics indicative of the *autonomous* stage, and compared their development with that of theories about men.

Though theories of adult development have been much criticized, we have found them helpful. The stories of most of the women could be well told in terms of Levinson's idea of age-linked life structures and transitions. However, the specific labels, divisions, and characterizations that Levinson used in his study of male lives apply better (not perfectly) to the four women whose lives were organized around work than to the three women with traditionally feminine commitments to partner and children. For example, the life structure of the family woman in our first case study changed at the times indicated by Levinson, but the relational themes that give continuity and content to her life are those elucidated by Gilligan. On the other hand, the lives of the career women are not well presented in Gilligan's terms.

The theories of Levinson and Gilligan both incorporate a gestalt of factors—sex role and physiology, gender roles, family structure, occupational structure, myth—though each highlights some of these and leaves others implicit. They are His and Her theories in both style and content, illuminating a man's life or a woman's life when these are lived under conditions one might call modern traditional. Each seems to us to have his or her limitations, the one oversystematized, the other interpersonally bound.

We were much impressed in this study that women with very different personalities, problems, and sources of challenge could attain a high level of ego-development. Our case studies illustrate the growth of two women who, though very different, both developed in relationships. We thought we chose these women because this kind of development has received little attention, where men's progress toward stature and independent identity has received a great deal. This is certainly true. However, another factor may be that neither Levinson's nor Gilligan's theory is a good fit for the women whose growth and identity come about primarily through their work. If there had been a man in the sample whose primary commitment was to his family, whose work was to care for them, we would not have found either theory a good fit for his life.

A theory is needed that can describe a wider variety of lives. One possibility is to describe lives in terms of the "social clock projects" undertaken in young and middle adulthood (Helson, Mitchell, & Moane, 1984), with recognition that commitments to family and work are not made strictly on the basis of gender, and that norms regulating the nature, timing, and coordinating of these commitments vary considerably from one period and place to another. A challenge for theory (and for the individual) is to fill in the enriching contexts of these nontraditional, atypical, or unfamiliar life patterns.

We regret having been unable to address such questions as whether or how and why each member of the seven changed in ego-level since college. We have tried to illustrate aspects of this interesting set of problems. We have found that Loevinger's concepts enrich those of both Levinson and Gilligan, and also that the ideas of Loevinger and Gilligan are enhanced by explicit contexts of development *in adults*. For example, case histories of family women suggest that the age 30 transition for them was a struggle to live at a higher ego-level, and also a shift from Gilligan's second stage toward her third stage—especially in relation to the partner. Again, the "rightness" of Gilligan's three stages and the reasons for the typically feminine conflict between selfishness and concern for others become maximally compelling when seen in the context of the family women's ego-development in the daughter-wife-mother roles of young and middle adulthood in a sexist society.

Different as the seven are among themselves, they share characteristics that Loevinger ascribes to the *autonomous* stage. To previous discussion of these characteristics we would add attention to the fact that, to an unusual degree, the seven sought out the challenges and suffered the hardships particular to their time in history. Thus, four of the seven had careers, two in fields where women had not tread before. Three family women have marked spiritual interests, and two experimented in communal living. Three of the four family women divorced at least once, two of them when their children were young. It is also noteworthy that three of the seven remained single at least until age forty, and these three have had no children. In the rest of the sample, only 10% show this pattern.

We reported that the childhoods of the seven were difficult. In later life, their pain and their processing of pain are suggested by the fact that four of them (57%) have had long-term psychotherapy, as compared with 27% of the rest of the sample. Studies of high ego-development in other samples and cohorts are needed, but the seven do not show the conventional adaptation that Vaillant (1977) believes generally to go along with maturity and ego-development. Vaillant studied Harvard men. Though Freud's observations about women's inability to grow after age 30 are disconfirmed not only by the seven but by our total sample (Helson & Moane, 1984), it may still be true that *autonomous* ways of thinking and behaving are so much discouraged in women that only those who have known pain or marginality develop a high ego-level, and those who have a high ego-level are unlikely to live a conventional life.

References

Barnett, R. C., & Baruch, G. K. (1978). Women in the middle years: A critique of research and theory. *Psychology of Women Quarterly*, 3, 187–198.

Broverman, I. K., Broverman, D. M., Clarkson, F. E., Rosenkrantz, P. S., & Vogel, S. R. (1970). Sex role stereotypes and clinical judgments of mental health. *Journal of Consulting and Clinical Psychology*, 34, 1–7.

Chodorow, N. (1974). Family structure and feminine personality. In M. Z. Rosaldo & L. Lamphere (Eds.), *Women, culture, and society* (pp. 43–66). Stanford, CA: Stanford University Press.

Costa, P. T., Jr., & McCrae, R. R. (1980). Still stable after all these years: Personality as a key to some issues in adulthood and old age. In P. B. Baltes & O. C. Brim (Eds.), *Life-span development and behavior* (Vol. 3, pp. 65–102). New York: Academic Press.

Freud, S. (1933). Femininity. In J. Strachey (Ed. and Trans.), *New introductory lectures on psychoanalysis* (Vol. 22). London: Hogarth Press.

Gilligan, C. (1982). *In a different voice.* Cambridge, MA: Harvard University Press.

Hauser, S. T. (1976). Loevinger's model and measure of ego development: A critical review. *Psychological Bulletin*, 83, 928–955.

Helson, R. (1966). Personality of women with imaginative and artistic interests: The role of masculinity, originality, and other factors in their creativity. *Journal of Personality*, 34, 1–25.

Helson, R. (1967). Personality characteristics and developmental history of creative college women. *Genetic Psychology Monographs*, 76, 205–256.

Helson, R., Mitchell, V., & Moane, G. (1984). Personality and patterns of adherence and nonadherence to the social clock. *Journal of Personality and Social Psychology*, 46, 1079–1096.

Helson, R., & Moane, G. (1984). *Personality change in women from college to midlife.* Unpublished manuscript.

Jung, C. G. (1966). Individuation. In *Two essays on analytical psychology* (Collected Works, Vol. 7, pp. 173–241). Princeton: Princeton University Press.

Kohut, H. (1977). *The restoration of the self.* New York: International Universities Press.

Lacy, W. B., & Hendricks, J. (1980). Developmental models of adult life: Myth or reality? *International Journal of Aging and Human Development*, 11, 89–110.

Levinson, D. J. (1978). *The seasons of a man's life.* New York: Knopf.

Loevinger, J. (1966). The meaning and measurement of ego-development. *American Psychologist*, **22**, 195–206.

Loevinger, J. (1976). *Ego development.* San Francisco: Jossey-Bass.

Loevinger, J. (1979). Construct validity in the Sentence Completion Test of ego-development. *Applied Psychological Measurement*, **3**, 281–311.

Loevinger, J., & Wessler, R. (1970). *Measuring ego development: Vol. 1. Construction and use of a sentence completion test.* San Francisco: Jossey-Bass.

Loevinger, J., Wessler, R., & Redmore, C. (1970). *Measuring ego development: Vol. 2. Scoring manual for women and girls.* San Francisco: Jossey-Bass.

O'Connell, A. N. (1976). The relationship between life style and identity synthesis and resynthesis in traditional, neotraditional, and nontraditional women. *Journal of Personality*, **44**, 675–688.

Picano, J. (1985). *Ego development and adaptation in middle-aged women.* Unpublished doctoral dissertation, California School of Professional Psychology, Berkeley.

Rossi, A. S. (1980). Life-span theories and women's lives. *Signs*, **6**, 4–32.

Vaillant, G. E. (1977). *Adaptation to Life.* Boston: Little Brown.

Wrightsman, L. S. (1981). Personal documents as data in conceptualizing adult personality development. *Personality and Social Psychology Bulletin*, **7**, 367–385.

Sex and sex role effects on achievement strivings: Dimensions of similarity and difference

William P. Gaeddert

Abstract

Models of gender differences in achievement were examined to explore their accuracy and redundancy. Self-reports of successes and failures of females and males were content analyzed. The eight dimensions postulated by Bakan (1966; agentic-communal), Stein and Bailey (1973; task-social), Kipnis (1974; other-directed, inner-directed), and Veroff (1977; impact-process) were collapsed into only two dimensions using factor analysis. A domain dimension was used to consider the task (agentic) vs. social (communal) nature of the achievement activities that were undertaken. A performance evaluation dimension referred to whether people used intrinsic (inner-directed, process) or extrinsic (other-directed, impact) factors in evaluating their performance. Analyses using measures of sex role identification, and the stereotypic masculinity or femininity of subjects' achievements suggested: (1) Sex role stereotypes are intimately related to the domains of achievement goals; however, women and men did not differ in the kinds of activities (domains) that they reported, and (2) women (intrinsic) and men (extrinsic) differed in how they defined success and failure, but these performance evaluation styles were not strongly related to sex role identification.

Contemporary research on achievement was initiated by the achievement motivation theory of Atkinson, McClelland, and colleagues (Atkinson & Raynor, 1974; McClelland, Atkinson, Clark, & Lowell, 1953). Sex differences in achievement behavior were apparent early in this work (McClelland et al., 1953), yet systematic research concerning women's achievement was not forthcoming for

This report is based on a dissertation submitted to the Graduate Faculty of Iowa State University in partial fulfillment of the requirements for the PhD degree. Portions of the current study were presented at the 1983 Meetings of the Eastern Psychological Association. Dr. Arnold Kahn deserves thanks for his encouragement and consultation on this research; Kim Sorenson, Nicole Zenian, and David Costello deserve recognition for their execution of their duties as content raters; and the suggestions of an anonymous reviewer are gratefully acknowledged.

nearly twenty years (Alper, 1974; Sarason & Smith, 1971). Research comparing women's and men's achievements suggests substantial gender differences. For example, men attain greater occupational pay and status than do women (Kreps, 1971), men's expectancies for success are higher than are women's in academic settings (Crandall, 1975) and on laboratory tasks (Feather, 1969; Lenny, 1977), and men outperform women in competitive settings (Horner, 1972).

Recent attempts to understand the effects of gender on achievement have focused on differences in women's and men's achievement goals (e.g., Bakan, 1966; Stein & Bailey, 1973) or their standards for accomplishment (e.g., Kipnis, 1974; Veroff, 1977). The current research examines the ability of these explanations to predict sex differences in achievement.

Domain Differences Models

Two explanations suggest that women and men choose different domains of activities for their achievement attempts. Bakan (1966) hypothesized that the life principles of agency and communion typify men's and women's achievement strivings. He proposed that men's achievement strivings are directed at the agentic concerns of self-enhancement, attainment of eminence, and mastery of the environment. Women's communal nature leads them to strive for accomplishments that are based on noncontractual cooperation, and which bring them into a state of harmony with others.

Although Bakan's (1966) agency-communion duality has been used to describe gender differences (e.g., Block, 1973; Buss, 1981; Spence & Helmreich, 1978) there have been few direct tests of his ideas. Carlson (1971) studied men's and women's descriptions of life experiences (not necessarily achievement related) and found that women's reports were more communal (experiences expressed in subjective and interpersonal terms) than were men's. Men's descriptions were more agentic (experiences expressed in objective, individualistic, and personally distant terms) than were women's. Hagen (1975) developed a measure of agency-communion and found it useful in predicting affiliative behavior. In another study (Gaeddert, 1979) this measure was used to predict achievement behavior in competitive (agentic) and cooperative (communal) settings; however, no differences in performance due to the agentic or communal orientation of females or males was observed.

Stein and Bailey (1973) suggested that sex role stereotypes are the carriers of the influence of different socialization for girls and boys (cf. Kagan & Moss, 1962; Hetherington, 1967). They reasoned that women adhere to the feminine role and direct their achievement strivings toward social or affiliative goals, whereas men follow the masculine stereotype and strive for excellence on objectively defined tasks or the mastery of tasks.

Although Stein and Bailey called for an emphasis on "... females' achievement strivings in self-selected activities ..." (1973, p. 345), very little research has directly examined their hypothesis. Travis, Burnett-Doering, and Reid (1982) categorized reports of success and failure events in college students' lives and found mild support for the prediction that women's achievements would be directed at social-affiliative goals. Travis et al. found that descriptions of achievements were focused on the mastery of objective tasks for all subjects; however, women were more likely than men to report affiliative accomplishments.

Performance Evaluation Models

Two explanations propose that women and men evaluate their performances differently. Kipnis (1974) assumed that the socialization of girls and boys leads them to define accomplishment differently. Reliance or peer groups for socialization and relatively loose parental supervision of boys (cf. Bronfenbrenner, 1970) leads them to use other people's performances as standards for determining their own success or failure (other-directed; Kipnis, 1974). Women's reliance on parental approval for achievement efforts (Crandall, Dewey, Katkovsky, & Preston, 1964) was taken as evidence of socialization that leads them to use internalized standards as guides in achievement (inner-directed; Kipnis, 1974).

Although Kipnis (1974) presented a cogent and intuitive argument, her model has not been examined by research designed to test the utility of the inner-directed vs. other-directed dimensions.

In developing a taxonomy of achievement motivation types, Veroff (1977) argued that men emphasize the effects, or impact, of their accomplishments using what was actually accomplished as a measure to define feelings of success. Women, according to Veroff, emphasize the process of accomplishment by reflecting on the effort expended or feelings of competence gained during the course of an achievement attempt in determining whether or not they feel successful.

The process vs. impact distinction was also used by Travis et al. (1982) to describe subjects' self-reports of successes and failures. They found evidence for greater impact orientation in males than in females, and greater process orientation in females than in males. Gaeddert (1979) used the process vs. impact dimension to describe types of achievement situations and found that while most people preferred process-oriented situations (e.g., a cooperative effort), they were preferred more by women than by men; however, no gender differences in performance in the different situations were found.

Purpose of the Present Study

Four models of sex differences in achievement strivings have been proposed. Although each of the models is empirically based, and some have been widely used as descriptions of achievement behavior, they have generated little research to test the accuracy of their predictions about achievement behavior directly. Furthermore, no previous study has compared these models to determine which is most accurate. The current research was aimed at providing these tests. In addition, the extent to which the models are independent or redundant in depicting sex differences in achievement was explored. To accomplish these goals, self-reports of actual success and failure experiences were obtained from female and male subjects. This type of investigation allowed women and men to express freely their preferences for different domains of achievement and their definitions of success vs. failure, rather than being restricted to manipulated tasks and outcomes as is typical of most achievement research.

According to the domain differences models of Bakan (1966) and Stein and Bailey (1973), men's reports should emphasize the mastery of a task and the separation of themselves from others through distinguished achievement to a greater extent than should those of women, whereas women more than men should describe experiences associated with strivings for interpersonal harmony and other affiliative goals.

Based on Kipnis' (1974) and Veroff's (1977) hypotheses concerning the locus of performance evaluation standards, the definitions of success for women should reflect a comparison with internal standards (for example, the effort expended or the steps involved in how the goal was attained) more than should men's definitions. Men's feelings of success should be based on comparisons with other people's performances (in terms of what was actually done) and the attainment of status to a greater degree than should those of women.

The effects of masculinity and femininity. The domain hypotheses of gender differences in achievement (particularly Stein & Bailey's) are based on the assumption that sex role stereotypes influence people's behavior. Psychological masculinity and femininity can be considered to indicate the extent to which individuals espouse sex role stereotypes. Masculinity and femininity are seen as personality characteristics by Spence and Helmreich (1978), who have developed a measure of these dimensions (Personal Attributes Questionnaire; Spence, Helmreich, & Stapp, 1974).

Spence and Helmreich (1978, 1979) have described their scale as measuring instrumentality (masculine) and expressiveness (feminine). Since the domain models of Bakan (1966) and Stein and Bailey (1973) stress the instrumental vs. expressive nature of males and females, it seems likely that scores on the Personal Attributes Questionnaire (PAQ) will be closely associated with differences in achievement domains. It is expected that masculinity will indicate agentic and task-mastery orientations, whereas femininity is expected to predict orientations to communal and social-affiliative accomplishments. Furthermore, it may be that masculinity is associated with other-directed and impact definitions of success, and femininity is associated with inner-directed and process definitions of success.

Method

Pilot Subjects

Twenty-two female and 22 male undergraduate students responded to open-ended questions concerning recent successes and failures, and filled out attribution and personality measures. These subjects' responses were not analyzed, but were used to insure that the achievement questions would elicit detailed responses, and to provide achievement essay protocols to be used in training the essay content raters.

Subjects

Data were collected from 134 undergraduate students who volunteered and received extra credit in psychology courses for their participation. Eleven subjects were dropped owing to their failure to complete attribution or personality measures. The achievement essays, attributions, demographic information, and personality scale responses of 57 female and 66 male subjects were used in analyses.

Subjects' Materials

Subjects received a six-page Essay Booklet and an eight-page Attitudes Booklet. Each booklet contained a cover page which provided instructions and information concerning informed consent.

The second and third pages of the Essay Booklet provided subjects with essay response forms. Success essays were elicited by the following instructions:

We are interested in the ways that people view accomplishment. Please think back over experiences you have had, and determine one instance in which you accomplished something important to you. You may describe any important experience that made you feel successful. Please respond to the following questions about your experience.

Subjects then responded to four questions in an open-ended fashion: "What did you accomplish?"; "Why did you want to succeed at that activity?"; "How did you know that you had succeeded?"; and "What was it about this experience that made you feel successful?".

Failure essays were elicited using the following instructions:

We are interested in the ways that people view experiences in which they do not accomplish something they set out to do. Please think back over experiences you have had and determine one instance in which you did not accomplish something important to you. You may describe any important experience in which you fell far short of achieving your goal. Please answer the following questions about your experience.

Subjects responded to the following four questions in an open-ended fashion: "What did you set out to accomplish?"; "Why did you want to succeed at that activity"; "How did you know that you had not accomplished your goal?"; and "What was it about this experience that made you feel that you had fallen far short of reaching your goal?".

Each subject responded to both success and failure instructions and questions. The order of presentation of success and failure response forms was counterbalanced across sex of subject.

The fourth and fifth pages of the Essay Booklet contained attribution measures. Subjects were asked to refer to the essays they had written, and indicate the extent to which the activity they had described would be hard for most people to accomplish, and the extent to which their ability, luck, the difficulty of what they had attempted, and their effort had affected their performance. Each of these items was presented in an anchored 15-point Likert style format. Subjects were also asked to indicate any other factors that contributed to their performance in an open-ended question. The last page of the Essay Booklet contained items which requested subjects to identify their sex, age, major in school, and cumulative grade point average.

The eight-page Attitudes Booklet contained the 24-item Personal Attributes Questionnaire (PAQ; Spence, Helmreich, & Stapp, 1974) and the 23-item Work and Family Orientation Questionnaire (WOFO; Helmreich & Spence, 1978).

The PAQ is divided into three scales of eight bipolar items each. Subjects responded to this measure on 5-point scales that reflected the extent to which they perceived the items to describe themselves. The scales were scored so that larger scores on the Masculinity Scale indicated masculinity, femininity on the Femininity Scale, and masculinity on the Masculinity-Femininity Scale. The WOFO consists of four scales, each scored on a 5-point agree-disagree format. Responses to the WOFO were tabulated so that high scores indicated competitiveness, emphasis on the efficacy of hard work, a desire for mastery, and little concern for the interpersonal consequences of achivement.

Procedure

Subjects were run in mixed sex groups of five to 20. When all subjects had arrived at the experimental room (3 by 10 meters) they were told that they would be asked to write about personal experiences and to fill out rating scales. Subjects were assured of the confidentiality of their data, the anonymity of their responses, and were instructed to be sure not to indicate their names on any of the response sheets. The Essay Booklets were distributed and after all subjects had completed their responses, the Attitudes Booklet was distributed. The order of presentation of success and failure questions, and PAQ and WOFO Scales was counterbalanced using four orders of presentation. After all subjects had completed the Attitudes Booklet they were provided with a brief explanation of the purpose of the experiment and dismissed.

Content Raters

Two female and two male raters examined subjects' achievement essays. Three of the raters (both females and one of the males) were upper level undergraduate psychology majors. Owing to difficulty in recruiting qualified male raters, the author served as the second male rater.

Rater's Materials

Prior to being content analyzed, each achievement essay was inspected by the author, and edited to remove references to the sex of the writer. For example, phrases such as "My failure has been not being in a sorority," were changed to delete the reference to the writer's sex: "My failure has been in not being in a Greek House." Two essays were deleted during this process (1 female success; 1 male failure), because they could not be edited without destroying the content of the essay.

Training of Raters

A Definition Booklet was prepared for use in training the raters. This booklet provided descriptions and examples of the ten achievement focus dimensions. The descriptions of these dimensions were prepared to provide condensed versions of the models of Bakan (1966; agency vs. communion duality), Stein and Bailey (1973; task vs. social domains), Kipnis (1974; inner- or other-directed achievement), Veroff (1977; process vs. impact orientations), and stereotypic masculinity and femininity. Appendix I contains a summary of these descriptions. Each of the ten dimensions was presented separately, and neither the author(s) of the models nor the expectation of sex differences on the dimensions was mentioned.

The raters met for two training sessions one week apart. The raters were given the Definition Booklet one week before the first training session. The first training session was focused on their understanding of the achievement focus dimensions. The dimensions were discussed, and the raters examined a small number of the achievement essays collected as pilot data.

The second training session stressed consistency and reliability in the content analysis. Raters received content rating sheets which contained the achievement focus scales (presented as 15-point scales), and spaces to provide word counts and the activity described in the essay. The order in which the achievement focus scales appeared on each content rating sheet was randomized and four different orders were used. The raters content analyzed pilot data essays and discussed their ratings of each essay on each of the achievement focus scales. This training session lasted until all ratings were within the same third of each scale for five successive essays.

Rating Procedure

Following the second training session, each rater was provided with rating scales, and a set of essays to be rated. Each edited achievement essay (56 female-success, 57 female-failure; 66-male-success, 65 male-failure) was content analyzed by both a male and a female rater. Sex of writer and success and failure essays were conterbalanced across raters.

The achievement essay content analysis was performed during the raters' spare time, over a period of three weeks.

Independent Variables

The primary independent variable of this research was sex of subject. A second independent variable was the psychological masculinity-femininity category for each subject. Subjects were categorized as masculine, feminine, androgynous, or undifferentiated based on a procedure identical to that recommended by Spence and Helmreich (1978). The distributions of Masculinity and Femininity Scale scores of the PAQ for female and male subjects were examined and approximate median splits were made (see Table 1).

Dependent Variables

The major dependent variable was derived from the content analysis of subjects' achievement essays. Each essay received scores from two raters on each of the ten achievement focus scales. It was found that the normality of the distributions of agentic focus, task focus, impact focus, and masculine orientation scores generated by one pair of raters and the distributions of the communal focus and other-directed scores for the essays rated by the other pair was enhanced by logarithmic transformations. The transformations were performed by taking the natural log of each score and using it as the data base.

After the distributions of achievement focus scores had been examined, the scores for each essay on each scale were standardized for each rater

Table 1. Masculinity-femininity categories.

Category	Cutoff scores	Numbers of subjects	
		Females	Males
Masculine	$M \geq 22$ $F \leq 22$	6	19
Feminine	$M \leq 21$ $F \geq 23$	17	10
Androgynous	$M \geq 22$ $F \geq 23$	16	10
Undifferentiated	$M \leq 21$ $F \leq 22$	8	15

Note.—M and F refer to scores on the Masculinity and Femininity Scales of the Personal Attributes Questionnaire, respectively.

separately. A final score for each essay, on each of the ten achievement focus scales, was derived by averaging the standardized ratings from the two raters who had examined that essay. This procedure was used to provide the achievement focus scores of each essay with enhanced stability, and to insure that a common metric was used for each essay.

The number of words in each achievement essay was counted by the raters. These word counts were then adjusted to return the word count to its preediting value and used in exploratory analysis.

The type of activity that was described in each essay was also determined by each rater. The described activity was coded into one of the following nine categories: scholastic activities; athletic endeavors; employment experiences; personal relationships; group membership concerns; contests and competitions; personal growth; and "other." The few (less than 5% of the categorizations) discrepancies that existed in the categorizations were identified and resolved by the author.

Attributions and WOFO Scale scores were not used in this report; results of analyses using these variables can be obtained from the author.

Results

Interrater Reliability

The extent to which each pair of raters agreed in their assessment of each essay's content was determined by computing Pearson correlation coefficients between the ratings on each of the ten achievement focus scales for each pair of raters. Inspection of these data suggested that some essays were too ambiguous to code accurately. In order to reduce error in subsequent analyses, these essays had to be deleted. Essays that were deleted were identified by the following characteristics: (a) Achievement Focus Scale scores from the two raters reflected little agreement about the content of the essay and (b) inspection of the essay (by the author) revealed that the subject had provided conflicting or confusing information regarding his or her success or failure experience. For example, a female whose accomplishment was attaining a "decent" grade point average wanted the goal in order to "... prove to myself, my family, and my friends that I would be able to deal with college life..." and knew that she had succeeded because "... the grade point showed it, too, my study habits began to improve...." However, she felt successful because she had "... made it with a decent grade point." These statements confound inner direction, other direction, impact, and process emphases in a manner that does not permit an accurate appraisal of the strength with which the subject relied on any particular definition of success. A total of 19 essays (10 males' and 9 females') met both conditions and were deleted.

Pearson correlation coefficients were computed for the reduced sample of achievement focus scale scores and estimates of the pooled reliability of raters were calculated using a procedure outlined by Strahan (1980). Interrater reliabilities for the scales used in the factor analyses ranged from 0.57 (impact focus) to 0.89 (social focus), with a mean of 0.72. Although these reliabilities are not uniformly high, it should be remembered that subjects' scores for the scales consisted of the average of standardized ratings, thus providing a common metric for each rater and enhanced stability.

The major hypotheses of this study were tested using scales based on factor analyses. Estimates of the reliabilities for the factor scores were 0.91 for domain dimension scores, 0.81 for performance evaluation dimension scores, and 0.74 for scores reflecting the stereotypic masculinity/femininity of the essay.

Relationships Among Achievement Focus Scores

The relationships among achievement focus scores were investigated in two factor analyses: one using achievement focus scores from success experiences only, and the other using achievement focus scores from failure experiences only. In both analyses, a principal components solution with iteration of the communality estimates was used for the data reduction step. The factors derived in this step were clarified using the Oblimin (oblique) method of rotation (cf. Cattell, 1957; Nunnally, 1967; Rummel, 1970).

Preliminary factor analyses were examined for success and failure experiences separately. These analyses indicated: (a) that sex of subject did not affect the pattern of relations among achievement focus scores, and (b) that based on a "scree test" (cf. Rummel, 1970) and the meaningfulness of the factors extracted, three factors should be rotated. The factor analyses of subjects' success experience achievement focus scores used the complete data from 110 persons. Table 2 contains summary information for the factor analysis in which three factors were rotated. The factor analysis using failure essays used data from 113 subjects, and yielded a factor structure very similar to that obtained using success essay scores. Table 3 contains a summary of this analysis.

In both analyses, the first factor was substantially defined by task and social foci, with agentic and communal foci also highly loaded. Factor I appears to be a task-mastery vs. social-affiliative domain factor. Factor II was primarily defined by inner- vs. other-directed orientations, with impact orientation highly loaded in the success experiences analysis. In the failure experiences analysis, impact orientation scores cross-loaded on Factor I. Factor II reflects an intrinsic vs. extrinsic performance evaluation dimension. The third factor was formed by the masculine or feminine focus of achievement essays, and appears to be a sex role stereotyped achievement factor.

Since the factors were subjected to oblique rotations, interfactor correlations were examined. Factors I and III were the only factors that were substantially correlated ($r = 0.45$ and -0.47 for the success and failure experience analyses respectively). Stereotypic masculinity was associated with task-mastery accomplishments.

Table 2. Summary of factor analysis using success experiences.

Variables	Factor pattern loadings		
	Factor I	Factor II	Factor III
agentic focus	0.44		
communal focus	− 0.57		
task focus	0.74		
social focus	− 0.92		
impact orientation		0.36	
process orientation		− 0.21	
other directed		0.83	
inner directed		− 0.81	
masculine			0.96
feminine			− 0.98
Eigenvalues	3.07	1.56	0.98
Proportion of variance	0.55	0.28	0.17

Note.—Cross-loaded variables are listed only if their loading exceeded 0.30.

Table 3. Summary of factor analysis using failure experiences.

	Factor pattern loadings		
Variables	Factor I	Factor II	Factor III
agentic focus	0.57		
communal focus	− 0.59		
task focus	0.72		
social focus	− 0.79		
impact orientation	0.38	0.31	
process orientation		− 0.31	
other directed		0.79	
inner directed		− 0.81	
masculine			− 0.98
feminine			0.94
Eigenvalues	3.21	1.84	0.88
Proportion of variance	0.54	0.31	0.15

Note.—Cross-loaded variables are listed only if their loadings exceeded 0.30.

Sex and Sex Role Effects on Achievement Orientations

In order to test the accuracy of the domain and performance evaluation hypotheses regarding sex and gender differences in achievement, subjects' scores on the domain, and performance evaluation factors were analyzed. In addition, sex and gender effects on the stereotypic masculinity/femininity of subjects' accomplishments were explored. Approximate factor scores were computed (cf. Rummel, 1970) so that higher scores reflected more task focus, more extrinsic orientation, and more stereotypic masculinity.

A series of 2 (Subject Sex) × 4 (PAQ Category) × 2 (Success vs. Failure Essays) ANOVAs with repeated measures on the success vs. failure variable were performed.[1] The analysis of subjects' domain factor scores yielded an interaction of success vs. failure and PAQ category, F (3,85) = 2.83, $p < .05$. Table 4 contains the means involved in this interaction and the results of Duncan's tests. Feminine subjects' success essays were more socially focused (less task focused) than were their failure essays and than were the success essays of masculine and undifferentiated subjects.

The analyses of subjects' performance evaluation factor scores revealed main effects of subject sex, F (1,85) = 9.31, $p < .01$, and PAQ category, F (3,85) = 2.70, $p < .05$. Females' performance

1. Preliminary analyses using order of presentation revealed no main effects for that variable, and no interactions of order and any of the other variables that qualified the results presented here. The analyses reported here were performed on the data collapsed across order of presentation.

Table 4. Interaction of PAQ category and Success vs. Failure essays on domain factor scores.

PAQ category	Success	Failure
masculine	− 0.14b	− 0.45ab
feminine	− 1.19a	0.16b
androgynous	− 0.52ab	− 0.29ab
undifferentiated	− 0.05b	− 0.39ab

Note.—Means not sharing common subscripts differ according to Duncan's tests, $p < .05$. Scores were computed so that high (i.e., positive) numbers indicate an emphasis on task-mastery goals and low (i.e., negative) numbers indicate a focus on social-affiliative goals.

evaluation scores revealed a greater reliance on internal standards ($M = − 0.26$) than did males' ($M = 0.17$). Duncan's tests of the means involved in the effect of PAQ category showed that androgynous subjects wrote more extrinsically oriented essays ($M = 0.25$) than did undifferentiated subjects ($M = − 0.30$). The performance evaluation scores of masculine and feminine subjects did not differ from each other or from the other two groups ($M = 0.02$ and $− 0.13$ respectively), all $p < .05$.

Subjects' stereotypic achievement factor scores revealed main effects for subject sex and success vs. failure, $F (1,85) = 12.31$ and 5.79, $p < .01$ and $.05$ respectively. Males' essays and subjects' success experiences were judged to be more stereotypically masculine ($M = 0.43$ and 0.31) than were females' essays and subjects' failure experiences ($M = − 0.26$ and $− 0.23$ respectively).

Essay Characteristics

The number of words subjects wrote in their essays was analyzed with 2 (Subject Sex) × 4 (PAQ Category) ANOVAs. These analyses revealed no differences in the number of words subjects wrote in their success essays; however, females wrote more words in their failure essays than did males, $F (1,105) = 10.44$, $p < .002$ ($M = 84.00$ and 64.38 words for females and males respectively).

Frequencies of the type of activity described in subjects' success and failure achievement essays were broken down by sex and PAQ category. Chi-square analyses of these frequencies revealed no significant differences due to sex or PAQ category. However, the bulk of the essays referred to scholastic accomplishments and failures (31% of the success and 32% of the failure essays).

Discussion

Summary of Results

Scores derived from content analyses of subjects' reports of important accomplishments and failures were factor analyzed, showing that three dimensions were important in describing the achievement experiences of males and females. These dimensions were found in both success and failure experiences, and thus seem to be stable characteristics of the data. Task-agentic vs. social-communal foci provided a domain dimension. An intrinsic vs. extrinsic locus of performance evaluation dimension was determined by impact-other-directed vs. inner-directed-process orientations. Also, subjects' experiences could be described by the extent to which they were stereotypically masculine vs. feminine. Intercorrelations of the factors showed that the stereotypic masculinity/femininity of essays' content was highly associated with differences in achievement domains, but not with the locus of performance evaluation.

Analyses of factor scores revealed that males and females differed in their locus of performance evaluation standards. As predicted by the performance evaluation models of Veroff (1977) and Kipnis (1974), males' experiences revealed greater extrinsic orientation than did females'. Females and males did not differ in the domains of their achievements and failures, nor in the types of activities they described as accomplishments or failures. However, subjects' sex role identity (measured by scores on the Personal Attributes Questionnaire) predicted the domains of their accomplishments: feminine persons' successes were more socially focused than were their failures and than the successes of masculine and androgynous persons. Furthermore, males' essays and success essays were more stereotypically masculine than were females' essays and failure essays, and androgynous persons used extrinsic performance evaluation standards to a greater extent than did undifferentiated persons.

Conclusions About the Domain Dimension

The models of Bakan (1966) and Stein and Bailey (1973) predict sex differences in achievement activities undertaken. The current research shows that although achievement experiences differed in the domains of activities attempted (task vs. social) and that sex role stereotypes were closely related to these domains (masculine-task; feminine-social), women's and men's achievements in this study did not differ in the domains of activities attempted.

Research used to develop the domain hypothesis of sex differences in achievement consisted largely of laboratory studies that linked achievement-related behaviors of girls and women with social or feminine activities (e.g., Crandall, Dewey, Katkovsky, & Preston, 1964; Stein, Pohly, & Mueller, 1971), or the arousal of achievement imagery in women due to socially oriented TAT instructions (e.g., McClelland, et al., 1953).

It appears that although women are able to perceive and react to demands for sex role appropriate behavior in structured (laboratory) situations, when given a choice they are not in fact more likely than are men to choose social relationships as achievement goals. In this study, sex roles (measured as personality dimensions) were associated with differences in achievement domains. This finding is consistent with Stein and Bailey's (1973) suggestion that sex role stereotypes are important in determining achievement domain choice. The failure of most researchers to follow Stein and Bailey's admonition to examine the self-selected achievements of women and men may have misled them to view achievement domains as associated with sex (i.e., males and females) rather than with sex roles (i.e., masculine and feminine roles).

Conclusions About the Performance Evaluation Dimension

The models of Kipnis (1974) and Veroff (1977) constitute performance evaluation hypotheses concerning gender differences in achievement. It was found that achievement experiences could be described by an intrinsic vs. extrinsic performance evaluation dimension, and that men were more likely than were women to define their success in terms of external referents (gaining prestige through accomplishment; pleasing other people through success). Women were more likely than were men to define success by referring to internal standards ("I did what I set out to do"). Performance evaluation styles were not highly related to measures of sex role stereotypes.

The performance evaluation hypothesis has received support from research using experimenter controlled tasks (e.g., Deci, 1972), survey research (Veroff, McClelland, & Marquis, 1971), and studies of subjects' self-selected accomplishments (Travis et al., 1982). It appears that women's and men's achievement strivings differ in the standards of performance evaluation that are used.

Implications for the Study of Sex and Sex Role Effects on Achievement

In this study, sex role stereotypes (measured both as personality characteristics and as characteristics of essays) were strongly related

to those aspects of achievement strivings that revealed no sex differences.[2]

This observation contrasts with much of the research used to
support domain hypotheses of sex differences in achievement. An
important difference between this study and the domain hypothesis
literature is that in the present study subjects were free to report
activities and orientations that were important to *them*. In most
studies used as support for the domain hypothesis, sex linkage of
tasks has been manipulated using instructions that evoke subjects'
expectations about the sex or sex role appropriateness of their
behavior. For example, Stein et al. (1971) used identical tasks in
feminine, masculine, and neutral task conditions; subjects were told
that the tasks were things that girls do well at, boys do well at, and
both boys and girls do equally well, respectively. Stein et al. revealed
the importance of expectancies in determining boys' and girls'
achievement: they did not study what women and men want to
accomplish, nor what women and men can accomplish, nor what
women and men do accomplish. Researchers interested in men's and
women's achievement behavior must heed arguments (e.g., Garnets
& Pleck, 1979; Lott, 1980) that strive to disassociate sex from sex
role stereotypes. Lott (1980) has argued that equating learned behaviors (sex role appropriate behavior) with sex or gender obscures
the malleability of the learned behavior. This argument and the
results of the current study should lead researchers to discover when
and if sex role stereotypes affect women's and men's behavior, and
not assume that they do.[3]

Subjects in this study differed in their use of intrinsic vs. extrinsic
performance evaluation standards: men were more likely than were
women to use external standards for determining success vs. failure.
It may be that men's use of extrinsic or competitive performance
evaluation standards is related to a striving for dominance or status.
Men use touching in interpersonal situations to display dominance

2.   A caveat regarding this conclusion may be warranted: College women and men
may be more similar in achievement goals than are other groups, therefore minimizing
the effects of differences in domains. Noncollege populations may be more diverse in
their achievement goals. Gaeddert and colleagues (1982) compared the achievement
orientations of college and noncollege persons aged 18 to 86 and found some evidence
that males aged 41 to 60 were more task-mastery focused than were women in that
age group. However, these researchers did not examine the specific accomplishments
reported by college vs. noncollege persons. Further research addressing this issue is
needed.

3.   It is interesting to note that people's success experiences were judged to be
more masculine than were their failure experiences. This result is consistent with the
definitions of masculinity/femininity used by the raters, and suggests further support
for the argument that researchers must separate sex and gender in order to describe
accurately their effects on achievement behavior.

and status (Henley, 1973), men's use of personal space connotes high status (cf. Sommer, 1969), and men perceive dominant acts (such as having others perform menial tasks) as more socially desirable than do women (Buss, 1981, Experiment 1). Men's greater use of extrinsic definitions of success and failure seems consistent with the view that men's behavior is often directed at the expression and use of status and power (cf. Kahn & Gaeddert, 1982; Unger, 1979). Researchers are encouraged to examine the self-selected accomplishments of women and men to determine the effects of performance evaluation styles and striving for status on achievement behavior.

Appendix I

Descriptions of Achievement Orientations

Dimension	Description Given to Raters
Communal	People who have a communal focus in achievement want to accomplish things that will make them feel as if they are a part of a group. They would help someone else achieve a goal and not expect anything in return. People with a communal focus toward achievement have the goal of being accepted by other people, and of having harmonious relationships with other people.
Agentic	People with an agentic focus in achievement want to accomplish things that benefit them. They are interested in achievement that sets them apart from other people. They are interested only in achieving their goal, and not with other people or other people's feelings.
Other directed	People who have an other focus in achievement want to achieve so that other people will think highly of them. They are not interested in accomplishment for its own sake. They are interested in achieving goals that will make them stand out in relation to their peers. The reason that they try to do well is to gain social approval.
Inner directed	People who have an inner focus in achievement want to accomplish their goals because it makes them feel good to succeed, whether anyone else knows about their accomplishment or not. People with inner focus desire to achieve because of their intrinsic motivation. They just want to be as good as they can possibly be.

Social orientation	People with a social focus in achievement are primarily interested in accomplishing good social relationships. They don't really care about grades, jobs, etc., what they really care about is their friends. People high in social focus would not want to compete with someone for a job because that competition might get in the way of their friendship. A social focus in achievement means that they try very hard to accomplish their goals, but their goals are mostly involved with having good relationships, being accepted, and being liked.
Task orientation	People with a task focus in achievement are mostly interested in accomplishing a task with a specific answer. Their main goal is to know that they have mastered a particular task, without caring very much how they go about accomplishing the task. They are not concerned with other people, they just want to get the job done.
Process orientation	People with a process focus in achievement would try to achieve things they had chosen to do. They would derive satisfaction from achievement due to the feeling that they had followed the rules and had done the thing right. The major focus is on *how* things are accomplished.
Impact orientation	People with an impact focus in achievement would want to accomplish something because their achievement would show that they had power over other people, or because they could "beat" someone. The person derives their feelings of accomplishment from looking only at the results of their efforts.
Masculine/feminine	Traditional sex roles indicate what is "right" and "wrong" for men and women to do. Men are "supposed to be" self-confident, persistent, aggressive, dominant, competitive, etc. Women are "supposed to be" warm, helpful, emotional, gentle, passive, etc.

Note.—Raters were also provided with experiences which were low and high on each dimension, and a more general description of each dimension.

References

Alper, T. G. (1974). Achievement motivation in college women: A now you see it now you don't phenomena. *American Psychologist, 29*, 194–203.

Atkinson, J. W., & Raynor, J. O. (1974). *Motivation and achievement.* Washington, DC: V. H. Winston & Sons.

Bakan, D. (1966). *The duality of human existence: Isolation and communion in Western man.* Boston: Beacon Press.

Block, J. H. (1973). Conceptions of sex role: Some cross-cultural and longitudinal perspectives. *American Psychologist*, 8, 512–526.

Bronfenbrenner, U. (1970). *Two worlds of childhood: U.S. and U.S.S.R.* New York: Russel Sage Foundation.

Buss, D. M. (1981). Sex differences in the evaluation and performance of dominant acts. *Journal of Personality and Social Psychology*, 40, 147–154.

Carlson, R. (1971). Sex differences in ego functioning: Exploratory studies of agency and communion. *Journal of Consulting and Clinical Psychology*, 37, 267–277.

Cattell, R. B. (1957). *Personality and motivation structure and measurements.* Yonkers-on-Hudson, NY: World Book Co.

Crandall, V. C. (1975). Sex differences in expectancy of intellectual and academic reinforcement. In R. K. Unger & F. L. Denmark (Eds.), *Women: Dependent or independent variable?* (pp. 649–685). New York: Psychological Dimensions Inc.

Crandall, V. J., Dewey, R., Katkovsky, W., & Preston, A. (1964). Parents' attitudes and behaviors and grade school childrens' academic achievements. *Journal of Genetic Psychology*, 104, 53–66.

Deci, E. L. (1972). Intrinsic motivation, extrinsic reinforcement, and inequity. *Journal of Personality and Social Psychology*, 22, 113–120.

Feather, N. T. (1969). Attributions of responsibility and valence of success and failure in relation to initial confidence and task performance. *Journal of Personality and Social Psychology*, 13, 129–144.

Gaeddert, W. P. (1979). *Effects of sex and situation congruence on achievement behavior.* Unpublished master's thesis, Iowa State University, Ames.

Gaeddert, W. P., Roberts, P., Merrens, M. R., Stiefel, G., Mullen, S., Bell, V., Allen, C., & McSweeney, S. (1982, November). *Achievement orientation in adulthood and old age.* Paper presented at the meeting of the Gerontological Society of America, Boston, MA.

Garnets, L., & Pleck, J. H. (1979). Sex role identity, androgyny, and sex role transcendence: A sex role strain analysis. *Psychology of Women Quarterly*, 3, 270–283.

Hagen, R. D. (1975) *Behavioral and introspective manifestations of agency and communion: An exploration.* Unpublished manuscript, Iowa State University, Ames.

Helmreich, R., & Spence, J. T. (1978). The work and family orientation scale (WOFO): An objective instrument to assess components of achievement motivation and attitudes toward family and career. *JSAS Catalog of Selected Documents in Psychology*, 8, 35–63 (Ms. No. 1677).

Henley, N. M. (1973). Status and sex: Some touching observations. *Bulletin of the Psychonomic Society*, 2, 91–93.

Hetherington, E. M. (1967). The effects of familial variables on sex typing, on parent-child similarity, and on imitation in children. In J. P. Hill (Ed.), *Minnesota Symposia on Child Psychology* (Vol. I, pp. 82–107). Minneapolis: University of Minnesota Press.

Horner, M. S. (1972). Toward an understanding of achievement related conflicts in women. *Journal of Social Issues*, 28, 157–176.

Kagan, J., & Moss, H. (1962). *Birth to maturity.* New York: Wiley.

Kahn, A., & Gaeddert, W. P. (1982 August). A status interpretation of gender effects in reward allocation. In A. Eagly (Chair), *Gender differences: The effects of status, power and competence.* Symposium at American Psychological Association.

Kipnis, D. M. (1974). Inner direction, other direction, and achievement motivation. *Human Development*, 17, 321–343.

Kreps, J. (1971). *Sex in the marketplace: American women at work.* Baltimore: John Hopkins Press.

Lenny, E. (1977). Women's self-confidence in achievement settings. *Psychological Bulletin*, 84, 1–13.

Lott, B. (1980). *A feminist critique of androgyny: Toward the elimination of gender attribution for learned behavior.* Unpublished manuscript, University of Rhode Island, Kingston.

McClelland, D. C., Atkinson, J. W., Clark, R. A., & Lowell, E. L. (1953). *The achievement motive*. New York: Irvington Publishers Inc.

Nunnally, J. C. (1967). *Psychometric theory*. New York: McGraw-Hill.

Rummel, R. J. (1970). *Applied factor analysis*. Evanston, Ill.: Northwestern University Press.

Sarason, I. G., & Smith, R. E. (1971). Personality. *Annual Review of Psychology*, 22, 393–446.

Sommer, R. (1969). *Personal space*. Englewood Cliffs, NJ: Prentice-Hall.

Spence, J. T., & Helmreich, R. L. (1978). *Masculinity and femininity: Their Psychological dimensions, correlates, and antecedents*. Austin: University of Texas Press.

Spence, J. T., & Helmreich, R. L. (1979). The many faces of androgyny: A reply to Locksley and Colten. *Journal of Personality and Social Psychology*, 37, 1032–1046.

Spence, J. T., Helmreich, R., & Stapp, J. (1974). The Personal Attributes Questionnaire: A measure of sex role stereotypes and masculinity-femininity. *JSAS Catalog of Selected Documents in Psychology*, 4, 43.

Stein, A. H., & Bailey, M. M. (1973). The socialization of achievement orientation in females. *Psychological Bulletin*, 80, 345–366.

Stein, A. H., Pohly, S. R., & Mueller, E. (1971). The influence of masculine, feminine and neutral tasks on children's achievement behavior, expectancies of success, and attainment values. *Child Development*, 42, 195–207.

Strahan, R. F. (1980). More on averaging judges' ratings: Determining the most reliable composite. *Journal of Consulting and Clinical Psychology*, 48, 587–589.

Travis, C. B., Burnett-Doering, J., & Reid, P. T. (1982). The impact of sex, achievement domain, and conceptual orientation on causal attributions. *Sex Roles*, 8, 443–454.

Unger, R. K. (1979). *Female and male: Psychological perspectives*. New York: Harper & Row.

Veroff, J. (1977). Process vs. impact in men's and women's achievement motivation. *Psychology of Women Quarterly*, 1, 283–293.

Veroff, J., McClelland, L., & Marquis, K. (1971). *Measuring intelligence and achievement motivation in surveys*. Final report to the U.S. Department of Health, Education and Welfare, Office and Economic Opportunity, Contract No. OEO–4180.

Individual differences in moral development: The relation of sex, gender, and personality to morality

Peter D. Lifton

Abstract[1]

Individual differences in moral development are examined, with a particular emphasis on sex and gender differences. This examination includes an extensive review of the empirical and theoretical literature in psychology on morality. Based on this review, it is concluded that sex differences occur with less frequency and with a less systematic favoring of males than is predicted by several theories of moral development. In addition, a study is presented which considers the relation of sex, gender, and personality to morality. Two age cohort samples, college sophomores ($n = 169$) and adults ($n = 151$), were assessed with the moral judgment scale of the cognitive-developmental model (Kohlberg, 1984) and a newly developed moral character template of the personological model (Lifton, in press). Participants also completed the CPI and MMPI personality inventories. Results of the study indicate (1) the absence of sex differences for either model, (2) the presence of gender differences favoring masculine persons for the cognitive-developmental but not personological model, and (3) that individual differences in moral development parallel individual differences in personality development. The implications of these findings are discussed with regard to Gilligan's (1982) claim that men and women differ in their moral orientations. Finally, it is argued that an individual difference approach, particu-

1. Editors' Note. In his article, Dr. Lifton distinguishes between sex as biology and physiology, and gender as psychology and sociology. Although we are in full agreement with the need to distinguish these two terms, his use of gender is narrower than the more structural analysis of power relations between women and men implied by some other authors when using this term in this issue. Readers should note these distinctions.

The author was supported, in part, by NIMH Training Grant No. 5-0-401-5235-38252, L. L. Thurstone Psychometric Laboratory, University of North Carolina, Chapel Hill. Portions of this article were written while the author was a research psychologist at the Institute of Personality Assessment and Research, University of California, Berkeley, and a visiting assistant professor in the Department of Psychological Sciences, Purdue University. The author gratefully acknowledges Harrison G. Gough, Wallace B. Hall, Ravenna Helson, Ellen Finver, David Schindler, Maya Kopell, Maria Eliopoulos, and Ellen D. Nannis for their generous assistance, and Abigail J. Stewart, M. Brinton Lykes, and three anonymous reviewers for their helpful comments in the revision of the manuscript.

larly one that emphasizes personality, would prove useful for future research on moral development.

Theories of moral development traditionally place greater emphasis on individual similarities than on individual differences. Theorists seek first to identify stages of morality, then to establish that most, if not all, persons progress through these stages by following the same developmental sequence over time. Some variation occurs; some persons complete their moral development at an earlier stage than do others. However, the developmental process, the path all persons follow toward moral maturity, is highly uniform. For example, the fundamental tenet of the cognitive-developmental model is that the six stages of morality form an invariant, nonregressive, and universal sequence of development (Colby, Kohlberg, Gibbs, & Lieberman, 1983).

Recently, emphasis has shifted to individual differences in moral development. Gilligan (1982) suggests that individual differences exist between the principles men and women employ as the basis for their moral reasoning. Men tend to prefer the moral principle of justice; women prefer the principle of caring. Hogan (1973, 1982) and Lifton (1983a, in press) suggest that individual differences in personality traits related to morality lead to subsequent differences in moral character. Haan (1978, 1982) posits individual differences in moral reasoning and action due to differences in ego functions and situational stresses.

In this article, individual differences in moral development are examined, with a particular emphasis on sex and gender differences. This examination includes a description of the position of several theories on the issue of sex and gender differences in moral development; a survey of empirical studies in the psychological literature which report on sex differences in moral development; and the presentation of findings from research concerned with the interrelation of sex, gender, personality, and moral development.

Among the issues examined are:

1. On the average, do men and women differ in their level of moral development? If differences exist, on the average are men morally superior to women, or women morally superior to men? Are these differences consistent throughout the entire developmental process?

2. If differences exist, are they sex differences or gender differences? Are they related to biology (sex) or socialization (gender)?

3. Are individual differences in moral development an indication of individual differences in personality development? Should moral

reasoning and behavior be studied within the broader context of personality psychology?

Definition of Terms

Several terms that appear throughout this examination of individual differences in moral development need to be defined. The first are *sex differences* and *gender differences*. These two terms often are used interchangeably in the psychological literature, at times leading to confusion and perhaps even mistaken conclusions. For present purposes, sex differences refer to biological and physiological distinctions between men and women (i.e., anatomy, genes, hormones). Conversely, gender differences refer to psychological and sociological distinctions (i.e., socialization, social roles, social expectations) which occur concomitant to the anatomical categorization of persons. (See Deaux, in press, for a similar discussion of sex and gender.)

Distinguishing between sex differences and gender differences has more than definitional importance. Despite the preponderance of articles purportedly examining sex differences in moral development, only the sociobiologists attribute such differences directly to biological factors (cf. Caplan, 1978; Stent, 1980; Wilson, 1975). Most other researchers who examine sex differences attribute such differences to psychological and sociological factors. By current definitions, they are examining gender differences, not sex differences. Confusion occurs because researchers categorize persons on the basis of their sex (male vs. female), not their gender (masculine vs. feminine). Therefore, it becomes critical to separate individual (sex) differences in moral development due to anatomical factors from individual (gender) differences in moral development due to psychological factors associated with the socialization of men and women.

A second term needing definition is *morality*. There is little consensus among psychologists on a definition. Theorists agree that morality involves judgments of right and wrong. Beyond that, there is broad disagreement.

There appear to be three general types of definitions of morality which correspond, not surprisingly, with three different theoretical perspectives. The first type views morality as synonymous with the rules, norms, values, and traditions of a particular society. Moral codes are equivalent to societal standards and hence vary from culture to culture. The psychoanalytic concept of the superego defines morality in this manner (Freud, 1923/1960, 1924/1961). The superego is an internal, psychological representation of external,

societal standards. These standards pass from society to the child
through the child's parents. Although some aspects of the superego
are common to all cultures (e.g., the taboo on incest), significant
aspects of the superego are unique to the particular culture within
which it forms (e.g., sexual orientation).

The second type of definition views morality as synonymous with
certain universal and transhistorical principles common to all hu-
mankind. These principles transcend the specific moral codes of any
particular person or culture. They are as fundamental to the natural
order of human existence as are principles governing the natural
order of the physical world (e.g., gravity, thermodynamics). The
cognitive-developmental perspective (Gilligan, 1982; Kohlberg,
1981, 1984; Piaget, 1932/1965) defines morality in this manner. In
particular, morality as justice (preservation of human rights and
human life, Kohlberg, 1981; Piaget, 1932/1965) is considered the
universal principle underlying all moral judgments. More recently,
morality as caring (preservation of fair and mutual relationships,
Gilligan, 1982) is offered as a second, complementary universal
principle.

The third type of definition views morality as synonymous with
values, standards, beliefs, and principles developed by a person for
the purpose of effective interaction with other persons. Morality is
a personal set of guidelines with which the individual monitors the
legitimacy and appropriateness of thoughts and behaviors within a
social context. Morality develops intrapersonally, shaped by the
uniqueness of personality, and interpersonally, shaped by the
uniqueness of social interactions. The interactional (Haan, 1978,
1982), socioanalytic (Hogan, 1973, 1982), and personological (Lifton, 1983a, in press) perspectives define morality in this manner.
These three theories, respectively, suggest that ego-processes (e.g.,
coping, defending), personality traits (e.g., socialization, empathy),
and social expectations (e.g., dependability, responsibility) influence
the unique moral judgments and moral actions of persons.

These three types of definitions of morality present three different
viewpoints concerning the etiology and nature of morality. The first
sees morality as a societal control imposed on a person; the second
sees morality as a philosophical principle revealed to a person; and
the third sees morality as a personal precept created by a person.
Given such fundamental differences, no single definition of morality
would be adequate, nor will one be offered. Instead, the exact
meaning of morality will vary depending on the theory of moral
development under discussion.

Despite the variety of definitions for the term morality itself, several other related terms can be defined more readily. *Moral development* is the transition over time of a person's moral beliefs; *moral level* is the sophistication of a person's moral beliefs at a particular time; *moral orientation* is the predominant moral belief of a person at any or all points in time; *moral maturity* is the highest moral level a person achieves and constitutes the endpoint of that person's moral development; *moral judgment* is evaluating right and wrong on the basis of moral beliefs; *moral character* is the psychological structure that serves to organize a person's moral beliefs; *moral reasoning* is cognitive activity based on moral beliefs; and *moral action* is behavioral activity based on moral beliefs.

The third and final term needing definition is *personality*. The definitional complexity of this word is well documented (see Allport, 1937, p. 24–54). For present purposes, particularly given the emphasis in this article on individual differences, personality refers to "more or less stable internal factors that make one person's behavior consistent from one time to another, and different from the behavior other people would manifest in comparable situations" (Child, 1968, p. 83).

Selection Procedure for Literature Review

The purpose of this article is not to provide an exhaustive survey of the empirical literature on sex differences in moral development (see Maccoby & Jacklin, 1974, and Walker, 1984, for more extensive reviews on this topic). Rather, the purpose is to provide some answers to the questions outlined earlier. Consequently, this review considers only studies in the psychological literature, published works through 1983, and most importantly, studies that specifically report either the presence or absence of sex differences in moral development.

This last point requires some elaboration. Virtually all researchers in psychology first analyze their data by sex, "if only to confirm that this variable can be ruled out for further analysis. If the analysis yields insignificant results, the researcher usually breathes a sigh of relief and sees fit not to report his (*sic*) negative findings in print" (Maccoby & Jacklin, 1974, p. 4). The overwhelming majority of studies in the psychological literature on moral development, where the specific issue under examination is not sex differences, report neither the presence nor absence of such differences. This failure to report findings on sex differences must be interpreted with caution. The presumption of this review (and some may disagree) is that these studies in fact found no significant differences. If the study had, the researcher would have reported such a finding. If one accepts this presumption, then the following literature review should be considered against the backdrop of hundreds of studies that failed to report, and therefore implicitly failed to find, any significant differences between men and women in their level of moral development.

Before the empirical literature is reviewed, the theoretical literature on sex differences in moral development is discussed.

Theories Positing Sex Differences in Moral Development

Freud's psychoanalytic theory of morality. Psychoanalysis is the first comprehensive theory of moral development to posit sex differences in favor of men. Moral character or the superego develops through resolution of the Oedipal conflict, an unconscious reenactment by children of primal sexual and aggressive instincts toward their parents. More specifically, children by age four years experience sexual desires toward their opposite-sex parent and feelings of hostility toward their same-sex parent, whom they view as a sexual rival. By age six years, these feelings begin to resolve themselves through defensive and anaclitic identification. The motivation behind these identifications is castration anxiety; the byproduct of these identifications is the superego (Freud, 1923/1960, 1930/1961).

Freud (1923/1960, 1924/1961, 1925/1961) states that castration anxiety is psychologically more threatening to boys for whom castration is a potential, prospective event than to girls for whom castration is an accomplished, retrospective event. "Freud made it clear that the motive for the male child's renunciation of the Oedipal impulses is a strong fear of being castrated by the father . . . The situation in the female child must be different since she does not possess a penis that could be castrated" (Turiel, 1967, p. 130). Since castration anxiety is *the* motivation for resolving Oedipal feelings, boys resolve the Oedipal conflict more successfully than do girls. Boys strongly repress their Oedipal desires; girls slowly renounce their Oedipal desires. Consequently, the relative strength of the superego varies between the sexes. The male superego, compared to the female superego, is a more internalized, rigid, and demanding intrapsychic structure. The general moral character of men, in turn, is more strongly defined than is the moral character of women.

Piaget's cognitive-developmental theory of morality. The belief that individual differences in moral development favor men is not limited to psychoanalysis. Piaget's cognitive-developmental theory of moral judgment posits a similar belief. According to Piaget (1932/1965), children progress from basing moral judgments on consideration of self only (egocentric morality); to basing moral judgments on the standards of other persons, typically adult authority figures (heteronomous morality); to basing moral judgments on their own logical consideration of all moral viewpoints (autonomous morality). Justice is the universal principle on which all children base their moral judgments.

Piaget (1932/1965, p. 315–317) discusses two types of justice. Retributive justice means that moral judgments are based on the consequences of actions, the absolute legitimacy of punishment, and the heteronomy of laws. Distributive justice means that moral judgments are based on the intentions behind actions, the relative legitimacy of punishment, and the autonomy of laws. Furthermore, "distributive justice can be reduced to the ideas of equality and equity" (Piaget, 1932/1965, p. 317). Justice as equality refers to notions of reciprocity, cooperation, and mutual respect. Justice as equity refers to notions of generosity, fairness, and substantive rights. Piaget considers moral judgments of equity superior to moral judgments of equality. "In the domain of distributive justice, equity means no longer thinking of law as identical for all but taking account of the personal circumstances of each (individual). Such an attitude tends to make justice more effectual than it was before" (Piaget, 1932/1965, p. 317). In other words, justice as equity is more useful than is justice as equality.

Most importantly, Piaget considers moral judgments of equity more common among boys while moral judgments of equality are more common among girls. "The most superficial observation is sufficient to show that in the main the legal sense (distributive justice) is far less developed in little girls than in boys. We did not succeed in finding a single collective game played by girls in which there were as many rules and, above all, as fine and consistent an organization and codification of these rules as in the games (played by boys)" (Piaget, 1932/1965, p. 77). In sum, the cognitive-developmental perspective posits that boys prefer the developmentally superior position of justice as equity as the basis for their moral judgments, while girls prefer the developmentally inferior position of justice as equality as the basis for their moral judgments.

Kohlberg's cognitive-developmental theory of morality. Kohlberg shares Piaget's belief that cognitive development underscores moral development and that justice is the universal principle on which all persons base their moral judgments. In contrast to Piaget's theory, which limits moral development to three stages, the highest reached during adolescence, Kohlberg's (1964, 1969, 1976, 1984) theory states that moral development follows a three level, six-stage sequence, the highest stages not reached until adulthood, if ever. Persons progress from basing moral judgments on fear of authority (preconventional level) to basing moral judgments on concern for the welfare of other persons and society (conventional level) to basing moral judgments on respect for the equal and universal rights of all persons. This sequence of stages represents a hierarchy of cognitive organization, each stage defined by an identifiable structure or set of rules for processing morally relevant information. Development involves the reorganization and transformation of prior stage structures, with the resultant new structure capable of processing increasingly intricate moral conflicts (cf. Lifton, 1982a).

Most men and women develop at least to the conventional level. However, within this level, women tend to prefer moral reasoning based on good intentions and gaining social approval (stage 3) while men tend to prefer moral reasoning based on societal laws and maintaining the social order (stage 4). As Holstein (1976) notes, "pure stage 3 reasoning is not compatible with the traditionally instrumental male role, nor is pure stage 4 compatible with the traditionally expressive female role" (p. 59).

Even more pronounced differences appear at the postconventional level. Men more than women prefer moral reasoning based on contractual obligations and democratic principles (stage 5) or individual conscience and universal ethics (stage 6). Only when women occupy professional, educational, and social positions equivalent to men's do they begin to reach the higher stages of morality. Until then, "while girls are moving from high school or college to motherhood, sizeable proportions of them are remaining at stage 3, while their male age mates are dropping stage 3 in favor of the stages above it. Stage 3 morality is a functional morality for housewives and mothers; it is not for businessmen and professionals (Kohlberg & Kramer, 1969, p. 108). (Kohlberg, 1984, p. 340 writes that he "has never directly stated that males have a more developed sense of justice than do females." The previous quotation suggests otherwise.)

Gilligan's cognitive-developmental theory of morality. Gilligan (1982) formulates a cognitive-developmental theory of morality that seeks to correct what she perceives as the inherent male bias of previous cognitive-developmental theories. Gilligan (1982, p. 18) proposes that in addition to justice, there exists a second universal moral principle, the principle of caring. Caring is defined as a morality of responsibility and relationships, a sensitivity to the needs of persons. For persons who base their moral judgments on the principle of caring, development progresses from concern for survival (caring for self), to concern for goodness (caring for others), to concern for truth (caring for self and others) (cf. Lifton, 1982b).

Gilligan (1982, pp. 18–19, 21–22) views men and women as preferring different, not superior or inferior, bases for their moral judgments. Men typically prefer to base their reasoning on justice, while women prefer caring. For men, moral development reflects a desire for separation, a goal compatible with the principle of justice. For women, moral development reflects a desire for attachment, a goal compatible with the principle of caring. Men favor formal and abstract reasoning about competing rights; women favor contextual and narrative reasoning about conflicting responsibilities. Gilligan argues that these differences suggest differences in the moral orientation of men and women, not in the level of their moral development; individual differences between the sexes exist but they are "more a commentary on society than a problem in women's development" (Gilligan, 1982, p. 171).

Theories Positing No Sex Differences in Moral Development

Haan's interactional and Hogan's socioanalytic theories. Not all systems of moral development posit differences between men and women as a theoretical construct. The interactional approach (Haan, 1982, 1983) considers morality a byproduct of interpersonal experiences, ego-defense mechanisms, and effective stress management. Two extensive studies of interactional morality indicate that the "relationship between . . . sex and (interactional) morality is neither strong nor extensive" (Haan, 1978, p. 295); "the variable of sex never makes a significant contribution" (Haan, in press).

The socioanalytic approach (Hogan, 1973, 1982; Hogan, Johnson, & Emler, 1978) considers morality associated with the development of the personality traits of socialization, empathy, and autonomy. Individual differences occur with respect to moral development, but they are a function of individual differences in personality, not sex; "a person's moral development . . . is fundamentally related to the structure of that person's personality" (Hogan & Busch, 1984, p. 238).

Lifton's personological theory of moral character. The personological approach (Lifton, 1983a, in press) considers morality to be a summary statement about the ethical nature of people's behavior. Morality is a dispositional attribute or personological label that people assign to themselves and other persons on the basis of extended periods of observation of behavior. As Hampshire (1953, p.

35) notes, dispositional attributes summarize the individual historical tendencies of people's behavior. If persons are moral, then the word moral "is so far the right word to summarize the general trend or tendency of their conduct."

Morality therefore is not a set of codified rules imposed by society on persons, nor a universal principle revealed to persons. Morality instead is an attribute or label persons assign as a short-hand, summary description of behavior which they judge to be ethical. Theoretically, the basis people use for assigning the dispositional attribute of morality may vary from person to person. In practice, it will be shown that variation is minimal.[2]

Morality considered as dispositional summary statements allows for several theoretical postulates. First, moral persons need not be moral in every situation. They simply need to show a consistent (not constant) level of moral behavior over time and across situations. Consequently, instances of moral courage and moral default (behaving more morally or less morally at a particular point in time compared with most other points in time) are not unexpected or uncommon.

Second, assigning the dispositional attribute of morality to someone does not, in itself, carry with it a prediction concerning future behavior. Morality is a descriptive summary of past behavior, not a prescriptive statement about future behavior. Consequently, the prediction of future moral behavior needs to be based on something other than the assignment of the label of moral to past or present behavior.

Third, assigning the dispositional attribute of morality to someone does not, in itself, carry with it a statement concerning the causality or determinant of moral behavior. As Hampshire (1953) and Buss and Craik (1983, p. 107) argue, dispositional attributes do not offer a causal explanation for behavioral manifestations. These behavioral manifestations instead must be explained on independent grounds and not with recourse to the dispositional attribute itself. The statement "He behaved morally because he is a moral person" is not valid; conversely, the statement "He is a moral person because he behaved morally" is valid.

The independent ground chosen by the personological approach is personality. Personality explains the consistency of past behavior,

2. For example, while persons may disagree on labeling any object on which someone sits a chair, most persons agree to assign the label of "chair" to an object with a seat, four legs, and a back. Agreement is achieved more readily with the second description because it includes the prototypic characteristics of a chair. Similarly, a description that includes the prototypic characteristics of moral behavior should achieve a comparable degree of consensual agreement.

provides a basis for the prediction of future behavior, and allows for causal or determinative statements about behavior. More specifically, personality provides the organizational structure for various psychological systems (e.g., traits, beliefs, thoughts, feelings), among them the system of moral, ethical, and personal beliefs. Note, emphasis is on personality as the organization of traits (Allport, 1937, p. 48), not as specific traits themselves.

The personological approach, therefore, seeks to identify that aspect of personality which serves to organize moral, ethical, and personal beliefs. It labels this suborganization within personality as moral character. Moral character is related to specific personality traits only to the extent that the traits reflect various moral beliefs (e.g., empathy as a belief in interpersonal sensitivity; socialization as a belief in the sanctity of societal rules and authority; responsibility as a belief in maintaining social contracts and obligations). However, moral character is more than simply the sum total of these traits. Moral character is the organizational structure that defines the relation among the traits, and among the moral beliefs reflected by each trait.

Moral character is operationally defined by an instrument known as the Moral Character Template (MCT). The MCT consists of a systematic set of statements descriptive of the behavioral and personological qualities associated with a prototypically moral person. These qualities, rank ordered from most characteristic to most uncharacteristic, form a consensual representation of the criteria or bases people typically employ in order to assign the label of "moral" to themselves or other people. The criteria include personality characteristics, behavioral tendencies, cognitive abilities, and personal and social expectations. The more a person's behavior, and to a lesser extent reasoning, resembles the criteria described by the MCT, the more the label of "moral" applies to that person.

Finally, the personological approach allows, in fact expects, individual differences in moral character. These differences are a function of personality and personality development, not such demographic variables as sex or age.

Empirical Studies of Sex Differences in Moral Development

The psychological literature through 1983 contains forty-five studies that specifically report either the presence or absence of sex differences in moral development. Sixty percent of these studies found no significant differences between men and women with respect to moral development; 40% found significant differences, though sometimes for only one sample studied but not another.

Studies Reporting No Significant Main Effect for Sex

Twenty-seven of forty-five studies surveyed report no significant main effect for sex. Sixteen studies use Kohlberg's Moral Judgment Scale (Bear & Richards, 1981; Berkowitz, Gibbs, & Broughton, 1980; Bielby & Papalia, 1975; Davidson, 1976; Froming, 1978; Haan, 1975, 1978; Haan, Stroud, & Holstein, 1973; Hoffman, 1975; Keasey, 1972; Lifton, 1983a; Maqsud, 1980 a and b; Saraswathi & Sundaresan, 1980; Selman, 1971; Singh, 1981; and Sullivan, Mc-Cullough, & Stager, 1970). Five studies use Rest's (1976) Defining Issues Test, an objective version of the MJS (Ernsberger, 1981; Fleetwood & Parish, 1976; Griffore & Lewis, 1978; Leahy & Eiter, 1980; Orchowsky & Jenkins, 1979). Three studies use Piaget's (1932/1965) moral dilemma stories (Fry, 1975; Jiminez, 1976; Magowan & Lee, 1970). Two studies use Haan's (1978) moral dilemma stories and games (Haan, 1978; Lifton, 1983a). Three studies use Hogan's (1973) empathy, socialization, and autonomy scales based on the California Psychological Inventory (Gough, 1957/1975) (Haier, 1977; Hogan, 1969; Lifton, 1983a). One uses Gilligan's (1982) moral dilemma stories (Pratt & Royer, 1982). Finally, one uses Lifton's (in press) moral character template (Lifton, 1983a).

Thirty-four different samples totaling 4,959 subjects were examined in these studies including 2,092 children, 872 adolescents, 992 college students, and 1,003 adults.

Studies Reporting A Significant Main Effect for Sex

Eighteen of forty-five studies surveyed report a significant main effect for sex.[3] Fourteen studies use Kohlberg's Moral Judgment Scale. Of these studies, five report findings in favor of females during childhood and adolescence (Biaggio, 1976; Freeman & Giebink, 1979; Krebs & Gillmore, 1982; Saltzstein, Diamond, & Belenky, 1972; Srivastava, 1977) and one reports findings in favor of females

3.   In a similar survey of the moral development literature, Walker (1984) finds that 6 of 41 samples of children and early adolescents, 10 of 46 samples of late adolescents and college students, and 4 of 21 samples of adults show a main effect for sex for Kohlberg's cognitive-developmental model. Differences during childhood and early adolescence tend to favor females, while differences during late adolescence through adulthood tend to favor males. Maccoby and Jacklin (1974) in their survey identify 10 of 27 studies reporting sex differences in moral development. Once again, differences during childhood favor females, while differences in adulthood favor males.

Table 1. Studies reporting on sex differences in moral development.

Study	Sample	n	Measure	Main effect for sex
Arbuthnot, 1983	college	207	MJS	$F > M$
Bear & Richards, 1981	child	60	MJS	ns
Berkowitz, Gibbs, & Broughton, 1980	college	82	MJS	ns
Biaggio, 1976	child	90	MJS	$F > M$
Bielby & Papalia, 1975	child	12	MJS	ns
	adol.	12	MJS	ns
	college	12	MJS	ns
	adult	36	MJS	ns
Bussey & Maughan, 1982	college	40	MJS	$M > F$
Davidson, 1976	child	176	MJS	ns
Ernsberger, 1981	adult	160	DIT	ns
Fleetwood & Parish, 1976	adol.	29	DIT	ns
Freeman & Giebink, 1979	adol.	240	MJS	$F > M$, 14 yrs.; no effect, 11 & 17 yrs.
Froming, 1978	college	200	MJS	ns
Fry, 1975	child	100	PMD	ns
Gottlieb, Taylor, & Ruderman, 1977	child	140	PMD	$F > M$, 5 yrs.; no effect, 3, 4, & 9 yrs.
Griffore & Lewis, 1978	adult	78	DIT	ns
Haan, 1975	college	310	MJS	ns
Haan, 1978	adol.	56	MJS & HMD	ns
Haan, Langer, & Kohlberg, 1976	adult	262	MJS	$M > F$
Haan, Smith, & Block, 1968	college	214	MJS	compared with total sample, 21% *F* & 11% *M* at stage 3; no effect at other stages nor average across all stages.
	adult	296	MJS	
Haan, Stroud, & Holstein, 1973	adol.	~15	MJS	ns for both samples combined.
	adult	~43	MJS	
Haier, 1977	college	132	SEA	ns
Hoffman, 1975	child	1137	MJS	ns
	adult	580	MJS	ns
Hogan, 1969	adol.	121	SEA	ns

Table 1.—Continued

Study	Sample	n	Measure	Main effect for sex
Holstein, 1976	adol.	53	MJS	$M > F$; modal for boys stage 4, modal for girls stage 3;
	adult	106	MJS	$M > F$; modal for men stages 4 & 5, modal for women stages 3 & 4.
Jiminez, 1976	child	216	PMD	ns
Kahn, 1982	adol.	508	DIT	$F > M$
Keasey, 1972	child	155	MJS	ns
Krebs & Gillmore, 1982	child	51	MJS	$F > M$
LaVoie, 1974	child	120	PMD	$F > M$
Leahy & Eiter, 1980	adol.	116	DIT	ns
Lifton, 1983a	college	100	MJS, HMD,	ns all 4 measures;
	adult	82	SEA, & MCT	ns all 4 measures.
Lyons, 1983	child	6	MJS & GMD	compared with total sample
	adol.	6	MJS & GMD	of females, "caring"
	college	12	MJS & GMD	theme predominant for
	adult	12	MJS & GMD	75% F; compared with total sample of males, "justice" theme predominant for 79% M.
Magowan & Lee, 1970	child	56	PMD	ns
Maqsud, 1980a, 1980b	adol.	210	MJS	ns
Orchowsky & Jenkins, 1979	college	84	DIT	ns
Parikh, 1980	adult	78	MJS	$M > F$
Poppen, 1974	college	104	MJS	$M > F$
Pratt & Royer, 1982	adol.	24	GMD (DIT)	ns for all samples (mea-
	college	72	GMD (DIT)	sured with a modified DIT
	adult	24	GMD (DIT)	to include "caring" themes).
Roberts & Dunston, 1980	child	120	PMD	$M > F$, preschoolers; $F > M$, 4th & 5th grade.
Saltzstein, Diamond, & Belenky, 1972	adol.	63	MJS	$F > M$
Saraswathi & Sundaresan, 1980	adol.	249	MJS	ns
Selman, 1971	child	60	MJS	ns

Table 1.—Continued

Study	Sample	n	Measure	Main effect for sex
Singh, 1981	child	120	MJS	ns
Srivastava, 1977	child	80	MJS	F > M
Sullivan, Mc-Cullough, & Stager, 1970	adol.	40	MJS	ns
Turiel, 1976	child	63	MJS	F > M, 10 yrs.; F > M, 13
	adol.	147	MJS	yrs.; M > F, 16 yrs.

Note—For sample category, *child* = 6–12 years old; *adolescent* = 13–18 years old; *college* = 18–22 years old; and *adult* = ≥ 23 years old.

For measure category, *DIT* = Rest's (1976) Defining Issues Test; *GMD* = Gilligan's (1982) Moral Dilemmas; *HMD* = Haan's (1978) Moral Dilemmas & Games; *MCT* = Lifton's (1983a) Moral Character Template; *MJS* = Kohlberg's (1984) Moral Judgment Scale; *PMD* = Piaget's (1932/1965) Moral Dilemmas; and *SEA* = Hogan's (1973) Socialization, Empathy, & Autonomy Scales based on the California Psychological Inventory (Gough, 1957/1975).

during early adolescence but males during late adolescence (Turiel, 1976). Six studies report findings in favor of males during college and adulthood (Bussey & Maughan, 1982; Haan, Langer, & Kohlberg, 1976; Haan, Smith, & Block, 1968; Holstein, 1976; Parikh, 1980; Poppen, 1974), one reports findings in favor of females during college (Arbuthnot, 1983). One final study reports differences in moral orientation, with males compared to females preferring the principle of the justice by a three to one ratio (Lyons, 1983).

One study using Rest's Defining Issues Test reports a difference favoring adolescent females over males (Kahn, 1982). Three studies use Piaget's moral dilemma stories and, in general, report a difference favoring female children to male (Gottlieb, Taylor, & Ruderman, 1977; LaVoie, 1974; Roberts & Dunston, 1980). One final study, using Gilligan's moral dilemma stories, reports a difference in moral orientation with females compared to males preferring the principle of caring by a five to one ratio (Lyons, 1983).

Twenty different samples totaling 3,018 subjects were examined in these studies including 672 children, 1,015 adolescents, 573 college students, and 758 adults.

Are There Sex Differences in Moral Development?

Sex differences in moral development appear more the exception than the rule. Furthermore, if one accepts the supposition offered earlier in this article, that failure to report sex differences in a study implies the probable absence of such differences, the occurrence of sex differences in moral development becomes an even rarer event.

When sex differences do occur, they are associated most often with Kohlberg's cognitive-developmental model. Of the thirty studies employing this model, 47% (14/30) report the presence of sex differences. By comparison, of the six studies employing either Haan's interactional, Hogan's socioanalytic, or Lifton's personological model, none reports sex differences. Walker (1984, p. 688), in a recent review of the psychological literature on sex differences, moral reasoning, and the cognitive-developmental model, concludes that "several studies yielding sex differences favoring men were methodologically flawed . . . and relied on early stage definitions and scoring procedures." Walker argues that if the cognitive-developmental model is sex biased in favor of men, the bias lies in the previous scoring manuals, not in the theoretical model itself.

However, if differences in moral development between men and women are due solely to the bias of scoring procedures or the methodological flaws of studies, one would expect this bias to favor one sex over the other consistently. Yet, as presented above, some studies have found the particular, though admittedly mercurial phenomenon of moral development during childhood favoring females and moral development during adulthood favoring males, with adolescence a period of transition or developmental crossover. Perhaps then individual differences in moral development between men and women are related more to social roles and expectations associated with each sex than to biological and anatomical qualities inherent to each sex.

In the following study, two hypotheses were examined: (1) individual differences in moral development are related more to gender (social roles and expectations) than to sex (biological and anatomical qualities); and (2) gender-related differences are reflective of individual differences in personality between men and women at comparable levels of moral development.

Method

Samples

Participants were from two developmentally distinctive populations, college sophomores and adults. The first group ($n = 169$) was predominantly white, middle to upper-middle class, University of California, Berkeley undergraduates randomly selected from the population of second-year students. The sample, whose average age was 19.2 years, contained slightly more females ($n = 86$) than males ($n = 83$).

The second group ($n = 151$) consisted of adults randomly solicited from predominantly white urban and suburban areas of the San Francisco Bay community. The sample of men ($n = 75$) ranged in age from 32 to 58 years, the women ($n = 76$) from 20 to 45 years. The average age for all adults was 34.5 years.

Design and Procedure

Persons participated ten at a time in a one-day assessment center program at the Institute of Personality Assessment and Research (IPAR), University of California, Berkeley. IPAR uses a methodological design that employs multiple observations of subjects by numerous assessors across a wide variety of assessment techniques. The observational descriptions by assessors of participants are based on life history interviews, personal and social values interviews, leaderless group discussions, "party games" (e.g., charades), and conversations during casual encounters (e.g., luncheon and dinner meals, cocktail hour). Data from descriptions by assessors are supplemented by self-report personality measures. (For a more detailed description of the IPAR assessment center program, see Lifton, 1983b and Wiggins, 1973, p. 515–603.)

Personality Measures

Two standard self-report personality measures were administered. One was the *California Psychological Inventory* (CPI) (Gough, 1957/1975), a measure concerned with everyday interpersonal behavior and social interactions. The other was the *Minnesota Multiphasic Personality Inventory* (MMPI) (Hathaway & McKinley, 1948/1967), a measure designed for psychiatric diagnosis of abnormal personality types.

Measures of Moral Development

Two measures assessed the moral development of the participants; one measured moral judgement, the other moral character.

Moral Judgment Scale. (Kohlberg, 1976, 1981). Moral judgment scores for Kohlberg's six stages of cognitive-development were obtained from the responses by participants to interview questions concerned with various moral issues. These included questions on alcohol, tobacco, and drug usage, contraception and abortion, childrearing practices, the role of women in modern life, political and religious beliefs, rehabilitation vs. punishment of criminals, and individual vs. societal rights. The transcribed interviews were scored blindly by four judges (noninterviewers) trained with the Moral Judgment Scale scoring manual (Kohlberg, Colby, Gibbs, & Speicher-Dubin, 1978).

A moral judgment score based on frequency of stage response was assigned to each participant's interview by each judge. These scores were composited across judges by weighting pure stage scores (e.g., stage 4) two points and transitional scores (e.g., stage 3/4) one point, per stage. If the summed weights of a stage exceeded two times the weights of any other stage then a pure stage score was assigned as the participant's overall level of moral judgment. Otherwise, a transitional stage score was assigned based on the

24 hours TEMPORARY HOLD

OLD UNTIL: 29/11/2000

r PATRON:
AME, Firstname

~~#ej~~ Hegenbarth
Ming

ODAY'S DATE:
TAFF INITIALS: 28/11/2000

ID

two highest weighted stages. For the college sophomore and adult samples combined, the average interrater reliability of the judges was .73 with a range from .56 to .81.

It should be noted that moral judgment scores were not derived from responses to the traditional hypothetical dilemma stories (e.g., Heinz, Officer Brown). The decision to deviate from the stories stemmed from the increasing evidence that hypothetical moral dilemmas elicit hypothetical responses of moral reasoning (Arendt, 1976; Haan, 1975; Gilligan, 1982; Lifton, 1983a; Rest, 1976). As Haan (1975) notes, "there are systematic differences between giving a story character fictitious moral advice, and formulating and acting on advice for oneself" (p. 269). She argues that one reason for these systematic differences comes from the increased personal investment or responsibility felt by persons in response to nonhypothetical moral dilemmas. Conversely, the absence of personal responsibility associated with hypothetical dilemmas makes it easier for persons to simply philosophize or "wax poetic" about their moral decisions.

Even Kohlberg now recognizes the important role personal responsibility plays in improving the validity of cognitive-developmental stage scores. Recently, Kohlberg (1984, pp. 252–257, 534–536) introduced the notion of a "substage B" or "judgment of responsibility" response into both the cognitive-developmental theory of moral judgment and the most recent scoring manual (Colby & Kohlberg, in press). This latest revision allows for some indication of the degree of personal responsibility felt by a person in response to a hypothetical moral dilemma. However, this major revision in theory and practice was not available at the time this research study was conducted in 1982 and 1983. Therefore, this study used nonhypothetical moral issues in the belief that they were an appropriate means for increasing the personal relevance and personal responsibility of responses by participants, thereby eliciting more valid information concerning the cognitive-developmental stage of moral reasoning of each participant.[4]

Moral Character Template. (Lifton, 1983a, in press). The moral character template is composed of items from the California Q-sort (Block, 1961), a measure well documented for its effectiveness in describing prototypic behaviors. The Q-sort consists of 100 statements, each one descriptive of a particular aspect of an individual's personality or behavior. The Q-sort is an ipsative measure; that is, the placement of each item depends on the placement of the other 99 items. Statements are grouped into one of nine categories ranging from "1" (most uncharacteristic) to "9" (most characteristic). Each category along this continuum is defined by a fixed number of items thereby ensuring a quasi-normal distribution.

The moral character template was developed from the Q-sort descriptions by twenty expert judges (10 male and 10 female faculty and advanced

4. The ability to assign stage scores to statements generated outside of the standard moral judgment interview procedure is well documented. Kohlberg and Candee (1984) have analyzed statements by participants in Milgram's experiments on obedience to authority (p. 546–548), soldiers involved in the My Lai massacre in Vietnam (p. 564–572), and Watergate defendants (p. 572–575).

graduate students in personality psychology) of an "ideally or prototypically moral" person. The composite of the experts' Q-sort descriptions was validated against the composite of Q-sort descriptions by sixty naive judges (30 male and 30 female college undergraduates). The correlation coefficient between the two composites was .79 ($p < .001$). No significant differences by sex of judge were found for any Q-sort item (all the t tests on each Q-sort item exceeded the .05, 2-tailed level of confidence). Only the Q-sort descriptions of the expert judges were used to create the MCT because these experts were presumed more knowledgeable about the psychology of morality, personality, and the Q-sort method itself. Alpha reliability for the 100-item MCT was .96.

In the study, five observers (assessors) used the California Q-sort to describe each participant. Their Q-sort descriptions were composited arithmetically, and the resultant composite resorted to retain the original quasi-normal distribution of items. For the college sophomore and adult samples combined, the average alpha reliability of the composite was .76 with a range from .40 to .92.

Moral character scores were derived by first correlating the template with the composited Q-sort descriptions by observers of the participants in the study, then converting the Pearson r coefficients to z scores. Moral character scores ranged from $+ 1.26$ to $- 1.08$ with a theoretical range from $+ 3.00$ to $- 3.00$. (For a more detailed description of the template matching methodology, see Bem & Funder, 1978.)

Table 2. Moral Character Template.[a,b]

Items most characteristic of a moral person	Actual mean	Q-sort value
Behaves in an ethically consistent manner.	9.00	9
Is a dependable and responsible person.	8.75	9
Straightforward and forthright with others.	8.25	9
Is concerned with philosophical problems.	8.17	9
Behaves in a giving way toward others.	7.83	9
•	•	•
•	•	•
•	•	•
Items most uncharacteristic of a moral person		
Extrapunitive; tends to transfer or project blame.	2.08	1
Creates and exploits dependency in people.	2.00	1
Negativistic; tends to undermine or obstruct.	1.92 (t)	1
Pushes limits; sees what she/he can get away with.	1.92 (t)	1
Is guileful, deceitful, manipulative, opportunistic.	1.00	1

[a] Item descriptions based on the California Q-sort (Block, 1961).
[b] Table 2 presents only the extreme items on the Moral Character Template. The complete template contains 100 items in descending order of magnitude. A copy of the entire Moral Character Template is available on request from the author.

Results

Sex Differences in Moral Development

Data were analyzed to determine if sex differences exist with respect to the distribution of scores for males and females on each measure of moral development. For Kohlberg's Moral Judgment Scale, χ^2 (10) = 6.75 (ns) and 5.36 (ns) for the college sophomore and adult samples, respectively. For Lifton's Moral Character Template, $t(168)$ = 1.34 (ns) and $t(150)$ = 1.31 (ns) for the respective samples. From these analyses, males and females appear to be at comparable levels of moral development.

Gender Differences in Moral Development

Data also were analyzed to determine if gender differences exist with respect to the distribution of scores for masculine and feminine persons on each measure of moral development. Mean splits of the Femininity (Fe) Scale based on norms in the California Psychological Inventory manual (Gough, 1957/1975) were used as the basis for categorizing persons as either masculine or feminine. For men, Fe scores ≤16 were masculine, ≥17 feminine. For women, Fe scores ≤22 were masculine, ≥23 feminine.

For Kohlberg's moral judgment scale, χ^2 (10) = 19.41 ($p < .05$) and 24.66 ($p < .01$) for the college sophomore and adult samples, respectively. For Lifton's moral character template, $t(168)$ = 0.98 (ns) and $t(150)$ = 1.12 (ns) for the respective samples. From these analyses, masculine persons appear at a higher stage of moral devel-

Table 3. Means and standard deviations for moral judgment and moral character scores by sex and gender.

Sex / Sample	n	Moral judgment M	σ	Moral character M	σ
Sophomores					
Male	83	3.49	.89	4.03	3.99
Female	86	3.23	.90	4.61	3.36
Adults					
Male	75	4.05	.75	5.30	3.55
Female	76	3.84	.69	5.62	3.26
Gender / Sample					
Sophomores					
Masculine	81	3.62	.96	4.40	3.90
Feminine	88	3.12	.83	4.24	3.45
Adults					
Masculine	74	4.35	.68	5.33	3.24
Feminine	77	3.54	.77	5.59	3.55

Note—Moral character scores multiplied by a constant of 10.

opment than feminine persons according to the cognitive-developmental model. Masculine and feminine persons appear comparable in level of moral development according to the personological model.

Personality Correlates of Moral Judgment and Moral Character

Moral judgment and moral character scores were correlated with standard and selected experimental scales of the CPI and MMPI to determine the personality characteristics associated with moral men and women. Analyses were computed within age (college sophomores vs. adults), sex (males vs. females), and theoretical model (moral judgment vs. moral character).

From the cognitive-developmental perspective, the moral judgment of young men (college sophomores) appears related to personality characteristics associated with the development of a sense of self-identity. Moral judgment correlates positively with social introversion (.26), anxiety (.25), and schizophrenia (.21), and negatively with psychological mindedness (− .41), sense of well-being (− .33), communality (− .21), ego-strength (− .21), and ego-control (− .21).

Conversely, the moral judgment of young women appears related to personality characteristics associated with the development of a sense of social identity. Moral judgment correlates positively with intellectual efficiency (.39), social dominance (.32), self-acceptance (.32), sociability (.28), ego-resiliency (.28), sense of well-being (.24), social responsibility (.23), achievement via conformance (.22), ego-strength (.22), and social presence (.21), and negatively with most types of psychopathology.

The moral judgment of older men and women (adults) appears related to personality characteristics associated with the development of mature, balanced, and symbiotic senses of self and social identity. For men, positive correlates of moral judgment and personality include ego-strength (.50), sense of well-being (.46), intellectual efficiency (.43), psychological mindedness (.43), social maturity (.43), socialization (.41), tolerance (.41), achievement via independence (.41), and ego-control (.40); negative correlates include femininity (− .23) and most types of psychopathology.

For women, positive correlates of moral judgment and personality include self-control (.42), achievement via conformance (.34), communality (.30), psychological mindedness (.29), ego-resiliency (.24), ego-control (.23), good impression (.23), and sense of well-being (.22); negative correlates include flexibility (− .35) and most types of psychopathology.

Table 4. California psychological inventory correlates with moral judgment and moral character scores.

	Moral judgment				Moral character			
	Sophomores		Adults		Sophomores		Adults	
	Males	Females	Males	Females	Males	Females	Males	Females
CPI	(n = 83)	(n = 86)	(n = 75)	(n = 76)	(n = 83)	(n = 86)	(n = 75)	(n = 76
Do	− .10	.32**	.16	.07	.20	.05	.29*	− .21*
Cs	.09	.16	.11	.17	.25*	.04	.29*	.07
Sy	− .07	.28*	.13	− .15	.30**	.36**	.30**	.01
Sp	.01	.21*	.02	− .07	.13	.15	.22*	.18
Sa	.05	.32**	.06	.12	.13	.15	.24*	− .15
Wb	− .33**	.24*	.46***	.22*	.26*	.07	.09	.33**
Re	.08	.23*	.35**	.21*	.16	.05	.33**	.20
So	− .10	.06	.41***	.11	.27*	.13	.31**	.33**
Sc	− .19	.08	.32**	.42***	.08	− .07	.04	.30**
To	− .14	.18	.41***	.12	− .03	.13	.17	.32**
Gi	− .06	.09	.21*	.23*	.16	− .14	− .01	− .06
Cm	− .21*	.07	.12	.30**	.04	.06	.21*	.21*
Ac	− .17	.22*	.26*	.34**	.24*	.12	.24*	.21*
Ai	− .04	.04	.41***	.04	− .03	.06	.37**	.21*
Ie	− .11	.39**	.43***	.17	.20	.06	.46***	.11
Py	− .41***	.07	.43***	.29*	.16	− .05	.02	.15
Fx	.06	− .06	.15	− .35**	− .21*	.14	.25*	− .01
Fe	.17	.09	− .23*	.14	− .19	.20	.05	.03
Em	.12	.17	.15	− .14	.11	.09	.26*	.01
In	.03	.20	.28*	.21*	.03	.10	.16	.06
SMI	.04	.17	.43***	− .02	.20	.25*	.45***	.27*

Note.—CPI Scales: *Do* = Dominance; *Cs* = Capacity for status; *Sy* = Sociability; *Sp* = Social presence; *Sa* = Self-acceptance; *Wb* = Sense of well-being; *Re* = Responsibility; *So* = Socialization; *Sc* = Self-control; *To* = Tolerance; *Gi* = Good impression; *Cm* = Communality; *Ac* = Achievement via conformance; *Ai* = Achievement via independence; *Ie* = Intellectual efficiency; *Py* = Psychological mindedness; *Fx* = Flexibility; *Fe* = Femininity; *Em* = Empathy; *In* = Independence; *SMI* = Social maturity index.
*** $p < .001$.
** $p < .01$.
* $p < .05$.

Hence, for the cognitive-developmental model, the moral development of young men is related to an almost neurotic concern for the development of a self-concept or self-identity. For these men, judgments about moral issues are predicated on consideration for the intrapersonal adequacy of the self. Conversely, the moral development of young women is related in a more psychologically facilitative manner to a concern for the development of a social self or social identity. For these women, judgments about moral issues are predicated on consideration for the interpersonal adequacy of the

Table 5. Minnesota multiphasic personality inventory correlates with moral judgment and moral character scores.

	Moral judgment				Moral character			
	Sophomores		Adults		Sophomores		Adults	
	Males	Females	Males	Females	Males	Females	Males	Females
MMPI	(n = 83)	(n =86)	(n = 75)	(n = 76)	(n = 83)	(n = 86)	(n = 75)	(n = 76)
L	.05	− .03	.14	.10	.05	.00	− .12	.08
F	.19	− .07	− .31**	.17	− .09	− .07	− .34**	− .31**
K	− .10	.05	.23*	.13	.07	.04	.03	.29*
Hs	− .05	− .22*	− .34**	− .26*	− .09	− .04	− .12	− .30**
D	.09	− .29*	− .09	.00	− .28*	− .18	− .30**	− .09
Hy	− .19	− .21*	− .19	− .03	− .19	.07	− .10	− .15
Pd	− .15	− .18	− .34**	− .09	− .15	− .08	− .30**	− .40***
Mf	.17	− .09	− .11	− .25*	− .29*	.21*	.11	.18
Pa	− .02	− .12	.01	− .26*	− .09	.11	− .12	− .17
Pt	− .03	− .28*	− .28*	− .35**	− .11	.00	− .17	− .27*
Sc	.21*	− .18	− .27*	− .30**	− .12	− .02	− .18	− .24*
Ma	.01	− .02	− .42***	− .29*	.16	.05	− .02	− .24*
Si	.26*	− .31**	− .15	.06	− .27*	− .19	− .20	− .10
A	.25*	− .19	− .27*	− .19	− .19	− .08	− .08	− .35**
R	− .04	− .11	.10	− .30**	− .24*	− .10	− .15	.11
ES	− .21*	.22*	.50***	.15	.07	.04	.22*	.09
EC	− .21*	− .18	.40***	.23*	.05	− .04	.01	.33**
ER	− .12	.28*	.24*	.24*	.13	.04	.00	.43***

Note.—MMPI Scales: *L* = Lie; *F* = Frequency; *K* = Correction; *Hs* = Hypochondriasis; *D* = Depression; *Hy* = Hysteria; *Pd* = Psychopathic deviate; *Mf* = Masculinity-femininity; *Pa* = Paranoia; *Pt* = Psychasthenia; *Sc* = Schizophrenia; *Ma* = Hypomania; *Si* = Social introversion; *A* = Anxiety; *R* = Repression; *ES* = Ego strength; *EC* = Ego control; *ER* = Ego resiliency.
*** p < .001.
** p < .01.
* p < .05.

self. Finally, the moral development of older men and women is related to the development of an integrated sense of self and social identity. For these men and women, judgments about moral issues are predicated on consideration for both the intrapersonal and interpersonal adequacy of the self.

From the personological perspective, the moral character of young men and women (college sophomores) appears related to personality characteristics associated with the development of a sense of social identity or social self. For men, moral character correlates positively with sociability (.30), socialization (.27), sense of well-being (.26), capacity for status (.25), and achievement via conformance (.25); negative correlates include social introversion (− .27) and flexibility (− .21). For women, moral character correlates positively with sociability (.36) and social maturity (.25).

The moral character of older men and women (adults) appears related to personality characteristics associated with the development of a balanced sense of self and social identity. For men, positive correlates of moral character and personality include social maturity (.45), intellectual efficiency (.46), achievement via independence (.37), social responsibility (.33), socialization (.31), and sociability (.30). For women, positive correlates of moral character and personality include ego-resiliency (.43), ego-control (.33), sense of well-being (.33), socialization (.33), tolerance (.32), and social maturity (.27); negative correlates include social dominance ($-$.21) and most types of psychopathology.

Hence, for the personological model, the moral character of young men and women is related to their development of a sense of social identity. The moral character of older men and women is related to their development of an integrated sense of social and self identity.

Discussion

There are several points that now can be discussed concerning the relation of sex, gender, and personality to morality.

First, sex differences occur with less frequency and with a less systematic favoring of males than is predicted by several theories of moral development. The inaccuracy of these predictions may be due, in part, to the initial observations by theorists of predominantly if not exclusively male populations.

Second, those studies that do report the presence of sex differences find them mainly for the cognitive-developmental model. Walker (1984) suggests that this phenomenon is more reflective of past deficiencies in the procedures used to assign moral judgment stage scores than of the concept of morality itself. The results of the study reported in this article suggest support for Walker's claim. No significant sex differences were found for either the college sophomore or adult samples, each assessed for stage of moral judgment by a procedure paralleling the more current interview and scoring procedures. Equally important, no sex differences were found using the moral character template, lending credence to the viewpoint that sex as a variable is essentially irrelevant to moral development.

Third, gender differences may be related to morality, particularly morality as defined and operationalized by the cognitive-developmental model. Significant differences in stage of moral judgment were found between masculine and feminine persons for both the college sophomore and adult samples. This suggests qualified support for Gilligan's (1982) contention that men and women differ in their moral orientations, with men preferring the universal principle of justice, women the universal principle of caring. Gilligan correctly views the cognitive-developmental model as favoring moral reasoning based on justice over moral reasoning based on caring. However, she incorrectly concludes that the model, in turn, favors males over females (sex differences) when instead the model may favor masculine over feminine persons (gender differences).

For the personological approach, which defines morality as personal rather than universal principles necessary for social interaction, gender is unrelated to moral development. This suggests that gender differences may be related more to the theoretical assumptions underlying models of morality than to the concept of morality itself. Further studies on gender and moral development are needed, studies that examine gender differences using dissimilar theoretical and definitional approaches to morality.

The apparent differences in moral orientation due to gender may provide an additional, post hoc explanation for why some studies but not others found sex differences in level of moral reasoning. In subject populations where sex is consistent with gender (i.e., a predominance of masculine men and feminine women), individual differences in level of moral reasoning would be found. These differences understandably though probably incorrectly would be attributed to sex rather than to gender. Arbuthnot (1975), in a study of college undergraduates, found no main effect for sex, but a significant interaction for sex role identity and level of moral reasoning as measured by the Moral Judgment Scale. Higher moral reasoning for both sexes was related to nontraditional sex role identities. Hence gender, not sex, may prove the more useful individual difference variable in the study of moral reasoning.

Fourth and finally, individual differences in moral development appear to parallel individual differences in personality development. Moral judgment and moral character scores correlate in a meaningful and substantial manner with CPI and MMPI personality scales. For both models of morality, moral development is related to the development and integration of self (intrapersonal) and social (interpersonal) identities. For the cognitive-developmental model, intrapersonal aspects of personality correlate most strongly with morality in men; interpersonal aspects correlate most strongly in women. If, as Gilligan (1982, p. 18) argues, justice is a more intrapersonal moral principle and caring a more interpersonal moral principle, then these individual differences in personality may offer yet another explanation for any differences in moral orientation between men and women. For the personological model, interpersonal aspects of personality correlate most strongly with morality in both men and women. This finding is consistent with the theoretical assumptions of the personological model which views moral development as an interactive rather than solitary process.

Why individual differences in morality parallel individual differences in personality remains an open question, but one which should receive increased attention by researchers and theorists. The findings and conclusions presented in this article indicate that an individual difference approach to the study of morality, particularly one that emphasizes personality, would prove a most useful path for psychologists to follow in the future.

References

Allport, G. (1937). *Personality: A psychological interpretation*. NY: Holt & Company.

Arbuthnot, J. (1975). Level of moral judgment as a function of sex and sex role identity. *Journal of Social Psychology*, 97, 297–298.

Arbuthnot, J. (1983). Attributions of responsibility by simulated jurors: Stage of moral reasoning and guilt by association. *Psychological Reports*, 52, 287–298.

Arendt, A. (1976). Maturity of moral reasoning about hypothetical dilemmas and behavior in an actual situation. *Dissertation Abstracts International*, 37, 435B.

Bear, G., & Richards, H. (1981). Moral reasoning and conduct problems in the classroom. *Journal of Educational Psychology*, 73, 664–670.

Bem, D., & Funder, D. (1978). Predicting more of the people more of the time. *Psychological Review*, 85, 485–501.

Berkowitz, M., Gibbs, J., & Broughton, J. (1980). The relation of moral judgment stage disparity to developmental effects of peer dialogues. *Merrill-Palmer Quarterly*, 26, 341–357.

Biaggio, A. (1976). A developmental study of moral judgment of Brazilian children and adolescents. *Revista Interamericana de Psicologia*, 10, 71–78.

Bielby, D., & Papalia, D. (1975). Moral development and perceptual role-taking egocentrism. *International Journal of Aging and Human Development*, 6, 293–308.

Block, J. (1961). *The Q-sort method in personality assessment and psychiatric research*. Palo Alto, CA: Consulting Psychologists Press.

Buss, D., & Craik, K. (1983). The act frequency approach to personality. *Psychological Review*, 90, 105–126.

Bussey, K., & Maughan, B. (1982). Gender differences in moral reasoning. *Journal of Personality and Social Psychology*, 42, 701–706.

Caplan, A. (1978). *The sociobiology debate*. NY: Harper & Row.

Child, I. (1968). Personality in culture. In E. Borgatta & W. Lambert (Eds.), *Handbook of personality theory and research* (pp. 82–145). Chicago: Rand McNally.

Colby, A., & Kohlberg, L. (in press). *The measurement of moral judgment*. NY: Cambridge University Press.

Colby, A., Kohlberg, L., Gibbs, J., & Lieberman, M. (1983). A longitudinal study of moral development. *Monographs of the Society for Research in Child Development*, 48, 1–124.

Davidson, F. (1976). Ability to respect persons compared to ethnic prejudice in childhood. *Journal of Personality and Social Psychology*, 34, 1256–1267.

Deaux, K. (in press). Sex and gender. *Annual Review of Psychology*, 36.

Ernsberger, D. (1981). Moral development, intrinsic/extrinsic religious orientation, and denominational teaching. *Genetic Psychology Monograph*, 104, 23–41.

Fleetwood, R., & Parish, T. (1976). Relationship between moral development test scores of juvenile delinquents and their inclusion in a moral dilemma discussion group. *Psychological Reports, 39*, 1075–1080.

Freeman, S., & Giebink, J. (1979). Moral judgment as a function of age, sex, and stimulus. *Journal of Psychology, 102*, 43–47.

Freud, S. (1960). *The ego and the id.* NY: Norton. (Original work published 1923)

Freud, S. (1961). *The dissolution of the Oedipus complex.* NY: Norton. (Original work published 1924)

Freud, S. (1961). *Some psychical consequences of the anatomical distinction between the sexes.* NY: Norton. (Original work published 1925)

Freud, S. (1961). *Civilization and its discontents.* NY: Norton. (Original work published 1930)

Froming, W. (1978). The relationship of moral judgment, self-awareness, and sex to compliance behavior. *Journal of Research in Personality, 12*, 396–409.

Fry, P. (1975). Moral judgment and parental identification among children. *Journal of Clinical Psychology, 31*, 476–483.

Gilligan, C. (1982). *In a different voice.* Cambridge: Harvard University Press.

Gottlieb, D., Taylor, S., & Ruderman, A. (1977). Cognitive bases of children's moral judgments. *Developmental Psychology, 13*, 547–556.

Gough, H. (1975). *Manual for the California Psychological Inventory.* Palo Alto, CA: Consulting Psychologists Press. (Original work published 1957)

Griffore, R., & Lewis, J. (1978). Characteristics of teacher's moral judgment. *Educational Research Quarterly, 3*, 20–30.

Haan, N. (1975). Hypothetical and actual moral reasoning in a situation of civil disobedience. *Journal of Personality and Social Psychology, 32*, 255–270.

Haan, N. (1978). Two moralities in action contexts. *Journal of Personality and Social Psychology, 36*, 286–305.

Haan, N. (1982). Can research on morality be scientific? *American Psychologist, 37*, 1096–1104.

Haan, N. (1983). An interactional morality of everyday life. In N. Haan, R. Bellah, P. Rabinow, & W. Sullivan (Eds.), *Social Science as moral inquiry* (pp. 218–250). NY: Columbia University Press.

Haan, N. (in press). Systematic variability in the quality of moral action. *Journal of Personality and Social Psychology.*

Haan, N., Langer, J., & Kohlberg, L. (1976). Family patterns of moral reasoning. *Child Development, 47*, 1204–1206.

Haan, N., Smith, B., & Block, J. (1968). Moral reasoning of young adults. *Journal of Personality and Social Psychology, 10*, 183–201.

Haan, N., Stroud, J., & Holstein, C. (1973). Moral and ego stages in relationship to ego processes. *Journal of Personality, 41*, 596–612.

Haier, R. (1977). Moral reasoning and moral character. *Psychological Reports, 40*, 215–226.

Hampshire, S. (1953). Dispositions. *Analysis, 14*, 5–11.

Hathaway, S., & McKinley, J. (1967). *Manual for the Minnesota Multiphasic Personality Inventory.* NY: Psychological Corporation. (Original work published 1948)

Hoffman, M. (1975). Sex differences in moral internalization and values. *Journal of Personality and Social Psychology, 32*, 720–729.

Hogan, R. (1969). Development of an empathy scale. *Journal of Consulting and Clinical Psychology, 33*, 307–316.

Hogan, R. (1973). Moral conduct and moral character. *Psychological Bulletin, 79*, 217–232.

Hogan, R. (1982). A socioanalytic theory of personality. In M. Page (Ed.), *Nebraska symposium on motivation* (Vol. 29, pp. 55–89). Lincoln: University of Nebraska Press.

Hogan, R., & Busch, C. (1984). Moral action as autointerpretation. In W. Kurtines & J. Gewirtz (Eds.), *Morality, moral behavior, and moral development* (pp. 227–240). NY: Wiley.

Hogan, R., Johnson, J., & Emler, N. (1978). A socioanalytic theory of moral development. In W. Damon (Ed.), *New directions in child development* (Vol. 2, pp. 1–18). San Francisco: Jossey-Bass.

Holstein, C. (1976). Irreversible, stepwise sequence in the development of moral judgment: A longitudinal study of males and females. *Child Development, 47,* 51–61.

Jiminez, M. (1976). The development of moral judgment in Filipino urban children. *Philippine Journal of Psychology, 9,* 3–33.

Kahn, J. (1982). Moral reasoning in Irish children and adolescents as measured by the Defining Issues Test. *Irish Journal of Psychology, 5,* 96–108.

Keasey, C. (1972). The lack of sex differences in the moral judgments of preadolescents. *Journal of Social Psychology, 86,* 157–158.

Kohlberg, L. (1964). Development of moral character and moral ideology. In M. Hoffman & L. Hoffman (Eds.), *Review of child development research* (Vol. 1, pp. 383–431). NY: Russell Sage Foundation.

Kohlberg, L. (1969). Stage and sequence: The cognitive-developmental approach to socialization. In D. Goslin (Ed.), *Handbook of socialization theory and research* (pp. 347–480). Chicago: Rand McNally.

Kohlberg, L. (1976). Moral stages and moralization. In T. Lickona (Ed.), *Moral development and behavior* (pp. 31–53). NY: Holt, Rinehart, & Winston.

Kohlberg, L. (1981). *The philosophy of moral development.* San Francisco: Harper & Row.

Kohlberg, L. (1984). *The psychology of moral development.* San Francisco: Harper & Row.

Kohlberg, L., & Candee, D. (1984). The relationship of moral judgment to moral action. In L. Kohlberg, *The psychology of moral development* (pp. 498–581). San Francisco: Harper & Row.

Kohlberg, L., Colby, A., Gibbs, J., & Speicher-Dubin, B. (1978). *Standard form scoring manual.* Cambridge: Harvard University.

Kohlberg, L., & Kramer, R. (1969). Continuities and discontinuities in childhood and adult moral development. *Human Development, 12,* 93–120.

Krebs, D., & Gilmore, J. (1982). The relationship among the first stages of cognitive development, role-taking abilities, and moral development. *Child Development, 53,* 877–886.

La Voie, J. (1974). Cognitive determinants of resistance to deviation in children in low and high maturity of moral judgment. *Developmental Psychology, 10,* 393–403.

Leahy, R., & Eiter, M. (1980). Moral judgment and the development of real and ideal androgynous self-image during adolescence and young adulthood. *Developmental Psychology, 16,* 362–370.

Lifton, P. (1982a). Should Heinz read this book? [Review of *The philosophy of moral development*]. *Journal of Personality Assessment, 46,* 323–324.

Lifton, P. (1982b). Should Heinz's wife read this book? [Review of *In a different voice*]. *Journal of Personality Assessment, 46,* 550–551.

Lifton, P. (1983a). *Personality and morality: An empirical and theoretical examination of personality development, moral reasoning, and moral behavior.* Unpublished doctoral dissertation, University of California, Berkeley.

Lifton, P. (1983b). Assessment centers: The AT & T and IPAR methods. *Journal of Personality Assessment, 47,* 442–445.

Lifton, P. (in press). Personological and psychodynamic explanations of moral development. In G. Sapp (Ed.), *Moral development: Models, processes, and techniques.* Birmingham, AL: Religious Education Press.

Lyons, N. (1983). Two perspectives: On self, relationships, and morality. *Harvard Educational Review, 53,* 125–145.

Maccoby, E., & Jacklin, C. (1974). *The psychology of sex differences.* Stanford: Stanford University Press.

Magowan, S., & Lee, T. (1970). Some sources of error in the use of the projective method for the measurement of moral judgment. *British Journal of Psychology*, 61, 535–543.

Maqsud, M. (1980a). Locus of control and stages of moral reasoning. *Psychological Reports*, 46, 1243–1248.

Maqsud, M. (1980b). Relationships between personal control, moral reasoning, and socioeconomic status in Nigerian Hausa adolescents. *Journal of Youth and Adolescence*, 9, 281–288.

Orchowsky, S., & Jenkins, L. (1979). Sex biases in the measurement of moral judgment. *Psychological Reports*, 44, 1040.

Parikh, B. (1980). Development of moral judgment and its relation to family environmental factors in Indian and American families. *Child Development*, 51, 1030–1039.

Piaget, J. (1965). *The moral judgment of the child*. NY: Free Press. (Original work published 1932)

Poppen, P. (1974). Sex differences in moral judgment. *Personality and Social Psychology Bulletin*, 1, 313–315.

Pratt, M., & Royer, J. (1982). When rights and responsibilities don't mix: Sex and sex role patterns in moral judgment orientation. *Canadian Journal of Behavioral Science*, 14, 190–204.

Rest, J. (1976). New approaches in the assessment of moral judgment. In T. Lickona (Ed.), *Moral development and behavior* (pp. 198–218). NY: Holt, Rinehart, & Winston.

Roberts, A., & Dunston, P. (1980). Effect of a conflict manipulation on children's moral judgment. *Psychological Reports*, 46, 1305–1306.

Saltzstein, H., Diamond, R., & Belenky, M. (1972). Moral judgment level and confirmity behavior. *Developmental Psychology*, 7, 327–336.

Saraswathi, T., & Sundaresan, J. (1980). Perceived maternal disciplinary practices and their relation to development of moral judgment. *International Journal of Behavioral Development*, 3, 91–109.

Selman, R. (1971). The relation of role taking to the development of moral judgment in children. *Child Development*, 42, 79–91.

Singh, R. (1981). Study of certain moral functions in relation to some demographic factors. *Indian Psychological Review*, 20, 7–12.

Srivastava, R. (1977). Cultural differences in moral judgment. *Indian Journal of Behavior*, 1, 24–25.

Stent, G. (1980). *Morality as a biological phenomenon*. Berkeley: University of California Press.

Sullivan, E., McCullough, G., & Stager, M. (1970). A developmental study of the relationship between conceptual, ego, and moral development. *Child Development*, 41, 399–411.

Turiel, E. (1967). An historical analysis of the Freudian conception of the superego. *The Psychoanalytic Review*, 54, 118–140.

Turiel, E. (1976). A comparative analysis of moral knowledge and moral judgment in males and females. *Journal of Personality*, 44, 195–208.

Walker, L. (1984). Sex differences in the development of moral reasoning: A critical review. *Child Development*, 55, 677–691.

Wiggins, J. (1973). *Personality and prediction*. Reading, MA: Addison-Wesley.

Wilson, E. (1975). *Sociobiology*. Cambridge: Harvard University Press.

Responsibility and the power motive in women and men

David G. Winter and Nicole B. Barenbaum

Abstract

Previous research on the correlates of power motivation in women and men had shown no gender differences, when the presence of younger siblings (reflecting responsibility training) was used as a moderator variable. This study reports development of an empirically derived direct TAT measure of responsibility as a moderator variable for the power motive. The new measure includes mention of legal or moral standards, obligation, concern about others, concern about consequences, and self-judgment. It is related to perceived parental expectations concerning responsibility. Among women and men high in responsibility, power motivation predicts responsible social power actions; but among women and men low in responsibility, power motivation predicts a variety of profligate, impulsive actions. Responsibility, then, rather than gender, appears to determine the ways in which the power motive is expressed.

Themes of power and responsibility are at the heart of both the realities and the myths about gender differences and gender relationships. Although there are variations over time and across societies, men generally have higher status and more power than do women, and women are often seen as more responsible than are men (see Sanday, 1981; Stewart & Winter, 1977; Whiting & Whiting, 1975). Such power as women do have, moreover, is often circumscribed and restricted on account of their special "responsibilities" (see Gorer, 1948). Perhaps because of these realities, the topics of power, responsibility, and gender are wrapped in a rich mythology.

One myth is that men are interested in getting power or motivated to seek power, while women are not. Another myth is that men and women differ in their styles of seeking and exercising power. Men,

We are grateful to Augusto Blasi, Joseph M. Healy, Jr., Janet E. Malley, David C. McClelland, and Abigail J. Stewart for discussions of issues, making available data, and assistance in the development of the scoring system. This research was supported by a grant to the first author from the John and Mary R. Markle Foundation.

for example, are said to seek power for egoistic reasons and wield it in an assertive, sometimes domineering manner. Women, in contrast, are thought to seek and use power in more "responsible" and "nurturant" ways, most commonly for the sake of another person (see McClelland, 1975, chaps. 2 and 3; Miller, 1982). Sometimes these two styles are given the familiar but imprecise labels of "instrumental" and "expressive," respectively (see Zelditch, 1955). While supposed gender differences of this kind may be put forward in all academic innocence, in fact they lend easy intellectual support to a social doctrine of separate spheres, in which men's so-called assertive power entitles them to occupy leadership roles in society, while women's more "responsible" power fits (and obliges) them to stay at home raising children.

This paper presents research on a new measure of responsibility, together with a review and secondary analysis of previous research on the power motive, in an effort to distinguish myth from reality in the area of power, responsibility, and gender—an area closely connected with stereotypes and political issues.

Studies of Gender and Power Motivation

Gender and the Nature of Power Motivation

A recent review of research on power motivation in women (Winter, 1983), and a general review of gender and motivation research (Stewart & Chester, 1982), challenge both myths. Working in the McClelland-Atkinson tradition, in which motives are experimentally aroused and then measured by their effects on fantasy or thematic apperception (Atkinson, 1958), Winter (1973) had developed a revised measure of the power motive, or a concern for having impact on others and maintaining prestige. (See Winter, 1973, and Winter & Stewart, 1978, for a review of the psychometric characteristics and action correlates of the power motive measure.) Stewart and Winter (1976) had already shown that the same experiences arouse power motivation, thus defined, in both women and men.

Addressing the first myth of gender differences in the *level* of the power motive, Winter (1983) reviewed some 27 studies in which women and men had been tested together (or in similar situations), writing Thematic Apperception Test (TAT) stories to the same set of pictures of other stimuli. Finding that women scored higher in 13 studies and men in 14 studies, he concluded that there were essentially no gender differences in the strength of power motivation.

Gender and the Expression of Power Motivation

Addressing the second myth of gender differences in power style, Winter concluded from the studies reviewed that power motivation predicted many of the same actions in women and men: becoming "visible" to others, getting positions of formal social power and pursuing power-related careers, and acquiring possessions that reflect prestige. Initially, however, there seemed to be one persistent gender difference. Power-motivated men often act in "profligate impulsive" ways: drinking, multiple drug use, gambling, verbal and physical aggression, sexual exploitation, interest in "vicarious" sex and aggression by reading magazines such as *Playboy*, and difficulty in intimate relations with the opposite sex. These actions were almost never associated with the power motive in women. (The focus here is on gender differences in the *correlations* of these activities with power motivation, not gender differences in the average *levels* of the actions themselves.)

Initially, then, it seemed that women's power motivation was indeed more "responsible" and less "profligate" (and thereby perhaps less "assertive") than men's. Further secondary analyses of several of these studies, however, suggested that these apparent gender differences virtually disappeared with the introduction of a simple moderator variable—whether the person had any younger siblings. Having younger siblings is associated with responsibility training, according to Whiting and Whiting (1975, pp. 133–134). Women (and men) with younger siblings showed correlations between power motivation and the "leadership" actions involving formal social power. Among men (and women) with no younger siblings, the power motive was associated with most of the profligate actions. In a 15-year study of members of the class of 1964 at "Ivy College" (a prestigious liberal arts institution in the Eastern United States), Winter, McClelland, and Stewart (1981, pp. 107–111) found that having children acted in similar ways as a moderator variable, for both women and men.

Considering these results in the light of anthropological evidence about the origins of egoistic and prosocial or responsible dominance tendencies (e.g., Ember, 1981; Whiting & Edwards, 1973; Whiting & Whiting, 1975), Winter tentatively concluded that responsibility socialization was responsible for the differences in style of expression of the power motive, and that there were no inherent gender differences as such in the expression of power or responsibility. (Such a conclusion is also consistent with the evidence presented by Bass, 1981, p. 500; Falbo, 1977; Frodi, Macaulay, & Thome, 1977;

Klein & Willerman, 1979; and Richardson, Bernstein, & Taylor, 1979.)

This paper is designed to extend and support Winter's (1983) interpretation. First, it presents a new and direct thematic apperceptive measure of "responsibility." This measure is then validated both in terms of its content and also by its relation to responsibility socialization experiences. Finally, the new responsibility measure is shown to moderate power motivation, among both women and men, in ways similar to having younger siblings or having children. Among people high in responsibility, it will be shown, power motivation predicts "responsible" leadership; but among people who score low in responsibility, the power motive is associated with a variety of profligate, impulsive actions.

Measuring Responsibility in Thematic Apperception

Method

Development of a Responsibility Measure

Subjects

Since having younger siblings and later in life having children were both important antecedents of responsibility on theoretical grounds and also highly successful as moderator variables for power motivation, they were used to define two contrasting groups for developing a new TAT measure of responsibility. For the 240 male members of the class of 1964 at Ivy College who had taken TATs in their first year of college, longitudinal information about both children and (in some cases) siblings was available. From among those men who scored at least one-half standard deviation above the mean in power motivation, five subjects who also had at least one child by the time of the follow-up (at least three of whom also had younger siblings), and five subjects who did not have children (at least three of whom did not have younger siblings) were selected for the initial development of the responsibility TAT scoring system. In terms of their scores on power motivation and the two moderator variables, they represented the two extremes of "responsible" and "profligate" power styles, respectively.

Procedure

The technique of deriving and cross-validating TAT scoring systems has been fully described by Winter (1973, chap. 3). In the present case, it involved several processes, each repeated several times in combination with each other: (*a*) search for themes or elements of content that reflect the major theoretical and empirical discussions of responsibility in the literature (e.g., Barnard, 1938, chap. 17; Blasi, 1983, 1984; Gilligan, 1982; Sartre, 1947), (*b*) simple empirical comparison of stories from each group, (*c*) informal testing of preliminary categories, and (*d*) recombination and redefinition of categories to broaden the coverage of story themes and sharpen the differentiation between the TATs of the two groups. After intense study of the two groups of TATs, seven themes or categories of story content were identified as present more often in the "responsible power" group. Since the final scoring system is more fully described in Appendix 1, they will be mentioned only briefly here:

1. *Moral standard.* Reference in the story to an abstract standard involving morality or intrinsic quality. This can involve legal standards (legal/illegal), moral standards (moral/immoral), codes of manners (polite/rude), and behavior that is fitting and appropriate (or inappropriate) to the situation.

2. *Obligation.* Character in the story is obliged to act because of a rule, regulation, impersonal imperative, or inner obligation.

3. *Concern for others.* One character helps or shows sympathetic concern for another.

4. *Concern about consequences.* Character is concerned about the consequences of own action.

5. *Escaping consequences.* Character avoids or escapes consequences of own action.

6. *Endurance.* Character endures a difficult, unhappy, or unsatisfying situation.

7. *Self-judgment.* Character critically evaluates own character, wisdom, or good sense.

These seven themes reflect some of the different connotations of responsibility that are emphasized by different theorists: responsibility as an obligation or dependability (category 2 and perhaps also 1), that a person "means it," feels an inner obligation to do what is known to be right, and can be "counted upon" (Barnard, 1938, chap. 17; Blasi, 1983, 1984); responsibility as self-control (category 4 and perhaps also 6), as when a parent exhorts a young person to "show a little responsibility;" responsibility as acknowledging or "owning" one's actions (category 7), as in "being responsible" for something (Sartre, 1947); and responsibility as altruism (category 3), being responsible for someone else, or prosocial motivation (Gilligan, 1982; Hoffman, 1982).

The five categories that were eventually adopted as the TAT scoring system for responsibility (see below) were then cross-checked for their differentiating power with small groups of TATs from three other data sets drawn from Stewart, Sokol, Healy, Chester, and Weinstock-Savoy (1982). Becoming a parent for the first time should increase one's sense of responsibility, so stories from seven new fathers (all of whom also had younger siblings) were compared with stories from seven male M.B.A. degree candidates (none of whom had children and only four of whom had younger siblings). From a sample of sixth-grade students, stories written by three eldest children with two younger siblings each were compared with stories from three youngest children with two or more older siblings each. Finally, from a high-school sample, six male students who had younger siblings and who were responsible for performing many chores or household tasks were compared with six students who had no younger siblings and few chores or household responsibilities. (Here and in all further studies, a TAT story received a score of +1 for each responsibility category that was present in that story.) In each case, the scoring system clearly differentiated the "more responsible" group from the "less responsible" group. Pooling across the three studies, the combined sixteen "high responsibility" subjects had a mean score of 2.19, significantly higher than the mean score of .81 for the sixteen "low responsibility" subjects, $t(30) = 3.23$, $p < .01$. Standardizing the scores separately within each study gives the same result. Each of the five categories, as well, was more frequently present in the combined high group than in the combined low group.

Cross-validation

The major cross-validation of the scoring system, therefore, was carried out on TATs written by students in two large introductory psychology courses at Wesleyan University ($Ns = 70$ and 86). Extensive information about household chore responsibilities and other parental expectations and training in the area of responsibility was also available for both groups, so that the TAT measure could be validated against a criterion of responsibility training that is both more direct and also more complex than the mere presence of younger siblings. In a questionnaire, the Wesleyan students had been asked to indicate (on a 4-point scale) how much their parents had expected from them, during grade school and junior high school, in the following nine areas: take care of other children, prepare food, clean up after meals, clean the house, do well at school, do well at some outside activity, do well at sports, be popular and have lots of friends, and be polite and well-mannered. Child-care and cooking are considered key aspects of responsibility training cross-culturally (see Whiting & Edwards, 1973), while the other areas reflect common parental emphases in American culture. (Parental expectations involving shopping, pet care, and paid employment were not included because they are affected by family income and type of residence.)

Four-picture TATs from both classes were scored by the second author, who had learned the responsibility scoring system to a high standard of reliability (average Category Agreement with expert scoring for two practice sets = .86; see Winter, 1973, pp. 248–249), and who was blind to any other knowledge about the subjects (e.g., gender or childhood chore experience). Factor analyses of the category scores were carried out for each class separately, and the rotated loadings for the 3-factor solutions are shown in Table 1. The overall factor structures are somewhat similar for the two classes. In each case, five of the subcategories load on what are essentially the same two factors. The first factor is defined by *moral standards, obligation,* and *self-judgment*; it might be labelled "responsibility as obligation." The second factor, defined by *concern for others*, might be labelled "responsibility as altruism." As shown in the table, *legal standards* and *concern about consequences* switch factors between the two classes. In both cases, however,

Table 1. Factor structure of TAT responsibility scoring system.

Category	Rotated loading on factor:					
	I		II		III	
	Class 1	Class 2	Class 1	Class 2	Class 1	Class 2
Standards:						
Legal	.51	.03	− .43	.54	.35	.01
Moral	.74	.77	− .24	− .06	− .05	− .05
Manners	− .07	.22	.01	− .44	.85	− .22
Appropriateness	− .23	− .15	− .38	.34	− .26	− .28
Obligation	.60	.75	.02	− .06	.10	− .19
Concern for others	.02	.14	.62	.78	.27	− .02
Concern about consequences	− .02	.40	.69	.09	− .10	.22
Escaping consequences	− .05	.05	.12	.35	.59	.75
Endurance	.40	− .09	.08	− .17	− .15	.75
Self-judgment	.64	.64	− .29	− .04	− .08	.05
Sum of squares	1.81	1.82	1.35	1.38	1.39	1.35

the "obligation" and "altruism" factors taken together include the same set of categories.

Escaping consequences and *endurance* constituted a third factor by themselves, and did not consistently load on either of the first two factors. For this reason, as well as on account of their dubious theoretical relevance and infrequent occurrence, they were dropped from the final scoring system. Because the "manners" and "appropriateness" standards subcategories did not load consistently on any factor, they were also dropped, so that the *standards* category was defined only in terms of legal or moral standards. The final responsibility scoring system, therefore, included five categories, each of which is scored as either present (+1) or absent (0) in a TAT story. The overall responsibility score is the sum of the scores for each story. Appendix 1 presents brief definitions and examples for each category.[1]

Do the categories of the responsibility scoring system relate to other measures of responsibility socialization? To weight the nine parental expectations equally, each was standard-scored ($M = 50$, $SD = 10$) before combining into an overall average parental expectations score. Combining women and men, the correlation between TAT responsibility and average parental expectations was .25 ($N = 154$, $p < .01$). For the women, the correlation was .23 ($N = 81$, $p < .05$), and for the men it was .30 ($N = 73$, $p < .05$). As

1. These definitions are not adequate for scoring purposes. Copies of the complete scoring system, with practice materials and expert scoring, are available at cost from the first author at the Department of Psychology, Wesleyan University, Middletown CT 06457.

expected, the women reported significantly higher average parental expectations than did the men, $Ms = 51.69$ and 48.02, respectively; $t (152) = 4.67$, $p = .001$, and had TAT responsibility scores that were higher than the men's, though not significantly so ($Ms = 1.33$ and 1.23, respectively). The relation of each of the five TAT categories to each task, separately for the women and men and for each class, were also checked.

Results

To summarize the results, all 36 correlations for each TAT scoring category (nine tasks by two genders by two classes) were grouped together and evaluated with a sign test for positive direction (considered as supporting the cross-validation) or negative direction (considered as not supporting the cross-validation). (See Rosenthal, 1978, in support of this procedure of aggregating results.) For each category, the sign test for proportion of positive correlations is significant at less than the .01 level, except for *self-judgment*, a relatively infrequent category.

These results suggest that for both women and men, the TAT responsibility score reflects perceived parental emphasis on responsibility in all senses of the word—dependability, owning one's actions, and taking care of others. Thus the TAT scoring system, derived from comparing the stories of power-motivated people with younger siblings with the stories of power-motivated people with no younger siblings, cross-validates on a very different criterion of early responsibility training, both as a whole and in terms of its individual categories. It is true that perceived parental expectations account for a little less than 10% of the variance in TAT scores. This is to be expected, however, since "responsibility" is probably the result of many other factors.[2]

Responsibility as a Moderator of Power Motivation

After introducing the new measure of responsibility, the other major purpose of this paper is to show that the measure moderates the expression of power motivation in the same ways for both women and men. To put the question another way: Is the expression of power motivation in "leadership" or "profligate" channels a function of gender (as initially seemed to be the case) or of responsibility? To answer these questions, TATs from several previous studies were

2. For example, among the men, responsibility is also associated with growing up in a single-parent family, $r = .36$, $n = 42$, $p < .05$. There is no relation among women, $r = - .06$. If a single-parent family usually means a father-absent family, then the pressure for a boy to assume the father's role would probably increase responsibility more than for girls.

scored for responsibility with the new scoring system, and the data were reanalyzed. All three studies to be discussed below involve secondary analysis of existing data sets containing power motivation scores and numerous dependent variables. The original published studies (McClelland, 1975, chap. 2; Stewart & Winter, 1974; Winter, 1973) should be consulted for details about subjects, instruments, procedures, and prior data analysis.

Method

Two Studies of College Students

Like most areas of personality research, power motivation research is largely based on studies of college student subjects. From among those studies for which the original data sets were available, two were selected on the basis of comparability of subjects and range of available dependent variables. Unfortunately, different TAT pictures were used and different questions were asked in the two studies, thus limiting the comparability of the results. Still, these two studies were reasonably parallel and are a useful first step toward identifying the effects of responsibility on the expression of power motivation.

Subjects and Procedures

In 1968, as a part of the original validation research for *The Power Motive*, Winter (1973) administered a 6-picture TAT and several other questionnaire measures to 40 male undergraduates in an advanced psychology course at Wesleyan University (at the time still an all-male institution). Two years later, 68 students at a small New England women's liberal arts college wrote stories to a 6-picture TAT and filled out an extensive activities questionnaire (Stewart & Winter, 1974).

For the present analysis, the second author scored each set of TATs for responsibility, without knowledge of any other information about the subjects. Responsibility scores were then split at the median (between 1 and 2 in each sample) to classify subjects as high or low. Each study originally included many isolated dependent variables. For the present analysis, only those variables relevant to the responsible-profligate power distinction were considered. As described below in the results section, these highly specific variables (often of low frequency) were aggregated into more stable and meaningful clusters on the basis of theory. In fact, both studies included only one or two variables that could seriously be considered as reflecting "responsible leadership"—holding office and membership in organizations. Even these are somewhat suspect because in college they rarely involve having "real" social power and genuine responsibility. During college, the best way to prepare for responsible power in the future might be conscientious hard work. For the women, it was possible to create a "conscientious student" cluster, made up of self-reported daily hours of study, attending summer school (usually for extra courses and not remedial work), spending a semester at another college, and handing in a paper early. The "profligate impulsivity" style is adequately represented in terms of previously studied variables such as drinking liquor, reading "vicarious" magazines, and traffic accidents. The various clusters are not highly intercorrelated (rs range from a high of + .33 between office-holding and the profligate cluster among women to − .36 between the responsible and profligate clusters among men).

Results

Tables 2 and 3 present the results for the women college student sample and the men college student sample, respectively. For the women, responsibility moderates the relation between power motivation and each of the profligacy variables in the predicted direction. Thus for women low in responsibility, the various profligacy measures (drinking liquor, reading vicarious magazines, and traffic accidents) are positively associated with the power motive; but for women high in responsibility, the relations reverse. Considering the aggregate profligacy cluster score, which is the mean of the standard-

Table 2. Effects of responsibility on expression of power motivation in college women.

| | Correlations with: | | |
| | | Power motivation and: | |
Variable	Power motivation ($n = 68$)	Responsibility high ($n = 30$)	Responsibility low ($n = 38$)
Officer	− .03	− .15	.13
Conscientious student cluster	− .05	.27 *	− .44**
Daily hours of study	− .10	.11	− .26
Paper handed in early	− .02	.23 *	− .30
Summer school	.04	.23 *	− .17
Semester away	− .03	.10	− .21
Profligacy cluster	.19	.03 *	.41*
Liquor	.05	− .24 *	.32
Vicarious magazines	.09	− .22 *	.36*
Traffic accidents	.14	− .04 *	.36*

Note.—Cluster scores are the means of standard-scored component scores. Asterisks *between* correlations refer to the one-tailed probability of the difference between adjacent correlations, in the predicted direction.
 * $p < .05$
 ** $p < .01$ (2-tailed)

Table 3. Effects of responsibility on expression of power motivation in college men.

| | | Correlations with: | |
| | | Power motivation and: | |
Variable	Power motivation (n = 40)	Responsibility high (n = 19)	Responsibility low (n = 21)
Responsibility cluster	.30	.29	.28
Officer	.34*	.31	.32
Adjusted officer[a]		.36	.27
College organizations	.24	.26	.21
Profligacy cluster	.00	− .71*** **	.40
Liquor	.05	− .67** **	.38
Vicarious magazines	.15	− .24 *	.41
Traffic accidents	.21	− .05	.32
Physical fights	− .31	− .50*	− .22
Impulsive acts[b]	− .20	− .55* *	.01
Sexual possessiveness[c]	.25	− .42 **	.87**

Note.—Cluster scores are the means of standard-scored component scores. Asterisks *between* correlations refer to the one-tailed probability of the difference between adjacent correlations, in the predicted direction.

[a] with effect of fraternity membership partialled out.
[b] see Winter (1973, p. 135).
[c] answers to two open-ended questions about reaction to a rival's successful alienation of a dating partner's affections, scored for possessive jealousy and summed.

* $p < .05$
** $p < .01$
*** $p < .001$ (2-tailed)

scored components, the effects are strong and the difference between the correlations quite significant. The moderator effects of responsibility on holding office in college organizations are slightly (though not significantly) in the direction opposite to that predicted, though they are significantly in the predicted direction for the "conscientious student" cluster and most of its components. Taken together, then, the results are somewhat mixed. They are important, however, because they do define a group of women (i.e., those low in responsibility) in which the power motive is positively related to the profligacy set of behaviors.

Roughly the same conclusions apply to the male data, as shown in Table 3. The responsibility measure moderates the relations between the power motive and the profligacy variables in ways predicted from theory. The difference between the correlations of power motivation with the profligacy cluster score for the high and low responsibility groups is striking. Neither moderator variable works well with the two measures of "responsible power," although the responsibility-moderated correlations are at least all in the right direction, if the influence of fraternity membership (positively correlated with office-holding and negatively correlated with responsibility) is partialled out.

As far as they go, the two college student studies offer some modest support for the notion that responsibility moderates the responsible-vs.-profligate orientation of the power motive in both women and men. In fact, the results for the "responsible power" orientation are rather weak, presumably because the available measures are both few in number and also not very persuasive as indicators of responsible power. Still, at the very least these studies can be said to show that several kinds of profligate behavior are correlated with power motivation among both women and men, *if* they are also low in the TAT responsibility measure. This suggests that there is no "mystery" about power motivation and female profligacy.

A Study of Middle-class Adults

Method

Subjects and Procedures

The ideal sample for studying the moderating effects of responsibility would be a large group of women and men, tested together with the same TAT pictures, who were then asked about all of the important actions associated with the power motive, with special attention to those involving responsible leadership and profligate impulsivity. Because the adult women and men studied by McClelland (1975, chap. 2) fit many of these criteria, they are an obvious choice for secondary analysis. One hundred and fifteen adult women and 85 adult men had been recruited by a newpaper advertisement for a study of power-motivation focussed especially on drinking and other behavior related to different psychological stages of development, and on the content of inner experience. All subjects wrote stories to a 4-picture TAT, in gender-mixed groups, and then filled out a lengthy questionnaire. They were paid $8 for participation.

While there are many advantages to this data set, there are several problems as well. Subjects were very heterogeneous with respect to age, social class, and other background variables. Since at least one-third of the dependent variables were significantly correlated with either age or social class, this introduces considerable complexity into any analysis. Moreover, Winter (1973, pp. 134–136) had shown that social class and age interact with the power motive in complex ways. Only sparse information is available for some important background variables (e.g., precise occupation for men) and no information is available for others (e.g., whether women subjects worked at all and whether they had children, two variables which have substantial effects on many other behaviors and outcomes for women).

Despite these problems, however, the McClelland sample is probably the best available adult data set and was therefore used for the present study. In order to reduce the heterogeneity of subjects' ages and backgrounds, only those persons who were indubitably middle-class (completed 16 or more years of education) and either young or young middle-aged adults (ages between 25 and 39) were included in the analysis. With the only social class information available—years of education—it was impossible to define a clearly working-class group of subjects. For example, 14 years of education could mean some college (probably middle-class) *or* a two-year vocational course (probably skilled labor and working class), and the number of subjects who had completed *only* high school or less was too small for separate analysis. Thus delimited to college-educated people between 25 and 39, the sample included 38 women and 36 men. As in the other studies reported in this paper, all TATs were scored by the second author without knowledge of any other information (including gender) about the subjects. Responsibility scores for all subjects were then split at the median (between 1 and 2) to classify subjects as high or low.

Dependent Variable Clusters

Because of the wide variety and great specificity of the dependent variables, the aggregation into clusters was more complicated and deserves some discussion. Appendix 2 presents the components of each cluster. (Cluster scores are simply the means of the standard-scored components.) Regarding the first cluster, having a power-related job (see Winter, 1973, pp. 105–113) and having many memberships in voluntary organizations are both straightforward forms of responsible power, as discussed by Winter and Stewart (1978). The third component variable, finding that work is "often a source of enjoyment" (rather than "boring and tedious" or "often a distraction from things you would rather be doing"), was included because it suggests a dutiful but positive conscientiousness which seems to be an important aspect of responsible power, as shown above in the "conscientious student" cluster of Table 2. The components of the profligate impulsivity cluster (II) were simply drawn from previous studies of power motivation: drinking a lot of liquor often (quantity times frequency product above the median), having a number of "problem" reasons for drinking (such as "to forget everything"), reading vicarious magazines, and a having a nonmonogamous attitude toward members of the opposite sex (preferring "several relationships" or "one relationship with freedom" to "a single stable relationship").

The other two "positive" clusters involve variables which have not been widely studied in relation to power motivation. They are included here because they connote effective, mature, and outgoing functioning in a social world and therefore suggest responsible forms of power. Cluster III includes a measure of maturity of psychological adaptation to the environment

(Stewart, 1982) applied both to TATs and to dream reports, a *low* level of symptoms (such as trouble sleeping, loss of appetite, finding it difficult to get up in the morning, or feeling unable to get going), and feeling that "people regard me as a very responsible person." Thus people who score high on this cluster are mature, effective contributors to society. Cluster IV reflects something akin to Rogers' (1961) "openness to experience," in the senses of both being open to new stimuli (such as traveling to new places and eating new foods), and also disclosing relatively more (about matters such as health, income, sex, feelings, and fitness) to other people. While openness may be associated with optimal functioning of all kinds, as Rogers maintains, it is especially relevant to the exercise of responsible power, where trust, support, and loyalty must be built up and maintained in continually changing and novel situations. These four clusters are not highly intercorrelated (rs range from + .19 for I and III to − .24 for II and III). Cluster V, which reflects an overall combined responsible vs. profligate power style, is simply an additive combination of the other four clusters, with cluster II given negative weight. It summarizes all of the dependent variables into a single score.

Results

Tables 4 and 5 present the results for both women and men. Table 4 gives descriptive statistics on the major variables. Among the adults as among the introductory psychology students, there are no gender differences in overall responsibility score. In contrast to the students, however, the adult women and men do show differences in scores on some of the component categories of responsibility. Women score significantly higher in *concern for others*, while men score higher in legal and moral *standards*. So far as they go, these differences are consistent with the analyses of Gilligan (1982), among many others, about gender differences in the structure and orientation of responsibility and morality. The men score higher in power motivation, although in previous studies this was not a consistent gender difference (see above, and Stewart & Chester, 1982). Among the power-style clusters of dependent variables, the men's higher score on cluster II (profligacy) is the only difference that approaches statistical significance. This trend is largely due to the men's higher score on number of vicarious magazines read, Ms = 1.05 for men and .28 for women; t (72) = 3.50, $p < .001$. The only other difference on the component variables is a tendency for men, more than women, to say that they enjoy travelling to new places, Ms = 3.41 and 2.83, respectively; t (72) = 2.79, $p < .01$. Finally, among both women and men, the responsibility measure has a moderate but not significant correlation with power motivation (rs = .22 for women and .31 for men).

Table 5 presents the results on the five cluster scores. Here the

Table 4. Scores on responsibility, power motivation, and power style clusters for adult women and men.

	Scores for:				
	Women (n = 36)		Men (n = 38)		
Variable	M	SD	M	SD	Difference
TAT responsibility score	1.33	1.31	1.29	.94	.04
Legal/moral standards	.11	.31	.37	.48	− .26 *t* = 2.67, *p* < .01
Obligation	.47	.65	.37	.58	.10
Concern for others	.36	.59	.13	.34	.23 *t* = 2.05, *p* < .05
Concern about consequences	.25	.43	.32	.57	.07
Self-judgment	.14	.42	.11	.38	.03
Power motivation	4.89	3.37	6.79	3.74	− 1.90 *t* = 2.26, *p* < .05
I. Responsible social power	50.60	6.48	49.33	6.77	1.27
II. Profligacy	48.90	3.42	51.05	5.98	− 2.15 *t* = 1.86, *p* < .10
III. Effective functioning	49.18	4.78	50.80	6.23	− 1.62
IV. Openness to experience	50.03	6.25	49.97	6.17	.06
V. Combined responsible vs. profligate power style (I−II+III+IV)	100.91	12.25	99.05	13.60	1.86

general hypothesis of this paper is broadly and strongly confirmed for both women and men: For people high in responsiblity, power motivation predicts high scores on the responsible social power, the effective functioning, and the openness clusters and low profligacy scores; among those low in responsibility, the power motive is associated with high profligacy scores and low scores on the other clusters.[3] (When having younger siblings is used as a moderator

---

3. While in the correct direction, the results for women on the responsible social power cluster are not strong. This is probably due to the fact that some of the women had careers outside the home and some did not, and some had young children and some did not. Unfortunately, full and precise information about these very important variables was not available to test this explanation.

A further problem involves the fact that while the moderated results for women and men are parallel and in accord with predictions, the simple unmoderated correlations between power motivation and profligacy (for men) and responsible power behavior (for women and men), which have typically been found in previous studies (often with college student subjects) are not shown in this sample. Perhaps power motivation is more decisively moderated one way or the other in adulthood, or perhaps the profligacy expressions of power motivation are more often found among working-class men (see Winter, 1973, pp. 134–135).

Table 5. Effects of responsibility on expression of power motivation in adult women and men.

		Correlations among women			Correlations among men	
			Power motivation,			Power motivation,
	Power motivation	Responsibility		Power motivation	Responsibility	
		high	low		high	low
Variable	(n = 36)	(n = 12)	(n = 24)	(n = 38)	(n = 14)	(n = 24)
I. Responsible social power	− .05	.12	− .14	.03	.52 **	− .38
II. Profligacy	.17	− .10	.30	.11	− .11 *	.51*
III. Effective functioning	− .08	.27 *	− .29*	.05	.52 *	− .24
IV. Openness to experience	.04	.57 **	− .40	.30	.58*	.26
V. Combined responsible vs. profligate power style (I−II+III+IV)	− .09	.49* **	− .46*	.12	.64* ***	− .49*

Note.—Cluster scores are the means of standard-scored component scores. Asterisks *between* correlations refer to the one-tailed probability of difference between the adjacent correlations, in the predicted direction.
   * $p < .05$
   ** $p < .01$

variable, the effects for all clusters are much weaker, though usually in the same direction, for both women and men.)

The combined cluster V shows the moderator effect of the TAT responsibility measure at its most dramatic and statistically significant. Because this combined score can be taken as the distilled responsibility vs. profligacy essence of all the other variables, it is further used as the dependent variable in an analysis of variance that represents the most succinct test of the central hypothesis of this paper—that apparent gender differences in power motive expression are really differences in responsibility socialization that, for socio-historical reasons, merely happen to be associated with gender in twentieth-century middle-class American culture. When a three-way analysis of variance on the combined power style score is performed, with gender, responsibility (high vs. low), and power motivation (high vs. low) as the independent variables, only the power-by-responsibility interaction effect reaches significance. All interactions involving gender, as well as the gender main effect itself, have only small and nonsignificant effects. (The results are about the same for three-way analyses of variance of each of the four cluster scores that make up the combined cluster, and are not substantially affected by covariance adjustments for age and years of education.) These results suggest that responsibility rather than gender determines the channels through which the college-educated adult women and men in this sample express their power motivation. Table 6 shows the analysis of variance results.

Conclusion

For reasons of economy, religion, political structure, education, demography, and perhaps psychology, women and men usually differ in status and power (see Stewart & Winter, 1977). Often as well women and men appear to differ in their styles of expressing power, even though their motivation for power is on average about the same. Many myths, cultural symbols, and religious legends are built on these latter apparent differences. A review of the power motive research literature suggests that power-motivated women and power-motivated men both seek responsible social power. Often power-motivated men act in profligate, impulsive ways as well. At first it seemed as though power-motivated women did not. On closer examination, however, what seemed to be a *gender* difference was really a *socialization* difference, revealed initially with a background or sociological variable (having younger siblings; see Winter, 1983). In the present paper these presumed socialization effects are even more sharply delineated with a new and directly psychological measure of responsibility. Both responsible women and responsible

Table 6. Variance table for combined responsible vs. profligate power style scores.

| Source | df | Variance table | |
		MS	F
Power motivation	1	1.13	.01
Responsibility	1	397.86	2.49
Gender	1	34.49	.22
Power × Responsibility	1	1361.86	8.52**
Power × Gender	1	.14	.003
Responsibility × Gender	1	6.92	.04
Power × Responsibility × Gender	1	30.10	.19
Within cell	66	159.81	

** $p < .01$

men who want power seek it in responsible ways; and both "irresponsible" women and "irresponsible" men who want power seek it in irresponsible or profligate ways.

These results are based only on secondary analyses of several data sets. If confirmed by further research, however, they would suggest a more general shift in the models used to interpret differences in personality and behavior associated with gender. Often as a function of social structures and mythological superstructures, we may initially interpret differences between women and men as psychological consequences of the anatomical distinctions between them. With changes in the *zeitgeist* and a new perspective, however, the interpretation may shift. Other variables, having little to do with anatomy (as in the present case of parental socialization for responsibility), are found to explain a good deal of the variance, thereby reducing much of the explanatory and interpretive scope of gender as such. Numerous other examples of shift in the basis of interpretation (for example, away from nationality or race) can be found in the history of psychology and the other social sciences.

Finally, the new responsibility measure deserves further psychometric scrutiny and study in its own right. Does it really reflect "responsibility" as the term has been used by many different theorists? Or is it active only as a moderator variable? Does it moderate other motives (e.g., achievement or affiliation-intimacy) as well as power?

The present results do raise one problem with the TAT measure of responsibility. On theoretical grounds, we might expect that women would score higher than men. This would also follow from the fact that power motivation often shows a significant simple (unmoderated) correlation with profligate behavior for men but not for women. In both samples of the present study where women and men were tested together with the same TAT pictures this did not happen, although there were gender differences in some of the components of responsibility and also gender differences in the parental expectations of responsible behavior that are presumably the antecedents of the TAT measure. This lack of gender difference in the TAT score is a little surprising, and suggests that need for further study with subjects of different backgrounds and demographic characteristics. Considering that all subjects in the present studies were college students or college graduates, we might speculate that higher education effaces "characteristic" gender differences resulting from early socialization or other differences (see Winter, McClelland, & Stewart, 1981).

Future research, then, is needed to identify the developmental antecedents of responsibility as measured by the new TAT scoring system. Are there experiences in adult life (e.g., schooling, institutions, therapeutic interventions) that could increase responsibility when early socialization was weak or nonexistent? Answers to such questions could have great theoretical significance for our understanding of the growth of responsibility, as well as practical significance for our social efforts to channel and "tame" people's power motivation.

Appendix 1

Brief Outline of the TAT Scoring System for Responsibility°

1. *Moral standard.* Scored when actions, people, or things in the story are explicitly described in terms of some abstract standard that involves either morality or legality. Standards are not inferred from outcomes or consequences. Examples: "The man entered the country illegally." "She wants to do the right thing."

2. *Obligation.* Scored when a character in the story is obliged to act because of a rule, regulation, order, instruction, or other imperative that is *impersonal* in origin. Also scored if there is an inner feeling of obligation or compulsion to act (as an end itself and not simply as a means-end relation). Examples: "He broke a rule." "She must get back to her office."

3. *Concern for others.* Scored when one character helps or intends to help (whether solicited or not), or shows sympathetic concern for another. Examples: "The parents are worried about their daughter's future." "The boss will understand the problem and give the worker a raise."

4. *Concern about consequences.* Scored when a character is worried, anxious, upset, or just reflects about possible negative consequences of her or his actions. Mere concern about success or failure is not scored. Examples: "She now regrets her haste." "The captain is hesitant to let the man on board, because of his instructions."

5. *Self-judgment.* Scored when a character critically evaluates her or his character, wisdom, self-control, good sense, etc. These sentiments must refer to the self and not merely to the outcome of an action. Examples: "The young man realizes he has done wrong." "They are embarrassed by the ridiculousness of their behavior."

Appendix 2

Components of Power Style Clusters in Study of Adult Women and Men

I. *Responsible social power*:
   —Currently in a power-related job (see Winter, 1973, pp. 105–113)

° This outline is not adequate for scoring purposes. Copies of the scoring system, together with practice materials, are available as discussed in text Footnote 1.

—Number of organizational memberships
—Belief that work is "often a source of enjoyment," rather than "a distraction from things [I'd] rather be doing" or "boring and tedious"

II. *Profligacy*:
—Liquor consumption (quantity times frequency) high
—Number of reasons for drinking that are associated with having a drinking problem
—Number of vicarious magazines read
—Prefer "several relationships" with the opposite sex to one relationship

III. *Effective functioning*:
—Mean stage of adaptation score (Stewart, 1982) of two dream reports
—Mean TAT stage of adaptation score (Stewart, 1982) of TAT
—Few symptoms
—Believe self to be a "responsible person" in the eyes of others

IV. *Openness to experience*:
—High on disclosure (of work, pride, health, income, sex, feelings, fitness) to others (father, mother, male friend, female friend, spouse)
—Enjoy (and often do) travelling alone in new places
—Enjoy (and often do) trying new things to eat

References

Atkinson, J. W. (Ed.). (1958). *Motives in fantasy, action, and society*. Princeton, NJ: Van Nostrand.

Barnard, C. (1938). *The functions of the executive*. Cambridge, MA: Harvard University Press.

Bass, B. M. (1981). *Stogdill's handbook of leadership*. New York: Free Press.

Blasi, A. (1983). Moral cognition and moral action: A theoretical perspective. *Developmental Review, 3*, 178–210.

Blasi, A. (1984). Autonomie im Gehorsam: Die Entwicklung des Distanzierungsvermögens im Sozializierten Handeln [Autonomy in obedience: The development of distancing in socialized action]. In W. Edelstein & J. Habermas (Eds.), *Soziale Interaktion und soziales Verstehen* (pp. 300–347). Frankfurt A/M: Suhrkamp Verlag.

Ember, C. R. (1981). A cross-cultural perspective on sex differences. In R. H. Munroe, R. L. Munroe, & B. M. Whiting (Eds.), *Handbook of cross-cultural human development* (pp. 531–580). New York: Garland STPM Press.

Falbo, T. (1977). Relationship between sex, sex role, and social influence. *Psychology of Women Quarterly, 2*, 62–72.

Frodi, A., Macaulay, J., & Thome, P. R. (1977). Are women always less aggressive than men? A review of the experimental literature. *Psychological Bulletin, 84*, 634–660.

Gilligan, C. (1982). *In a different voice*. Cambridge MA: Harvard University Press.

Gorer, G. (1948). *The American people*. New York: Norton.

Hoffman, M. L. (1982). The development of prosocial motivation: Empathy and guilt. In N. Eisenberg (Ed.), *The development of prosocial behavior* (pp. 281–313). New York: Academic Press.

Klein, H. M., & Willerman, L. (1979). Psychological masculinity and femininity and typical and maximal dominance expression in women. *Journal of Personality and Social Psychology, 37*, 2059–2070.

McClelland, D. C. (1975). *Power: The inner experience*. New York: Irvington.

Miller, J. B. (1982). *Women in power*. (Work in Progress No. 82-01). Wellesley, MA: Wellesley College, Stone Center for Developmental Services and Studies.

Richardson, D. C., Bernstein, S., & Taylor, S. P. (1979). The effect of situational contingencies on female retaliative behavior. *Journal of Personality and Social Psychology*, **37**, 2044–2048.

Rogers, C. R. (1961). *On becoming a person.* Boston: Houghton Mifflin.

Rosenthal, R. (1978). Combining results of independent studies. *Psychological Bulletin*, **85**, 185–193.

Sanday, P. R. (1981). *Female power and male dominance: One the origins of sexual inequality.* Cambridge and New York: Cambridge University Press.

Sartre, J. P. (1947). *Existentialism* (B. Frechtman, Trans.). New York: Philosophical Library. (Original work published 1945)

Stewart, A. J. (1982). The course of individual adaptation to life changes. *Journal of Personality and Social Psychology*, **42**, 1100–1113.

Stewart, A. J., & Chester, N. L. (1982). The exploration of sex differences in human social motives: Achievement, affiliation, and power. In A. J. Stewart (Ed.), *Motivation and society* (pp. 172–218). San Francisco: Jossey-Bass.

Stewart, A. J., Sokol, M., Healy, J. M., Jr., Chester, N. L., & Weinstock-Savoy, D. (1982). Adaptation to life changes in children and adults: Cross-sectional studies. *Journal of Personality and Social Psychology*, **43**, 1270–1281.

Stewart, A. J., & Winter, D. G. (1974). Self-definition and social definition in women. *Journal of Personality*, **42**, 238–259.

Stewart, A. J., & Winter, D. G. (1976). Arousal of the power motive in women. *Journal of Consulting and Clinical Psychology*, **44**, 495–496.

Stewart, A. J., & Winter, D. G. (1977). The nature and causes of female suppression. *Signs: Journal of Women in Culture and Society*, **2**, 531–553.

Whiting, B., & Edwards, C. (1973). A cross-cultural analysis of sex differences in the behavior of children aged three through eleven. *Journal of Social Psychology*, **91**, 171–188.

Whiting, B., & Whiting, J. W. M. (1975). *Children of sex cultures: A psycho-cultural analysis.* Cambridge, MA: Harvard University Press.

Winter, D. G. (1973). *The power motive.* New York: Free Press.

Winter, D. G. (1983). *The power motive in women—and men.* Manuscript submitted for publication.

Winter, D. G., McClelland, D. C., & Stewart, A. J. (1981). *A new case for the liberal arts.* San Francisco: Jossey-Bass.

Winter, D. G., & Stewart, A. J. (1978). Power motivation. In H. London & J. Exner (Eds.), *Dimensions of personality* (pp. 391–447). New York: Wiley.

Zelditch, M. (1955). Role differentiation in the nuclear family. In T. Parsons & R. F. Bales (Eds.), *Family, socialization and interaction process* (pp. 307–352). Glencoe, IL: Free Press.

Gender and individualistic vs. collectivist notions about the self

M. Brinton Lykes

Abstract

This article provides a critique of traditional psychological theories of the self that emphasize autonomy, separation, and independence, and ignore the inherently social character of the self. Evidence from an empirical investigation of selected experiences of 84 white adult women and men who evidence two different notions of the self (autonomous individualism and social individuality) suggest that the culturally dominant notion of the self, rooted in assumptions of autonomy, independence, and separation, is but one orientation to the self. A contrasting notion, social individuality, reflects a dialectical understanding of individuality and sociality grounded in an experience of social relations characterized by inequalities of power. Preliminary research suggests that differences between women's and men's notions of the self are grounded in their different experiences of power. These findings support a larger argument that research on the self in psychology must be grounded in an analysis of material social reality and reflect the dialectical relation of individuality and sociality.

Psychological theories of the self developed in the West and based on the dominant view of the self as an autonomous and separate individual consistently ignore both the socio-historical context of the "subjects" whose self-understandings we seek to describe (Finison, 1980; see also, e.g., Gergen, 1973, 1978; Israel, 1979; Sampson, 1978) and the social context which shapes the development of our psychological knowledge per se (Buss, 1975). Many of the descriptions of self elaborated through positivistic, ahistorical psychological research have been found to describe accurately only one particular group of persons, that is, white, middle-class, college-educated, American males. More recently, Bell (1982) and Pleck (1981) have argued that even the experiences of that group are not accurately reflected in these theories.

Extensive theoretical and empirical evidence has been presented to argue convincingly that the experiences of women (see, e.g.,

Broverman, Broverman, Clarkson, Rosenkrantz, & Vogel, 1970; Joseph & Lewis, 1981; Miller, 1976), Blacks and other persons of color (see, e.g., Fanon, 1968; Jones, 1972; White, 1984; Willie, 1979) and persons from the lower end of the economic structure (see, e.g., Hollingshead & Redlich, 1958; Mishler, Amarasingham, Hauser, Liem, Osherson, & Waxler, 1981) are not faithfully represented by self-theories that emphasize autonomy and individualism. More sustained attention to the experiences of these groups, in particular to women's voices (Gilligan, 1982, 1984; Lyons, 1983), promises both a better understanding of women's psycho-social reality and fundamental revisions of currently biased psychological theories about the self and human development (Miller, 1984).

Consideration of the cultural meaning of studying the self shifts one's focus from the cognitive or social characteristics of the self as "subject" or "object" to major ideas about the self reflective of a given society's resolution of the problem of the relationship of the individual and society. Resolutions of this problem differ among cultures (Shweder & Bourne, 1982) and have an influence on how people ask questions about the self, the answers to which may influence how they think about and guide their lives and be evident in a given individual's "notion of the self."

Two dominant resolutions of the problem of the relationship of the individual and society can be categorized in understandings of the self as either "egocentric contractual" or as "sociocentric organic" (Shweder & Bourne, 1982). The former resolution, dominant in Western cultures, emphasizes the self as autonomous individual, whereas the latter focuses on the collectivity, often to the point of dissolution of any notion of individuality. These seemingly antithetical perspectives, grounded in different social experiences, are not contradictory, but are best understood in relation to each other. The unity thus revealed suggests a notion of the self as an "ensemble of social relations" (Schaff, 1970).

My investigation of two alternative bases for ideas about the self in women's and men's experiences of individualism and collectivity provides evidence of a reconstructed and synthesized notion of the self, social individuality. This view contrasts with both the interactionist perspective, rooted in an assumption of an autonomous entity interacting with other entities, and with perspectives that emphasize the organic unity of the social whole and negate all forms of individuality. Evidence from a recent empirical investigation is presented and discussed more fully to amplify this conception of the self as social individuality. Implications of this notion for conceptualizing gender in research in personality psychology are elaborated.

*Women's Lives: A Base from which to Theorize about the
Self*

A growing body of psychological theory, rooted in an analysis of
women's experiences, suggests that women's sense of self is best
characterized by an emphasis on caring (Gilligan, 1982), "being-in-
relationship" (Miller, 1984), and a "fluidity" in self development
(Kaplan, 1984; Kaplan & Surrey, 1984), not by the dominant model
of an autonomous and independent self.

Women's different voice. Initial efforts to reevaluate critically the
forms of affiliation and caring expressed in women's lives led to the
formulation of several theories of "women's sense of self." These
theories draw on Chodorow's (1978) suggestion that women are
more relational and empathetic than are men and that these gender
differences are due to the fact that women, universally, are largely
responsible for early child-care ("women's mothering is one of the
few universal and enduring elements of the sexual division of labor,"
p. 3). The sources of male and female affective, cognitive, and
behavioral differences are also traced to the fact that females (in
contrast to males) are nurtured by a same-sex caretaker; and to the
exploitative nature of our socio-economic system, rooted in a profit
system that values creativity, aggression, and independence in the
marketplace and beyond (Hsu, 1983) and devalues and exploits
women (Hartsock, 1983).

Drawing on this analysis, Gilligan (1982) hypothesized gender
differences in moral development. In contrast to Kohlberg's (1969)
emphasis on a self defined through separation and autonomy wherein
responsible action is judged in terms of abstract moral principles
(i.e., fairness, justice, rights, the Golden Rule), Gilligan suggests that
women's sense of self is rooted in experiences of relationship and
connection, wherein moral or responsible action is evaluated by
principles of caring. According to Gilligan, attachment, relationship,
and interdependence form a contextual web through which the
woman comes to understand herself and to define moral behavior.

The suggested link between women's reasoning about moral dilemmas and women's "sense of self" was explored empirically by
Lyons (1983). She argued that *all* individuals are likely to provide
self-descriptions that indicate a relational component but that people
use two distinct modes in describing the self-in-relation (see Lyons,
1983, Appendix C, p. 145). One mode, reflected in the responses of
a majority of the 22 females in her study, describes a self connected
or interdependent in its relations with others and reveals a preoccupation with doing good for another. Relationships are conceived

as givens and one's abilities are described in terms of making or sustaining connection and doing things for others. The other mode, more frequently found in the responses of the 14 males in her sample, describes a self as separate in its relationships with others. Relationships, described as part of one's obligations or commitments, are evaluated in terms of one's "ability" or "skill in interacting with others." As predicted, these alternative modes of describing the self-in-relation were systematically related to gender differences in approaches to solving moral dilemmas. However, despite these differences in modes of self-definition, Lyons (1983, p. 140) found that approximately equal proportions of men (86%) and women (81%) include a relational component in their self-descriptions, suggesting that both women and men tend to emphasize some form of interconnection or relatedness to others in their self-definitions, and pointing towards a reconceptualization of the self in social relations.

Self-in-relation. Miller's (1984) description of women's sense of self as a "self-in-relation" represents another effort to reconceptualize the dominant view of the self as autonomous individual. According to Miller, women, in contrast to men, stay with and build on their earliest experiences of attachment and affiliation. Women have traditionally been constrained to affiliate with others from a subservient position and have been restricted from developing autonomy or self-determination (valued in male development). However, subservience is not intrinsic to the definition of affiliation and many women experience affiliation as both a fundamental strength and a source of empowerment.

One's sense of self-in-relation begins in the mother-child relationship wherein the child's first internal representation of self emerges from what she or he is actually doing. ". . . The beginnings of the concept of self are not those of a static and lone self being ministered to by another . . . but much more of a self inseparable from a dynamic interaction" (Miller, 1984, p. 4). The child's earliest representations of self include feeling the other's emotions and one's own in an interplay (Miller, 1984, p. 3–4). Interconnection is a "natural" way of being and acting, not a threat to one's autonomy, or a detraction from one's goal of "self-development."

This theoretical formulation moves beyond previous interactionist descriptions of the self-other relationship by focusing on the "mutually enhancing dimension of the connection wherein the woman is confirmed in the validity of her own self as a person-in-relationship" (Jordan, 1984, p. 10). Absence of relationship is thus experienced as a "failure of the self" for many women. Despite the conclusions that this sense of self-in-relationship is more characteristic of women than of men, Miller (1976) suggests that individual development for women and men "proceeds only by means of affiliation" (p. 83).

The Self and Social Structure

Critical Reflections on "Women's Sense of Self"

By emphasizing the centrality of social relations and the importance of interconnection, the theorists of a self-in-relation provide a more accurate description of the lived experiences of the women in the research and clinical work they describe and suggest an important alternative to the dominant model of the self embedded in an assumption of autonomous individualism. However, these theories retain certain problematic characteristics that prevent the full articulation of a notion of a social self. The relationship of mother and child described in these theories is abstracted from its socio-historical context and discussed apart from any specific organization of material life. The dyadic relationship, defined as key to women's self-understanding, is described independently of the social totality in which it is grounded.

There are at least two negative consequences of this acontextual description of the essential qualities of mothering. First, such descriptions inevitably raise questions about *why* it is that women, universally, raise children. By focusing at least implicitly on the universal quality of women's experiences that are associated with women's subordinate status, that is, the self-in-relation, man's dominant role is implied and both "facts" take on an ahistorical and permanent quality (see Smith, 1983, for a similar point). These theories further reflect inherently flawed efforts to reduce biology or individuality and environment or sociality to separate elements (Lowe & Hubbard, 1983). The highly variable relationships that comprise different societies and contextualize and create meaning for the "self-in-relation" are thus extrinsic to its very definition.

Second, "the social" implied in these theories of the "self-in-relation" reflects an understanding of the social extracted from the dynamics of power or coercion and devoid of social structural character. Society is seen as "great cooperative community process," a "myriad of direct and indirect mutual relationships" (Schutz, 1967, 1970) or the "generalized other" (Mead, 1962). On the one hand, the model of the self in connection found in Lyons' and Gilligan's work resembles the social interactionist perspective wherein two separate entities are described as intimately "connected" or "other-directed" and the underlying conceptualization of self is of a separate entity (or self) who interconnects with another separate entity (or other). This view reflects a "female" variation of the dominant "male" model of the "egocentric contractual" idea of the self (Shweder & Bourne, 1982) that dominates Western models wherein two autonomous selves interact. The "social" is thereby reduced to a mechanism in the individual's attainment of a sense of self-in-relation and society is defined simply as "more than one" or "many" individuals. The notion of an autonomous and independent self is extended by suggesting two (not one) interdependent (not independent) selves, but the underlying assumption of individualism is retained.

Alternatively society is defined at least implicitly as a set of exploitative and repressive structures, constraining women's true "sociability" and preventing their full development (Lewis, 1976; Miller, 1976). From this perspective the social is experienced as an almost monolithic structure that stands outside of and over against women. The social is then a more global generalized other, a "unitary force" (Holland, 1977, p. 103), experienced through the constraining forces of male power or of a super-ego. Neither the social structural variability characteristic of all societies nor the facilitative qualities of some organizations are fully articulated in such an undifferentiated view of society. Women's individual and collective resistances to oppressive forces are underestimated within this view of society.

Although psychologists cannot be expected to do the work of sociologists or anthropologists in developing a fully elaborated theory of society, all psychological theories are based on a set of assumptions that, at least implicitly, include such definitions. What is problematic in these theories of the self-in-relation, therefore, is the absence of an alternative understanding of the social that would allow for a truly social notion of the self.

Collectivist Bases for Notions about the Self

Evidence from analysis of the relationship of the social organization of material life and the mother-child experience provide a perspective on the importance of collective experiences for developing a notion of the social self. Leacock's (1983) descriptions of societies organized communally in kin groups where networks of exchange relations are egalitarian in form, children are cared for by the kin-based collective and women are not economically dependent on men, suggest a link between the social organization of material life and the parent-child experience (see also Turnbull's, 1984, description of the Mbuti for a similar point). The Whitings' (1975; see also, Minturn & Lambert, 1964) psycho-cultural analyses of mothers and children in six cultures suggests further that child-training practices are based upon "certain conditions in the natural and social environment" that make them necessary for survival (Whiting, cited in Minturn & Lambert, 1964, p. 291).

If, as Chodorow argues, the sex gender system (see also, Rubin, 1975) is a socio-cultural construction, surely mothering in kin-based collectives and in hierarchically ordered nuclear families was and is differentially experienced and enacted. Knowledge of such differences is critical to an understanding of the individual's developing sense of self grounded in an analysis of the mother-child relationship.

Carol Stack (1974) makes a similar point in her descriptions of the ties of kinship and friendship in a poor Black urban community in the United States today. The sense of self that emerges from these kin-based networks where "the recognized mother, the 'mama' . . . determines the child's kinship affiliations through females" (p. 49) is not of a single autonomous individual interacting but of a coacting network of relationships embedded in an intricate system of social exchanges and obligations. Stack argues that these experiences of mother and child reflect this people's creative response to the harsh economic realities of poverty and racism.

Joseph (Joseph & Lewis, 1981) refers to Black mothers' and daughters' experiences as a "dynamic dyad," as a "communication/interaction process" (p. 82). The Black daughters in her national survey describe their mothers in terms of qualities understood within a context of community, for example, "her creativity and talents in keeping the family together in spite of the difficulties she had to face" (p. 125). Although white daughters in a comparison sample frequently mentioned the same characteristics, that is, "creativity" or "talent," their descriptions reflected a tendency to abstract their mothers from a context, an attempt to capture some essential quality or trait possessed by an individual. For the Black women in Joseph's sample, mothering and daughtering are particular, dynamic changing processes whose meaning develops within a broader social and historical context. The framework developed by white psychologists to describe the mother-daughter relationship fails to capture adequately this quality which is reflective of both the strong traditions of Black family patterns rooted in African cultures and the structural oppression of racism that both constrains the resources available to Blacks for adequate parenting and shapes the messages they must communicate early on to their children. (See Joseph, 1984, for a similar point and Bell-Scott & Guy-Sheftall, 1984, for a fuller treatment of Black mothers and daughters.)

In these examples, community or collective experiences are fundamental to the articulations of individuality and relationship that emerge. The experiential basis for the idea of the self-in-relation is the community, grounded in the totality of social relations. This contrasts both with the dominant view of autonomous individualism and with the view reflected in societies whose dominant resolution of the individual-society problem in collectivism results in the dissolution or negation of individuality (see, for example, Taylor, 1972, on the "group-mindedness" of the Zuni; Tuan, 1982, on the "sense of group self" of the Kaingang; Dumont, 1970, 1980, on India). An elaboration of experiences of "community" and "collectivity" in our society and of the ways in which these experiences are constrained by differential access to power and resources (i.e., of the material fabric of these experiences) provides a critical base for developing a notion of the self as social.

The Self as an Ensemble of Social Relations

The human individual is thus both conscious subject, creator of history, and an object, a product of nature or biology and of historical conditions. Our physical and historical environments are systematically organized in social structures that serve multiple functions in maintaining human social life. These structures differentially affect women and men, Blacks and whites, workers and those in positions of economic power and are frequently experienced as objectifying or alienating.

The theories of self-in-relation discussed above suggest that consciousness itself is also initially formed in a dynamically active relational system. The infant-mother interaction is one in which the self is inseparable from a dynamic ecological system, a system that shapes both child and mother. These theories suggest that individuality is developed most fully through closeness in contrast to traditional theories that focus on developing autonomy through separation. However, the mother-child relationship, which includes separateness and connection in inextricable unity, is only fully articulated in its grounding in social experiences.

To ignore either institutional alienations or dynamic relationship is to fail to understand human activity, that is, to fail to grasp the full potential of human social consciousness and the potential for social transformation. The infant's experience of "being-in-relationship" so powerfully described by Miller and Lewis can only be fully understood within the context of institutional arrangements of motherhood in Western capitalist society. To abstract the affective dimension of the experience and suggest that it can be defined and understood as some universal, irrespective of context, is to fail to grasp the truly social nature of the human. These social factors do not stand outside of the individual exerting an influence on her or his individual development. Rather the individual can be fully understood only when the dialectical relationship of self and social is articulated.

The Relationship between Notions of the Self and Social Experience

Notions of the self are embedded in and reconstructed from social arrangements. The notion of the self as an ensemble of social relations reflects the inextricable unity of individuality and sociality evidenced in one's sense of self. However, the dominant and pervasive view of the self in our culture, sustained by powerful, ideological, and structural forces remains that of autonomous individualism (see, e.g., Hogan, 1975; Hsu, 1983; Kanfer, 1979; Lewis, 1979; Smith, 1978; Wikse, 1977). We can, therefore, anticipate differences in people's notions of the self deriving from social experiences both at the group level (e.g., as a member of a social group excluded from power) and at the individual level (e.g., experiences in collective activities for social change).

Individuals from majority groups (e.g., white upper class males) whose material conditions and social relations are most likely to be consonant with individualism would be more likely to have a notion of the self as autonomous individualism. Persons in less powerful groups (e.g., women, people of color, working class people) are more likely to perceive contradictions between the assumptions of autonomous individualism and their social experiences. These individuals may also experience group solidarity or some sense of the "given-ness" of "being-in-relation," for their survival as a group may seem possible only in relationship (Hooks, 1984). The contradiction between the dominant perspective of the self as a separate and autonomous entity and an awareness or apperception of the indivisibility of the self and the social requires resolution. Resolution might be achieved through resignation to the dominant model in, for example, self-blame. Alternatively, resolution might include an active reconstruction through a change in consciousness and/or through praxis. Persons from less powerful groups should be more likely than those from more powerful groups to have notions of the self as social individuality. However, persons from any social group may get involved in socially responsible collective activities that sensitize them to the inherently collective basis of their sense of self and to the view of the self as social individuality.

The research described below was undertaken to investigate empirically this notion of the self. In the absence of prior empirical evidence, it seemed appropriate to use multiple indices to measure social individuality at various levels of cognitive functioning. Four indices—cognitive-perceptual styles, apperception, ideology, and reasoning about moral dilemmas—were selected to measure the notion of the self as social individuality. These indices were expected to be positively correlated, thus demonstrating social individuality to be a coherent construct. Finally, the notion of the self as social individuality was expected to be evidenced by persons from groups whose social position is less powerful and/or those who have engaged in collective activities.

Method

Participants in the Study

Participants for this study were purposively selected to include at least some individuals who were known to have had some of the experiences expected to relate to the understanding of the self as social individuality.

Fifteen groups or organizations, including a statewide tenants' organization, a labor studies program at a local college for public and community service, and several other urban adult education programs in the greater Boston area, agreed to invite their members, colleagues, students, or workers to participate in the study.

Background and demographic characteristics. Participants in the study included 54 white females and 30 white males ranging in age from 19 to 72 years. The mean age of the sample was 34.5 years; 48% of the sample had less than a BA degree, while 28% had completed college and 20% had MA or PhD degrees. Each participant's occupation was coded using the Michigan Occupation Code. These 50 coding categories were subsequently reduced to three categories, and, of the 79 participants for whom an occupational level could be coded, 20% were manual or service workers, 42% worked in the minor professions, and 38% in the major professions. Although a diverse group, the sample is, of course, not representative of the general population and the evidence presented in the results section must be evaluated with this in mind.

Procedures

All participants were given a questionnaire including the four measures described below. Respondents were also asked questions about their background and participation in a range of groups. Men and women received the same questionnaire with the exception of the responsibility measure in which the sex of the main character in the dilemmas was the same as that of the respondent (see Lykes, 1984, for copies of the questionnaire, descriptions of the measures, complete coding manuals and more detailed descriptions of the validity and reliability of each instrument).

The women in the sample also participated in follow-up interviews in which they were asked questions about their current families, neighborhoods, and work experiences, and about their families and neighborhoods in childhood. Each interview took from 20 minutes to an hour.

Measures

Cognitive-perceptual styles. The tendency to perceive the inextricable link between individuality and sociality might be reflected in basic perceptual processes. A tendency to perceive unspecified objects or forms as related, integrated, or synthesized wholes thus provides an aperture on the notion of the self as social individuality. A slightly modified version of the multiple choice form of the Rorschach Inkblot (Rorschach, 1942/1975), developed by Harrower & Steiner (1973), was included to assess this cognitive-perceptual style and was administered to each participant in the study.

Guidelines for coding, derived from Harrower & Steiner (1973) and Rorschach (see Beck, 1949), were used to score the number of integration choices selected by each respondent. Responses coded for integration corresponded to Rorschach's descriptions of an organized whole, that is, the respondents readily identify both a whole and its constituent parts, reflecting the respondent's synthesizing activity. These wholes were instantly, not additively, organized and reflected a tendency to see the part as inextricably linked to the whole. For example, in response to Inkblot II one respondent described "two grotesque figures in a tableau" (Beck, 1949, p. 18). Similarly, a second respondent described Inkblot I as "two people on a merry-go-round." In contrast, responses of "a bat" to Inkblot I were coded as an instant whole whereas that of a "little temple high up" (in response to Inkblot II) was coded as a detail, that is, as identifying only isolated individual parts. Neither of these latter responses captures any synthesizing or integrating tendency. The score on cognitive-perceptual style reflects the total number of integrative responses selected by the participant, across six inkblots. Scores for this sample ranged from 0 to 6 with a mean of 3.31.

Apperception of the social. Social individuality also presumes a tendency to perceive the self as embedded in or expressing the social forces of a particular context. This perception can be contrasted with a tendency to view each individual as a separate or autonomous entity in interaction with other autonomous entities and to ignore the corporate or group process. The Thematic Apperception Test (Atkinson, 1958) was used to assess social apperception. Pictures were selected to include both men and women and a collection of people who could be perceived either as an aggregation of autonomous individuals or as a collectivity. Subjects were given three picture cues and the standard TAT instructions and asked to write stories in response to the cues.

Five scoring criteria were developed for scoring stories for the degree of social apperception reflected. (See Appendix 1 for a brief summary of this scoring system.) Each of these five categories was scored as present (1) or absent (0) for its inclusion in the story told by the respondent.

Several examples provide a summary view of the five categories and should further clarify differences among individuals' apperception of the social. The following story was coded as reflecting the perspective on the self described as social individuality.

> This family situation is one of much sorrow and pain. The father of the family is sitting at the table talking to the young children of the family. His wife looks on, trying to offer support and comfort. Their aunt (the young children's) has just died. Her husband is also seated at the table at the right. He doesn't show much sorrow or pain because it was an expected death. The elders of the family are relieved that her suffering has ended. The third brother . . . has his back turned so as to hide his pain from the youngsters. The two boys . . . hold on and support each other—they don't know what the trouble is yet but from the atmosphere of the family they know it is serious.
>
> The young girl is also filled with the pain and sorrow of her aunt's death. She was very close to her aunt and was not aware of the seriousness of her illness. They will prepare the children for the funeral and then offer prayer and comfort to each other.

The storyteller clearly identifies a collective body, this family unit, that is comforting itself in the face of a member's death. Individual responses of particular family members give us a sense both of the particular members and of how the family functions as a whole. The story further suggests that the family members are collaborating in the effort to deal with this death both emotionally and practically.

The themes presented in a second story were coded as reflecting an understanding of the self as autonomous individualism.

> There is a discussion taking place around a table. Seated at the table are two men on one side and two men and a woman on the other side. There is a man standing staring out of a window, and another woman standing by the table watching the discussion.
>
> It appears to be taking place around a dining room table. The discussion is a very intense one and not all of the people agree. The people around the table are all related, either by blood or through sisters and their families. They are discussing whether or not to put their mother in a nursing home. Two are in favor and two are not and it has become a very emotional, very tense afternoon.

The people around the table are described individually and their possible interrelations are only mentioned in passing. The problem itself is somehow seen as outside of the context, rather than as a matter that they must engage. Although words like "very emotional" and "very tense" are used, they are tags or labels and do not reveal multiple points of view of interrelated participants in a process.

Protocols from pilot subjects were used to establish interrater reliability between a student coder and myself. Reliability was computed as a percentage of twice the number of agreements between the two coders divided by the sum of the number of items coded by each coder (see Winter, 1973, chap. 2). Reliability scores, computed for each picture separately with agreements and disagreements on each category enumerated, ranged from .87 to .92. Scores for each picture ranged from 0 to 5 with mean scores of 1.45, 1.81, and 1.41 on pictures 1, 2, and 3 respectively. Initial analyses revealed positive correlations among the five coding categories within and across pictures. A total score for social apperception was therefore computed by summing the five category scores across all three pictures; total scores for this sample ranged from 2 to 13, with a mean of 4.67, and were used in subsequent analyses.

Ideology. The third measure, ideology or one's fundamental belief system, was designed to differentiate those persons whose basic beliefs about how people function in the world are expressed with a primary focus on the autonomous individual from those who are more likely to see social reality and interactions as driven by collective or corporate forces or activities. This measure was derived from an ideology scale (Ryan, Lykes, & Bertner, 1983) which has been found to correlate significantly with adherence to meritocratic or antimeritocratic principles and with one's position on a number of social policy issues.

Thirteen items reflecting the centrality of the individual, the primacy of a social grouping, and the importance of collective action relative to individual action were included in a longer Philosophy of Life Questionnaire. These items included several explicit statements of beliefs about the self (e.g., "No matter how much of our lives are lived in groups we are first and foremost individuals, separate from one another" and "If you think about life you realize that each person is a separate individual leading his or her own individual life"). Statements designed to elicit a more automatic response (e.g., "There is a lot of wisdom in the old Dutch proverb, 'If each before his or her own stoop sweeps, the village will be clean'" and "'Paddle your own canoe' is a good principle to live by") that may be less susceptible to the problem of social desirability and more likely to elicit the individual's unquestioned assumptions were also included.

A Likert-type scale of 7 points ranging from strongly disagree (1) to strongly agree (7) allowed participants to indicate their opinions on these items. Items were counterbalanced and their order randomly determined.

In scoring the questionnaire responses, specific items were reversed so that high numbers (i.e., 5–7) indicated a collectivist response and low numbers (i.e., 1–3) indicated an individualistic response. Based on initial factor analyses 9 of the original 13 items were selected as the best measure of individual-collective ideology. Mean scores were derived from each participant with scores for this sample ranging from 2 to 5.78 with a sample mean of 3.97.

Reasoning about moral dilemmas: Social responsibility. The fourth measure assessed the extent to which the subject envisioned her- or himself as a socially responsible actor embedded in and constrained by some social context. Subjects' reasoning about a hypothetical moral dilemma was scored as socially responsible if they described acting directly in the situation in which they encountered the problem and acknowledged or interacted with the constraint of the social group or unit.

Three hypothetical dilemmas were presented and a set of questions raised after each dilemma. Subjects were asked to read the hypothetical dilemmas and to imagine themselves as the main character. They were asked to describe (1) what they saw as the conflict, (2) what they thought they must accomplish in the situation and why, (3) how they would go about it, and (4) what outcomes they would find acceptable. Each set of responses to the four questions was then coded using a system developed by the author. (See Appendix 2 for a brief summary of this scoring system.) Each subject received a score ranging from − 1 to + 3 for each of the three dilemmas. Interrater reliability, on coding done with sample protocols that included all three responsibility dilemmas, was high ($r = .86$, time 1 and $r = .88$, time 2).

Several examples may help to clarify these scoring categories. In the third dilemma the main character (Estelle or Hank) who is currently unemployed and receiving benefits and food stamps must decide whether or not to accept a friend's offer to join in a business venture while continuing to receive benefits. Although future prospects are good he/she would be only modestly remunerated for at least the first six months in the business. Yet she/he has a family to support and must decide whether to take the position or more importantly whether or not to discontinue receiving benefits or to continue getting the benefits and lie about this work.

In response to questions following Dilemma 3, one respondent described Estelle's problem as making a decision "her conscience can live with." She decided that Estelle should "take [her friends'] offer and see how much she makes," deferring until later a decision whether or not to "go off unemployment benefits." At no point did this respondent mention anything about obligations to other potential or actual beneficiaries of these government-subsidized programs or more generally about the illegality of the actions her friends propose. She failed to identify any constraint due to the social framework. Since she did recommend some action directed at the problem the story is scored − 1.

In response to questions following this same dilemma, another respondent recommended that Estelle "work for Betty and Helen, collect unemployment and look for a new job." She neither recognized the social constraints of the dilemma nor chose one action over another; thus she did not deal directly with the dilemma. This response set is scored 0.

A third respondent saw Estelle's problem as a conflict between one's own (and one's family's) benefit and a set of "general rules designed to benefit you and others." Breaking the rules was described by this respondent as "cheating others," thus reflecting her awareness of the social nature of the constraints in this dilemma. Although she did not actively engage the constraint of this social context, she did recommend direct action and her response is scored + 2.

Initial descriptive statistics indicated very low frequencies on Categories 2 and 5 and led to the reduction in the number of distinct Categories from 5 to 3 with scores on each dilemma ranging from 1 to 3 and a high score indicating a more socially responsible response. An overall score for each respondent, derived by summing the scores across all 3 stories, was used in subsequent analyses. Scores for this sample ranged from 3 to 9, with a mean score of 5.24.

Life Experiences

A full demonstration of the construct social individuality necessitates a description of its existence in particular groups with particular social experiences. Fixed-alternative (closed) questions about the respondents' background and current activities were included to assess their social groupings and their present or recent experiences in collective activities. All participants were asked to indicate whether or not they participated in groups or organizations, which kinds, and which of these groups was the most important to them and why. The groups of interest in these analyses included neighborhood groups, political groups, community groups, and unions. A variable coding different levels of participation in these groups was computed with scores ranging from 1 through 3. A score of 3 indicates that one actively participated in at least one of the four kinds of groups of interest and identified one of these groups as important. A score of 2 indicates that the person actively participated in at least one of the four groups but did not select any of them as "most important." A score of 1 indicates that a person did not participate in any of the four groups.

Results

Evidence of a Conception of the Self as Social Individuality

Results from the major analyses supported the expectation that the four measures described above would interrelate in a way that reflects an orientation to the self that is described as social individuality. Associations among selected background variables, current life experiences, the four individual measures, and a composite score of social individuality also generally confirmed the initial expectations. (See Lykes, 1984, for a detailed description of these validational analyses.) The specific analyses having to do with gender and one's conception of the self are of particular relevance for this discussion.

Gender and social individuality. Although the gender differences in mean levels on the four individual indices of social individuality were only slight (women's notions of the self being significantly more likely than men's to reflect the notion of the self as social individuality on the measure of apperception), examination of the intercorrelation of the four measures revealed gender differences in the patterns of relations among the various indices. In general, the measures were positively and significantly correlated for the sample of women whereas the relations were weaker and mostly nonsignificant for the sample of men (see Table 1). Those women whose cognitive-perceptual style reflected a tendency to perceive integrated wholes (in contrast to simple wholes or small details) were also more likely to apperceive the social dimensions of human interactions, to express a collectivist ideology and to describe the resolution of moral dilemmas using strategies that reflect themes of social responsibility. Of all possible intercorrelations, only the relation between social responsibility and ideology did not reach statistical significance in this correlation matrix.

In contrast, the pattern for men was not as consistent. Although the pattern of relations among cognitive perceptual styles, social apperception, and social responsibility for men was similar to that obtained for women, there was either no relation between the ideology measure and the perceptual measures or there was a negative relation (i.e., between ideology and social responsibility). Rather than revealing the relatively cohesive gestalt of relations identified for the sample of women, this matrix reveals a more complex set of relations suggesting either (1) that aspects of social individuality may operate in different ways at different levels of

Table 1. Intercorrelation matrix by gender groups: Four apertures on social individuality.

	Social apperception	Indiv-coll ideology	Social responsibility
Women[a]			
Cognitive-perceptual style	.29*	.36**	.28*
Social apperception		.39**	.30*
Indiv-coll ideology			.14
Men[b]			
Cognitive-perceptual style	.14	.07	.26[t]
Social apperception		.07	.37*
Indiv-coll ideology			− .10

[a] ns range from 50 to 54 due to missing data.
[b] $n = 30$.
[t] $p < .10$.
* $p < .05$.
** $p < .01$.

awareness for women and men, or (2) that social individuality is a less pervasive orientation for men, or (3) that social individuality exists at a different stage of development for women and men. However, the small sample size for men suggests caution in interpreting these data as indicative of strong gender differences.

Additional social experiences and social individuality. The data suggest that social individuality may be better understood in examining variations within, not across, gender. Thus, the quantitative and qualitative data providing some evidence of relations between women's differing social experiences and their notions of the self are of considerable interest. A combined score measuring social individuality was regressed on the six variables expected to predict this way of understanding the self. As expected (see Table 2), these six variables account for a significant amount of the variation (35%) in social individuality (multiple $R = .59$, $p < .01$). More specifically, participation in collective activities, higher levels of education, and

Table 2. Selected life experiences and social individuality for women.

Predictors	Standardized Beta coefficients	F (df) (at step entered)	
Educational level	.45** (—)	12.07** (1,50)	(—)
Group participation	.34* (.34*)	9.50)** (2,49)	(6.64*) (1,50)
Service & manual workers	.45^t (.22)	7.04** (3,48)	(2.31^t) (5,46)
Group participation by workers	− .33 (− .33)	6.02** (4,47)	(2.75*) (4.47)
Group participation by minor professionals	.11 (.15)	4.84** (5,46)	(3.27*) (3,48)
Minor professionals	− .05 (− .29)	3.97** (6,45)	(4.23*) (2,49)
Multiple R	.59** (.44^t)		
r squared	.35 (.20)		

Note.—*F*s and Betas in parentheses represent scores in stepwise regression *excluding* educational level.
$^t p < .10.$
$^* p < .05.$
$^{**} p < .01.$

lower occupational levels are associated with higher scores on the measure of social individuality for the women in this sample.

As expected, those working in service or manual jobs, representing those in the sample with the lowest occupational levels (who have similarly low levels of education), are more likely than are minor or major professionals (in higher occupational levels with similarly higher educational levels) to evidence a notion of the self as social individuality. Those with higher levels of education also evidenced a notion of the self as social individuality. However, since lower occupational levels are positively associated with lower levels of education (in the general population and in this sample, $r = .49$, $p <$ .001) and with social individuality, the positive association between social individuality and higher levels of education needs explanation.

Minimally these relations suggest that education and occupational level are not measuring the same or equivalent characteristics of one's social position. Perhaps for those who benefit in some way from existing social arrangements (i.e., minor or major professionals) education provides a way of understanding one's experiences relative to a larger context, revealing its social nature in contrast to the dominant perspective of autonomous individualism. However, as Bowles & Gintis (1976), among others, have demonstrated, education can also sustain oppressive, dominant, and exclusive social systems where the individualism of Horatio Alger is the dominant ideology. Alternatively, the positive association between education and social individuality may reflect either that in school one may acquire the cognitive skills reflected by these measures or that the skills assessed by the measures enable one to get more education. Additional research is needed to clarify this relation.

A closer look at the role of group participation in collective activities indicates that despite the fact that women overall were less likely than were men to participate in collective activities [χ^2 (2, N = 82) = 7.56, $p < .05$], such participation seemed to be associated significantly with their notions of the self. Sixty percent of those women who participated in at least one group working for social change scored above the mean on the measure of social individuality whereas only 30% of those women who did not participate in any collective activities scored above the mean. Women who have some experience in collective activities are more likely than are women not engaged in such activities to perceive the self as social.

These analyses suggest that selected life-experiences, some that vary due to membership in a social grouping (e.g., gender or occupational level) and others rooted in early or current life activities (e.g., participation in collective activities), are systematically associated with one's conceptualization of the self. Interviews with women in the sample were examined to provide additional, more qualitative, descriptions of their life experiences so that we might better understand the experiential correlates of this notion of the self as social individuality.

Descriptions of collective experiences. In general, the interviews suggested differences in the ways in which women scoring high in social individuality, referred to as social individuals, and women scoring low in social individuality, referred to as autonomous individualists, describe the breadth and depth of their relationships and their levels of current community involvement. Social individuals are more likely than are autonomous individualists to evidence both a widening circle of relationships from childhood to adulthood, including family, friends, neighborhood and community, and a tendency actively to participate in these communities, in addition to work and family responsibilities. For example, social individuals tend to describe themselves in terms of relatedness to friends, family, neighborhood and society. Frequent acknowledgement of political and social differences with family or friends suggests that interconnection does not negate particularity or difference.

For example, one social individual said: "When I go home to see my folks I find something I do in my life that they do in theirs, usually something in relationship to people, for example, in the way we both joke with people. . . . It's important for me to see the links between who I am and them. . . . We've had some hard times. I ran away when I was in college. It was the Vietnam era. My folks are Republican. They've challenged me lots and I've challenged them. We share things, like how we are relationally, but experiences I've had have really led me in different directions than them. . . . "

Social individuals are active and involved in circles well beyond immediate family or neighborhood and describe work as one vehicle for such involvement. They participate in a range of activities, many of which reflect both a sense of their own individuality or particularity and a commitment to social change through collaborative or collective action. They also cherish time alone and many of them mentioned the need for having such time for themselves.

In contrast, autonomous individualists tend to describe their current communities in terms of physical characteristics and not in terms of human relations or interconnections. Independence and autonomy are themes that emerge in their descriptions of their personal and work lives. There is little evidence in these interviews of commitment to or engagement in action for social change.

Typical of this group is the woman who said that although most of her family of origin still lives in the area, family members "don't spend much time together." She added: "I really like the shore. . . . I have a whole set of values that I've established for myself and I'm not living that way [now]. I want to own my own house in a fairly well-to-do suburb. . . . At this point in my life I'm into materialism." This woman also stated that she values "flexibility and autonomy" in her current job and describes it as a place where she works "very independently." In addition to work-related professional groups in which she is active, she belongs to an exercise group that provides an "outlet for stress and tension. I am much more productive and more satisfied with myself physically and emotionally."

Autonomous individualists are also involved in a range of activities but, in contrast to social individuals, they tend to stress their independence or separateness in these activities, rather than viewing them as contexts for relationships or as opportunities for making connections. Few autonomous individualists are actively involved in their communities and even fewer are engaged in collective activities for social change. Few of these women mention an interest in or valuing of spending time alone.

Although both groups of women identify multiple activities and involvements, the descriptions of these activities for those whose underlying notion of the self is social individuality revealed a focus on connection and separateness. Although the "need to be alone" may conflict with the "demands of children and community" at any given moment, the two are seen as part of the same reality, codefining their sense of self. Conflict and difference with parents is real and often painful, but the separateness is revealed in its totality only by also focusing on the connection. The emphasis on separateness thus presupposes ties or connection. Similarly, to need time alone is a dialectical confirmation of one's relatedness.

Summary

Evidence from the quantitative analyses was confirmed by the interview material and supports the expectations that women, particularly those working at the lower ends of the occupational ladder, are more likely to perceive the interrelation of self and others and the self-defining/defined nature of social experiences. Involvement in activities that focus on the transformation of oppressive structures, in which one acts on a belief in the interdependence of all people or through which one is reinforced in one's sense of belonging through community, may serve both to concretize an abstract sense of oneself as "an ensemble of social relations" and to provide a place where consciousness and action converge.

Discussion

The research described here supports my initial argument that an examination of women's experiences must look beyond individual, interpersonal relationships and identify the collective bases of our social interactions. Although the notion of the "self-in-relation" is an important extension of notions of autonomy and independence underlying most conceptualizations of the self, this notion retains some of its problems. By focusing on an alternative base for one's sense of self, collective experiences, and emphasizing the inextricable link between lived experiences and sense of self, I have identified an alternative notion of self, social individuality, and provided some evidence of it as revealed through the perceptions and words of some women.

Although limited by reductionistic methods that operationalize rich and complex social experiences (e.g., gender and occupational standing) using categorical variables (male or female, low, middle, or high occupational level), this research sought to clarify the inextricable link between one's notion of self and one's social experiences. Differences in conceptions of self were not therefore hypothesized as varying from one individual to the next but were presented as alternative notions of the self that would be systematically revealed by individuals from particular social groups with particular social experiences. This initial effort to articulate these relations has not asked the more basic question of how these alternative conceptions come to exist and to be expressed by individuals. Nor has it adequately or fully described the diversities of women's and men's social experiences. Additional work is needed to examine this notion of the self within various communities, for example, Black, Asian, or Hispanic, and to explore relations between education and social individuality.

The relations between gender and social individuality identified above are suggestive. Variations in women's and men's positions in society relative to the distribution of power and not to biology were critical for understanding variations in their sense of self. Sex differences in level or degree of social individuality were not found. Variations within gender groups were evident in the differing patterns of relations among the multiple measures of social individuality for women and men. Other social experiences (e.g., occupation, education, and collective activities) were equally important in accounting for intrasex variability in notions of the self. Additional research is needed further to clarify relations between gender and notions of the self.

Despite this, the initial effort reported here, however methodologically provisional, suggests several important directions for future research and theorizing about gender in personality research on the self. First, the effort to identify a theory of self rooted in an analysis of the *essential* qualities of the mother-child relationship overlooks the complex set of relationships that constrain that notion and that define its meaning for social participants. Identification of female mothering as a nearly universal experience and as the critical and foundational relationship for understanding one's sense of self is problematic. I do not mean to suggest that knowing and understanding the mother-child attachment/separateness is not critical for understanding the self and our notions of the self. Nor do I mean to argue against a position that suggests that all women may share some characteristics, even biologically based characteristics (Lewis, 1976), in common.

I have argued rather that a failure to focus on the particularity of mother-child relating and the cross-cultural and cross-contextual variations in the meaning of adult-child attachment-separateness reduces the highly variable social bases for our notions of the self to a base of individualism that can only support an individualistic understanding of the self. Such efforts are also embedded in inherently flawed efforts to reduce biology or individuality and environment or sociality to separate elements (Lowe & Hubbard, 1983).

Second, despite the important development of a woman's sense of self as intrinsically relational, that is, as codetermined by a mutually affirming relationship that confirms ". . . the validity of your own self as a person-in-relationship" (Kaplan, 1984, p. 10), the basis upon which this understanding rests remains individual, interpersonal experience. Such interactionist views of the self-in-relation support a lopsided focus on attachment, while the self can only be fully understood with equal focus on separateness.

Jordan (1984) suggests that the relation between the two processes is paradoxical, yet urges our consideration of "human activity," in contrast to the human entities engaged in activities and describes the "emergent self as a structure of coherent separateness and meaningful connection (p. 11). Similarly, Lewis (1976) refers to the dialectical nature of the mother-child relationship. Finally, Gilligan (1984), drawing on work by Vygotsky (1978), stresses the importance of envisioning relationships between, for example, parent and child, researcher and subject, not only in terms of inequality but in

terms of their interdependence. Yet each of these dialectical statements remains underdeveloped in the work discussed. Perhaps it is,
at least in part, as Heilbroner (1980) suggests: The language of
dialectics although grasped intuitively yields with great resistance to
intellectual discussion or explication.

Despite this, these comments point beyond interactionism to a
notion of self that simultaneously focuses on individuality and sociality, that sees the unity in these supposed oppositions and that is
revealed in human activity. Soviet psychologists, among others, have
argued that activity is key to understanding human experiences and
psychological development (see, for example, Vygotsky, 1978;
Wertsch, 1981). Although their understanding of activity is often
difficult to fully grasp (see, Wertsch, 1981), the focus on human
activity suggests a unit of analysis that "includes both the individual
and his/her culturally defined environment" (Wertsch, p. viii). Human activity is a dialectic of subject and object wherein subject and
object interpenetrate. ". . . Man's activity is conceived of by Marx as
a dialectic of subject and object; it is an objectivization of the subject
and a deobjectivization of the object. In activity, subject and object
interpenetrate" (cited by Wertsch, 1981 p. 12). This understanding
is critical in more fully developing a social sense of the self.

Personality research and theorizing about gender and the self must
therefore focus on human activity and on examining the multiple
and interrelated levels of understanding revealed through a study of
particular activities. Concepts describing the self developed in a
socially grounded personality theory would focus on the articulation
of individuality in the activity of social interrelatedness. Such concepts subsequently alter our views of various human experiences as,
for example, our discussion of mothering suggests or as evidenced
in Fine's (1983–1984) contextually based reanalysis of the experience of rape or in Bunch's (1975) discussion of women's struggles
for self-definition and for political survival.

Although ambitious in scope, the research strategy suggested here
expands on the processes reported by Gilligan and Lyons in their
studies of women's and men's differing voices or by Kaplan, Jordan,
and Miller in their therapeutic interviews with women. On the one
hand, it reflects a faithfulness to describing a broader range of
women's experiences, using a methodology that captures the dialectical relation between the self and social experiences and suggests a
more fully articulated alternative to previous efforts to develop an
understanding of the self as social. On the other hand, it attempts to
ground this theoretical orientation in a systematic empirical investigation. Fruitful next steps might include an effort to extend the

perspective described here to the research relationship itself through use of a method grounded in the dialectical relationship between participant and researcher. This would be consistent with some current methodologies (see, e.g., Roberts, 1981) and would further enhance our understanding of social individuality.

Author's Notes

The data reported in this paper were collected as a part of my doctoral dissertation submitted to the Faculty of the Department of Psychology of Boston College in partial fulfillment of the requirements for the PhD degree. Portions of this study were presented at the 1984 meetings of the American Psychological Association.

I would like to thank William Ryan, G. Ramsay Liem, and Abigail J. Stewart for their critical collaboration, support, and challenge at all stages in the development of that research. My thanks also to Joseph Healy and Susan Miolla for assistance in coding the data and, most particularly, to the women and men who so generously gave of their time to participate in this study.

I would also like to thank Hortensia Amaro, Oliva Espin, Margaret Fearey, Barbara Gruber, Anne Mulvey, Loraine Obler, Marianne Paget, and Shulamit Reinharz with whom I meet in a Feminist Methodology Research Group. Our individual and collective reflections have been critical to the elaboration of my ideas. Finally, I am grateful to Michele Fine, Mary Parlee, Shulamit Reinharz, and Abigail J. Stewart for their comments on an earlier draft of this manuscript.

Copies of the questionnaire, including the measures and interview questions, the coding manuals, and descriptions of the validity and reliability of the measures are in my dissertation, *Autonomous individualism vs. social individuality: Towards an alternative conceptualization of the self*, which is available from University Microfilms International, 300 N. Zeeb Road, Ann Arbor, MI 48106.

Appendix 1

Brief Summary of the Scoring System for Apperception°

1. *A unitary action is performed by a corporate entity and individual members participate in varied ways.* In order for a story to be scored for the presence of this category both the unitary action and individual participation must be present.

2. *Integration and differentiation,* that is, the scene described must be characterized by the integration of the various persons and aspects of the context described and include descriptions incorporating some details about the parts, exemplifying their concrete nature.

3. *Action is described, as opposed to a static picture and the action helps define the nature of the collectivity.* The person or groups described are

actively engaged in the scenario presented and this action helps provide a fuller description of the group or collectivity.

4. *The enacted roles pick up some of their meaning from the fact of being part of a collectivity and/or in a shared context,* that is, the persons who are engaged in creative action are also embedded in and shaped by the social context which they are creating.

5. *The capacity to experience multiple points of view is cognitively and/ or affectively expressed.* The storyteller exhibits an ability to imagine a number of perspectives and describes a scene in terms of a number of different persons' thoughts or feelings.

° This summary is not adequate for scoring purposes. Copies of the complete scoring system with practice materials and expert scoring are available at cost from me at the Department of Psychology, Rhode Island College, Providence, RI 02908.

Appendix 2

Brief Summary of Scoring System for Responsibility in Reasoning about Hypothetical Moral Dilemmas°

Each response set (including responses to all four questions following a single dilemma) was coded according to the following criteria. Each set received one of the following five scores:

1. acting directly, without an awareness of the constraint of the social, scored − 1;
2. neither acting directly nor identifying the constraint of the social, scored 0;
3. identifying the constraint of the social framework and taking some direct action, scored + 1;
4. acknowledging the social nature of the constraint and taking some direct action, scored + 2;
5. interacting with or engaging the social framework/context (e.g., identifying the social nature of the constraint and actively engaging the social context), scored + 3.

° This summary is not adequate for scoring purposes. Copies of the complete scoring system with practice materials and expert scoring are available at cost from me at the Department of Psychology, Rhode Island College, Providence, RI 02908.

References

Atkinson, J. W. (Ed.). (1958). *Motives in fantasy, action, and society.* Princeton, NJ: Van Nostrand.

Beck, S. J. (1949). *Rorschach's test* (Vol 1, 2nd ed.). New York: Grune & Stratton.

Bell, D. H. (1982). *Being a man: The paradox of masculinity.* Lexington, MA: The Lewis Publishing Co.

Bell-Scott, P., & Guy-Sheftall, B. (Eds.). (1984). Mothers and daughters [Special issue]. *Sage: A Scholarly Journal on Black Women, 1* (2).

Bowles, S., & Gintis, H. (1976). *Schooling in capitalist America: Educational reform and the contradictions of economic life.* New York: Basic Books.

Broverman, I. K., Broverman, D., Clarkson, F. E., Rosenkrantz, P. S., & Vogel, S. R.

(1970). Sex role stereotypes and clinical judgments of mental health. *Journal of Consulting and Clinical Psychology, 34* (1), 1–7.

Bunch, C. (1975). Self-definition and political survival. *Quest, 1* (3), 2–15.

Buss, A. R. (1975). The emerging field of the sociology of psychological knowledge. *American Psychologist, 30* (10), 988–1002.

Chodorow, N. (1978). *The reproduction of mothering: Psychoanalysis and the sociology of gender.* Berkeley, CA: University of California Press.

Dumont, L. (1970). The individual as an impediment to sociological comparison and Indian history. In L. Dumont (Ed.), *Religion, politics, and history in India: Collected papers in Indian sociology* (Chap. 7). Paris/The Hague: Mouton Publishers.

Dumont, L. (1980). *Homo hierarchicus: The caste system and its implications.* (M. Sainsbury, L. Dumont, & B. Gulati, Trans.). Chicago, IL: University of Chicago Press. (Original work published 1966)

Fanon, F. (1968). *The wretched of the earth* (Constance Farrington, Trans.). New York: Grove Press. (Original work published 1961)

Fine, M. (1983–1984). Coping with rape: Critical perspectives on consciousness. *Imagination, Cognition, and Personality, 3* (3), 249–267.

Finison, L. (1980, April). *Social action in historical perspective.* Discussion-workshop at the meeting of the New England Social Psychological Association, Boston, MA.

Gergen, K. (1973). Social psychology as history. *Journal of Personality and Social Psychology, 26,* 309–320.

Gergen, K. (1978). Experimentation in social psychology: A reappraisal. *European Journal of Social Psychology, 36* (11), 1344–1360.

Gilligan, C. (1982). *In a different voice: Psychological theory and women's development.* Cambridge, MA: Harvard University Press.

Gilligan, C. (1984). *Remapping development: The power of divergent data.* Unpublished manuscript. (Available from C. Gilligan, Harvard University, School of Education, Cambridge, MA 02138)

Harrower, M. R., & Steiner, M. A. (1973). *Large scale Rorschach techniques* (2nd ed.). Springfield, IL: Charles C. Thomas.

Hartsock, N. (1983). *Money, sex, and power: Towards a feminist historical materialism.* New York: Longman.

Heilbroner R. (1980, March). The dialectical vision. *The New Republic* (pp. 25–31).

Hogan, J. (1975). Theoretical egocentrism and the problem of compliance. *American Psychologist, 30* (5), 533–540.

Holland, R. (1977). *Self and social context.* London, England: MacMillan Press, Ltd.

Hollingshead, A. B., & Redlich, F. C. (1958). *Social class and mental illness.* New York: John Wiley & Sons.

Hooks, B. (1984). *Feminist theory: From margin to center.* Boston, MA: South End Press.

Hsu, F. L. K. (1883). *Rugged individualism reconsidered: Essays in psychological anthropology.* Knoxville, TN: The University of Tennessee Press.

Israel, J. (1979). From level of aspiration to dissonance (or, what the middle class worries about). In A. R. Buss (Ed.), *Psychology in social context* (pp. 239–257). New York: Irvington.

Jones, J. (1972). *Prejudice and racism.* Reading, MA: Addison-Wesley.

Jordan, J. V. (1984). *Empathy and self boundaries.* (Working Papers in Progress, No. 85–05). Wellesley, MA: Wellesley College, The Stone Center.

Joseph, G. (1984). Black mothers and daughters: Traditional and new populations. *Sage: A Scholarly Journal on Black Women, 1* (2), 17–21.

Joseph, G., & Lewis, J. (1981). *Common differences: Conflicts in black and white feminist perspectives.* Garden City, NY: Anchor Press/Doubleday.

Kanfer, F. H. (1979). Personal control, social control, and altruism: Can society survive the age of individualism? *American Psychologist, 34* (3), 231–239.

Kaplan, A. G. (1984). *The "self-in-relation": Implications for depression in women.* (Working Papers in Progress, No. 84–03). Wellesley, MA: Wellesley College, The Stone Center.

Kaplan, A., & Surrey, J. L. (1984). The relational self in women: Developmental theory and public policy. In L. E. Walker (Ed.), *Women and mental health policy*, (pp. 79–94). Beverly Hills, CA: Sage.

Kohlberg, L. (1969). Stage and sequence: The cognitive-developmental approach to socialization. In D. Goslin (Ed.), *Handbook of socialization theory and research* (pp. 347–480). New York: Rand McNally.

Leacock, E. (1983). Ideologies of male dominance as divide and rule politics: An anthropologist's view. In M. Lowe & R. Hubbard (Eds.), *Woman's nature: Rationalizations of inequality* (pp. 111–121). New York: Pergamon Press.

Lewis, H. B. (1976). *Psychic war in men and women*. New York: New York University Press.

Lewis, M. (1979). *The culture of inequality*. New York: New American Library.

Lowe, M., & Hubbard, R. (Eds.). (1983). *Woman's nature: Rationalizations of inequality*. New York: Pergamon Press.

Lykes, M. B. (1984). Autonomous individualism versus social individuality: Towards an alternative understanding of the self. *Dissertation Abstracts International, 45* (4), 1322B. (University Microfilms No. DA8416004)

Lyons, N. P. (1983). Two perspectives: On self, relationships, and morality. *Harvard Educational Review, 53* (2), 125–145.

Mead, G. H. (1962). *Mind, self, and society* (C. W. Morris, Ed.). (Vol. 1). Chicago, IL: University of Chicago Press. (Original work published 1934)

Miller, J. B. (1976). *Toward a new psychology of women*. Boston, MA: Beacon Press.

Miller, J. B. (1984). *The development of women's sense of self*. (Work in Progress Papers, No. 84–01). Wellesley, MA: Wellesley College, The Stone Center.

Minturn, L., & Lambert, W. W. (1964). *Mothers of six cultures: Antecedents of childrearing*. New York: John Wiley & Sons.

Mishler, E. G., Amarasingham, L. R., Hauser, S. T., Liem, R., Osherson, S. D., & Waxler, N. E. (1981). *Social contexts of health, illness, and patient care*. Cambridge, England: Cambridge University Press.

Pleck, J. H. (1981). *The myth of masculinity*. Cambridge, MA: The MIT Press.

Roberts, H. (Ed.). (1981). *Doing feminist research*. Boston, MA: Routledge & Kegan Paul.

Rorschach, H. (1975). *Psychodiagnostics* (8th ed.). New York: Grune & Stratton. (Original work published 1942)

Rubin, G. (1975). The traffic in women: Notes on the 'political economy' of sex. In R. R. Reiter (Ed.), *Toward an anthropology of women* (pp. 157–210). New York: Monthly Review Press.

Ryan, W., Lykes, M. B., & Bertner, B. (1983, April). *Assessing ideology: The influence of fundamental belief systems on social and political opinions*. Paper presented at the 54th Annual Meeting of the Eastern Psychological Association, Philadelphia, PA.

Sampson, E. E. (1978). Scientific paradigms and social values: Wanted—a scientific revolution. *Journal of Personality and Social Psychology, 36* (11), 1332–1343.

Schaff, A. (1970). *Marxism and the human individual*. (Based on a translation by O. Wojtasiewicz; R. S. Cohen, Ed.). New York: McGraw–Hill. (Original work published 1965)

Schutz, A. (1967). *The phenomenology of the social world* (G. Walsh & F. Lehnert, Eds.). Chicago, IL: Northwestern University Press. (Original work published 1932)

Schutz, A. (1970). *On phenomenology and social relations. Selected writings* (H. R. Wagner, Ed.). Chicago, IL: University of Chicago Press.

Shweder, R. A., & Bourne, E. J. (1982). Does the concept of the person vary cross-culturally? In A. J. Marsella & G. M. White (Eds.), *Cultural conceptions of mental health and therapy* (pp. 97–137). London: Reidel.

Smith, J. (1983). Feminist analysis of gender: A mystique. In M. Lowe & R. Hubbard (Eds.), *Woman's nature: Rationalizations of inequality* (pp. 89–109). New York: Pergamon Press.

Smith, M. B. (1978). Perspectives on selfhood. *American Psychologist, 33* (12), 1053–1063.

Stack, C. B. (1974). *All our kin: Strategies for survival in a Black community.* New York: Harper & Row.

Taylor, G. R. (1972). *Rethink: A paraprimitive solution.* London: Secker & Warburg.

Tuan, Yi-Fu. (1982). *Segmented worlds and self: Group life and individual consciousness.* Minneapolis, MN: University of Minnesota Press.

Turnbull, C. M. (1984). The individual, community, and society: Rights and responsibilities from an anthropological perspective. *Washington & Lee Law Review, 41* (1), 77–132.

Vygotsky, L. S. (1978). *Mind in society: The development of higher psychological processes* (M. Cole, V. John-Steiner, S. Scribner, & E. Souberman, Eds.). Cambridge, MA; Harvard University Press. (Original work published 1930)

Wertsch, J. V. (1981). (Ed. & Trans.). *The concept of activity in Soviet psychology.* Armonk, NY: M. E. Sharpe, Inc.

White, J. L. (1984). *The psychology of Blacks: An Afro-American perspective.* Englewood Cliffs, NJ: Prentice Hall.

Whiting, B. B., & Whiting, J. W. M. (1975). *Children of six cultures: A psycho-cultural analysis.* Cambridge, MA: Harvard University Press.

Wikse, C. V. (1977). *About possession: The self as private property.* University Park, PA: Pennsylvania State University Press.

Willie, C. V. (1979). *Caste and class controversy.* Bayside, NY: General Hall, Inc.

Winter, D. (1973). *The power motive.* New York: The Free Press.

Masculine/Feminine:
A personological perspective
Rae Carlson

Abstract

How might our expanding knowledge of *gender* contribute to a deeper understanding of *personality*? This paper offers a personological perspective for considering the import of contemporary work, and focuses on the ten substantive papers included in this issue of the *Journal of Personality*. An agenda for our future inquiry is proposed that includes (*a*) revising our ideology of science in a postpositivist era, (*b*) recognizing the complexity of personality as a domain distinguished from "human being theory," (*c*) developing richer and more comprehensive personality theory, and (*d*) studying persons over time. The papers reported in this issue contribute in various ways to the enrichment of personological understanding.

Prologue

Imagine a symbolic drama portraying a group of intrepid explorers seeking to map the unknown terrain of gender and personality. This is a drama in five acts, three of which precede the opening of my paper.

Act I. Our explorers meet, circa 1950, to review ancient literature, travelers' anecdotes, and artistic depictions of the fabled continent. They have every reason to believe the quest will prove exciting and fruitful, for there has always been documented knowledge of the importance of gender in human society. However, the object of this investigation is to discover how such knowledge bears upon an understanding of *personality*. The most important directives come from psychodynamic theories of Freud and Jung, and these are now supplemented with a few promising empirical studies. "Identification," "socialization," and "bisexuality" offer the most significant landmarks.

Act II. Nearly 20 years later, our explorers are huddled together, weary and discouraged, ready to abandon their provisional maps. Landmarks have disappeared; only bare desert surrounds them.

Consulting the most authoritative of new works, the 5-volume *Hand-book of Social Psychology* (Lindzey & Aronson, 1969), they recognize that the quest is hopeless. The sole indexed reference to "femininity" turns out to be a paragraph about hypomasculinity in preadolescent *boys*. Clearly there is no such psychological territory as gender *or* personality. They are about to abandon the project until they hear a good deal of murmuring and shouting from unidentified sources. So they decide to press on longer.

Act III. Ten years later (now it's the late 1970s) our explorers stumble onto our current civilization, and are totally unprepared for the experience. They have come from the desert into a neon jungle. Gender is everything: androgyny, sex roles, gender-identity counseling, feminist therapy, gay liberation, politics of reproduction, alternative life-styles. Above all, there is now a vast psychological industry newly created to harvest the fruits of the women's movement of the 1960s and early 1970s. Initially beguiled by all of these riches and distractions, our explorers cling to their original goal. They ask: What does all of this tell us about *personality*?

Act IV takes place (partially) in this issue of the *Journal of Personality*, and *Act V* somewhere in the future. This paper is an attempt to draw new and better maps for our explorers by aligning our new knowledge of gender with the neglected task of studying personality.

A Personological Perspective

The drama sketched above is not wholly imaginary, for it describes some of my own explorations of the gender-and-personality terrain. A quarter-century ago (Carlson & Carlson, 1960) I noted that women were rarely included (and their absence unnoted) in personality research of that era. Later studies suggested that masculine/feminine qualities in personality could be discerned, if approached as a theoretical problem (Carlson, 1965, 1971a), but that the scientific ideology and methodological preoccupations of the field precluded any thoughtful study of the issues (Carlson, 1971b, 1984). Welcoming the rise of feminist scholarship, I urged that its greatest potential contribution would be that of enriching our impoverished conceptions of personality; but I worried that the early fruits of our raised consciousness (in the angry phase of feminism) were leading women psychologists to adopt the very constructs and methods of the "oppressive" scientific establishment (Carlson, 1972). Essentially, I was pleading for a personological perspective, one that would accept the challenge of taking *personality* seriously, as against mere accretion of "significant differences" on one or another currently fashionable personality variable.

Thus the occasion of a special issue of the *Journal of Personality* devoted to exploring gender and personality is a happy one. As a framework for discussion of the papers included in this issue, I propose a few key ideas that may help in identifying their import for personality study, as contrasted with their contributions to "group differences," "psychology of women," or social criticism.

Personality as a Field of Inquiry

Personality is so daunting in its complexity that psychologists have made their task easier via convenient simplifications. Personal dispositions become summarized as "traits" that can be further reduced to "individual differences" amenable to nomothetic, quantitative analyses of data from any convenient sample. A person's intrinsic embeddedness in some socio-historical milieu invites the economy of looking *only* at social directives (e.g., "sex roles") for explanatory constructs. Wary of positing biological bases of personality, but attracted all the same, we alternate between celebrating and denouncing organic determinants. Individual development is hard to conceptualize and extremely expensive to study; thus we posit "stages" of development, and opt for group snapshots for verification, rather than taking sound-movies of persons over time. Above all, our scientific superegos have required us to produce empirical data to support—or challenge—any proposition; and here we have been more anxious to demonstrate the uncontaminated *purity* of our variables than to consider the explanatory *power* of our theoretical formulations.

Assumptions of our "normal science" have proven so unhelpful in arriving at a deeper understanding of personality that major revisions are now underway. Not all of the new developments seem equally promising for our future. (For example, much of "critical theory" tends to dismiss personality as an intellectual tool of capitalistic oppression; elsewhere, sophisticated techniques for analysis of "narrative structure" render ever more abstract and ephemeral the concrete reality of an individual life.) Rediscovering the personological perspective originally advanced by Murray and his colleagues in *Explorations in Personality* (Murray, 1938; White, 1981) offers a refreshing sense of the importance and vitality of *persons* that we have missed for a long time (Carlson, 1984).

From the rich framework suggested by a personological perspective, a few central ideas seem especially useful in discussing the papers offered in this issue.

Revising our ideology of science. Psychology has been overripe for alternatives to its failed paradigms and positivistic heritage. Feminist scholarship has been helpful, in a somewhat indirect way, by focusing on the incredible neglect of women's experience as an agenda for psychological inquiry. But our task is more general than either making a special place for a psychology of women or adopting any of the various "contextualist," " dialectical," "ethogenic," "interactional," or "transactional" approaches that are currently advocated. (An important contribution—but one that I cannot develop here—may be found in Tomkins' [1965, 1984] formulation of ideological scripts. This personological approach to the psychology of knowledge invokes personality theory to account for broad trends of social thought as well as an investigator's resonance to "humanistic" or "normative" worldviews that are independent of specific intellectual content. Dominant trends in psychology—its insistence on large samples, quantitative data, and relentless pursuit of error at the expense of increments in knowledge—are clearly normative, as I have suggested elsewhere—Carlson, 1984a.)

Human being theory vs. personality theory. Personologists' strongest criticism of mainstream research in personality is only superficially based on traditional nomothetic method or positivistic ideology of science. A more fundamental issue is a failure at the heart of our theorizing, the failure to distinguish between "human being theory" (an account of shared endowments of all human beings) and "personality theory" (an account of ways in which common ingredients result in highly individual recipes for living). This confusion underlies our allegiance to nomothetic method. Personologists recognize as "given" that the individual person is an active, intentional agent—an evolutionary emergent for whom biology and culture are *ground* and individual life the *figure* of our inquiry. Personologists hold themselves responsible for mastering our expanding knowledge of both biological and cultural directives; but this is a prelude to the study of individual lives. There is an implicit division of labor often obscured. What all human beings share is largely the province of general psychology; how these endowments are channeled by sociocultural forces is the province of social scientists. But the intersection of biology and culture, as managed (or mismanaged) by the individual person is central to our work.

Some important clarifications follow. Too much of our published research deals only with the nomothetic boundaries of human being theory. It relies too heavily on aggregate data, inappropriate metrics from the "individual differences" perspective (Lamiell, 1981), investigator-imposed categories, and deliberate "control" of unwelcome variance stemming from the person's activity and intentionality. A more appropriate use of human being theory would be that of focusing on the most *human* of our evolutionary endowments—our capacities for differentiated feeling and thought—as the starting-point for personological inquiry.

The personological perspective poses a special problem for research on gender and personality. Insofar as we define gender in terms of *differences* between males and females (or masculine/feminine qualities in either sex), we risk losing important insights. Ask yourself twin questions: How important is gender? How is gender important? The first question could be answered by citing abundant data reminding us that gender differences are routinely found when sought. The second question asks us to explore the significance of gender in individual lives, a question that we rarely pose.

Gender surely plays a significant part in any life, but it is not always the same part. To take an extreme example, Jan Morris (1974) has given us a poignant portrayal of a life in which gender-identity of a transsexual was magnified into a major script. Her account is rich with theoretical implications, as well as insightful reflections on experience in both masculine and feminine identities. For most of us, gender-identity rarely occupies so much of our life-space. There are probably particular points in development when gender is figural as a conscious concern—Oedipal conflict, the conformist stage of ego development (Loevinger, 1976), certain of the psychosocial crises that Erikson (1950) has discussed. Most often gender is a silent, unnoticed correlate of other matters that we care about, reflected perhaps in our styles of dealing with experience. Studying gender effects in aggregate data, we may be tapping only habitual, social scripts (though these are not trivial) without recognizing the highly individual ways in which gender may signify something of importance in an individual life.

Developing personality theory. For nearly a half-century, serious theoretical work in personality has been moribund. Between the introduction of Kelly's (1955) personal construct theory and Tomkins' (1979, 1984) script theory, no comprehensive new personality theory has been advanced. We "make do" with fragments of psychodynamic theories (and even nontheories of personality) in the burgeoning field of textbook writing. Unready to tackle the enormous complexity of the personality domain, psychologists have generated a host of "midlevel theories" in which great ingenuity is expended in constructing formal models of pet variables. The intellectual cost of such endeavors has been trenchantly accounted by Maddi (1984).

Yet the scene may not be so dismal as now appears. Psychologists have come to appreciate the activity and intentionality of persons— and thus to accept Tyler's (1959) urging that we focus on "choice" and "organization" as basic issues in the study of personality. Some of the liveliest new work comes from contemporary psychoanalysts whose traditional concern for detailed study of the individual is joined by freedom from some of the constraints of Freudian metapsychology and openness to more personological modes of inquiry.

Whatever the specific premises of tomorrow's theory of personality, such work must recognize the complexity and heterogeneity of intrapsychic structures as well as the diversity of personalities. Meanwhile, theoretical development may proceed by "making connections" among previously isolated facts, and by "making corrections" of dominant theories. Two papers in this issue, to be discussed below, exemplify these helpful trends.

Studying lives over time. While we *know* that an intellectual account of personality depends on an understanding of individual lives, our psychological literature is nearly devoid of such inquiry (Carlson, 1971b, 1984b). Psychobiographical studies hold great potential promise, but these are rarely cited (much less developed) in our research literature. At least three problems may be identified, beyond the fact that historians, literary scholars, and political scientists are doing "our" work. First, by concentrating on "eminent" people, such studies necessarily leave unexplored a great variety of personality patterns to be found among ordinary people. Second, psychobiographical work has relied almost exclusively on psychoanalytic theory as a conceptual framework that is assumed, rather than tested. Third, and quite appropriately, most psychobiographies are intended to illumine a life-history as an end in itself, rather than to contribute to a larger and more systematic understanding of personality.

"Studying personality the long way" (White, 1981) is difficult, expensive, rarely fundable, and unlikely to lead to academic tenure. Conceivably such constraints account for the poverty of personological work. Yet I think that ideological commitments (welcomed or enforced) play a larger part. Happily, a shift in our *zeitgeist* is now discernible. The life span emphasis in developmental psychology encourages longitudinal study. Methodological directives (Runyan, 1982) are newly available, as are demonstrations of idiographic approaches to the study of identities (Rosenberg & Gara, 1985).

Longitudinal study per se is no panacea. When such work is

variable-centered (e.g., Costa & McRae, 1980) it yields abundant evidence of the consistency and stability of selected personality dimensions, but tells us little about more fundamental issues. Elegant longitudinal studies, informed by theory and expert use of appropriate methods (e.g., Block, 1971; Helson, Mitchell, & Moane, 1984) are rare, and uniquely valuable. Yet more modest projects are worth pursuing. Even short-term single-case studies (Carlson, 1981) are capable of illuminating theoretical issues. Resources available to investigators could be greatly expanded by the use of rich materials available in published work (e.g., Lewis' *The Children of Sanchez*). We need only to recognize the potentialities of personological study of lives over time.

Looking ahead, there are reasons to hope for more consequential personality study in our future. Feminist scholarship will surely contribute to this trend. For, stereotype or not, "feminine" styles of inquiry have typically shown the engagement in complexities, the patience required to track development, and the willingness to challenge received wisdom, that are much needed in the field.

On Reading and Enjoying This Issue

Packed within these pages are some of the best efforts to comprehend issues of gender and personality to be found in contemporary psychology. Invited to provide a conceptual framework, I have been somewhat fierce in asserting the value of a personological perspective. Readers who disparage personology (few, I hope!) will also learn much from the work presented here.

Revising Our Ideology of Science

The decline of positivism, the ascendance of new models of inquiry, and the power of feminist thought are by now familiar. Two papers in this issue accept such revisions of our former ways of construing inquiry and go beyond familiar critiques to pose more challenging questions.

Morawski (this issue) leads us on an historical tour of the gender-and-personality domain since the turn of the century, revealing implications that most of us missed. Underlying our "progress" over the past 90 years there runs a constant thread: the search for evidence supporting the "real" gender differences given in our cultural categories. Equally constant are the unspoken constraints on our scientific inquiry: assumptions of our "expert" status, the need to disguise measures of masculinity/femininity as "too hot" for ordinary people to confront directly, and a rather flexible faith in our measures and quantitative analyses.

Our recent preoccupation with "androgyny," as Morawski demonstrates, reproduced rather faithfully the core assumptions of the intellectual tradition that it meant to replace. Why did so many feminists seem to adopt the notion of androgyny as a breakthrough? Largely because it appeared to liberate women from the negative implications of passivity and weakness associated with "appropriate sex roles." More subtly, androgyny research may have been self-serving for young professional women who found in it a model and a rationale for their own aspirations in the male-dominated world of psychology, and an affirmation of the positivistic values interiorized in their scientific socialization. Morawski asks us to consider our scientific work reflexively, to confront our history, and to devise more thoughtful ways of examining gender and personality.

Perhaps it is misleading to comment on Lykes' paper (this issue) in terms of ideology, for it contains substantive work as well as ideological criticism. Yet I believe her message is primarily ideological. Treating the central issue of *selfhood*, Lykes goes beyond current feminist ideas to question the notion of attachment as central to woman's identity. How ought we to consider selfhood? Contextually, in the rather special sense advanced by critical theory, by examining relationships to a larger social order. This somewhat abstract approach is given concrete focus with an empirical study of community adults chosen on the basis of their experience as social activists. Lykes' concern with the disempowered members of our society provides a corrective for our usual reliance on convenience samples. Many of her respondents were *from* disempowered groups, but sought and attained "responsible" power in contributing to community life. Thus their experiences of selfhood tell us important things that we could not learn from college freshmen or from formal political leaders. Lykes' proposal of "social individuality" is a valuable focus for future inquiry.

Reassessing Our Empirical Knowledge

Much of our received knowledge of gender and personality rests on ad hoc findings of sex differences emerging from diverse empirical studies. As we begin to make gender and personality the focus of our work, a double reassessment of such knowledge is needed: first, to examine its contribution to an understanding of gender per se, and then to weigh its import for personality. Five papers in this collection attempt such clarifications.

Emotional development in males and females. As we attempt to sort out what we know about people-in-general from what we know about personality, few areas of inquiry are more important than the study of affect and affective-cognitive complexes. Brody (this issue) offers a review and synthesis of a vast literature on emotional development in terms of gender differences in defense and display rules, emotional expressiveness, emotional recognition, affect experience, and the socialization of affect.

Brody is appropriately critical of much existing work, noting that research has been constrained by both theoretical and methodological limitations. Her heroic work in organizing the literature and proposing directions for future work will be helpful to many investigators. I would like to add comments on three problems that arise from the tendency to confuse human being theory with personality theory.

There is now wide agreement that the affect system, along with our cognitive systems, is uniquely important among our evolutionary endowments. The conjunction of affect with cognition gives rise to the individual's freedom from "instinctual" directives and extraordinary capacity for constructing a truly personal life. Personality theory *begins* with acceptance of such universal potentialities, and proceeds to study their deployment in generating the diversity of personality structures that we intuitively recognize. What, then, are the difficulties?

First, there is considerable confusion in "defining" emotions. Important clarifications are possible, I believe, if we respect the affect system as a biological given (Tomkins, 1962, 1963) in which discrete affects with intrinsically rewarding/punishing qualities are evolutionarily endowed. Affects are endlessly combinable with cognitions; these give rise to affective-cognitive complexes often misidentified as "basic emotions." Now we are approaching the level of personality theory. Tomkins (1981 a and b) has portrayed the historical mix-up that generated so much confusion in defining emotions and has clarified the distinction between our basic endowments and what we make of these.

Second, most of our knowledge of the affect domain rests on aggregate data. Nomothetic data are useful in affording clues to sex typical differences in temperament and culture-specific ways in which socialization of affect occurs. Such knowledge is important base-line data. When we go beyond recording gender-typical responses to standard stimuli and ask people to *construct* affect-laden scenes, we come closer to an appreciation of how affect is handled in personally meaningful ways. (See Carlson & Carlson, 1984 for one example of such a study.)

Third, there is a more pervasive and subtle consequence of our habitual ways of studying emotions. Affect is far more ubiquitous than we have recognized in our conceptualizations, or than our research designs enable us to learn. Studying affective processes in isolation, we are not alerted to the specific affects that power such culturally valued qualities as "achievement," "competence," "creativity," and the like—in these cases the affects of excitement and anger that are traditionally encouraged in masculine development and discouraged in feminine socialization. (To consider this issue reflexively, as Morawski recommends, the present paper may serve as an example. I am suddenly conscious of the *excitement* imagery— where I speak of "exploring" unknown terrain, of "taking off" for new lines of inquiry, of "illuminating" puzzles—and of *anger* in the milder form of impatience with psychologists' long neglect of feminine experience and their continuing neglect of personality as the central intellectual problem of the field.)

Abundant evidence tells us that our tradition of Western thought imposes (or builds upon) affect-specialization, such that the masculine affects of excitement, anger, contempt, and disgust are culturally acceptable, while feminine joy, distress, fear, and shame are more likely to be recognized as "emotional." Thus the very language of our social science tends to perpetuate the ideas that emotions: (*a*) depend on prior cognitive appraisals (thus confusing affect and affective-cognitive complexes), (*b*) are the special domain of women, and (*c*) are somewhat irrational intrusions into competent performances. Such parochialism seems to be changing in recent years, but has yet to be fully understood in our academic circles.

Victimized women. Our knowledge of "battered women," reassessed by Walker and Browne (this issue), deals with a more pervasive problem than we have fully appreciated. Epidemiological studies, the authors tell us, estimate that one in four women will be raped and/or battered by their mates. Where earlier work sought to identify masochistic personality patterns that invite such victimization, Walker and Browne examined data on patterns of interaction with violent men (and abusing families) that result in such pathology and sometimes lead to desperate acts of homicide.

This problem is surely gender-related, and surely has profound implications for the study of personality. Yet the conceptual tools of "learned helplessness" and "modeling" scarcely seem adequate to organize the poignant data presented in the paper. (Mindful of Morawski's advice to examine our science reflexively, one wonders whether the exclusive use of these limited constructs may not *ex-emplify* the learned-helplessness and modeling behavior of investigators caught in the grip of an academically powerful research ideology?)

How might battered women be understood in more personological terms? One formulation might suggest that: (1) their lives are dominated by negative affect scripts in which positive moments are mainly "relief affect" from transient reductions of distress and terror, (2) their earlier socialization experiences afforded little opportunity to experience the self as capable of commanding rewarding relationships, (3) their commitments to abusive mates are at once a kind of "faithfulness" and an acceptance of shame and fear as the natural conditions of connectedness, (4) their inconsistent ways of dealing with their own children both replay and attempt to counteract their own childhood experience; and (5) the "solution" of homicide represents an heroic counteraction of intolerable terror and disgust. Such a formulation does not "explain" the life situation of battered women, but may offer a rich way of studying it.

Power, achievement, and morality reconsidered. A trio of empirical papers, all based on nomothetic inquiry, offer clarification of gender effects on major variables of personality.

Folk wisdom holds that males more "naturally" seek power—a notion that has been supported in empirical research. Here Winter and Barenbaum (this issue) offer new evidence that "what seemed to be a *gender* difference was really a *socialization* difference." How so? Because a refined measure of "responsibility" tells us that gender effects in empirical correlates of TAT measures of power motivation disappear when a person's experience of responsibility (for younger siblings, for own children) is considered. Such findings require us to examine more closely the texture of individual lives, rather than assimilating data to preconceived notions of sex roles. If "profligate" power still appears to be a masculine domain, "responsible" power is now seen as gender-neutral; the sheer experience of responsibility (chosen or not) seems to alter the construction of one's life.

Psychologists' concern with achievement motivation at once reflects a dominant cultural value, a concern in the careers of investigators, and a chronic empirical puzzle. (Why can't a woman be more like a man?) Gaeddert's examination of gender and sex effects (this issue) employed a study of college students in which the "domain" of personal achievement episodes was crossed with "process of evaluation." Although the findings were a bit cloudy (neither sex nor gender identity accounted for any main effects), the implications may be clear enough. Serious inquiry into the experience and/or the evaluation of "achievement" must weight the importance of success or failure episodes in a differentiated (and more personological) fashion.

For at least two decades the nature of moral development has preoccupied developmental psychologists. Far from being a neutral matter, the nature of moral conduct and moral judgement has profound implications for personality; such concerns are amplified by the centrality of morality as a concern in current political and social life. Lifton's paper (this issue) attempts to sort out the conflicting messages about sex and gender differences in our literature with an exhaustive review of published work, new empirical data, and a conceptual clarification of alternative theoretical formulations. What do we learn? Both much and little. The facts are clear enough: when significant gender effects are found, these seem to be based on the Kohlberg cognitive developmental model in which "rational" principles of moral judgement are criterial, and thus give the edge to males. Alternative models such as Gilligan's or a "personological" (actually, an individual-differences) model proposed by the author yield little evidence of gender differences. Lifton has accomplished a thoughtful review of massive empirical literature that will be useful to many investigators. Yet the fundamental issues remain elusive because linkages between morality and other facets of personality development rest on aggregation of nomothetic data. This is a promising start in the sense of clarifying some misconceptions and broadening our view of moral implications of personal life.

The variable-centered inquiry that informed five major papers in this issue will be illuminating and useful to some readers, dispiriting to others. For further meaning to emerge from such inquiry, we will need broader theoretical directives, an issue pursued in the next section of this paper.

Developing personality theory. The "midlevel" theorizing (Maddi, 1984) familiar in contemporary psychology is simply incapable of guiding personological inquiry, so that our most useful frameworks still rest on the more comprehensive vision of psychoanalytic theory. Two papers in this issue begin with the premises of Freudian or Eriksonian thought and go on to offer searching appraisals of what is needed for making connections or corrections.

Lewis (this issue) begins with a deceptively modest introduction: How are we to understand why women are subject to depressive disorders, and men to paranoid (or schizophrenic) disorders? The empirical data are clear enough, and are not trivial. Lewis takes off from this observation for a searching exploration of the entire gender and personality domain. At the risk of fatal oversimplification, I might capture the import of her paper with a few assertions. (1) The human being is intrinsically a "social" animal, so that distortions of sociality observed in clinical work mirror the more general conditions of masculine/feminine development. (2) Both constitutional and cultural directives push women toward advanced development of sociality, and men toward individualistic neglect or denial of social bonds, with consequences for distinctive patterns of ordinary life, as well as patterns of mental illness. (3) Consequences of such gender specialization are found in superego structures that rest on feminine "shame" and masculine "guilt," as observed in the course of psychotherapy. (4) Shame and guilt, in turn, are related to the voluminous work on field dependence/independence; these cognitive styles also clarify the nature of psychotherapeutic process. (5) Contrary to stereotypes, males are actually the more vulnerable. ("Women get sick; men die.") They seem more vulnerable to distortions of basic human sociality, and thus to the more intractable kinds of pathology. Covering a vast range of scholarship, Lewis' formulation is broad in scope, specific in detail, and will surely power more thoughtful inquiry into gender and personality.

Erik Erikson's work has undoubtedly been the most influential theoretical framework invoked in the study of life span personality development. Early feminist protests of the "inner space" concept were frequently based on a wholesale rejection of the psychoanalytic ("anatomy is destiny") approach rather than a careful reading of Erikson's message. Yet the single pathway of development implied in Erikson's familiar epigenetic sequence *does* seem to mask distinctive differences in experiences, timing, and outcomes for males and females. Franz and White (this issue) address this problem with the most meticulous examination of Eriksonian theory I have yet encountered. Their solution is not simply one of rewriting the epigenetic charts for women. Rather, they propose a *double helix* model "in which the two parallel but interconnected strands or pathways— the pathways of psychological individuation and attachment—ascend in a spiral representing the life cycle . . . " for males and females alike. The two-path model is offered in a chronological sequence in which the Eriksonian individuation strand is supplemented with an attachment strand provisionally adapted from Selman's work on sociocognitive development and from Mahler's object-relations approach. Thus, a developmental perspective is offered that is consistent with, but may enrich, the familiar dialectical conceptions of Bakan, Jung, and others. Again, we have a thoughtful piece of conceptual work that will be exciting to many readers.

Studying lives over time. This issue is blessed with a gem of personological work in a report from Ravenna Helson's longitudinal study of college women. Helson and her colleagues have previously contributed several illuminating papers from this project (Helson, 1966, 1967; Helson, Mitchell, & Moane, 1984; Helson & Moane, 1984). Here Helson, Mitchell, and Hart (this issue) offer something very special: a review of the lives of the seven women (among 90) who achieved the highest levels of ego development on Loevinger's sentence completion test in terms of three major theories of personality development. Levinson's formulation of "life structures" derived from the study of adult men, Gilligan's model of female development, and Loevinger's (1976) theory of ego development all "fit" to some degree these complex lives; but these formulations are complementary, rather than competitive.

Uniquely valuable in this paper is the combination of first-person accounts of experience from articulate women and skillful pursuit of theoretical implications on the part of the authors. We are allowed to enter "real lives" with the benefit of expert and unobtrusive guides, and we find both confirmations and surprises. Most challenging, perhaps, are the surprises. Our theories would not prepare us for the pain and difficulties that marked the development of these women, the extraordinary diversity of their personalities, or the drama of their postcollege years. Helson et al. have touched upon the ideological and theoretical issues raised by other contributors to this issue in the most intellectually satisfying way—with a richly personological account of personality development.

Epilogue

As the curtain descends on Act IV of our imaginary drama, we have an Intermission. If we were simply the audience, we might enjoy brief chats with friends and then return to witness the final act. But we are the playwrights, and this is a long intermission: Act V is still to be written by our collaborative efforts.

Happily, we find that this issue of the *Journal of Personality* is so replete with insights that the next act writes itself. We are the explorers, and we have better (if still incomplete) maps of the terrain. Surely Act V will portray our liberation from methodological dogma, a more reflexive notion of our own science, more comprehensive theorizing, and if we are very lucky, a series of studies of *individual* lives to deepen and extend our knowledge of gender and personality.

References

Bakan, D. (1966). *The duality of human existence.* Chicago: Rand, McNally.
Block, J. (1971). *Lives through time.* Berkeley, CA: Bancroft Books.

Brody, L. R. (1985). Gender differences in emotional development: A review of theories and research. *Journal of Personality, 53,* 102–149.

Carlson, E., & Carlson, R. (1960). Male and female subjects in personality research. *Journal of Abnormal and Social Psychology, 61,* 482–483.

Carlson, L., & Carlson, R. (1984). Affect and psychological magnification: Derivations from Tomkin's script theory. *Journal of Personality, 52,* 36–45.

Carlson, R. (1965). Stability and change in the adolescent's self-image. *Child Development, 36,* 659–666.

Carlson, R. (1971a). Sex differences in ego functioning: Exploratory studies of agency and communion. *Journal of Consulting and Clinical Psychology, 37,* 267–277.

Carlson, R. (1971). Where is the person in personality research? *Psychological Bulletin, 75,* 203–219.

Carlson, R. (1972). Understanding women: Implications for personality theory and research. *Journal of Social Issues, 28,* 17–30.

Carlson, R. (1981). Studies in script theory: I. Adult analogs of a childhood nuclear scene. *Journal of Personality and Social Psychology, 40,* 501–510.

Carlson, R. (1984a). Affects, ideology, and scripts in social policy and developmental psychology. Paper presented at Chapel Hill conference, July, 1984.

Carlson, R. (1984b). What's social about social psychology? Where's the person in personality research? *Journal of Personality and Social Psychology, 47,* 1304–1309.

Costa, P. T., Jr., & McCrae, R. R. (1980). Still stable after all these years: Personality as a key to some issues in adulthood and old age. In P. B. Baltes & O. C. Brim (Eds.), *Life-span development and behavior* (Vol. 3, pp. 65–102). New York: Academic Press.

Erikson, E. (1950). *Childhood and society.* New York: Norton.

Franz, C. E., & White, K. M. (1985). Individuation and attachment in personality development: Extending Erikson's theory. *Journal of Personality, 53,* 224–256.

Gaeddert, W. P. (1985). Sex and sex role effects on achievement strivings: Dimensions of similarity and difference. *Journal of Personality, 53,* 286–305.

Gilligan, C. (1982). *In a different voice.* Cambridge: Harvard University Press.

Helson, R. (1966). Personality of women with imaginative and artistic interests: The role of masculinity, originality, and other factors in their creativity. *Journal of Personality, 34,* 1–25.

Helson, R. (1967). Personality characteristics and developmental history of creative college women. *Genetic Psychology Monographs, 76,* 205–256.

Helson, R., Mitchell, V., & Hart, B. (1985). Lives of women who became autonomous. *Journal of Personality, 53,* 257–285.

Helson, R., Mitchell, V., & Moane, G. (1984). Personality and patterns of adherence and nonadherence to the social clock. *Journal of Personality and Social Psychology, 46,* 1079–1096.

Helson, R., & Moane, G. (1984). Personality change in women from college to midlife. Unpublished manuscript.

Kelly, G. A. (1955). *The psychology of personal constructs.* New York: Norton.

Kohlberg, L. (1964). Development of moral character and moral ideology. In M. Hoffman and L. Hoffman (Eds.), *Review of child development research* (Vol. 1, pp. 383–431). New York: Russell Sage Foundation.

Lamiell, J. T. (1981). Toward an idiothetic psychology of personality. *American Psychologist, 36,* 276–289.

Lewis, H. B. (1985). Depression vs. paranoia: Why are there sex differences in mental illness? *Journal of Personality, 53,* 150–178.

Lewis, O. (1961). *The children of Sanchez: Autobiography of a Mexican family.* New York. Random House.

Lifton, P. D. (1985). Individual differences in moral development: The relation of sex, gender, and personality to morality. *Journal of Personality, 53,* 306–334.

Lindzey, G., & Aronson, E. (eds.) (1969). *Handbook of social psychology* (2nd ed.). Reading, MA: Addison-Wesley. 5 vols.

Loevinger, J. (1976). *Ego development.* San Francisco: Jossey-Bass.

Lykes, M. B. (1985). Gender and individualistic vs. collectivist notions about the self. *Journal of Personality, 53*, 356–383.

Maddi, S. R. (1985, June). The practical dangers of middle-level theorizing. Paper presented to the Society for Personology, Chicago.

Mahler, M. S., & McDevitt, J. B. (1980). The separation-individuation process and identity formation. In S. I. Greenspan & G. H. Pollock (Eds.), *The course of life: Psychoanalytic contributions toward understanding personality development, Vol. 1. Infancy and early childhood*. National Institute of Mental Health.

Morawski, J. G. (1985). The measurement of masculinity and feminity: Engendering categorical realities. *Journal of Personality, 53*, 196–223.

Morris, J. (1974). *Conundrum*. NY: Harcourt Brace Jovanovich.

Murray, H. A. (1938). *Explorations in personality*. New York: Oxford.

Rosenberg, S., & Gara, M. (in press). The multiplicity of personal identity. *Review of Personality and Social Psychology*.

Runyan, W. McK. (1982). *Life histories and psychobiography*. NY: Oxford Press.

Selman, R. L. (1980). *The growth of interpersonal understanding: Developmental and clinical analyses*. New York: Academic Press.

Tomkins, S. S. (1962). *Affect, imagery, consciousness. Vol. 1. The positive affects*. New York: Springer.

Tomkins, S. S. (1963). *Affect, imagery, consciousness. Vol. 2. The negative affects*. New York: Springer.

Tomkins, S. S. (1965). Affect and the psychology of knowledge. In S. S. Tomkins & C. Izard (Eds.), *Affect, cognition, and personality*. New York: Springer.

Tomkins, S. S. (1979). Script theory: Differential magnification of affects. In H. E. Howe Jr. & R. A. Dienstbier (Eds.), *Nebraska Symposium on Motivation* (Vol. 26). Lincoln: University of Nebraska Press.

Tomkins, S. S. (1981a). The quest for primary motives: Biography and autobiography of an idea. *Journal of Personality and Social Psychology, 41*, 306–329.

Tomkins, S. S. (1984, June). Script theory. Paper presented to Society for Personology, Asilomar, California.

Tomkins, S. S. (1981b). The rise, fall, and resurrection of the study of personality. *Journal of Mind and Behavior, 2*, 443–452.

Tyler, L. (1959). Toward a workable psychology of individuality. *American Psychologist, 14*, 75–81.

Walker, L. E. A., & Browne, A. (1985). Gender and victimization by intimates. *Journal of Personality, 53*, 179–195.

White, R. W. (1981). Studying personality the long way. In A. I. Rabin, J. Aronoff, A. M. Barclay, & R. A. Zucker (Eds.), *Further explorations in personality* (pp. 3–19). New York: Wiley.

Winter, D. G., & Barenbaum, N. B. (1985). Responsibility and the power motive in women and men. *Journal of Personality, 53*, 335–355.

Ironies in the contemporary study of gender
Deborah Belle

The papers in this issue capture well the excitement of contemporary research on sex and gender as well as many ironies implicit in this body of research. In attempting to learn about the intrinsic differences between male and female we have generally learned more about our own preconceptions and about our own tendencies to reify images of starkly contrasting male and female personalities. Sex difference research, when critically examined, has generally failed to find the sex differences that were expected (see Brody and Lifton papers in this issue). Reflections on the history of sex difference research have illuminated the social schemas and unstated political agendas that have influenced both social scientists and laypersons (Morawski, this issue). Yet investigations of women's perspectives and experiences have forced provocative reexaminations and reworkings of classic psychological theories pertaining to both men and women and have opened our eyes to new visions of the human experience (see Franz and White, Lewis, and Lykes papers in this issue).

Despite widespread belief to the contrary, virtually all studies of sex differences in cognitive skills, temperament, and social behavior as elicited in laboratory settings show striking similarity between men and women. Even when sex differences are reliably found (as in studies of visual-spatial ability and the decoding of nonverbal behavior) sex of subject appears to account for less than 5% of the variance in behavior (Deaux, 1984). Laboratory studies probably elicit an individual's potential rather than his or her most likely behavior in a more natural environment. The repeated finding of minimal or no sex differences across a wide variety of skills, styles, and behaviors argues against the notion that the two sexes differ sharply in their intrinsic capacities for cognitive and social behavior.

Our persistence in holding unsubstantiated beliefs about the sexes is certainly attributable in part to the political and social agendas discussed by Morawski. As she argues, sex difference research has often served a prescriptive as well as a descriptive role, bolstering notions of stereotypic femininity and masculinity in times of wide-spread "alterations and confusions of gender images and roles." Historically, gender researchers began their research with the assumption that masculinity and femininity were real and distinct psychological qualities, paralleling the socially prescribed social roles for men and women. When research findings failed to confirm such assumptions, as when girls actually outscored boys on early intelligence tests, it was typically the findings rather than the assumptions that were rejected.

Perhaps some of our reluctance to give up unproven and even disproven beliefs about the sexes can also be explained by the very fact that there are only two sexes, and that there is a human tendency to focus on differences when confronted by two of anything. Barnes (1984) found that when parents described their children, those parents with two children tended to describe each in contrast to the other. "Charles is shy and timid . . . Bobby will tell you off." "Michelle is a leader; Jimmie is a follower" (p. 43). While all of the parents in two-child families described their two children in contrasting terms, only a minority of the parents of three children and none of the parents of four children did so. Instead, parents with larger families focused on unique aspects of each child. One parent of four children, for instance, noted that child A was sociable and liked to read and fix things, child B liked art, drawing, music and was good at songs, child C was interested in fashion and clothes, and child D worked with his hands and loved sports.

In a similar vein, Gregory Bateson (1968) once noted that anthropologists who did fieldwork in just two cultures tended to emphasize the differences between these cultures, while anthropologists with wider field experience noted, instead, the diversity of human adaptations. There is no way to give researchers any "wider field experience" with a third or fourth sex, but one must wonder to what extent the existence of only two sexes focuses our attention inappropriately on areas of possible contrast. The issue is heightened, of course, by the fact that any single researcher belongs to one of the two groups being contrasted. As Eagly and Carli (1981) showed, authors are more likely to report sex differences that reflect credit on their own sex. Such a result again demonstrates the not-too-deeply hidden agendas that have influenced the study of sex differences.

Perhaps our preoccupation with bipolar contrasts also inhibits us from studying the ways in which gender is "nuanced" by other social characteristics such as race, class, employment status, parental status, and age. Studies of nonverbal behavior, for instance, have examined sex differences and race differences but rarely the interaction of sex and race (Smith, 1983). The scarcity of research on such interactive effects then contributes to the impression of monolithic sex differences.

The stereotype of women as fragile, loving, submissive, and innocent, well-suited for family life and motherhood, but poorly equipped for the public sphere, corresponds to the "cult of true womanhood" (Perkins, 1983). Women socialized in this tradition probably did come to embody many of the virtues and deficiencies for which they were powerfully rewarded. Yet many women were excluded from this vision of femininity by virtue of their class or race: black women, immigrant women, and poor women faced vastly different expectations. It must often have been such women who most effectively challenged the generalizations of fragility and weakness that were used to justify limitations on all women. What could have been a more effective challenge to those who saw women as too delicate and ineffectual to vote than Sojourner Truth's words and the reality of her lived experience?

> Look at my arm! I have ploughed and planted and gathered into barns . . . and ain't I a woman? I could work as much and eat as much as a man—when I could get it—and bear the lash as well . . . I have borne thirteen children and seen most of 'em sold into slavery, and when I cried out with my mother's grief, none but Jesus helped me—and ain't I a woman? (Friedan, 1974, p. 88.)

We will certainly learn more about the potentialities of being female and male as we pay closer attention to women and men who occupy diverse positions in society and who have been socialized in different traditions concerning the meaning of femininity and masculinity.

The behavior, attitudes, and psychological responses of the sexes are strongly shaped by social roles, which create their own imperative demands, and which tend to be allocated differentially by sex. One rarely finds men who are low-income single parents, battered spouses, day-care providers, or secretaries, or women who are school superintendents, day laborers, bank presidents, or soldiers. The "feminization of poverty" (Pearce, 1979) has also meant that economic insecurity and deprivation characterize the lives of women more than those of men. These aspects of the lived experiences of men and women contribute to the divergencies between men and women that are noted in adult life.

Sex is also a powerful social category that influences our judgments about ourselves and others. Young children actively organize their understanding of the social world through the use of social categories such as gender. Children's earnestness in discovering regularities associated with gender and in enforcing their categorical systems are often amusing. Frieze, Parsons, Johnson, Ruble, and Zellman (1978) discuss one young boy who insisted that a male adult not drink the coffee he had been offered. The child argued that, "Only mommies drink coffee" (p. 124). The boy had never been told that coffee drinking was sex role related, but his observations of his own parents led him to this conclusion. Violations of the child's schema were upsetting to him, although they could also lead to modifications in his understanding of gender-linked behavior.

In adult life our expectations for males and females (and for ourselves, as one or the other) continue to reflect our use of gender as a social category and organizing principle. We continue to resist change in the sex stereotypes we have learned through personal observation or explicit cultural teaching. Deaux (1984) has reviewed evidence that men and women alter their interactional behavior to conform to the expected sex and sex role attitudes of their interactional partners. Their partners, in turn, are more likely to enact sex-typed behavior when it appears to have been expected of them. Even if men are not intrinsically more competitive and less warm than women, they are generally expected to be so. Thus, beliefs in such stereotypes often become self-fulfilling prophecies, as we try to act out culturally sanctioned norms and expect this of others.

Such sex stereotypes, particularly the exalted cultural image of men as independent, unemotional, and agentic, are also reflected in the limitations of many of our psychological theories, which denigrate or misperceive the "feminine" issues of vulnerability and attachment (Miller, 1976). If men are not supposed to make interpersonal relationships central to their lives, then these must not be critical elements for healthy psychological development. As Lewis notes in this issue, women carry the burden of our "culture's devaluation of sociability." Many of our terms for interpersonal attachment and relatedness are remarkably pejorative: dependency, enmeshment, fusion. The word "dependency" is often used indiscriminately to refer both to the helpless neediness of the young child and to the mature investment of an adult woman in relationships with her kin.

The female stereotype, while devaluing women for their presumed emotionality and interpersonal neediness, does point to the importance of human relationships for adult development, identity, and well-being. Researchers and clinicians who attended closely to the meaning of interpersonal connection in women's lives then came to see such connection as a potential source of strength, rather than a weakness.

In reworking theory so that it begins to capture women's experiences, investigators have begun to rehabilitate sociability and attachment, discovering new ways in which interpersonal connection is critical to development and to identity for both men and women. Franz and White (this issue) note that Erikson's theory of life-span personality development fails to account fully for the process of attachment over the lifespan, and that this failure is made salient by the theory's difficulty in encompassing female as well as male development. Franz and White's extension of Erikson's theory into a two-path model that incorporates both attachment and individuation issues at every stage of development is not only a more adequate model of female development; it is a more adequate model of male development as well. Similarly, Lykes's exploration (this issue) of the concept of "social individuality" to capture women's sense of self as embedded in and expressing particular social contexts while contributing to those contexts proves a useful lens through which to view male personality as well.

Thus, paradoxically, the study of gender has been least successful in elucidating the mysteries of sex differences, and most successful in illuminating an idea that transcends gender: the lifelong critical importance of interpersonal attachments and connections as these contribute to identity and to mature development.

References

Barnes, W. S. (1984). Sibling influences within family and school contexts. Unpublished doctoral dissertation. Harvard Graduate School of Education.
Bateson, G. (1968) Insight in a bicultural context. *Philippine Studies*, **16**, 605–621.
Deaux, K. (1984). From individual differences to social categories: Analysis of a decade's research on gender. *American Psychologist*, **39**(2), 105–116.
Eagly, A. H., & Carli, L. L. (1981). Sex of researchers and sex-typed communications as determinants of sex differences in influenceability: A meta-analysis of social influence studies. *Psychological Bulletin*, **90**, 1–20.
Franz, C. E., & White, K. M. (1985). Individuation and attachment in personality development: Extending Erikson's theory. *Journal of Personality*, **53**, 224–256.
Friedan, B. (1974). *The feminine mystique.* New York: Dell.
Frieze, I. H., Parsons, J. E., Johnson, P. B., Ruble, D. N., & Zellman, G. L. (1978). *Women and sex roles: A social psychological perspective.* New York: W. W. Norton.
Lewis, H. B. (1985). Depression vs. paranoia: Why are there sex differences in mental illness? *Journal of Personality*, **53**, 150–178.
Lykes, M. B. (1985). Gender and individualistic vs. collectivist notions about the self. *Journal of Personality*, **53**, 356–383.
Miller, J. B. (1976). *Toward a new psychology of women.* Boston: Beacon Press.
Morawski, J. G. (1985). The measurement of masculinity and femininity: Engendering categorical realities. *Journal of Personality*, **53**, 196–223.

Pearce, D. (1979). Women, work, and welfare: The feminization of poverty. In K. W. Feinstein (Ed.), *Working women and families*. Beverly Hills: Sage.

Perkins, L. M. (1983). The impact of the "cult of true womanhood" on the education of black women. *Journal of Social Issues, 39*, 17–28.

Smith, A. (1983). Nonverbal communication among black female dyads: An assessment of intimacy, gender, and race. *Journal of Social Issues, 39*(3), 55–67.

Index

Abuse. *See* Violence

Achievement, 5, 11, 23, 52, 172, 176, 179, 198–215, 238, 240–241, 306; extrinsic rewards, 11, 198, 208–209, 211–213; intrinsic rewards, 11, 198, 208, 211–212

Achievement motivation, 198, 264, 306–307. *See also* Motivation

Affect. *See* Emotion

Affiliation, 11, 23, 79, 199–201, 208, 264, 270–272. *See also* Communion; Relationships and relatedness

Agency, 6, 80, 109, 127, 137, 165, 198–199, 201–202, 204–205, 208, 211, 214. *See also* Individuation; Mastery/competence

Aggression/aggressiveness, 15, 20–22, 24, 39, 43, 45, 50–52, 62, 64–65, 68–69, 72, 75, 77–78, 80, 85–86, 91–94, 96–97, 104, 119, 121, 141, 157, 164, 223, 249, 270. *See also* Battered women; Violence

Androgyny, 3, 10, 15, 108, 110, 124–129, 165, 211, 303

Anger (hostility, rage, fury), 9, 14, 17–19, 21–22, 24, 28–29, 31–33, 37, 39, 42–46, 50–52, 75, 78, 82–84, 91–92, 95, 104, 143, 157, 223

Anxiety, 24, 28–29, 45, 65, 82, 143; castration, 223; separation and stranger, 28, 32, 71. *See also* Fear

Archer, D., 34–36

Atkinson, J. W., 198, 248, 278

Attachment, 10, 23, 63, 70–72, 74, 81, 85–86, 136–138, 140, 145–146, 151–153, 156, 158–159, 161–166, 172, 226, 270–271, 289, 303, 308, 315–316. *See also* Relationships and relatedness

Attribution, 39, 45–47, 51, 84

Autonomous individualism, 5, 11, 268–290. *See also* Social individuality

Autonomy, 79, 82, 92, 139, 152, 158, 162–163, 165, 189–194, 226, 229, 268–271, 273, 276, 286–287. *See also* Individuation

Bailey, M. M., 198–202, 204, 211–212

Bakan, D., 80, 137, 165, 198–199, 201–202, 204, 211, 308

Battered women, 51, 91–105, 305–306. *See also* Violence, victim

Bem, S., 3, 124–126

Bem Sex Role Inventory (BSRI), 124–126

Birnbaum, D., 19, 32, 44, 47

Blanck, P., 35–36, 44

Block, J., 235, 302

Block, J. H., 43, 45, 232

Bowlby, J., 2, 71, 83

Brody, L., 6–9, 17, 26, 32, 34, 37–39, 42, 47, 50–51, 53, 304, 312

Broverman, D. M., 26, 169, 269

Broverman, I. K., 26, 169, 269

Browne, A., 6–8, 9, 51, 97–98, 100–102, 305

Buck, R., 16, 18, 20–21, 27, 29, 32–33, 35, 38, 40–41, 43, 46, 50

Buechler, S., 16–17, 50

Bugental, D., 27, 33, 46

California Psychological Inventory (CPI), 121–122, 218, 229, 234, 237–238, 242

Caring. *See* Relationships and relatedness

Carlson, R., 3, 11, 124, 137, 199, 297–298, 301–302, 305

THE EDITORS

Abigail J. Stewart is an Associate Professor of Psychology at Boston University. She served as director of the Henry A. Murray Research Center of Radcliffe College (a center for the study of women's lives) from 1978 to 1980. She received her master's degree from the London School of Economics in 1972 and her doctorate from Harvard University in 1975. She has coedited two issues of the *Journal of Social Issues*, which is devoted to approaches to studying women's lives, and has published a number of research articles in the area. Her main research interest is the study of change at the individual and social levels.

M. Brinton Lykes is an Assistant Professor of Psychology at Rhode Island College. She received her doctorate from the Community-Social Psychology Program at Boston College. She served as Coordinator of Women's Programs at Harvard Divinity School from 1973 to 1977. Her current work builds on her efforts to create feminist, multicultural educational models. Her research interests include a cross-cultural exploration of a social understanding of the self that contrasts with the dominant North American notion of self, autonomous individualism.

CONTRIBUTORS

Nicole B. Barenbaum, Department of Psychology, Boston University

Deborah Belle, Department of Psychology, Boston University

Leslie R. Brody, Department of Psychology, Boston University

Angela Browne, University of New Hampshire

Rae Carlson, Department of Psychology, Rutgers, The State University

Carol E. Franz, Department of Psychology, Boston University

William P. Gaeddert, Department of Psychology, SUNY, Plattsburgh

Barbara Hart, Institute of Personality Assessment and Research, University of
   California, Berkeley

Ravenna Helson, Institute of Personality Assessment and Research, University
   of California, Berkeley

Helen Block Lewis, Yale University

Peter D. Lifton, Department of Psychology, University of North Carolina, Chapel
   Hill

M. Brinton Lykes, Department of Psychology, Rhode Island College

Valory Mitchell, Institute of Personality Assessment and Research, University
   of California, Berkeley

J. G. Morawski, Department of Psychology, Wesleyan University

Abigail J. Stewart, Department of Psychology, Boston University

Lenore E. Auerbach Walker, Walker and Associates

Kathleen M. White, Department of Psychology, Boston University

David G. Winter, Department of Psychology, Wesleyan University

β